PERSPECTIVES ON FICTION

PERSPECTIVES ON FICTION

EDITED BY

JAMES L. CALDERWOOD

AND

HAROLD E. TOLIVER

UNIVERSITY OF CALIFORNIA, IRVINE

New York
OXFORD UNIVERSITY PRESS
London   Toronto
1968

PREFACE

The essays collected here examine a number of recurrent problems in the reading and analysis of fiction. Though their emphasis falls collectively on modern prose fiction and its special problems of style, point of view, characterization, and plot, a few also range among epics, myths, sagas, and folktales. One examines fictional representation in general and another the effects of printing on form.

On the assumption that essays by various hands are better suited to raise than to settle questions, we have not attempted to impose a unified theoretical framework on them or to iron out their differences. But certain problems crop up whenever fiction is discussed, and perhaps the most important of these is that formidable dragon, the tension between form and content, or to shift to its customary modal variation, between romance and realism. It threatens to devour lesser issues because fiction is by definition artful and untrue, yet is often committed to minute descriptions of the daily acts of eating, growing, dying, money- and love-making, fighting and politicking. Nearly anything that human beings are prepared to do or to think about doing, fiction is prepared to tell us about, either romanticizing it or being formlessly frank. The difficulty is that it tells the truth as falsehood and falsehood as the truth. It gives us verifiable fact but not in a scientific manner; or it gives us outlandish make-believe but in the scrupulous manner of the druggist carefully measuring out milligrams. It makes use of past tense indicative sentences and narrative chronology much like history, reporting, biography, and autobiography; yet unlike these sister forms, wears them as masks, sporting with them. Behind its masks, it may be as historical or utopian, philosophical or imaginative, bizarre or commonplace as it chooses.

The least we can say, then, is that fiction follows its own laws and is not intimidated by paradox. The problem for both theoretical and practical critics is that no given work is all fable or all fact: each work forces some aspect of realism to lie down with some aspect of the fairy tale. This is true of modern fiction no less than older forms of myth and fable. Some of the most fruitful of the modern experiments in fiction are combinations of romance and social or psychological reporting, as in the major works of Melville, Emily Brontë, Joyce, Beckett, Barth, Conrad, Faulkner, Nathanael West, William Golding, Malamud, and further back, in Cervantes's fabled knight, who carries his book-fed imagination into battle against treacherous inns, incorrigible rascals, and scolding swine-maidens. So deep does the reciprocity between romance and realism run that self-conscious writers such as Cervantes, Beckett, and Doris Lessing (in *The Golden Notebook*) are tempted to write novels about novels and their distortions of reality.

Perhaps the initial difficulty with the marriage of realism and romance is that reality itself is anything but romantic or artistic. At best it presents the writer with merely incipient orders and fragments of structure. Historical fact, observation, investigation, sensation, and mimetic character by necessity lead him toward formlessness and often dullness, whereas his inventive or fabulous bent can be trusted to lead toward predetermined ends, purposefulness, symmetry, coherence, and heightened interest. For at one extreme, in myth, the imagination invents gods in perfect control of nature who may command large stretches of geography and history and shape all actions to their wills; but at the other extreme, realism offers only unheroic men neither favored by gods nor able to transcend their daily entanglements. The primitive storyteller united the two more comfortably because his culture often assured him that historical reality represented the will of the gods. But in sophisticated societies, a writer who wishes to combine minute documentation and fable must have double vision and stylistic agility. He cannot escape the uneasy feeling that whatever shape and coherence he discovers in his subject he has very possibly put there in the act of seeing and writing.

Hence an aesthetics of fiction cannot be entirely severed from a metaphysics of fiction: its various modes are ways of seeing and imagining as well as writing. The problem is compounded by the fact that the number of modes between naturalism and fantasy is almost infinite and each contains its own view of reality, inherent in its particular selection and reordering of material. But the essays here make significant advances on these problems, both in theory and in the practical criticism of particular texts. That they overflow the general index headings by which we have grouped them is testimony to the inseparability of their subjects. They have enough inherent dialectic to encourage a search for the comprehensive view of fiction they cannot fully define.

In both this volume and companion collections on drama and poetry, we have received valuable assistance from Dianne Ewing, Sue Smith, Virginia McQuaid, and Betty Becker, whose contributions have been graciously offered.

Irvine, California   J. L. C.
February 1968   H. E. T.

CONTENTS

PERSPECTIVES ON FICTION

NATURE AND METHOD OF FICTION

Some events in fiction have actually happened in history; others have not happened but conceivably might have and are situated in familiar contexts that make them seem plausible, such as New York, London, or Hardy's Wessex country. Still others, though they contain recognizable elements, are basically fantastic, dreamlike, or surrealistic; and in at least one variety of fiction, the tall story, the events are exaggerated in such a way as to test the storyteller's ingenuity in explaining the impossible. In all these forms, a given subject may be screened through narrative, dramatic, discursive, descriptive, or stream of consciousness technique, each of which translates its materials differently and imposes a different structure on them. Generally speaking, the translation of a flow of sensations into an associative stream of words makes the least displacement of raw materials, while discursive or didactic commentary causes the greatest displacement. Narrative, dramatic, and descriptive techniques are partly interpretive and partly mimetic in reflecting the nature of the event in style and movement.

Erich Auerbach's essay from *Mimesis: The Representation of Reality in Western Literature* establishes Homeric and Hebraic methods of narration as models of two quite different modes, one primarily realistic and the other symbolic. Homeric narrative represents phenomena "in

3

a fully externalized form, visible and palpable in all their parts and completely fixed in their spatial and temporal relations." Each detail as it is narrated carries its own weight: all is foreground and immediate presence in the sequential parade of the things themselves. Scriptural narration, on the other hand, "has no present," and its details point to things that they cannot fully manifest. Both motives and surrounding circumstances are left partly to inference. The prime mover of Abraham's story, for instance, is God, who for obvious reasons cannot be fully externalized but must remain a mysterious voice from an invisible background. Principles of style such as syntax, dialogue, and characterization are influenced by the abrupt intrusions of such hidden plot strands and motive forces.

If we consider Homeric narrative with the idea of the hidden Cause in mind, we perceive that even a comparatively realistic mode has similar forces at work upon it—not mysterious and personal, perhaps, but nonetheless imperative. For every narrative work that has a method also has goals and patterns that require our transcendence of immediate detail. At every point of the reading we must look into what has happened and anticipate what is about to happen, constantly comparing, predicting, and assessing. These buried aspects of a story form the background to the present and define its purpose and direction. Hence one might say that the plan-of-the-whole is a "prime mover" quite as dictatorial as the voice that Abraham hears. It demands certain things of characters and twists individual sentences in certain ways that no other story does. Whether or not a story withholds its principle of order until a sudden deus ex machina comes forth to declare it, then, something is always invisible until the plot is completed, and all relationships among all parts bear upon the meaning of each particular part.

It becomes obvious in Auerbach's analysis of the two examples that what a work of fiction reveals to us is inseparable from the manner in which it does so: as far as art is concerned, reality *is* representation. But in his examination of Fielding's stylistic mixtures, Leonard Lutwack suggests that a given work need not adhere too rigidly to a *single* decorum. Though a Kafka dream sequence would obviously be out of place in the mind of Robinson Crusoe, a work may accommodate different styles without making its stance toward its subject inconsistent. If it succeeds, the result is an ironic or complex rather than a uniform mode. The question is whether or not the various styles are compatible—whether, for instance, narrative, description, and authorial intrusions have a common perspective.

Hugh Kenner associates style and method with the problem of medium, deriving form from printed as opposed to spoken words. From the placing of an adverb in the individual sentence to the arrangement of the entire work, the method of Joyce's *Ulysses* depends upon the fixed, intricately cross-referenced means of the printed inventory. Without the printing press and the bound book, this kind of novel would be as inconceivable as certain kinds of visual connectives and sequences without motion pictures, or certain ways of establishing motifs and rhythms without music.

In her discussion of the kinds of statement that fiction makes, Margaret MacDonald assesses several of these problems in general philosophical terms, passing from fictional "lies" and pseudo-designation to procedure and the relationship that a particular mode has to reality. At this level of abstraction, it is possible to distinguish fictional method from other forms of expression lacking the indirection of fable. But as the tentative ending of the essay indicates, the critic is also left with the task of analyzing "different types of plausibility" as particular works illustrate them—in other words, the task of defining distinct modes and the style of individual works within the general method that all works of fiction share.

ERICH AUERBACH

Odysseus' Scar

Readers of the *Odyssey* will remember the well-prepared and touching scene in book 19, when Odysseus has at last come home, the scene in which the old housekeeper Euryclea, who had been his nurse, recognizes him by a scar on his thigh. The stranger has won Penelope's good will; at his request she tells the housekeeper to wash his feet which, in all old stories, is the first duty of hospitality toward a tired traveler. Euryclea busies herself fetching water and mixing cold with hot, meanwhile speaking sadly of her absent master, who is probably of the same age as the guest, and who perhaps, like the guest, is even now wandering somewhere, a stranger; and she remarks how astonishingly like him the guest looks. Meanwhile Odysseus, remembering his scar, moves back out of the light; he knows that, despite his efforts to hide his identity, Euryclea will now recognize him, but he wants at least to keep Penelope in ignorance. No sooner has the old woman touched the scar than, in her joyous surprise, she lets Odysseus' foot drop into the basin; the water spills over, she is about to cry out her joy; Odysseus restrains her with whispered threats and endearments; she recovers herself and conceals her emotion. Penelope, whose attention Athena's foresight had diverted from the incident, has observed nothing.

All this is scrupulously externalized and narrated in leisurely fashion. The two women express their feelings in copious direct discourse. Feelings though they are, with only a slight admixture of the most general considerations upon human destiny, the syntactical connection between part and part is perfectly clear, no contour is blurred. There is also room and time for orderly, perfectly well-articulated, uniformly illuminated descriptions of implements, ministrations, and gestures; even in the dramatic moment of recognition, Homer does not omit to tell the reader that it is with his right hand that Odysseus takes the old woman by the throat to keep her from speaking, at the same time that he draws her closer to him with his left. Clearly outlined, brightly and uniformly illuminated, men and things stand out in a realm where everything is visible; and not less clear—wholly expressed, orderly even in their ardor—are the feelings and thoughts of the persons involved.

In my account of the incident I have so far passed over a whole series of verses which interrupt it in the middle. There are more than seventy of these verses—while to the incident itself some forty are devoted before the interruption and some forty after it. The interruption, which comes just at the point when the housekeeper recognizes the scar—that is, at the moment of crisis—describes the origin of the scar, a hunting accident which occurred in Odysseus' boyhood, at a boar hunt, during the time of his visit to his grandfather Autolycus. This first affords an opportunity to inform the reader about Autolycus, his house, the precise degree of the kinship, his character, and, no less exhaustively than touchingly, his behavior after the birth of his grandson; then follows the visit of Odysseus, now grown to be a youth; the exchange of greetings, the banquet with which he is welcomed, sleep and waking, the early start for the hunt, the tracking of the beast, the struggle, Odysseus' being wounded by the boar's tusk, his recovery, his return to Ithaca, his parents' anxious questions—all is narrated, again with such a complete externalization of all the elements of the story and of their interconnections as to leave nothing in obscurity. Not until then does the narrator return to Penelope's chamber, not until then, the digression having run its course, does Euryclea, who had recognized the scar before the digression began, let Odysseus' foot fall back into the basin.

The first thought of a modern reader—that this is a device to increase suspense—is, if not wholly wrong, at least not the essential explanation of this Homeric procedure. For the element of suspense is very slight in the Homeric poems; nothing in their entire style is calculated to keep the reader or hearer breathless. The digressions are not meant to keep the reader in suspense, but rather to relax the tension. And this frequently occurs, as in the passage before us. The broadly narrated, charming, and subtly fashioned story of the hunt, with all its elegance and self-sufficiency, its wealth of idyllic pictures, seeks to win the reader over wholly to itself as long as he is hearing it, to make him forget what had just taken place during the foot-washing. But an episode that will increase suspense by retarding the action must be so constructed that it will not fill the present entirely, will not put the crisis, whose resolution is being awaited, entirely out of the reader's mind, and thereby destroy the mood of suspense; the crisis and the suspense must continue, must remain vibrant in the background. But Homer—and to this we shall have to return later—knows no background. What he narrates is for the time being the only present, and fills both the stage and the reader's mind completely. So it is with the passage before us. When the young Euryclea (vv. 401ff.) sets the infant Odysseus on his grandfather Autolycus' lap after the banquet, the aged Euryclea, who a few lines earlier had touched the wanderer's foot, has entirely vanished from the stage and from the reader's mind.

Goethe and Schiller, who, though not referring to this particular episode, exchanged letters in April 1797 on the subject of "the retarding element" in the Homeric poems in general, put it in direct opposition to the element of suspense—the latter word is not used, but is clearly implied when the "retarding" procedure is opposed, as something proper to epic, to tragic procedure (letters of April 19, 21, and 22). The "retarding element," the "going back and forth" by means of episodes, seems to me, too, in the Homeric poems, to be opposed to any tensional and suspensive striving toward a goal, and doubtless Schiller is right in regard to Homer when he says that what he gives us is "simply the quiet existence and operation of things in accordance with their natures"; Homer's goal is "already present in every point of his progress." But both Schiller and Goethe raise Homer's procedure to the level of a law for epic poetry in general, and Schiller's words quoted above are meant to be universally binding upon the epic poet, in contradistinction from the tragic. Yet in both modern and ancient times, there are important epic works which are composed throughout with no "retarding element" in this sense but, on the contrary, with suspense throughout, and which perpetually "rob us of our emotional freedom"— which power Schiller will grant only to the tragic poet. And besides it seems to me undemonstrable and improbable that this procedure of Homeric poetry was directed by aesthetic considerations or even by an aesthetic feeling of the sort postulated by Goethe and Schiller. The effect, to be sure, is precisely that which they describe, and is, furthermore, the actual source of the conception of epic which they themselves hold, and with them all writers decisively influenced by classical antiquity. But the true cause of the impression of "retardation" appears to me to lie elsewhere—namely, in the need of the Homeric style to leave nothing which it mentions half in darkness and unexternalized.

The excursus upon the origin of Odysseus' scar is not basically different from the many passages in which a newly introduced character, or even a newly appearing object or implement, though it be in the thick of a battle, is described as to its nature and origin; or in which, upon the appearance of a god, we are told where he last was, what he was doing there, and by what road he reached the scene; indeed, even the Homeric epithets seem to me in the final analysis to be traceable to the same need for an externalization of phenomena in terms perceptible to the senses. Here is the scar, which comes up in the course of the narrative; and Homer's feeling simply will not permit him to see it appear out of the darkness of an unilluminated past; it must be set in full light, and with it a portion of the hero's boyhood—just as, in the *Iliad,* when the first ship is already burning and the Myrmidons finally arm that they may hasten to help, there is still time not only for the wonderful simile of the wolf, not only for the order of the Mymirdon host, but also for a detailed account of the ancestry of several subordinate leaders (16, vv. 155ff.). To be sure, the aesthetic effect thus produced was soon noticed and thereafter consciously sought; but the more original cause must have lain in the basic impulse of the Homeric style; to represent phenomena in a fully externalized form, visible and palpable in all their parts, and completely fixed in their spatial and temporal relations. Nor do psychological processes receive any other treatment: here too nothing must remain hidden and unexpressed. With the utmost fullness, with an orderliness which even passion does not disturb, Homer's personages vent their inmost hearts in speech; what they do not say to others, they speak in their own minds, so that the reader is informed of it. Much that is terrible takes place in the Homeric poems, but it seldom takes place wordlessly: Polyphemus talks to Odysseus; Odysseus talks to the suitors when he begins to kill them; Hector and Achilles talk at length, before battle and after; and no speech is so filled with anger or scorn that the particles which express logical and grammatical connections are lacking or out of place. This last observation is true, of course, not only of speeches but of the presentation in general. The separate elements of a phenomenon are most clearly placed in relation to one another; a large number of conjunctions, adverbs, particles, and other syntactical tools, all clearly circumscribed and delicately differentiated in meaning, delimit persons, things, and portions of incidents in respect to one another, and at the same time bring them together in a continuous and ever flexible connection; like the separate phenomena themselves, their relationships— their temporal, local, causal, final, consecutive, comparative, concessive, antithetical, and conditional limitations—are brought to light in perfect fullness; so that a continuous rhythmic procession of phenomena passes by, and never is there a form left fragmentary or half-illuminated, never a lacuna, never a gap, never a glimpse of unplumbed depths.

And this procession of phenomena takes place in the foreground—that is, in a local and temporal present which is absolute. One might think that the many interpolations, the frequent moving back and forth, would create a sort of perspective in time and place; but the Homeric style never gives any such impression. The way in which any impression of perspective is avoided can be clearly observed in the procedure for introducing episodes, a syntactical construction with which every reader of Homer is familiar; it is used in the passage we are considering, but can also be found in cases when the episodes are much shorter. To the word scar (v. 393) there is first attached a relative clause ("which once long ago a boar . . ."), which enlarges into a voluminous syntactical parenthesis; into this an independent sentence unexpectedly intrudes (v. 396: "A god himself gave him . . ."), which quietly disentangles itself from syntactical subordination, until, with verse 399, an equally free syntactical treatment of the new content begins a new present which continues unchallenged until, with verse 467 ("The old woman now touched it . . ."), the scene which had been broken off is resumed. To be sure, in the case of such long episodes as the one we are considering, a purely syntactical connection with the principal theme would hardly have been possible; but a connection with it through perspective would have been all the easier had the content been arranged with that end in view; if, that is, the entire story of the scar had been presented as a recollection which awakens in Odysseus' mind at this particular moment. It would have been perfectly easy to do; the story of the scar had only to be inserted two verses earlier, at the first mention of the word scar, where the motifs "Odysseus" and "recollection" were already at hand. But any such subjectivistic-perspectivistic procedure, creating a foreground and background, resulting in the present lying open to the depths of the past, is entirely foreign to the Homeric style; the Homeric style knows only a foreground, only a uniformly illuminated, uniformly objective present. And so the excursus does not begin until two lines later, when Euryclea has discovered the scar—the possibility for a perspectivistic connection no longer exists, and the story of the wound becomes an independent and exclusive present.

The genius of the Homeric style becomes even more apparent when it is compared with an equally ancient and equally epic style from a different world of forms. I shall attempt this comparison with the account of the sacrifice of Isaac, a homogeneous narrative produced by the so-called Elohist. The King James version translates the opening as follows (Genesis 22: 1): "And it came to pass after these things, that God did tempt Abraham, and said to him, Abraham! and he said, Behold, here I am." Even this opening startles us when we come to it from Homer. Where are the two speakers? We are not told. The reader, however, knows that they are not normally to be found together in one place on earth, that one of them, God, in order to speak to Abraham, must come from somewhere, must enter the earthly realm from some unknown heights or depths. Whence does he come, whence does he call to Abraham? We are not told. He does not come, like Zeus or Poseidon, from the Aethiopians, where he has been enjoying a sacrificial feast. Nor are we told anything of his reasons for tempting Abraham so terribly. He has not, like Zeus, discussed them in set speeches with other gods gathered in council; nor have the deliberations in his own heart been presented to us; unexpected and mysterious, he enters the scene from some unknown height or depth and calls: Abraham! It will at once be said that this is to be explained by the particular concept of God which the Jews held and which was wholly different from that of the Greeks. True enough—but this constitutes no objection. For how is the Jewish concept of God to be explained? Even their earlier God of the desert was not fixed in form and content, and was alone; his lack of form, his lack of local habitation, his singleness, was in the end not only maintained but developed even further in competition with the comparatively far more manifest gods of the surrounding Near Eastern world. The concept of God held by the Jews is less a cause than a symptom of their manner of comprehending and representing things.

This becomes still clearer if we now turn to the other person in the dialogue, to Abraham. Where is he? We do not know. He says, indeed: Here I am—but the Hebrew word means only something like "behold me," and in any case is not meant to indicate the actual place where Abraham is, but a moral position in respect to God, who has called to him—Here am I awaiting thy command. Where he is actually, whether in Beersheba or elsewhere, whether indoors or in the open air, is not stated; it does not interest the narrator, the reader is not informed; and what Abraham was doing when God called to him is left in the same obscurity. To realize the difference, consider Hermes' visit to Calypso, for example, where command, journey, arrival and reception of the visitor, situation and occupation of the person visited, are set forth in many verses; and even on occasions when gods appear suddenly and briefly, whether to help one of their favorites or to deceive or destroy some mortal whom they hate, their bodily forms, and usually the manner of their coming and going, are given in detail. Here, however, God appears without bodily form (yet he "appears"), coming from some unspecified place—we only hear his voice, and that utters nothing but a name, a name without an adjective, without a descriptive epithet for the person spoken to, such as is the rule in every Homeric address; and of Abraham too nothing is made perceptible except the words in which he answers God: *Hinne-ni*, Behold me here—with which, to be sure, a most touching gesture expressive of obedience and readiness is suggested, but it is left to the reader to visualize it. Moreover the two speakers are not on the same level: if we conceive of Abraham in the foreground, where it might be possible to picture him as prostrate or kneeling or bowing with outspread arms or gazing upward, God is not there too: Abraham's words and gestures are directed toward the depths of the picture or upward, but in any case the undetermined, dark place from which the voice comes to him is not in the foreground.

After this opening, God gives his command, and the story itself begins: everyone knows it; it unrolls with no episodes in a few independent sentences whose syntactical connection is of the most rudimentary sort. In this atmosphere it is unthinkable that an implement, a landscape through which the travelers passed, the serving-men, or the ass, should be described, that their origin or descent or material or appearance or usefulness should be set forth in terms of praise; they do not even admit an adjective: they are serving-men, ass, wood, and knife, and nothing else, without an epithet; they are there to serve the end which God has commanded; what in other respects they were, are, or will be, remains in darkness. A journey is made, because God has designated the place where the sacrifice is to be performed; but we are told nothing about the journey except that it took three days, and even that we are told in a mysterious way: Abraham and his followers rose "early in the morning" and "went unto" the place of which God had told him; on the third day he lifted up his eyes and saw the place from afar. That gesture is the only gesture, is indeed the only occurrence during the whole journey, of which we are told; and though its motivation lies in the fact that the place is elevated, its uniqueness still heightens the impression that the journey took place through a vacuum; it is as if, while he traveled on, Abraham had looked neither to the right nor to the left, had suppressed any sign of life in his followers and himself save only their footfalls.

Thus the journey is like a silent progress through the indeterminate and the contingent, a holding of the breath, a process which has no present, which is inserted, like a blank duration, between what has passed and what lies ahead, and which yet is measured: three days! Three such days positively demand the symbolic interpretation which they later received. They began "early in the morning." But at what time on the third day did Abraham lift up his eyes and see his goal? The text says nothing on the subject. Obviously not "late in the evening," for it seems that there was still time enough to climb the mountain and make the sacrifice. So "early in the morning" is given, not as an indication of time, but for the sake of its ethical significance; it is intended to express the resolution, the promptness, the punctual obedience of the sorely tried Abraham. Bitter to him is the early morning in which he saddles his ass, calls his serving-men and his son Isaac, and sets out; but he obeys, he walks on until the third day, then lifts up his eyes and sees the place. Whence he comes, we do not know, but the goal is clearly stated: Jeruel in the land of Moriah. What place this is meant to indicate is not clear—"Moriah" especially may be a later correction of some other word. But in any case the goal was given, and in any case it is a matter of some sacred spot which was to receive a particular consecration by being connected with Abraham's sacrifice. Just as little as "early in the morning" serves as a temporal indication does "Jeruel in the land of Moriah" serve as a geographical indication; and in both cases alike, the complementary indication is not given, for we know as little of the hour at which Abraham lifted up his eyes as we do of the place from which he set forth—Jeruel is significant not so much as the goal of an earthly journey, in its geographical relation to other places, as through its special election, through its relation to God, who designated it as the scene of the act, and therefore it must be named.

In the narrative itself, a third chief character appears: Isaac. While God and Abraham, the serving-men, the ass, and the implements are simply named, without mention of any qualities or any other sort of definition, Isaac once receives an appositive; God says, "Take Isaac, thine only son, whom thou lovest." But this is not a characterization of Isaac as a person, apart from his relation to his father and apart from the story; he may be handsome or ugly, intelligent or stupid, tall or short, pleasant or unpleasant—we are not told. Only what we need to know about him as a personage in the action, here and now, is illuminated, so that it may become apparent how terrible Abraham's temptation is, and that God is fully aware of it. By this example of the contrary, we see the significance of the descriptive adjectives and digressions of the Homeric poems; with their indications of the earlier and as it were absolute existence of the persons described, they prevent the reader from concentrating exclusively on a present crisis; even when the most terrible things are occurring, they prevent the establishment of an overwhelming suspense. But here, in the story of Abraham's sacrifice, the overwhelming suspense is present; what Schiller makes the goal of the tragic poet—to rob us of our emotional freedom, to turn our intellectual and spiritual powers (Schiller says "our activity") in one direction, to concentrate them there—is effected in this Biblical narrative, which certainly deserves the epithet epic.

We find the same contrast if we compare the two uses of direct discourse. The personages speak in the Bible story too; but their speech does not serve, as does speech in Homer, to manifest, to externalize thoughts—on the contrary, it serves to indicate thoughts which remain unexpressed. God gives his command in direct discourse, but he leaves his motives and his purpose unexpressed; Abraham, receiving the command, says nothing and does what he has been told to do. The conversation between Abraham and Isaac on the way to the place of sacrifice is only an interruption of the heavy silence and makes it all the more burdensome. The two of them, Isaac carrying the wood and Abraham with fire and a knife, "went together." Hesitantly, Isaac ventures to ask about the ram, and Abraham gives the well-known answer. Then the text repeats: "So they went both of them together." Everything remains unexpressed.

It would be difficult, then, to imagine styles more contrasted than those of these two equally ancient and equally epic texts. On the one hand, externalized, uniformly illuminated phenomena, at a definite time and in a definite place, connected together without lacunae in a perpetual foreground; thoughts and feeling completely expressed; events taking place in leisurely fashion and with very little of suspense. On the other hand, the externalization of only so much of the phenomena as is necessary for the purpose of the narrative, all else left in obscurity; the decisive points of the narrative alone are emphasized, what lies between is nonexistent; time and place are undefined and call for interpretation; thoughts and feeling remain unexpressed, are only suggested by the silence and the fragmentary speeches; the whole, permeated with the most unrelieved suspense and directed toward a single goal (and to that extent far more of a unity), remains mysterious and "fraught with background."

I will discuss this term in some detail, lest it be misunderstood. I said above that the Homeric style was "of the foreground" because, despite much going back and forth, it yet causes what is momentarily being narrated to give the impression that it is the only present, pure and without perspective. A consideration of the Elohistic text teaches us that our term is capable of a broader and deeper application. It shows that even the separate personages can be represented as possessing "background"; God is always so represented in the Bible, for he is not comprehensible in his presence, as is Zeus; it is always only "something" of him that appears, he always extends into depths. But even the human beings in the Biblical stories have greater depths of time, fate, and consciousness than do the human beings in Homer; although they are nearly always caught up in an event engaging all their faculties, they are not so entirely immersed in its present that they do not remain continually conscious of what has happened to them earlier and elsewhere; their thoughts and feelings have more layers, are more entangled. Abraham's actions are explained not only by what is happening to him at the moment, nor yet only by his character (as Achilles' actions by his courage and his pride, and Odysseus' by his versatility and foresightedness), but by his previous history; he remembers, he is constantly conscious of, what God has promised him and what God has already accomplished for him—his soul is torn between desperate rebellion and hopeful expectation; his silent obedience is multilayered, has background. Such a problematic psychological situation as this is impossible for any of the Homeric heroes, whose destiny is clearly defined and who wake every morning as if it were the first day of their lives: their emotions, though strong, are simple and find expression instantly.

How fraught with background, in comparison, are characters like Saul and David! How entangled and stratified are such human relations as those between David and Absalom, between David and Joab! Any such "background" quality of the psychological situation as that which the story of Absalom's death and its sequel (II Samuel 18 and 19, by the so-called Jahvist) rather suggests than expresses, is unthinkable in Homer. Here we are confronted not merely with the psychological processes of characters whose depth of background is veritably abysmal, but with a purely geographical background too. For David is absent from the battlefield; but the influence of his will and his feelings continues to operate, they affect even Joab in his rebellion and disregard for the consequences of his actions; in the magnificent scene with the two messengers, both the physical and psychological background is fully manifest, though the latter is never expressed. With this, compare, for example, how Achilles, who sends Patroclus first to scout and then into battle, loses almost all "presentness" so long as he is not physically present. But the most important thing is the "multilayeredness" of the individual character; this is hardly to be met with in Homer, or at most in the form of a conscious hesitation between two possible courses of action; otherwise, in Homer, the complexity of the psychological life is shown only in the succession and alternation of emotions; whereas the Jewish writers are able to express the simultaneous existence of various layers of consciousness and the conflict between them.

The Homeric poems, then, though their intellectual, linguistic, and above all syntactical culture appears to be so much more highly developed, are yet comparatively simple in their picture of human beings; and no less so in their relation to the real life which they describe in general. Delight in physical existence is everything to them, and their highest aim is to make that delight perceptible to us. Between battles and passions, adventures and perils, they show us hunts, banquets, palaces and shepherds' cots, athletic contests and washing days—in order that we may see the heroes in their ordinary life, and seeing them so, may take pleasure in their manner of enjoying their savory present, a present which sends strong roots down into social usages, landscape, and daily life. And thus they bewitch us and ingratiate themselves to us until we live with them in the reality of their lives; so long as we are reading or hearing the poems, it does not matter whether we know that all this is only legend, "make-believe." The oft-repeated reproach that Homer is a liar takes nothing from his effectiveness, he does not need to base his story on historical reality, his reality is powerful enough in itself; it ensnares us, weaving its web around us, and that suffices him. And this "real" world into which we are lured, exists for itself, contains nothing but itself; the Homeric poems conceal nothing, they contain no teaching and no secret second meaning. Homer can be analyzed, as we have essayed to do here, but he cannot be interpreted. Later allegorizing trends have tried their arts of interpretation upon him, but to no avail. He resists any such treatment; the interpretations are forced and foreign, they do not crystallize into a unified doctrine.

The general considerations which occasionally occur (in our episode, for example, v. 360: that in misfortune men age quickly) reveal a calm acceptance of the basic facts of human existence, but with no compulsion to brood over them, still less any passionate impulse either to rebel against them or to embrace them in an ecstasy of submission.

It is all very different in the Biblical stories. Their aim is not to bewitch the senses, and if nevertheless they produce lively sensory effects, it is only because the moral, religious, and psychological phenomena which are their sole concern are made concrete in the sensible matter of life. But their religious intent involves an absolute claim to historical truth. The story of Abraham and Isaac is not better established than the story of Odysseus, Penelope, and Euryclea; both are legendary. But the Biblical narrator, the Elohist, had to believe in the objective truth of the story of Abraham's sacrifice—the existence of the sacred ordinances of life rested upon the truth of this and similar stories. He had to believe in it passionately; or else (as many rationalistic interpreters believed and perhaps still believe) he had to be a conscious liar—no harmless liar like Homer, who lied to give pleasure, but a political liar with a definite end in view, lying in the interest of a claim to absolute authority.

To me, the rationalistic interpretation seems psychologically absurd; but even if we take it into consideration, the relation of the Elohist to the truth of his story still remains a far more passionate and definite one than is Homer's relation. The Biblical narrator was obliged to write exactly what his belief in the truth of the tradition (or, from the rationalistic standpoint, his interest in the truth of it) demanded of him—in either case, his freedom in creative or representative imagination was severely limited; his activity was perforce reduced to composing an effective version of the pious tradition. What he produced, then, was not primarily oriented toward "realism" (if he succeeded in being realistic, it was merely a means, not an end); it was oriented toward truth. Woe to the man who did not believe it! One can perfectly well entertain historical doubts on the subject of the Trojan War or of Odysseus' wanderings, and still, when reading Homer, feel precisely the effects he sought to produce; but without believing in Abraham's sacrifice, it is impossible to put the narrative of it to the use for which it was written. Indeed, we must go even further. The Bible's claim to truth is not only far more urgent than Homer's, it is tyrannical—it excludes all other claims. The world of the Scripture stories is not satisfied with claiming to be a historically true reality—it insists that it is the only real world, is destined for autocracy. All other scenes, issues, and ordinances have no right to appear independently of it, and it is promised that all of them, the history of all mankind, will be given their due place within its frame, will be subordinated to it. The Scripture stories do not, like Homer's, court our favor, they do not flatter us that they may please us and enchant us—they seek to subject us, and if we refuse to be subjected we are rebels.

Let no one object that this goes too far, that not the stories, but the religious doctrine, raises the claim to absolute authority; because the stories are not, like Homer's, simply narrated "reality." Doctrine and promise are incarnate in them and inseparable from them; for that very reason they are fraught with "background" and mysterious, containing a second, concealed meaning. In the story of Isaac, it is not only God's intervention at the beginning and the end, but even the factual and psychological elements which come between, that are mysterious, merely touched upon, fraught with background; and therefore they require subtle investigation and interpretation, they demand them. Since so much in the story is dark and incomplete, and since the reader knows that God is a hidden God, his effort to interpret it constantly finds something new to feed upon. Doctrine and the search for enlightenment are inextricably connected with the physical side of the narrative—the latter being more than simple "reality"; indeed they are in constant danger of losing their own reality, as very soon happened when interpretation reached such proportions that the real vanished.

If the text of the Biblical narrative, then, is so greatly in need of interpretation on the basis of its own content, its claim to absolute authority forces it still further in the same direction. Far from seeking, like Homer, merely to make us forget our own reality for a few hours, it seeks to overcome our reality: we are to fit our own life into its world, feel ourselves to be elements in its structure of universal history. This becomes increasingly difficult the further our historical environment is removed from that of the Biblical books; and if these nevertheless maintain their claim to absolute authority, it is inevitable that they themselves be adapted through interpretative transformation. This was for a long time comparatively easy; as late as the European Middle Ages it was possible to represent Biblical events as ordinary phenomena of contemporary life, the methods of interpretation themselves forming the basis for such a treatment. But when, through too great a change in environment and through the awakening of a critical consciousness, this becomes impossible, the Biblical claim to absolute authority is jeopardized; the method of interpretation is scorned and rejected, the Biblical stories become ancient legends, and the doctrine they had contained, now dissevered from them, becomes a disembodied image.

As a result of this claim to absolute authority, the method of interpretation spread to traditions other than the Jewish. The Homeric poems present a definite complex of events whose boundaries in space and time are clearly delimited; before it, beside it, and after it, other complexes of events, which do not depend upon it, can be conceived without conflict and without difficulty. The Old Testament, on the other hand, presents universal history: it begins with the beginning of time, with the creation of the world, and will end with the Last Days, the fulfilling of the Covenant, with which the world will come to an end. Everything else that happens in the world can only be conceived as an element in this sequence; into it everything that is known about the world, or at least everything that touches upon the history of the Jews, must be fitted as an ingredient of the divine plan; and as this too became possible only by interpreting the new material as it poured in, the need for interpretation reaches out beyond the original Jewish-Israelitish realm of reality—for example to Assyrian, Babylonian, Persian, and Roman history; interpretation in a determined direction becomes a general method of comprehending reality; the new and strange world which now comes into view and which, in the form in which it presents itself, proves to be wholly unutilizable within the Jewish religious frame, must be so interpreted that it can find a place there. But this process nearly always also reacts upon the frame, which requires enlarging and modifying. The most striking piece of interpretation of this sort occurred in the first century of the Christian era, in consequence of Paul's mission to the Gentiles: Paul and the Church Fathers reinterpreted the entire Jewish tradition as a succession of figures prognosticating the appearance of Christ, and assigned the Roman Empire its proper place in the divine plan of salvation. Thus while, on the one hand, the reality of the Old Testament presents itself as complete truth with a claim to sole authority, on the other hand that very claim forces it to a constant interpretative change in is own content; for millennia it undergoes an incessant and active development with the life of man in Europe.

The claim of the Old Testament stories to represent universal history, their insistent relation—a relation constantly redefined by conflicts—to a single and hidden God, who yet shows himself and who guides uni-

versal history by promise and exaction, gives these stories an entirely
different perspective from any the Homeric poems can possess. As a
composition, the Old Testament is incomparably less unified than the
Homeric poems, it is more obviously pieced together—but the various
components all belong to one concept of universal history and its interpretation. If certain elements survived which did not immediately fit
in, interpretation took care of them; and so the reader is at every
moment aware of the universal religio-historical perspective which
gives the individual stories their general meaning and purpose. The
greater the separateness and horizontal disconnection of the stories and
groups of stories in relation to one another, compared with the *Iliad*
and the *Odyssey*, the stronger is their general vertical connection,
which holds them all together and which is entirely lacking in Homer.
Each of the great figures of the Old Testament, from Adam to the
prophets, embodies a moment of this vertical connection. God chose
and formed these men to the end of embodying his essence and will—
yet choice and formation do not coincide, for the latter proceeds
gradually, historically, during the earthly life of him upon whom the
choice has fallen. How the process is accomplished, what terrible trials
such a formation inflicts, can be seen from our story of Abraham's
sacrifice. Herein lies the reason why the great figures of the Old Testament are so much more fully developed, so much more fraught with
their own biographical past, so much more distinct as individuals, than
are the Homeric heroes. Achilles and Odysseus are splendidly described
in many well-ordered words, epithets cling to them, their emotions are
constantly displayed in their words and deeds—but they have no development, and their life-histories are clearly set forth once and for all.
So little are the Homeric heroes presented as developing or having
developed, that most of them—Nestor, Agamemnon, Achilles—appear to
be of an age fixed from the very first. Even Odysseus, in whose case
the long lapse of time and the many events which occurred offer so
much opportunity for biographical development, shows almost nothing
of it. Odysseus on his return is exactly the same as he was when he left
Ithaca two decades earlier. But what a road, what a fate, lie between
the Jacob who cheated his father out of his blessing and the old man
whose favorite son has been torn to pieces by a wild beast!—between
David the harp player, persecuted by his lord's jealousy, and the old
king, surrounded by violent intrigues, whom Abishag the Shunnamite
warmed in his bed, and he knew her not! The old man, of whom we
know how he has become what he is, is more of an individual than the

young man; for it is only during the course of an eventful life that men are differentiated into full individuality; and it is this history of a personality which the Old Testament presents to us as the formation undergone by those whom God has chosen to be examples. Fraught with their development, sometimes even aged to the verge of dissolution, they show a distinct stamp of individuality entirely foreign to the Homeric heroes. Time can touch the latter only outwardly, and even that change is brought to our observation as little as possible; whereas the stern hand of God is ever upon the Old Testament figures; he has not only made them once and for all and chosen them, but he continues to work upon them, bends them and kneads them, and, without destroying them in essence, produces from them forms which their youth gave no grounds for anticipating. The objection that the biographical element of the Old Testament often springs from the combination of several legendary personages does not apply; for this combination is a part of the development of the text. And how much wider is the pendulum swing of their lives than that of the Homeric heroes! For they are bearers of the divine will, and yet they are fallible, subject to misfortune and humiliation—and in the widst of misfortune and in their humiliation their acts and words reveal the transcendent majesty of God. There is hardly one of them who does not, like Adam, undergo the deepest humiliation—and hardly one who is not deemed worthy of God's personal intervention and personal inspiration. Humiliation and elevation go far deeper and far higher than in Homer, and they belong basically together. The poor beggar Odysseus is only masquerading, but Adam is really cast down, Jacob really a refugee, Joseph really in the pit and then a slave to be bought and sold. But their greatness, rising out of humiliation, is almost superhuman and an image of God's greatness. The reader clearly feels how the extent of the pendulum's swing is connected with the intensity of the personal history—precisely the most extreme circumstances, in which we are immeasurably forsaken and in despair, or immeasurably joyous and exalted, give us, if we survive them, a personal stamp which is recognized as the product of a rich existence, a rich development. And very often, indeed generally, this element of development gives the Old Testament stories a historical character, even when the subject is purely legendary and traditional.

Homer remains within the legendary with all his material, whereas the material of the Old Testament comes closer and closer to history as the narrative proceeds; in the stories of David the historical report predominates. Here too, much that is legendary still remains, as for example the story of David and Goliath; but much—and the most essential—consists in things which the narrators knew from their own experience or from firsthand testimony. Now the difference between legend and history is in most cases easily perceived by a reasonably experienced reader. It is a difficult matter, requiring careful historical and philological training, to distinguish the true from the synthetic or the biased in a historical presentation; but it is easy to separate the historical from the legendary in general. Their structure is different. Even where the legendary does not immediately betray itself by elements of the miraculous, by the repetition of well-known standard motives, typical patterns and themes, through neglect of clear details of time and place, and the like, it is generally quickly recognizable by its composition. It runs far too smoothly. All cross-currents, all friction, all that is casual, secondary to the main events and themes, everything unresolved, truncated, and uncertain, which confuses the clear progress of the action and the simple orientation of the actors, has disappeared. The historical event which we witness, or learn from the testimony of those who witnessed it, runs much more variously, contradictorily, and confusedly; not until it has produced results in a definite domain are we able, with their help, to classify it to a certain extent; and how often the order to which we think we have attained becomes doubtful again, how often we ask ourselves if the data before us have not led us to a far too simple classification of the original events! Legend arranges its material in a simple and straightforward way; it detaches it from its contemporary historical context, so that the latter will not confuse it; it knows only clearly outlined men who act from few and simple motives and the continuity of whose feelings and actions remains uninterrupted. In the legends of martyrs, for example, a stiff-necked and fanatical persecutor stands over against an equally stiff-necked and fanatical victim; and a situation so complicated—that is to say, so real and historical—as that in which the "persecutor" Pliny finds himself in his celebrated letter to Trajan on the subject of Christians, is unfit for legend. And that is still a comparatively simple case. Let the reader think of the history which we are ourselves witnessing; anyone who, for example, evaluates the behavior of individual men and groups of men at the time of the rise of National Socialism in Germany, or the behavior of individual peoples and states before and during the last war, will feel how difficult it is to represent historical themes in general, and how unfit they are for legend; the historical comprises a great number of contradictory motives in each individual, a hesitation and ambiguous groping on the part of groups; only seldom (as in the last war) does a more or less plain situation, comparatively simple to describe, arise, and even such a situation is subject to division below the surface, is indeed almost constantly in danger of losing its simplicity; and the motives of all the interested parties are so complex that the slogans of propaganda can be composed only through the crudest simplification—with the result that friend and foe alike can often employ the same ones. To write history is so difficult that most historians are forced to make concessions to the technique of legend.

It is clear that a large part of the life of David as given in the Bible contains history and not legend. In Absalom's rebellion, for example, or in the scenes from David's last days, the contradictions and crossing of motives both in individuals and in the general action have become so concrete that it is impossible to doubt the historicity of the information conveyed. Now the men who composed the historical parts are often the same who edited the older legends too; their peculiar religious concept of man in history, which we have attempted to describe above, in no way led them to a legendary simplification of events; and so it is only natural that, in the legendary passages of the Old Testament, historical structure is frequently discernible—of course, not in the sense that the traditions are examined as to their credibility according to the methods of scientific criticism; but simply to the extent that the tendency to a smoothing down and harmonizing of events, to a simplification of motives, to a static definition of characters which avoids conflict, vacillation, and development, such as are natural to legendary structure, does not predominate in the Old Testament world of legend. Abraham, Jacob, or even Moses produces a more concrete, direct, and historical impression than the figures of the Homeric world —not because they are better described in terms of sense (the contrary is the case) but because the confused, contradictory multiplicity of events, the psychological and factual cross-purposes, which true history reveals, have not disappeared in the representation but still remain clearly perceptible. In the stories of David, the legendary, which only later scientific criticism makes recognizable as such, imperceptibly passes into the historical; and even in the legendary, the problem of the classification and interpretation of human history is already passionately apprehended—a problem which later shatters the framework of historical composition and completely overruns it with prophecy; thus the Old Testament, in so far as it is concerned with human events, ranges through all three domains: legend, historical reporting, and interpretative historical theology.

Connected with the matters just discussed is the fact that the Greek text seems more limited and more static in respect to the circle of personages involved in the action and to their political activity. In the recognition scene with which we began, there appears, aside from Odysseus and Penelope, the housekeeper Euryclea, a slave whom Odysseus' father Laertes had bought long before. She, like the swineherd Eumaeus, has spent her life in the service of Laertes' family; like Eumaeus, she is closely connected with their fate, she loves them and shares their interests and feelings. But she has no life of her own, no feelings of her own; she has only the life and feelings of her master. Eumaeus too, though he still remembers that he was born a freeman and indeed of a noble house (he was stolen as a boy), has, not only in fact but also in his own feeling, no longer a life of his own, he is entirely involved in the life of his masters. Yet these two characters are the only ones whom Homer brings to life who do not belong to the ruling class. Thus we become conscious of the fact that in the Homeric poems life is enacted only among the ruling class—others appear only in the role of servants to that class. The ruling class is still so strongly patriarchal, and still itself so involved in the daily activities of domestic life, that one is sometimes likely to forget their rank. But they are unmistakably a sort of feudal aristocracy, whose men divide their lives between war, hunting, marketplace councils, and feasting, while the women supervise the maids in the house. As a social picture, this world is completely stable; wars take place only between different groups of the ruling class; nothing ever pushes up from below. In the early stories of the Old Testament the patriarchal condition is dominant too, but since the people involved are individual nomadic or half-nomadic tribal leaders, the social picture gives a much less stable impression; class distinctions are not felt. As soon as the people completely emerges—that is, after the exodus from Egypt—its activity is always discernible, it is often in ferment, it frequently intervenes in events not only as a whole but also in separate groups and through the medium of separate individuals who come forward; the origins of prophecy seem to lie in the irrepressible politico-religious spontaneity of the people. We receive the impression that the movements emerging from the depths of the people of Israel-Judah must have been of a wholly different nature from those even of the later ancient democracies—of a different nature and far more elemental.

With the more profound historicity and the more profound social activity of the Old Testament text, there is connected yet another important distinction from Homer: namely, that a different conception of the elevated style and of the sublime is to be found here. Homer, of course, is not afraid to let the realism of daily life enter into the sublime and tragic; our episode of the scar is an example, we see how the quietly depicted, domestic scene of the foot-washing is incorporated into the pathetic and sublime action of Odysseus' home-coming. From the rule of the separation of styles which was later almost universally accepted and which specified that the realistic depiction of daily life was incompatible with the sublime and had a place only in comedy or, carefully stylized, in idyl—from any such rule Homer is still far removed. And yet he is closer to it than is the Old Testament. For the great and sublime events in the Homeric poems take place far more exclusively and unmistakably among the members of a ruling class; and these are far more untouched in their heroic elevation than are the Old Testament figures, who can fall much lower in dignity (consider, for example, Adam, Noah, David, Job); and finally, domestic realism, the representation of daily life, remains in Homer in the peaceful realm of the idyllic, whereas, from the very first, in the Old Testament stories, the sublime, tragic, and problematic take shape precisely in the domestic and commonplace: scenes such as those between Cain and Abel, between Noah and his sons, betweeen Abraham, Sarah, and Hagar, between Rebekah, Jacob, and Esau, and so on, are inconceivable in the Homeric style. The entirely different ways of developing conflicts are enough to account for this. In the Old Testament stories the peace of daily life in the house, in the fields, and among the flocks, is undermined by jealousy over election and the promise of a blessing, and complications arise which would be utterly incomprehensible to the Homeric heroes. The latter must have palpable and clearly expressible reasons for their conflicts and enmities, and these work themselves out in free battles; whereas, with the former, the perpetually smouldering jealousy and the connection between the domestic and the spiritual, between the paternal blessing and the divine blessing, lead to daily life being permeated with the stuff of conflict, often with poison. The sublime influence of God here reaches so deeply into the everyday that the two realms of the sublime and the everyday are not only actually unseparated but basically inseparable.

We have compared these two texts, and, with them, the two kinds of style they embody, in order to reach a starting point for an investigation into the literary representation of reality in European culture. The two styles, in their opposition, represent basic types: on the one hand fully externalized description, uniform illumination, uninterrupted connection, free expression, all events in the foreground, displaying unmistakable meanings, few elements of historical development and of psychological perspective; on the other hand, certain parts brought into high relief, others left obscure, abruptness, suggestive influence of the unexpressed, "background" quality, multiplicity of meanings and the need for interpretation, universal-historic claims, development of the concept of the historically becoming, and preoccupation with the problematic.

LEONARD LUTWACK

Mixed and Uniform Prose Styles in the Novel

A distinction may be made between a novel in which more than one prose style is used and a novel which is written in a single, uniform style throughout. *Tom Jones* and *Ulysses* are mixed style novels, *Pamela* and *The Ambassadors* are uniform style novels. The object of this paper is to define the distinction and to work out some of the implications it may have in the study of the novel.

Tom Jones is an early specimen of a novel with mixed prose styles that originate from the author's ironical attitude towards his material and from his compartmentalized treatment of the three genres of which fiction is composed: narrative, essay, and drama. At least three narrative styles are used by Fielding. Tom's rescue of Mrs. Waters from Northerton is a passage of "mere narrative":

> He had not entered far into the wood before he beheld a most shocking sight indeed, a woman stripped half naked, under the hands of a ruffian, who had put his garter round her neck, and was endeavouring to draw her up to a tree. Jones asked no questions at this interval, but fell instantly upon the villain, and made such good use of his trusty oaken stick that he laid him sprawling on the ground before he could defend himself, indeed almost before he knew he was attacked; nor did he cease the prosecution of his blows till the woman herself begged him to forbear, saying, she believed he had sufficiently done his business.

Although excrescences of abstract diction slip into these lines, they are few and do no injury to the narrative force of the style. This prose is

From *The Journal of Aesthetics and Art Criticism,* March 1960. Copyright 1960 by The American Society for Aesthetics. Reprinted by permission of publisher and author.

almost purely objective, with only the slightest suggestion of authorial atttitude towards its content; it is prose that takes its subject seriously. The syntax is a matter of the simple compounding of short clauses that make absolutely clear the persons, objects, and time sequence of the action.

Against this plain narrative style Fielding sets his "Homerican style," which parodies the heroic manner of narration in epic poetry and romance:

> Now the dogs of war being let loose, began to lick their bloody lips; now Victory, with golden wings, hung hovering in the air; now Fortune, taking her scales from her shelf, began to weigh the fates of Tom Jones, his female companion, and Partridge, against the landlord, his wife, and maid . . .

In Fielding's third narrative style, the formal, periodic manner of the eighteenth-century essay is used to overlay the plain narrative contents. After Tom's rescue of Mrs. Waters, the two repair to an inn where the landlady is not anxious to receive them:

> Now it required no very blamable degree of suspicion to imagine that Mr. Jones and his ragged companion had certain purposes in their intention, which, though tolerated in some Christian countries, connived at in others, and practiced in all, are however as expressly forbidden as murder, or any other horrid vice, by that religion which is universally believed in those countries. The landlady, therefore, had no sooner received an intimation of the entrance of the above-said persons than she began to meditate the most expeditious means for their expulsion. In order to do this, she had provided herself with a long and deadly instrument, with which, in times of peace, the chambermaid was wont to demolish the labours of the industrious spider. In vulgar phrase, she had taken up the broomstick, and was just about to sally from the kitchen, when Jones accosted her with a demand of a gown and other vestments to cover the half-naked woman up-stairs.

Both the essay and the heroic styles of narration, besides being amusing in themselves as burlesque and mock-heroic, are the result of Fielding's ambiguous attitude towards the material used in a novel. They also effectively point up the unsuitability in the novel of the "elevation of style" used in more traditional forms of narrative writing. By comparison the plain style is made to appear without question to be the best for the novel. The variety of narrative styles at the disposal of the novelist is succinctly illustrated by Fielding in *Joseph Andrews* on the occasion of one of the many beatings suffered by Parson Adams, whose assailant this time "belaboured the body of Adams till he was weary, and indeed till he concluded (to use the language of fighting) that he had done his business; or, in the language of poetry, 'that he had sent him to the shades below'; in plain English, 'that he was dead.'" And yet Fielding cannot take quite seriously the behavior of the "comic class" which his plain narrative style is so well calculated to report; his parodies and burlesques, like those of Joyce in *Ulysses*, exhibit the risibility of the world he is rendering and restore the ironical viewpoint of the author.

In addition to the three different narrative styles in *Tom Jones*, the style of the eighteenth-century essay is put to normal use in the well-known introductory chapters, "composed of observation and reflection," as well as in the course of the story itself when authorial comment seems appropriate. And to make the variety of styles even richer, Fielding, borrowing the principle of verisimilar speech from the drama, makes liberal use of many different speaking styles: the learned jargon of Square and Thwackum, the tiresome commonplace chatter of Mrs. Honour, the local dialects of barmaids, servants, and Squire Western.

Fielding's practice suggests the principle that the more independently the three genres composing the novel are developed, the more sharply differentiated will be the several prose styles of a novel, or the greater divergence there will be between the language that conveys the story, the language that conceptualizes and analyzes, and the language in which the characters speak. The structure of such a novel will tend to be episodic, the pattern of styles, paratactic: that is, blocks of varied material will be set beside each other without much coordination and modulation, and prose styles of sharply differing character will be juxtaposed. *Moby Dick*, even more than *Tom Jones*, is a prime example of a novel with mixed styles growing out of unassimilated genres and the divided mind of the author who regarded his material as both common whale blubber and rare mythic poetry. The narrative is presented in prose that is economical, concrete, and direct; exposition and authorial observations and reflections are presented ironically in a mixture of the "hopping," intimate style of the whimsical essay and the public style of oratory; the dialogue has the quality of heroic poetry, which Melville takes seriously as imitation, not parody, of Elizabethan blank verse. While all of these styles make a remarkable blend in *Moby Dick*, the special quality of each is preserved.

Being itself a compound of genres, each with a more fixed character than the novel and each having a different stylistic potential, the novel has always offered opportunities for a mixture of styles. And yet the novel has never imposed the necessity of being written in mixed styles. Indeed, from the very beginning, novelists have easily avoided the mixture of styles that the hybrid form and uncertain status of the novel seem to encourage. Far from being the rule, the mixed style novel has been the anomaly in the history of fiction, the kind of work that it is so difficult to justify as belonging at all to the genre.

The concentration on one of the component genres of the novel to the exclusion of the others has been one method to avoid a mixture of styles. Uniformity of style in *Clarissa* was made possible by the adaptation of the moral essay to fictional purposes; in *Tristram Shandy*, by the exploitation of that aspect of the personal essay that lends itself to facetious rhetoric and parenthesis. Concentration on the essayistic or analytic potential of prose produced uniform style in the later James and Proust, just as the scrupulous avoidance of analytic prose and an almost complete dependence upon narrative and drama yielded a uniform plain style in Hemingway.

In *The Ambassadors*, Maria Gostrey and Strether discover that they have in Waymarsh a mutual acquaintance:

> "Oh yes," he replied, "my very well-known friend. He's to meet me here, coming up from Malvern, and I supposed he would already have arrived. But he doesn't come till later, and I'm relieved not to have kept him. Do you know him?" Strether wound up.
>
> It was not till after he had spoken that he became aware of how much there had been in him of response; when the tone of her own rejoinder, as well as the play of something more in her face—something more, that is, than its apparently usual restless light—seemed to notify him. "I've met him at Milrose—where I used sometimes, a good while ago, to stay; I had friends there who were friends of his, and I've been at his house. I won't answer for it that he would know me," Strether's interlocutress pursued; "but I should be delighted to see him.

Perhaps," she added, "I shall—for I'm staying over." She paused an instant, while our friend took in these things, and it was as if a good deal of talk had already passed. They even vaguely smiled at it, and Strether presently observed that Mr. Waymarsh would, no doubt, be easily to be seen. This, however, appeared to affect the lady as if she might have advanced too far. She was frank about everything. "Oh," she said, "he won't care!"—and she immediately thereupon remarked that she believed Strether knew the Munsters; the Munsters being the people he had seen her with at Liverpool.

The speeches of the characters, the motions of Strether's consciousness as it begins to play on a new phenomenon, and the author's objective record of the scene are all of a piece stylistically. There is no break from one kind of material to another; stiff-jointed syntax carries the burden of meticulous analysis. Colloquial usage gets into the recording prose of the author ("our friend took in these things"), and the formality of the author's manner gets into the speeches ("I supposed he would already have arrived").

A different kind of uniformity is achieved by Hemingway. The ambulance of Lieutenant Henry is bogged down in the mud:

> The thing to do now was to dig out in front of the wheels, put in brush so that the chains could grip, and then push until the car was on the road. We were all down on the road around the car. The two sergeants looked at the car and examined the wheels. Then they started off down the road without a word. I went after them.
>
> "Come on," I said. "Cut some brush."
>
> "We have to go," one said.
>
> "Get busy," I said, "and cut brush."
>
> "We have to go," one said. The other said nothing. They were in a hurry to start. They would not look at me.
>
> "I order you to come back to the car and cut brush," I said. The one sergeant turned. "We have to go on. In a little while you will be cut off. You can't order us. You're not our officer."
>
> "I order you to cut brush," I said. They turned and started down the road.
>
> "Halt," I said. They kept on down the muddy road, the hedge on either side. "I order you to halt," I called. They

went a little faster. I opened up my holster, took the pistol, aimed at the one who had talked the most, and fired.

The same style is used for both action and dialogue and never varies throughout the book. No differentiation is made between the speeches of the narrator, an American who is presumably speaking simple Italian, and the speeches of the sergeant, a native Italian. No analysis is made of the characters' thought; it must be deduced from what they do and say: Lieutenant Henry "aimed at the one who had talked the most." There is no attempt in *A Farewell To Arms* to go beyond the plain recording of simple action and speech, except on one occasion when the mind of Lieutenant Henry is rendered as it succumbs to sleep and on another when an unspoken prayer for Catherine's recovery passes through the mind of the narrator.

Although competition among the three original genres of the novel has always been a condition in the writing of fiction, it is to be noted that in the earliest and latest years of the history of the novel this competition has been more pronounced than in the middle period, the nineteenth century. At that time the principle of assimilation prevailed: that is, the narrative, essayistic, and dramatic ingredients of the novel were not treated independently, each with a different potential fully realized, but were combined in a single genre and presented under a single aspect of language. Henry James stated the principle of assimilation when he wrote:

> I cannot imagine composition existing in a series of blocks, nor conceive, in any novel worth discussing at all, of a passage of description that is not in its intention narrative, a passage of dialogue that is not in its intention descriptive, a touch of truth of any sort that does not partake of the nature of incident. . . . A novel is a living thing, all one and continuous, . . . in each of the parts there is something of each of the other parts.

In a novel of such closely articulated parts—and the works of James's middle phase are among the best examples—the essayistic material ("a touch of the truth"), the dramatic material, and the narrative ("incident") have no existence as independent genres and are presented in a prose style that is essentially uniform. Moreover, the elements of narrative, essay, and drama are held in more or less equal proportions: there is not more essay material than dramatic, no more dramatic material than narrative. The balancing of novelistic ingredients and the presentation of all in a uniform style characterize the greatest achievements in the novel of the nineteenth century. A uniform style was thus the result of the assimilation of the component genres of the novel, and uniform style was also the means by which assimilation was helped.

Concentration on the essayistic element in fiction is likely to result in a complex prose style of a personal rather than conventional quality. Conversely, the assimilation and balancing of the novel's three component genres more readily leads to a plain style of conventional character, the language of narrative and drama acting as correctives to the tendency of essayistic prose to become syntactically complex and verbally abstract. The prose style of nineteenth-century English, French, and Russian fiction is distinguished by its plainness and by its lack of literary distinction. It was not far removed from the common style used in all sorts of contemporary writing that made a close approach to the plain facts of existence. Being close to the style of journalism, it was an easy and a popular style, well suited to the purposes of realism.

Whatever variety there was in this unspecialized and general style for fiction was gained by differentiating the speeches of characters. Such variety places most nineteenth-century fiction somewhere between the pure extremes of mixed and uniform style novels. It was of course the spirit of realism and the principle of verisimilar speech practiced in the drama that had prompted novelists as early as Fielding to contrive a mixture of speaking styles appropriate for various character types: dialect speakers, exotics like Scott's Highlanders and Cooper's Indians, and eccentrics whose peculiarities were better displayed in their speech than in their behavior. All of these speakers had numerous prototypes in Shakespeare and the contemporary stage, and most spoke in the novel "for the jest-sake," as Fielding put it, and for the purpose of injecting into the plain prose of the nineteenth-century novel a touch of "quaint," strange, or poetic language. Their varied speaking styles were not to be taken quite seriously, however, never to be accorded the same high value associated with the speaking style of the proper heroes and heroines. Since these spoke in the same style used in the essay and narrative material of the novel, the general effect of uniform style thus remained in spite of the speeches of amusing and exotic characters, whose divergent styles supplied only occasional color to the common fabric of the prose.

The normative or base style of the typical nineteenth-century novel can be described as polite, "literary," book prose, greatly relaxed and loosened by the influence of journalism—what Carlyle contemptuously labelled "ready-writing" and Thoreau "fluent writing." Undistinguished as such a style was, it served the purpose of the best fiction of the time. It had two important advantages for the novel of that time: its fluency and prolixity supported the sense of continuous and detailed existence that the novel tried to render, and its gentility constituted a valuable means of reader edification and reader identification with the point of view of the author. An equable and consistent view of reality was presented in a consistent and unpointed flow of language. Every narrative incident, every authorial comment was assured of a respectful response by reason of its being conveyed in a style common to both writer and reader. Characters of irregular habit or disposition were easily identified and evaluated according to their degree of departure from the normative style of the hero and the author.

Uniform style in fiction employing first-person narration is of course a formal requirement to reflect limited point of view. Some variety of style is secured by the narrator's total recall of the speeches of characters he encounters. When partial recall is used, as in *Huckleberry Finn*, the recorded speaking styles are accommodated to the style of the narrator, so that while there is some difference between the style of the narrator and other characters, it is not as great as in a novel like *David Copperfield*, in which the narrator preserves exactly the strikingly different qualities of Micawber and Mrs. Mowcher. Absolute uniformity of style in a first-person novel is achieved simply by making no concessions whatever to individual differences. Interest is made to center so exclusively on the narrator's particular response to reality and on a set of characters closely resembling the narrator, that no expectation of stylistic variation has to be met by the writer. Walter Shandy and his guests are rhetoricians of the same school as Tristram; the narrators of James and Hemingway present worlds that are closed to any character and any style that is not of a piece with the narrator's.

While verisimilar speech was widely used for amusing and exotic characters in novels before the last quarter of the nineteenth century, little attempt was made to have the first-person narrator deliver his fiction in a verisimilar speaking style. Convention required that the narrator "write" his account in the style generally expected in all fiction rather than "speak" it in a special personal style. The prose of a narrator like David Copperfield differs not at all from the prose used by Dickens in his third-person novels. David Copperfield's personality is of course revealed, but not through the kind of prose style he employs. The manner in which he tells his story is calculated less to individualize his character than to supply the stabilizing and evaluative function of a conventional style. *Tristram Shandy* and *Moby Dick* represent early attempts to depart from the conventional style for first-person narration by exploiting the idiosyncrasies of the narrator's language. Tristram drives traditional rhetorical devices to unconventional extremes, and Ishmael resorts to archaic essay styles. Neither uses a verisimilar speaking style, although this is speciously suggested by their addressing the reader on almost every page. In neither case is a new style for fiction developed or even intended; the striking effect in each book depends upon the highly mannered application to fiction of prose styles that are outrageously unsuited for fiction.

It was not until the latter part of the nineteenth century, when the fully developed theory of realism embraced the serious use of dialect styles, that verisimilar speech was considered appropriate for first-person narrators. Mark Twain proved that a special dialect style could support a masterpiece, and Hemingway later proved that a general colloquial style is equally capable of sustaining a novel. But these are singular achievements of stylistic imitation and hold no promise either for the continued creativeness of a writer or for the novel in general.

Uniform style is characteristic of the naturalistic novel that specializes in the breadth rather than the depth of its *tranche de vie*. Since the naturalist takes no commanding view of his fiction, narrative and essay materials are presented in a style not far removed from the dull, unpointed speaking style of the characters, who are representative of average humanity. The result is a monolithic dullness of language. In the later development of naturalism, however, the limitations of simple syntax and colorless diction became an intolerable burden, and we find naturalists resorting to a modified mixed style novel. By the use of "interchapters" that range in style from the newspaper headline to the stream of consciousness, Dos Passos sought ways of varying the uniform dullness of his prose and gaining access to subjective and even poetic expression. Steinbeck, in *The Grapes of Wrath*, carries his tribe of Joads into Canaan almost entirely in the low dialect style of their speech, but, quite appropriately for a story that is a latter-day Exodus, his interchapters reflect the style of the King James Version.

The tendency towards mixed styles in the naturalistic novel proves the inadequacy of a prose style based exclusively on the low tone of ordinary speech, or what Henry James called the "unutterable depths" of the "bastard vernacular" of modern communities. An uncommon dialect speaker like Huck Finn commands interest, and his speech may even rise to heights of poetic expressiveness; a common colloquial narrator, like Frederick Henry in *A Farewell To Arms*, attracts because of his artful selection from the common store of colloquial diction and rhythm. But the unrelieved, common slush of prose characteristic of Studs Lonigan cannot fail to be dull. The naturalists as well as their critics recognized this, and their interchapters suggest the close of another period of uniform prose and the return of the novel to a mixture of styles.

In naturalistic novels that specialize in depth, the stream of consciousness technique constitutes an extreme development of the earlier principle of verisimilar speech. When the content of a character's consciousness is composed of ideas, of thought, it must be conveyed in language that approaches closer to the quality of speech than to the style of either essay or narrative. It is speech without the use of syntax, or speech in which conventional syntax is replaced by a personal rhetoric of associations employed just below the level of communication. The style of such passages must be an appropriate imitation of potential or incipient speech, just as speaking style in conventional fiction imitates actual or achieved speech. When the content of a character's consciousness is composed of sensations, however, the style cannot be modeled upon speech patterns but must depend upon the nonimitative imagination of the novelist working with the syntax and vocabulary of poetry. In either event, opportunities for mixed style novels have been immeasurably increased by the stream of consciousness technique; for in a single novel there may be as may styles as there are characters, and a single character may have more than one style assigned to him, depending upon the levels of consciousness in which he is revealed.

No historical or evolutionary principle explains the incidence of mixed and uniform styles in the novel. The possibilities of both methods were realized in the earliest novels, and both methods are in use today. The least one can safely say is that between *Moby Dick* and *Ulysses* the novel was committed to a uniform plain style. *Moby Dick* is the last specimen of the early mixed style novel, and *Ulysses* begins the return of the contemporary novel to mixed styles. In the period between these two works, the novel attained a degree of stylistic stability that made possible the perfection of the genre in that time.

Uniform style novels may result from the operation of some formal principle such as first-person narration, the assimilation of the three component genres of fiction, or the exclusive dependence upon one. Uniform style in a novel generally depends upon the writer's settled conviction of the single, unambiguous nature of his materials and of the novel's adequacy as a vehicle for their serious presentment. In so far as style is a means of shutting out many possible views on a subject and directing attention to a few selected views, a uniform style has the effect of better narrowing the scope to a single, unified view of reality. A uniform style is assimilative in that it helps to create under a single aspect of language a single vision of the multiplicity of reality; it is a bond between author and reader, insuring that no different adjustment to language and viewpoint will be demanded from the reader than that established at the outset. In the nineteenth century it was confidently expected—and sometimes rigorously demanded as in the case of Melville and James—that every work of a novelist be in the same style as his first success. Our contemporary taste is just the reverse: it finds fault with a writer like Hemingway because his style repeats itself from one work to another, while nothing now creates more respect and attention than a change of style, as was evidenced in the recent stir in critical circles over Cozzens' *By Love Possessed*.

A mixed style novel may proceed from the variety that can be gained from exploiting the different potentials of the three genres composing the novel. It is the ideal vehicle for the writer who is motivated by the spirit of irony and parody and who finds it impossible to remain committed to a single vision of reality. A mixture of styles has the effect of making the reader pass through a succession of contradictory and ambiguous attitudes; it offers no sure stylistic norm by which the reader may orient himself permanently to the fiction and to the point of view of the author. He is conditioned to expect to change his position of witness as the style changes. Instead of being assimilative, the mixed style method is mimetic, or imitative of the inherent qualities of things and of the diverse attitudes with which reality may be viewed.

HUGH KENNER

James Joyce: Comedian of the Inventory

Flaubert, we know, was the connoisseur of the *mot juste,* lifted with tweezers from its leatherette box by a lapidary of choleric diligence. Paragraph after paragraph, page after page, his scores of special-purpose words certify, by their very air of uniqueness, to a resolute artistry for which stock parts would not suffice. His tight, burnished set pieces slacken considerably in translation; if we want to see something in English that resembles them, we cannot do better than consult *Ulysses,* where Bloom's cat "blinked up out of her avid shameclosing eyes," or "Frail from the housetops two plumes of smoke ascended, pluming, and in a flaw of softness softly were blown," or "Two shafts of soft daylight fell across the flagged floor from the high barbicans; and at the meeting of their rays a cloud of coalsmoke and fumes of friend grease floated, turning."

Such sentences, while they contain no difficulty of reference or content, might send a foreign reader to his dictionary, whether to find out the meaning of such words as "avid" and "barbicans," which while not recherche fall well outside a basic English vocabulary, or else to make sure that his difficulty in fitting less uncommon words together is not due to their possessing meanings of which he is unaware. Like Flaubert, Joyce in such passages throws the words into isolation, exposing their unmortared surfaces; when he assimilates them into idioms it is because he wants us to notice the idiom, which is commonly a borrowing or a parody.

It is by imagining the difficulties of a foreign reader that we can most readily see Joyce's characteristic way of dealing with the single word. For he continuously evades the normal English patterns to which structural linguists have devoted so much study. He places the adverbial phrase before the object ("her fingertip lifted to her mouth random crumbs"), sets the verb between the subject and phrases in apposition to the subject ("Down stage he strode some paces, grave, tall in affliction, his long arms outheld"), and is tirelessly resourceful in placing the adverb where it will exert stress against the other members of the sentence. ("He passed, dallying, the windows of Brown Thomas, silk mercers.") These are not the manoeuvres of a man speaking, but of a man writing: a man setting down twelve or fourteen selected words and determining in what order to arrange them. A man speaking arranges larger structural units than words. Frank Budgen recalls their discussion of what had been for Joyce a solid day's work: two sentences. "You have been seeking the *mot juste?*" "No," said Joyce, "I have the words already. What I am seeking is the perfect order of words in the sentence. There is an order in every way appropriate. I think I have it."

It is perfectly natural that *Ulysses* should have attracted the attention of a group of scholars who wanted practice in compiling a word-index to some extensive piece of prose. More than any other work of fiction, it suggests by its texture, often by the very look of its pages, that it has been painstakingly assembled out of single words, and that we may learn something by taking the words apart again and grouping them for alphabetical study. Thanks to Professor Miles Hanley and his collaborators, we therefore know exactly how many different words it contains (29,899); which one is used most often ("the"), and how many times (14,877); which, and how many (16,432), used once only. The Hanley Word-Index to *Ulysses* [1] simply carries to an extreme of thoroughness the sort of marginal cross-references every student of the book pencils on page after page of his copy.

For the reader of *Ulysses* holds a book in his hands. Homer envisaged no such possibility. Consider what it makes feasible. On page 488 we read, "Potato preservative against plague and pestilence, pray for us." Now just sixty pages earlier, if we were alert, we may have noted the phrase, "Poor mamma's panacea," murmured by Bloom as he feels his trouser pocket. And fully 372 pages before that, on the bottom line of page 56, we have Bloom feeling in his hip pocket for the latchkey and reflecting, "Potato I have." The serious reader's copy of *Ulysses* acquires cross-references at three points; and Bloom's potato, it is by now commonplace to remark, is but one trivial instance among hundreds of motifs treated very briefly at two or three widely separated points in the book, and not even intelligible until the recurrences have been collated. It is customary to note that Joyce makes very severe demands of his reader. To learn something new from this commonplace we have only to set down its corollary. The demands Joyce makes on the reader would be impossible ones if the reader did not have his hands on the book, in which he can turn to and fro at his pleasure. And more than that: the whole conception of *Ulysses* depends on the existence of something former writers took for granted as simply the envelope for their wares: a printed book whose pages are numbered.

II

Any book so conceived has broken with narrative, though it may go through certain forms of storytelling. Narrative implies that someone is talking. It is an art that unfolds its effects in time, like music. It holds us under the spell of a voice, or something analogous to a voice, and (again like music) it slowly gathers into a simplified whole in the memory. The supreme vividness of the present instant blends continually with times gone: words fade, past scenes blur, scenes and characters we had forgotten reappear with studied eclat in some late phase of the adventure; the voice presses on, and the effect is completed as the final words set up resonances among our recollections of all that has preceded. No one understood this better than Joseph Conrad, who is at such pains to subject us to the spell of the teller of a tale. Conrad, with his studied apparatus of spoken narrative discharged into a reflective silence, attempted to carry to some ideal limit the convention under which Dickens, for instance, had operated with such confidence: the convention that a tale is something told, an act of intrepidity on the part of the teller, who is venturing where he has really never been before; and that the tale is a whole only in the hearer's memory; and that the written book is simply a record of the telling, or purports to be such a record. If we press back to Dickens we find an even simpler convention: the written book is a script, to be brought to life in oral delivery, by some middle-class Englishman reading aloud at his fireside, or by the author on an American tour. Far back of Dickens, again, lies Homer, whose book is simply a graph of what the bard recited: something that lived exactly in his memory, and gets transferred to the listener's memory less exactly. A manuscript or printed book, entitled *The Odyssey*, has simply this function, that it takes the place of the rhapsode's memory, somewhat deadly, somewhat mechanically.

Homer, of course, also lies behind *Ulysses;* and the most profound of all Joyce's Homeric transformations is this, that the text of *Ulysses* is not organized in memory and unfolded in time, but both organized and unfolded in what we may call *technological space:* on printed pages for which it was designed from the beginning. The reader explores its discontinuous surface at whatever pace he likes; he makes marginal notes; he turns back whenever he chooses to an earlier page, without destroying the continuity of something that does not press on, but will wait until he resumes. He is manoeuvred, in fact, precisely into the role of the scholiasts whose marginalia encumbered the Alexandrian manuscripts of Homeric texts; only here is a text designed, as Homer's was not, precisely for this sort of study. It really *does* contain, as Homer's work was reputed to contain, a systematic compendium of arts, sciences and moral teachings; symbols, rituals and practical counsels; Irish history and the geography of the city of Dublin. If we are agreed that Homer's text does not designedly contain all the things that symbolic exegesis used to find there, it is because we are convinced that Homer spoke and sang but did not fuss over a manuscript. The Alexandrian scholars lived in a manuscript culture, whose conventions they projected onto their author. Joyce, however, did fuss over a manuscript, and a manuscript designed for a printer, and he pored over galley proofs and page proofs also. Joyce is acutely aware that the modern Homer must deal with neither an oral culture nor a manuscript one, but with a culture whose shape and whose attitude to its daily experience is determined by the omnipresence of the printed book.

He was very careful, therefore, to reproduce in his text the very quality of print, its reduction of language to a finite number of interchangeable and permutable parts. We have the impression, as we read the Circe episode, that we have encountered all its ingredients before, only in a different arrangement.

> Dennis Breen, whitetallhatted, with Wisdom Hely's sandwich-
> board, shuffles past them in carpet slippers, his dull beard
> thrust out, muttering to right and left. Little Alf Bergan,
> cloaked in the pall of the ace of spades, dogs him to left and
> right, doubled in laughter.

This combines Mr. Breen, the Mad Hatter's hat, the sandwichmen from page 152, a shuffling gait and the phrase "dull beard" from page 157, Breen's dream of the ace of spades from page 155, and Alf Bergan who on page 157 is named as the probable sender of a disturbing postcard. (This is a hasty census: I may have missed a few items.) There presides over this phantasmagoria precisely the faith that presides over the eighteenth century's rationalism, the faith that we can register all relevant phenomena in some book where we can find them again: in a dictionary, where human speech is dissociated into words which can be listed in alphabetical order, or in an encyclopaedia, where human knowledge is broken up into discontinuous fragments to be registered on a similar principle.

The Rev. Walter J. Ong, S.J., has argued brilliantly that printing was the efficient cause of those intellectual movements which in the sixteenth and seventeenth centuries destroyed the hierarchies of knowledge and rearranged the things we know for the sake of pedagogic convenience. Certainly it was printing which led us to think of speech as being composed of interchangeable parts, if only because printing and its by-product lexicography enforced a uniformity of spelling which gave each separate word a stable identity to the eye, whatever its equivocal status for the ear. After that, writing becomes a matter of locating and arranging words, as Joyce spent his celebrated day trying out different arrangements of fifteen words:

> Perfume of embraces all him assailed. With hungered flesh obscurely, he mutely craved to adore.

Those words he caused to lie within the gestures of the spoken voice, while conveying tensions that speech, which manipulates phrases rather than words, would never have discovered for itself.

Printing also leads to the manufacture of books, and to the nuisance of untalented authors. And here we encounter one of those loops in time, uniting the eighteenth and the twentieth centuries, which the student of Joyce's Dublin learns to anticipate, welcome, and explore. For the first author of talent to have been forcibly struck by the *nature* of the printed book appears to have been a compatriot of Joyce's and a great denizen of *Finnegans Wake*, by name Jonathan Swift.

III

There are many ways of describing *A Tale of a Tub;* let us call it one thing more, a parody of the book as a book. For its method is to emphasize to the point of grotesqueness exactly those features which distinguish the printed book *per se*, the printed book a technological arti-fact, from a human document. Human documents Swift is prepared to understand, though looking around him in 1704 or thereabouts, in the first dawn of the bookseller's paradise, he can discern precious few.

Between a human document and the thing that Gutenberg's monster typically disgorges, a distinction may be discovered which turns on the intimate nature of what the brain thinks and the hand writes. For Swift, a piece of writing is properly something that exists in a personal context, where one human being is seeking to gain the confidence and understanding of another. Pamphlets like the *Modest Proposal* or the *Argument Against Abolishing Christianity* depend for their effect on our understanding and approving this fact: their supposed author re-poses in a state of bland rapport with readers who will respond suitably to his insinuations and share his notions of rational conduct. Though the pamphlet is anonymous, its effect is not to efface the supposed author but to generalize him; he is the obedient humble servant of whatever reader is jackass enough to find him congenial. The rapport between them, while it depraves the rational intercourse of honest men, is still an intercourse between persons: as much so, Swift might add, as an act of sodomy. By contrast Swift finds in the typical con-temporary printed book no trace of the inviolable human person. *A Tale of a Tub* is not at bottom a civil letter, as a pamphlet is essentially a letter. It is anonymous because it is written by nobody, by no person, but by the autonomous book-compiling machine itself; and it addresses itself, like a public speech from the scaffold, to the public at large and to posterity—that is, to no one. *A Tale of a Tub* is the first comic ex-ploitation of that technological space which the words in a large printed book tend to inhabit. Commerce and capital had recently dis-covered that printing is not simply a way of disseminating manuscripts, but that a book is an artifact of a new kind. This discovery brought with it a host of technical gimmicks which Swift regards with fasci-nated disquiet. We have discovered in the same way that the motion picture is not simply a way of recording plays, but a different medium; and that television is not simply a way of disseminating motion pic-tures, but a different medium; and each of these discoveries has brought with it an embarrassing swarm of new techniques. So it was, in Swift's day, with the book: and *A Tale of a Tub* is the register of Gutenberg technology, discerned by a man who regarded each of the bookmaker's devices as a monstrous affront to the personal intercourse which letters in a dialogue culture had served to promote.

The book as book entails, then, Introductions, Prefaces, Apologies and Dedications; Headings, Subheadings; Tables, Footnotes, Indices; even Pictures. The way in which some of these help mechanize the act of discourse is perfectly plain. Take the footnote, for instance.[2] The footnote's relation to the passage from which it depends is established wholly by visual and typographic means, and will typically defeat all efforts of the speaking voice to clarify it without visual aid. Parentheses, like commas, tell the voice what to do: an asterisk tells the voice that it can do nothing. You cannot read a passage of prose aloud, interpolating the footnotes, and make the subordination of the footnotes clear,[3] and keep the whole sounding natural. The language has forsaken a vocal milieu, and a context of oral communication between persons, and commenced to take advantage of the expressive possibilities of technological space.

This ventriloqual gadget, the footnote, deserves some attention, partly because Swift became a great virtuoso on this new instrument, and Joyce later devoted a whole section of *Finnegans Wake* to ringing changes on the footnote and its cousin the marginalium. One would like to know when it was invented; it is as radical a discovery as the scissors or the rocking chair, and presumably as anonymous. The man who writes a marginal comment is conducting a dialogue with the text he is reading; but the man who composes a footnote, and sends it to the printer along with his text, has discovered among the devices of printed language something analogous with counterpoint: a way of speaking in two voices at once, or of ballasting or modifying or even bombarding with exceptions [4] his own discourse without interrupting it. It is a step in the direction of discontinuity: of organizing blocks of discourse simultaneously in space rather than consecutively in time. We encounter its finest flower in the immense scheme of annotation to the final edition of the *Dunciad Variorum,* a project in which it is customary to discern Swift's hand. *The Dunciad,* like *A Tale of a Tub,* is not only a satire against the abuses of the Gutenberg era, but an exploitation of technical devices made available by that era. Because print enables us to distinguish verse from prose at once by eye, we may here observe, page by page, an Attic column of verse standing on a thick pedestal of miscellaneous learning. Or the verse plunges majestically forward amid a strangely orderly babel of commentaries, assailed at random by every fly in Grub Street. Very often the note is needed to complete a poetic effect; Mr. Empson has analyzed a famous instance of this. And Pope's intricate mosaic of allusions to other poems, it is pertinent to remark, depends for its witty precision on a prime assumption of the Dunces, namely that poetry is to be found exclusively in books, that the texts of past classics are as stable as mosaic tiles (having been quick-frozen by the printer), and that someone with fingernail scissors and a little bottle of paste can rearrange the general stock of literature to produce new beauties. The Dunces themselves, of course, do this all the time; Pope is always careful to imitate their every mannerism with insolent fidelity; and it is the easier to do because metrical varieties have become so standardized, like that standardization of machine-screw threads which today makes possible an international technology.

We called the footnote [5] a device for organizing units of discourse discontinuously in space rather than serially in time. The same is true of the Introductions, Dedications and Digressions with which the *Tale* is so lavishly equipped. They all of them instance and exploit the essential discontinuity of the book as book. The introductory matter expands to a heroic scale certain printers' conventions. A conventional heading in large capital letters suffices to legitimize the presence in a book of almost anything the author and bookseller choose: flattery of some patron, for instance, which we can incorporate into any book at all simply by heading it *Dedication*. Swift allows the eponymous author of the *Tale* to plume himself mightily on his own capacity for sheer miscellaneousness, and carries this theme into the text itself by the device of interpolating immense Digressions, each headed "Digression" to prevent any earnest reader from supposing that he is losing the thread. The first section of the book proper (headed Section One: the Introduction) makes a great pother about the various conditions for the oral delivery of wisdom: from the pulpit, the stage itinerant, the scaffold and perhaps the bench; but nothing is clearer from the beginning of this book to the end than the fact that all conceivable modes of oral discourse are totally unrelated to it. The Digressions, indeed, treat not of speech or dialogue but of every aspect of bookmaking: notably indices, tables of contents, anthologies, compilations, the art of digression, the practice of criticism and the improvement of madness in the commonwealth.

Having mentioned Pope's witty precisions, we should mention Swift's in turn, for the two of them generate a stylistic curve which passes axially through *Ulysses* and *Finnegans Wake*. If their exactness of language pleases and surprises, it is by a sort of analogy with deft manufacture; we acknowledge as much when we apply a word like "precision," which in the twentieth century is a technological metaphor. The *mot juste* is a beauty we owe to the omnipresence of the printer, because oral delivery tends to blur it. Our interest in the *mot juste* is a function of our concern with the single word, its look, feel, weight, history, range, and denotation: a concern first fostered by the eighteenth-century interest in lexicography, which interest in turn belongs to the age of the book. A scholiast writing marginalia to the *Odyssey* may pause over a single word to consider how Homer is using it here; but a lexicographer abstracts it from all particular usage. Samuel Johnson may be described as the first writer to have examined individually in turn each of the words he employs, and without actually compiling dictionaries, writers have followed his example ever since. Certainly Joyce does. And in Johnson's lexicography there is crystallized an attitude to language already for half a century prevalent and dominant, sponsored by the concern of a whole society's intelligence with the production of printed books. (A word assembled from leaden cubes in a type case, as Father Ong has indicated, is already well on its way to being an interchangeable part.) When Pope writes of a heroic Dunce plunging into the Thames,

> Furious he dives, precipitately dull,

we know that the word "precipitately" has received from Pope a kind of attention which the word "incarnadine" did not receive from Shakespeare. Pope's wit consists in the exactness with which the word's etymology is being re-enacted in the line. Swift in the same way, reflecting on the posthumous fame of authors, is careful to arrange each of his individual words, clearly defined, into scintillation and balance.

> . . . whether it is that fame, being a fruit grafted on the body, can hardly grow, and much less ripen, till the stock is in the earth, or whether she be a bird of prey, and is lured, among the rest, to pursuit after the scent of a carcass: or whether she conceives her trumpet sounds best and farthest when she stands on a tomb, by the advantage of a rising ground, and the echo of a hollow vault.

We hear "carcass" start out from among the ceremonious euphemisms of decease, and hear the smart "advantage" offset the Virgilian "echo," and hear "rising ground" paralleled by "hollow vault," and no blur surrounds any of these effects, etched with lexicographic clarity. The effect is quite different from the effect that a similar terminology might have in a sermon of Donne's, because it is queerly unrelated to oral delivery: an eerie life stirs among words that have been briskly laid out to fill categories and complete tropes, in the stunned neutrality of print. Each term snaps magnetically into its place in the inviolable whole; each sentence is levelled like a course of bricks. To contrast these smartly articulated figures of thought, each one displayed and delimited like a little algebraic calculation, with some Shakespearean image groping obscurely among the roots of language for its own bases of relevance:

. . . Witness this army of such mass and charge . . .

is to perceive the kind of clarity that works by analogies with visual clarity and with the fact that we have before us a page to look at, where the backward glance to the beginning of any phrase, clearly indicated by the punctuation, will confirm the accuracy of every epithet. This is the precision which Joyce inherited from the first hey-day of the book, and exploited as no one had exploited it before, out of some conatural awareness of the nature of a civilization structured by print.

Though Leopold Bloom's knowledge, for example, most of it trace-able to books, is extremely inexact, it never produces on us an effect of confusion. There is no loss of outline: perfectly distinct words, each clearly remembered, have simply got into the wrong categories, or else sentences of which the beginnings have been fixed in his memory are incomplete because he has forgotten the endings.

> Where was that chap I saw in that picture somewhere? Ah, in the dead sea, floating on his back, reading a book with a parasol open. Couldn't sink if you tried: so thick with salt. Because the weight of water, no, the weight of the body in the water is equal to the weight of the. Or is it the volume is equal of the weight? It's a law something like that. Vance in high school cracking his finger-joints, teaching. The college curriculum. Cracking curriculum. What is weight really when you say the weight? Thirty-two feet per second, per second. Law of falling bodies; per second, per second. They all fall to the ground. The earth. It's the force of gravity of the earth is the weight.

Whatever the deficiencies of Bloom's understanding, there is no blur around any of these words, any more than around Swift's. The sentences do not achieve the formulations one might find in the physics textbooks Bloom is half remembering, but each word is clearly enunciated, and so far as lexicography can tell us, clearly understood. In fact the criterion of intellectual adequacy Bloom has inherited, the criterion to which he does not succeed in living up (and who could?), is a criterion based on the authority of the book. One is not expected to understand the phenomena; one is expected to get the formulas right, to lay hold of all the words and arrange them in the order in which the textbook arranges them. This proposition is easily tested: observe that we do not need to understand the physical laws involved to be sure that Bloom does not understand them. We need only note the incompleteness of his sentences, and their bathetic, anticlimactic rhythms. For words are interchangeable parts to be arranged, and there are authorized arrangements the recitation of which evinces confidence. Stephen Dedalus may understand what he is talking about or he may not, but he enjoys the confidence of the born word-man: "Ineluctable modality of the visible: at least that if no more, thought through my eyes. Signatures of all things I am here to read, seaspawn and seawrack, the nearing tide, that rusty boot."

That these examples touch principles which underlie the whole conception of *Ulysses,* is a fact obscurely recognized by the very large amount of critical energy that has been devoted to making wordlists for Joyce's books. The books, it is felt, are permutations of a stock of words which can be counted, enumerated, and classified. You can of course count, enumerate and classify Shakespeare's words, if you are so minded, but you are unlikely to attach any importance to the fact that a given word occurs in the canon, say, seven times. Or if you do attach importance to this fact, as the scholars do who explore Shakespeare's image-clusters, you will explain the fact on psychological grounds rather than assign it to deliberate technique. One does not think of Shakespeare as a man conscious that certain words, a large but finite number of them, enjoyed a proper existence, whereas any other words that came to his fancy were coinages. Joyce on the other hand, in a world where the dictionary and the printing press suggest limits to the authorized vocabulary, functions with a peculiar sardonic awareness of the fact that "catalectic," "consubstantial," and "costdrawer" are citizens in good standing of some large dictionary, that "contransmagnificandjewbangtantiality" is a molecule synthesized by him out of several such words, and that on a wholly different principle "lovelorn longlost lugubru Blooloohoom" is a comic coinage because it freezes in visual space some gesture of the tongue, the voice and the breath.

These auditory coinages deserve a bit of attention. Bloom's cat meows, and Joyce writes out the sound: "Mrkgnao!" Davy Byrne yawns, "Iiiiii-chaaaaaaach." The paperfolding machine speaks in its own way: "sltt." The fact that the dictionary gives no help to an author who wants to register phenomena of this kind attests to the divorce between printing-case language, inhabiting technological space, and acoustic language, the intelligible creation of human speech. The ordinary words we speak inhabit both dimensions, and we shift from the visual to the vocal manifestations of language with the negligence of lifelong habit. But let an intelligible sound which the dictionary has omitted to register be transcribed according to approved phonetic rules, and the result is taut, arbitrary and grotesque: something living has been imperfectly synthesized out of those twenty-six interchangeable parts to which every nuance of human discourse can allegedly be reduced: as though technology were offering to reproduce Helen of Troy with a Meccano set. There is something mechanical, Joyce never lets us forget, about all reductions of speech to arrangements of twenty-six letters. We see him playing in every possible way with the spatial organization of printed marks: inserting headlines; reducing the themes of an intricate Augustinian music to fifty-nine grotesque permutable phrases, each printed at the head of the Sirens episode on a separate line; entrusting the enervate languor of Eumaeus to grey unbroken paragraphs that numb the mind by tiring the eye, printing the questions and answers of the great catechism with emphatic intervening spaces, and the ultimate monologue of Mrs. Bloom with neither paragraphs, commas nor full stops; and delivering what one would expect to be the very epitome of the free and fluid, an immense drunken phantasmagoria a fifth of the book in length, into the keeping of the most rigid typographic formality he employs anywhere: discrete speeches, capitalized speakers, italicized narration: the status of everything visible at a glance.

What he thus freezes into a book is the life of Dublin, chiefly its vocal life. Ireland, it is relevant and even commonplace to observe, is unique in the West for the exclusiveness of its emphasis on oral rather than typographic culture, and *Ulysses* is built about the antithesis between the personal matrix of human speech and the unyielding formalisms of the book as book. It can hardly be accidental that two

Irishmen, Swift and Sterne,[6] exploited as long ago as the eighteenth century the peculiarities of the book to an extent no Anglo-Saxon has ever thought to emulate: nor is it accidental that the two of them link arms throughout *Finnegans Wake* like a pair of tutelary deities. Both of them were detached, as Joyce himself was later detached, from the assumptions of typographic culture: detached by the richer assumptions of a culture that thinks not of words but of voices, of the voice that states rather than the book that contains, of a matrix of speech in which person confronts person, not fact fact, of language generated by continuous acts of discourse rather than language delivered over to typographic storage. The Irish tradition of emitting pamphlets and broadsides rather than treatises, a tradition to which Joyce himself contributed in his youth, is an extension of these assumptions: the broadside is inalienably personal. It would be tempting to base a modern history of Ireland on the fact that the country has never sustained a large-scale publishing industry to erode its vocal and rhetorical bias, and polarize its sense of language toward the immutability of print rather than the coercive evanescence of breath. Even today it is customary for Dublin tavern wits to despise Joyce for practicing a lesser art than the talker's, a contempt sustained by something more than jealousy.

For nearly three centuries Ireland has mocked the book. Swift, we have seen, reached his most frenetic flights of ingenuity in the presence of the bookman's arsenal of techniques. Laurence Sterne availed himself of a hundred devices totally foreign to the storyteller but made possible by the book alone: not only the blank and marbled pages, the suppressed chapters represented only by headings, the blazonry of punctuation marks and the mimetic force of wavy lines, but also the suppression of narrative suspense—a suspense proper to the storyteller who holds us by curiosity concerning events unfolding in time—in favour of a bibliographic suspense which depends on our knowledge that the book in our hands is of a certain size and that the writer therefore has somehow reached the end of it—by what means? Nothing more completely separates typographic from oral narrative than the fact that, as we turn the pages, we can literally see the end coming. Following Swift and Sterne, Joyce shut a living world into a book, a heavy book that contains Dublin, kills it, and sets it into motion once again on a new plane: but a technological plane and a comic because finically precise motion. Dubliners tell discreditable stories about their enemies, and all Dublin knows the stories; but Joyce's revenge on

Oliver Gogarty was to shut him into a book: a deed that crushed Gogarty more, despite the limited number of Dubliners who inspected the result, than any number of rumours: for in a book Buck Mulligan enacts the same formal ballet of irreverence, and emits the same delimited witticisms, for ever: always on schedule, always in the same context, always on the same pages: a precise definition of imaginative hell, ineluctable, unstoppable, unmodifiable. This preoccupation of Dublin wits with the book continues: both Flann O'Brien in *At Swim-Two-Birds* and Samuel Beckett in his great trilogy of French novels capitalize on the antisocial quality of literature, the fact that the writer is not speaking, is not drinking, is confronting nobody warming and warming to nobody, but exists shut away in a room setting on pieces of paper word after word which once they have passed through Gutenberg's machinery no afterthought will ever efface: a deed the very antithesis of everything that Irish culture prides itself on being.

IV

Joyce's techniques—it is one of his principal lessons—are without exception derived from his subject, often excerpted from his subject. They are not means of representing the subject, and imperfectly; they are the subject's very members laid on the page, in eloquent or ludicrous *collage*. His subject is Dublin, and a past Dublin, much of it alive in perishable memory, much of its already reduced to printed lists or shut away in printed books. Before *Ulysses* itself comes to an end, it must incorporate portions of a newspaper that was being printed while some of its events were being transacted. From this paper we learn that the remains of the late Mr. Patrick Dignam were interred at Glasnevin in the presence of, *inter alia*, "L. Boom"; like *Bouvard et Pécuchet* the book goes through the motions of picking up its own documentation. This particular document is a forgery, but what newspaper is not? *Ulysses* itself is certainly the forgery Joyce later called it in *Finnegans Wake*, joining in some ideal archive the hundreds of other printed documents June 16, 1904, has left behind. For Joyce was competing with his own materials, writing, as he was, in the midst of an economy of print, surrounded by other books on which to draw. He possessed, for example, Thom's Dublin Directory for the year 1904. He possessed the newspapers for the day he had chosen. He possessed dictionaries, in which to find the day's words and verify their spelling (it is worth remembering that Shakespeare had no dictionary). He possessed other books, in which he could find lists of all kinds: the colours of the Mass vestments, for example, and their significance. As days die, in the modern world, they pass into records, not merely, as did Homer's days, into memory. A certain day exists eternally at the point where the City Directory is intersected by the newspaper, the Gregorian and Liturgical calendars, the race results, the weather bureau statistics, the police blotter, and a million letters, diaries, cancelled cheques, account books, betting tickets, laundry lists, birth certificates and cemetery registers.

Here we move beyond Flaubert; Flaubert, in quest of the general case, has none of Joyce's interest in lists. If many of Joyce's effects are the nearest English language equivalent to some of Flaubert's characteristic effects, yet even in brief examples one senses a pattern of difference, and the wider the range of examples the more marked the difference becomes. Consider, for instance, Joyce's concern with the arrangement of a limited number of words. He does this sentence by sentence and paragraph by paragraph (the Joycean paragraph deserves a chapter to itself; it is a unique creation), and by the time he has achieved the book we find it profitable, as Professor Hanley did, to regard the whole as a series of cunning permutations of some 30,000 different words. Or consider his collector's zeal. Frank Budgen once drew his attention to a word of Chatterton's and Joyce said, "It is a good word, and I shall probably use it": which he did. Or consider the care with which he stratifies the vocabulary of the various episodes, using in the lunchtime passage as many casual expressions derived from foodstuffs as he can collect, or in the funeral section a thousand mortuary turns of phrase. He appears to be working from lists, and for preference finite lists, beginning with the dictionary.

Discourse has become a finite list of words: at least potentially finite, since we can always imagine, without contradiction, a really complete dictionary, at least a really complete dictionary of the printed language. Dublin, 1904, in the same way has become the contents of Thom's Directory, in which it was possible for Joyce to verify in a moment the address of every business establishment, or the occupancy of every house (he was careful to install the Blooms at an address which, according to Thom's, was vacant). Theoretically, it would have been possible for him to name, somewhere in *Ulysses*, every person who inhabited Dublin on that day. Dublin, June 16, 1904, is documented in the newspapers of the day; Professor Richard Kain has shown with what care Joyce assimilated the names of the horses who were racing in the Gold Cup, or the details of the American steamboat disaster which occupied the Dublin headlines that morning. Even the nine participants in a quarter-mile footrace are embalmed forever in his text, name by name: M. C. Green, H. Thrift, T. M. Patey, C. Scaife, J. B. Jeffs, G. N. Morphy, F. Stevenson, C. Adderly and W. C. Huggard.

And we may note the congruence of such lists with other finite lists. There are twenty-four hours in a day, and he accounts for all but the ones spent by his characters in sleep. The spectrum has seven colours, and Bloom names them: roy g biv. The *Odyssey* can be dissociated into specific episodes, which Joyce accounts for. Shakespeare wrote some thirty-six plays; I do not know whether Joyce includes in the library scene an allusion to each of them, but it would not be surprising. The embryo lives nine months in the womb, or forty weeks; the body of the Oxen of the Sun episode has nine principal parts, in forty paragraphs, linked furthermore to a sequence of geological eras obtained from a list in a textbook.

We have heard of this side of Joyce often enough, but we have perhaps not heard the right things about it. As every commentator since Stuart Gilbert has discovered, nothing is easier than to disentangle, with patience, lists and more lists from the Protean text. What seems not to be dwelt upon is the fact that these lists are commonly finite, and that so far as he can, Joyce is at pains to include every item on them. What we can recover from his text is not a few samples, but the entire list. This is particularly clear in *Finnegans Wake*, where he had not, as in *Ulysses*, considerations of verisimilitude to impede him. Mr. James Atherton, in *The Books at the Wake*, has noted the presence in that work of all the titles of Shakespeare's plays, all of Moore's Irish Melodies, both the first line and the name of the tune, all the Books of the Bible, all the *suras* of the Koran (or not quite all; but whereas he speculates about the ones that are missing, it seems more likely that either he or Joyce simply overlooked them). Then there is the famous incorporation, into Anna Livia Plurabelle, of some six hundred rivers; probably not all the rivers of the world, but no doubt as many as Joyce could locate the names of. The same is true of the figures of rhetoric in the Aeolus episode of *Ulysses*; Mr. Gilbert, doubtless prompted by the author, cites ninety-four. I do not know whose enumeration Joyce followed, but I suspect he exhausted it, and if such a thing as an absolutely exhaustive list of figures of rhetoric were possible, and had been available to him, he would not have rested until he had accounted for every one.

This is the comedy of the Inventory, the comedy of exhaustion, comic precisely because exhaustive. The feeling proper to comic art, Joyce wrote, is joy, and by way of making clear what joy is, he distinguished it from desire. Now the virtue of exhaustiveness is this, that by it desire is utterly allayed. Nothing is missing. We have the double pleasure of knowing what should be present, and knowing that all of it is present. We have also what Bergson has taught us to regard as an indispensable component of the comic, a mechanical element; what is more mechanical than a check-list? And we have one other benison, an internal criterion of consistency. Celebrating a city, which once had walls and still has limits, which is laid out into streets and blocks, districts and zones, which can be represented by a map, or by a directory, Joyce is at pains to imitate all of these aspects of his subject in his book, which can be mapped and indexed, which has internal thoroughfares connecting points not textually contiguous, which contains zones defined and inimitably characterized (you could no more mistake a passage from "Eumaeus" for one from "Hades" than you could mistake Nighttown for Merrion Square).

NOTES

1. Madison, Wisconsin, 1937.
2. I do not mean the scholar's footnote which supplies a reference, but the footnote that supplements, qualifies, parallels, quips, digresses or elucidates.
3. And they are often less subordinated than counterpointed.
4. Some footnotes of course seem totally unrelated to the point in the text at which they are appended. They suggest an art form like the refrains in Yeats' late poems.
5. In the middle of the previous paragraph. Please pay attention.
6. I follow Joyce's usage, which makes Sterne an honorary Irishman. He was born in Ireland and spent much of his first ten years there.

MARGARET MACDONALD

The Language of Fiction

> Emma Woodhouse, handsome, clever and rich, with a com-
> fortable house and happy disposition seemed to unite some of
> the best blessings of existence and had lived nearly twenty-
> one years in the world with very little to distress or vex her.

The opening sentence of Jane Austen's novel *Emma* is a sentence from
fiction. *Emma* is a work in which the author tells a story of characters,
places and incidents almost all of which she has invented. I shall mean
by "fiction" any similar work. For unless a work is largely, if not wholly,
composed of what is invented, it will not correctly be called "fiction."
One which contains nothing imaginary may be history, science, detec-
tion, biography, but not fiction. I want to ask some questions about how
an author uses words and sentences in fiction. But my interest is logical,
not literary. I shall not discuss the style or artistic skill of any storyteller. Mine is the duller task of trying to understand some of the logic
of fictional language; to determine the logical character of its expressions. How do they resemble and differ from those in other contexts?
What are they understood to convey? Are they, e.g., true or false statements? If so, of or about what are they true or false? If not, what other
function do they perform? How are they connected? These are the
questions I shall chiefly discuss.

First of all, "fiction" is often used ambiguously both for what is fictitious and for that by which the fictitious is expressed. Thus "fiction" is
opposed to "fact" as what is imaginary to what is real. But one must
emphasize that a work of fiction itself is not imaginary, fictitious or
unreal. What is fictitious does not exist. There are no dragons in the
zoo. But the novels of Jane Austen do exist. The world, fortunately,

From *Proceedings of the Aristotelian Society*. Copyright 1954 by the
Aristotelian Society. Reprinted by permission of the Editor.

contains them just as it contained Jane Austen. They occupy many bookshelves. Works of fiction, stories, novels are additions to the universe. Any unreality attaches only to their subject matter.[1]

Secondly, everyone understands the expressions of fiction. Or, if they do not, the reason is technical, not logical. One may find it hard to understand some of the expressions of Gertrude Stein or *Finnegan's Wake* but this is due to the peculiar obscurity of their style and not to the fact they occur in works of fiction. No one who knows English could fail to understand the sentence quoted from *Emma*. That Emma Woodhouse was handsome, clever, and rich is understood just as easily as that Charlotte Brontë was plain, sickly and poor. Both are indicative sentences which appear to inform about their subjects. But while the sentence containing "Charlotte Brontë" expresses a true statement of which Charlotte Brontë is the subject, that containing "Emma Woodhouse," cannot work similarly, since Jane Austen's Emma did not exist and so cannot be the logical subject of any statement. "Emma Woodhouse" does not and cannot designate a girl of that name of whom Jane Austen wrote. This has puzzled philosophers.[2] If apparent statements about Emma Woodhouse are about no one, of what is Jane Austen writing and how is she to be understood? Perhaps a subsistent wraith in a logical limbo is her subject? This will not do; or, at least not in this form. Jane Austen is certainly "pretending" that there was a girl called Emma Woodhouse who had certain qualities and adventures. According to one view she is understood because we understand from non-fictional contexts the use of proper names and the general terms in which she describes Emma Woodhouse and her adventure. There is no Emma Woodhouse, so Jane Austen is not writing about her; rather is she writing about a number of properties, signified by the general terms she uses, and asserting that they belonged to someone. Since they did not, "Emma Woodhouse" is a pseudo-designation and the propositions are false, though significant. Readers of *Emma* need not, and usually do not, believe falsely that its propositions are true. A work of fiction is, or is about, "one big composite predicate" and is so understood by readers who need neither know nor believe that any subject was characterized by it. If, however, there had been, by chance, and unknown to Jane Austen, a girl called Emma Woodhouse who conformed faithfully to all the descriptions of the novel, its propositions would have been about and true of her and Jane Austen would have "accidentally" written biography and not fiction.[3]

This seems a somewhat strained account of a story. As Moore says,[4] it does seem false to deny that Jane Austen wrote about Emma Wood-house, Harriet Smith, Miss Bates, Mr. George Knightley and the rest, but is, instead, about such a peculiar object as a "composite predicate." He would, surely, find this quite unintelligible. It is also false to say that a work of fiction may be "accidentally" history or biography. For if there were ten girls called "Emma Woodhouse" of whom all that Jane Austen wrote were true, they are not the subject of *Emma,* for Jane Austen is not telling a story of any of them, but of a subject of her own invention. Moreover, it would not only be necessary that Emma Woodhouse should have a real counterpart but that such coun-terparts should exist for every other element of the novel. You cannot separate Emma from Highbury, her companions and the ball at the Crown. They all belong to the story. Such a coincidence would be almost miraculous. So Moore seems to be right when he says: [5]

> I think that what he (Dickens) meant by "Mr. Pickwick" and what we all understand is: "There was only one man of whom it is true both that *I am going to tell you about him* and that he was called 'Pickwick' *and* that, etc." In other words, he is saying from the beginning, that he has one and only one man in his mind's eye, about whom he is going to tell you a story. That he has is, of course, false; it is part of the fiction. It is this which gives unique reference to all subsequent uses of "Mr. Pickwick." And it is for this reason that Mr. Ryle's view that if, by coincidence, there happened to be a real man of whom everything related of Mr. Pickwick in the novel were true then "we could say that Dickens' propositions were true of somebody" is to be rejected . . . . . . *since Dickens was not telling us of him:* and that this is what is meant by saying that it is only "by coincidence" that there happened to be such a man.

I think this can be seen to be true even in circumstances which might appear to support Ryle's view. *Jane Eyre* and *Villette* are known to contain much autobiographical material. Charlotte Brontë knew her original as Dickens did not know of a "coincidental" Mr. Pickwick. Yet *Jane Eyre* and *Villette* are still works of fiction, not biography. They are no substitute for Mrs. Gaskell's *Life of Charlotte Brontë.* For although she may be *using* the facts of her own life, Charlotte Brontë is not writing "about" herself, but "about" Jane Eyre, Helen

Burns, Mr. Rochester, Lucy Snowe, Paul Emmanuel and the rest. Or, she is writing about herself in a very different sense from that in which she is writing about the subject matter of her novels.

Ryle and Moore agree, with many others, that the sentences of fiction express false statements and Moore adds, I think rightly, that, so far, at least, as these are fictional, they could not be true. But there is a more radical view for which there is also some excuse. If a story-teller tells what he knows to be false, is he not a deceiver and his works a "tissue of lies?" That storytelling is akin to, if not a form of, lying is a very common view. "To make up a tale," "to tell a yarn" are common euphemisms for "to tell a lie." A liar knows what is true, but deliberately says what is false. What else does the storyteller who pretends that there was a girl called "Emma Woodhouse," etc., when she knows this is false? A liar intends to, and does, deceive a hearer. Does not a storyteller do likewise? "Poets themselves," says Hume, "though liars by profession, always endeavor to give an air of truth to their fictions." [6] Hume is contrasting all other expressions as indifferently lies or fiction, with those which are true of matters of fact. Hume is quite wrong to classify all poetry with fiction, though some stories may be told in verse. But no one could correctly call, e.g., Shakespeare's Sonnets, Keats' Odes or Eliot's Four Quartets, works of fiction. Nor are they statements of fact, but their analysis is not my task here. I wish only to protest against a common tendency to consign to one dustbin all expressions which do not conform to the type of statement found in factual studies. Even though they are not factual statements, expressions in literature may be of many different logical types. It is clear, however, that for Hume storytelling is a form of lying. And, indeed, a storyteller not only says what he knows to be false but uses every device of art to induce his audience to accept his fancies. For what else are the ancient incantatory openings, "Once upon a time . . . ," "Not yesterday, not yesterday, but long ago . . . ," and their modern equivalents, but to put a spell upon an audience so that the critical faculties of its members are numbed and they willingly suspend disbelief to enter the state which Coleridge called "illusion" and likened to dreaming? [7] All this is true. Everyone must sometimes be informed, instructed, exhorted by others. There are facts to learn and attitudes to adopt. However dull, these processes must be endured. But no one is obliged to attend to another's fancies. Unless, therefore, a storyteller can convince, he will not hold an audience. So, among other devices, he "endeavors to give an air of truth to his fictions." It does not follow that what he says *is* true, nor that he is a deceiver. One must distinguish "trying to convince" from "seeking to mislead." To convince is a merit in a work of fiction. To induce someone to accept a fiction, however, is not necessarily to seduce him into a belief that it is real. It is true that some people may be deceived by fiction. They fail to distinguish conviction from deception. Such are those who write to the B.B.C. about Mrs. Dale and the Archers as if they believe themselves to be hearing the life histories of real families in these programs. But this does not show that the B.B.C. has deliberately beguiled these innocents. Finally, a liar may be "found out" in his lie. He is then discredited and his lie is useless. Nor is he easily believed again. But it would be absurd for someone to complain that since *Emma* was fiction he had "found out" Jane Austen and could never trust her again. The conviction induced by a story is the result of a mutual conspiracy, freely entered into, between author and audience. A storyteller does not lie, nor is a normal auditor deceived. Yet there are affinities between fiction and lying which excuse the comparison. Conviction, without belief or disbelief, as in art, is like, but also very different from, unwitting deception. And a liar, too, pretends but not all pretending is lying.

A fictional sentence does not, then, express a lying statement. Does it express a false statement which is not a lie? False statements are normally asserted from total or partial ignorance of the facts. Those who assert them mistakenly believe they are true. This is not true of the storyteller. Neither he nor his auditor normally believes that his statements are true. It is false that Jane Austen wrote *Pickwick Papers* but it is not nonsense to suggest that it might have been true. As already seen, however, no factual discovery can verify a fictional statement. It can then never be true. So it would seem to be necessarily false or logically impossible. But the expressions of fiction are neither self-contradictory nor nonsensical. Most of them are perfectly intelligible. Those which are not are so for reasons quite unconnected with truth and falsity. It is not because James Joyce's statements are false that they are unintelligible. For those of Jane Austen and Dickens are equally false, but not obscure.

Alternatively, it might be said that the propositions of fiction are false, but neither believed nor asserted. Their fictional character consists in the fact that they are merely proposed for consideration, like hypotheses. "Let us suppose there was a girl called Emma Woodhouse, who . . . etc." For a proposition may be entertained, but yet be false. So an author puts forward and his audience considers, but neither affirm, the false propositions of fiction.[8] Now, a storyteller does invite his audience to "Imagine that . . . ," "Pretend that . . ." and even "Suppose that . . ." or "Let it be granted that . . ." He does not often preface his story with just these remarks, but he issues a general invitation to exercise imagination. So far one may liken his attitude to that of some one proposing an hypothesis in other fields. An hypothesis, like a lie or a story, requires some invention; it is not a report of observed fact. But these suggested fictional hypotheses are also very different from all others. Non-fictional hypotheses are proposed to explain some fact or set of facts. "If the picture is by Van Dyck, then . . ."; "Suppose that malaria is transmitted by mosquitoes, then. . . ." They suggest, e.g., the origin of a painting or the cause of a disease. But a story is not told to solve any such problem. Moreover, a non-fictional hypothesis must be testable or be mere speculation without explanatory value. But, obviously, nothing can count as evidence in favor of a fictional story. And what no fact can confirm none can disconfirm either. So, if a story consists of propositions entertained for consideration, the purpose of such entertainment must be for ever frustrated since they can never be asserted as true, false, probable or improbable. I conclude, therefore, that the expressions of fiction do not function either as propositions or hypotheses.

Nevertheless, as I have said, one can easily understand why people are tempted to identify fictional expressions with lies, falsehoods, unverifiable hypotheses. For what it is worth, the English dictionary appears to support this view. "Fiction," it says, "the act of feigning, inventing or imagining: that which is feigned, i.e., a fictitious story, fable, fabrication, falsehood." If the last four terms are intended as synonyms, this certainly suggests that all fiction is falsehood. Both rationalist and religious parents have forbidden children to read fairy stories and novels lest they be led astray into false and immoral beliefs. Yet its logical difference from these seems to show that fiction is not false, lying or hypothetical statement. It is clear that "S pretends that p" cannot entail p. This is, again, the point of saying that the truth of p must be "coincidental." When discovered, no future S (or storyteller) could pretend that p, for one cannot pretend that a proposition is true when it is, and is known to be, true. But neither, in fiction, can "S pretends that p" entail "not-p," or even "Perhaps-p." So, fictional expressions must be of a different type from statements.

An alternative is the familiar emotive answer. This is associated chiefly with the name of I. A. Richards. I can mention it only briefly.

According to it, sentences in fiction, as in all non-informative contexts, express an emotional state of their author and seek to induce a similar state in his audience. A work is judged better or worse according to the amount of harmonious mental adjustment by which it was caused and which it effects. This view is difficult to estimate because of its vague use of the word "express." It tends to suggest that the expressions of fiction are disguised exclamations such as "Hurrah!" or "Alas!" Or that these could be substituted for them. This, of course, is impossible. No one could tell the story of *Emma* in a series of smiles, sighs, tears, shouts or the limited vocabulary which represents such emotive expressions. Most stories, one must reiterate, are told in normal English sentences which are common to fact and fiction and appropriately understood. This is, indeed, just the problem. If the expressions of Jane Austen were as easily distinguishable from factual statement as exclamation from articulate utterance no one would be puzzled. "Emotive expression" must, therefore, be compatible with understood sense.[9] It is true that emotional relationships play a large part in most fiction, but so does much else. Nor need these subjects coincide with the experience of either author or audience. No story, even though told in the first person, can be completely autobiographical without ceasing to be fiction. And whether or not a work of fiction uses autobiographical material, the actual, or suspected, direct intrusion of personal feeling by the author is liable to be fatal to the work.

> I opened it at chapter twelve and my eye was caught by the phrase "Anybody may blame me who likes." What were they blaming Charlotte Brontë for, I wondered? And I read how Jane Eyre used to go up on the roof when Mrs. Fairfax was making jellies and look over the fields at the distant view. And then she longed—and it was for this that they blamed her —that "then I longed for a power of vision which might overpass that limit . . . I desired more of practical experience . . . more of intercourse with my kind . . . I believed in the existence of other and more vivid kinds of goodness and what I believed in I wished to behold . . . Who blames me? Many no doubt and I shall be called discontented . . . When thus alone I not infrequently heard Grace Poole's laugh."
>
> That is an awkward break, I thought. It is upsetting to come upon Grace Poole all of a sudden. The continuity is disturbed. One might say, I continued . . . That the woman who wrote

these pages had genius . . . but if one reads them over and
marks that jerk in them, that indignation, one sees . . . that
her books will be deformed and twisted. (Virginia Woolf;
A Room of One's Own, p. 104.)

In short, Charlotte Brontë will, or will appear to, express her own
feelings too nakedly through her heroine, in order to induce a sympathetic emotional response in her readers, instead of telling her story.
Someone may protest that this amounts to *describing*, not expressing,
her emotions. But this is not ostensibly so. The passage is still a
soliloquy by Jane Eyre, not an introspective report by Charlotte Brontë.
Virginia Woolf is giving an interpretation of the passage, but this would
not be necessary if it were a simple description of Charlotte Brontë's
feelings. If her critic is right and if, nevertheless, the passage is not
what is meant by an expression of the author's emotion by fiction, this
cannot be because it is a straightforward description of fact. Another
objection might be that this is a crude example of expression and does
not prove that the task of fiction is not to express emotion. Skilful
expression is impersonal, almost anonymous. One cannot tell from their
works what Shakespeare or Jane Austen felt. Hence the floods of speculation by critics. One knows only too well from her novels what
Charlotte Brontë felt, so she is not truly expressing, but merely venting,
her emotions. But then, if one so often cannot tell whose, or even what,
emotion is being expressed, what is the point of saying that all fictional
expressions are emotive? Should the criterion be solely the effect on
their audience? Certainly, a tale may amuse, sadden, anger, or otherwise move a hearer. But is the fact that *Emma* may cause one to laugh
or sigh what distinguishes it as a work of fiction from a statement of
fact? This must be false for much that is not fiction has the same effect.
The answer to the theory is that a work of fiction, like any work of
literary art, causes a very special emotional effect, an harmonious
adjustment of impulses, a personal attitude, not otherwise obtainable.
But no independent evidence of any such pervasive effect is offered,
nor can I, for one, provide it from experience of reading fiction. So,
if one cannot distinguish fiction from fact by the normal emotional
effects which fiction sometimes causes, nor by the pervasive changes it
is alleged to cause, the theory only reformulates and does not explain
this distinction.

But the theory does emphasize that language has less pedestrian uses
than those of the laboratory, record office, police court and daily dis-

course. Also, that to create and appreciate fiction requires more than intellectual qualities. Most fiction would be incomprehensible to a being without emotions. One must be able to enter imaginatively into its emotional situations though its emotions need not be felt. One need not feel jealousy either to construct or understand Mr. Knightley's censorious attitude to Frank Churchill, but someone who had never felt this might find an account of it unconvincing. Authors differ, too, in what may vaguely be called "climate" or "atmosphere," which is emotional and moral as well as intellectual. The "worlds" of Jane Austen and Henry James, e.g., differ considerably from those of Emily Brontë and D. H. Lawrence. Also, much of the language of fiction is emotionally charged. For it depicts emotional situations which are part of its story. But none of these facts is positively illuminated by a theory which limits the language of fiction to the expression of an emotion transferred from author to auditor even if such a transaction were fully understood. It does not seem to be the feeling which generates them nor that which they cause which wholly differentiates the ironies of Gibbon from those of I. Compton Burnett. Nor is it either Tolstoy or ourselves in whom we are primarily interested when reading *War and Peace.* Rather is it the presentation of characters, actions and situations. The vast panorama of the novel shrinks into triviality as the instrument of the emotional adjustments of Tolstoy and his readers. I conclude, therefore, that the characteristic which differentiates fictional sentences from those which state facts is not that the former exclusively express anybody's emotions, though many of them have a very vital connection with emotion.

II

When someone reports a fact he may choose the language or symbolism of his report. He may choose to use this carefully or carelessly. But there is a sense in which he cannot choose what he will say. No one could report truly that Charlotte Brontë died in 1890; that she wrote *Villette* before *Jane Eyre;* that she was tall, handsome and a celebrated London hostess. No biography of Charlotte Brontë could contain such statements and remain a biography. For what is truly said of Charlotte Brontë must be controlled by what she was and what happened to her. But Jane Austen was under no such restraints with Emma Woodhouse. For Emma Woodhouse was her own invention. So she may have any qualities and undergo any adventures her author pleases. It is not even certain that these must be logically possible, i.e., not self-contradictory. For some stories, and not the worst, are extremely wild. There is *Finnegan's Wake* as well as *Emma*. A storyteller chooses not only the words and style but also, and I suggest with them, provides the material of a fictional story. I want to stress this fact that in fiction language is used to *create*. For it is this which chiefly differentiates it from factual statement. A storyteller performs; he does not —or not primarily—inform or misinform. To tell a story is to originate, not to report. Like the contents of dreams, the objects of fiction may pre-suppose, but do not compete with, those of ordinary life. Unlike those of dreams, however, they are deliberately contrived. Hence, they differ too from lunatic frenzies. A lunatic unintentionally offends against fact and logic. He intends to respect them. He thinks he is right, however wild his fancies, when he is always wrong. But a storyteller, though equally wild, is never deluded. He invents by choice, not accident.

As I have already said, most of a storyteller's words and sentences are understood to have the same meanings as the same words and grammatical forms in non-fictional contexts. For all who communicate use the same language, composed mainly of general terms. But language may be used differently to obtain different results. When a storyteller "pretends" he simulates factual description. He puts on an innocent air of informing. This is part of the pretence. But when he pretends, e.g., that there was a Becky Sharp, an adventuress, who finally came to grief, he does not inform or misinform about a real person called "Becky Sharp" or anyone else: he is creating Becky Sharp. And this is what a normal audience understands him to be doing. Of course, he does not thereby add to the population of the world. Becky Sharp is not registered at Somerset House. But this, too, is shown by language. A storyteller, like a dramatist, is not said to create persons, human beings, but *characters*. Characters, together with their settings and situations, are parts of a story. According to Ryle, although "it is correct to say that Charles Dickens created a story, it is wholly erroneous to speak as if Dickens created Mr. Pickwick." [10] But Dickens *did* create Mr. Pickwick and this is not equivalent to saying, as Ryle does, that what Dickens created was a "complex predicate." No one would ever say this. But it is perfectly ordinary and proper to say that an author has created certain characters and all that is required for them to function. "In Caliban," said Dryden, "Shakespeare seems to have *created* a being which was not in nature." [11] He was not in nature because he was part of *The Tempest* To create a story is to use language to create the contents of that story. To write "about" Emma Wood-house, Becky Sharp, Mr. Pickwick, Caliban, and the rest is to "bring about" these characters and their worlds. Human beings are not nor-mally called "characters." If they are, it is by analogy with art. One might say, "I met a queer character the other day; he might have been created by Dickens." This does not show that Dickens wrote or tried to write about such a person, but that his readers now view their fel-lows through Dickens' works. So may one now see Constable and Cézanne pictures in natural landscapes, which would not have been seen without these artists. Characters play a rôle; human beings live. a life. A character, like all else in pure fiction, is confined to its rôle in a story. Not even the longest biography exhausts what could be told of any human person, but what Jane Austen tells of Emma Woodhouse exhausts Emma Woodhouse. A character may be completely under-stood, but the simplest human being, if any human being is simple, is somewhere opaque to others. A character has no secrets but what are contained within five acts or between the covers of a book or the interval from suppper to bedtime.[12] A story may, indeed, have a sequel, but this is a new invention, not a report of what was omitted from the original.

This may be challenged. Surely, it will be said, many characters in fiction are as complex as human beings? Do not critics still dispute about the motives of Iago and the sex of Albertine? But to say that a character is limited to what is related of it in a story does not imply that this must always be indisputably obvious. All it implies is that the only way to find out about a character is to consult the author's text. This contains all there is to discover. No one can find independent evidence which the author has missed. Not even Dr. Ernest Jones for the alleged "complexes" of Hamlet. Assuming that the text is complete and authentic, there may be different interpretations of it and thus of a character but no new evidence such as may render out of date a biography. No one will find a diary or a cache of letters from Hamlet to his mother which will throw light upon his mental state. Nor must this be forever secret in the absence of such evidence. For Hamlet is what Shakespeare tells and what we understand from the text, and nothing more.

What is true of characters is true also of other fictional elements of a story. "Barchester" does not name a geographical place. It is the set-ting or scene of a number of Trollope's characters. So is his magic island for Prospero and his companions. The words used to "set the scene" of a story paint as it were the backcloth to its incidents. "Scene" is a term of art, a word from the language of the theatre. One would naturally say "The scene of Archdeacon Grantley's activities is laid in Barchester," but not, unless affecting histrionics, "The scene of this Conference is laid in Oxford." It would be more normal to say "This Conference is being held in Oxford." "Scene" is used of natural situations only when they are being treated artificially. Finally, the situations and incidents of a story form its plot. They conform to a contrived sequence of beginning, middle and end—or have some modern variety of this shape. But human life and natural events do not have, or conform to, a plot. They have no contrived shape.

It is thus, then, that we talk of works of fiction and their fictional contents. They are contrivances, artifacts. A story is more like a picture or a symphony than a theory or report. Characters, e.g., might for a change, be compared with musical "themes" rather than with human flesh and blood. A composer creates a symphony, but he also creates all its several parts. So does a storyteller, but his parts are the characters, settings and incidents which constitute his story. The similarity is obscure just because the storyteller does, and must, use common speech with its general terms, so that he appears to assert propositions about an independent reality in a manner similar to that of one who does or fails to report what is true. So, philosophers conclude, since pure fiction cannot be about physical objects, it must be about wraith-like simulacra of real objects or equally attenuated "predicates." I do not, however, want to claim a special mode of existence for fictional objects as the contents of fiction. And though it is obvious that fiction writers use our common tongue I do not think that what they do is illuminated by saying that they write about predicates or properties. It is agreed that a storyteller both creates a story, a verbal construction, and the contents of that story. I want to say that these activities are inseparable. Certainly, no one could create pure fiction without also creating the contents which are its parts. One cannot separate Emma Woodhouse from *Emma* as one can separate Napoleon from his biography. I do not say that Emma is simply identical with the words by which she is created. Emma is a "character." As such she can, in appropriate senses, be called charming, generous, foolish, and even "lifelike." No one could sensibly use these epithets of words. Nevertheless, a character is that of which it makes no sense to talk except in terms of the story in which he or she is a character. Just as, I think, it would make no sense to say that a flock of birds was carolling "by chance" the first movement of a symphony. For birds do not observe musical conventions. What is true of characters applies to the settings and incidents of pure fiction. To the questions "Where will they be found?"; "Where do they exist?," the answer is "In such and such a story," and that is all. For they are the elements or parts of stories and this is shown by our language about them.

But the content of very little fiction is wholly fictitious. London also forms part of the setting of *Emma* as it does of many of Dickens' novels; Russia of *War and Peace* and India of *A Passage to India*. Historical persons and events also seem to invade fiction. They are indeed the very stuff of "historical" novels. Do not the sentences in which the designations or descriptions of such places, persons and incidents occur express true or false statements? It is true that these real objects and events are mentioned in such fictional expressions. Nevertheless, they certainly do not function wholly as in a typographical or historical record. They are still part of a story. A storyteller is not discredited as a reporter by rearranging London's squares or adding an unknown street to serve his purpose. Nor by crediting an historical personage with speeches and adventures unknown to historians. An historical novel is not judged by the same standards as a history book. Inaccuracies are condemned, if they are, not because they are bad history or geography, but because they are bad art. A story which introduces Napoleon or Cromwell but which departs wildly from historical accuracy will not have verisimilitude which appears to be its object and will be unplausible and tedious. Or if, nevertheless, interesting will provoke the question, "But why call this character Oliver Cromwell, Lord Protector of England?" Similarly, for places. If somewhere called "London" is quite unrecognizable, its name will have no point.

So I am inclined to say that a storyteller is not making informative assertions about real persons, places and incidents even when these are mentioned in fictional sentences. But rather that these also function like purely fictional elements, with which they are always mingled in a story. Russia as the setting for the Rostovs differs from the Russia which Napoleon invaded which did not contain the Rostovs. There was a battle of Waterloo, but George Osborne was not one of its casualties, except in Thackeray's novel. Tolstoy did not create Russia, nor Thackeray the battle of Waterloo. Yet one might say that Tolstoy did create Russia-as-the-background-of-the-Rostovs and that Thackeray created Waterloo-as-the-scene-of-George-Osborne's-death. One might say that the mention of realities plays a dual rôle in fiction; to refer to a real object and to contribute to the development of a story. But I cannot pursue this, except to say that this situation differs from that in which, e.g., Charlotte Brontë uses the real events of her life in *Jane Eyre*. For she does not *mention* herself nor the real places and incidents upon which her story is modelled.

I have tried to say how the expressions of fiction operate and to show that they differ both from statements and emotive expressions. I also began by asking how they are connected. It is clear that their order need not be dictated by that of any matter of fact. Nor are they always even bound by the principles of logic. Do their connections, then, follow any rule or procedure? Is there a conception by which their transitions may be described? Since a work of fiction is a creative performance, however, it may be thought senseless to ask for such rules or such a conception. Is not the creation of that which is new and original, independent of logic and existence, just that to which no rules are appropriate and no conception adequate? But the creation of a work of fiction, however remarkable, is not a miracle. Nor is its author's use of language entirely lawless and vagabond but is directed by some purpose. Certainly, no set of rules will enable anyone to write a good novel or produce a good scientific hypothesis. But a scientist employs his ingenuity to invent a hypothesis to connect certain facts and predict others. He provides an organizing concept related to the facts to be organized and governed by the probability that it provides the correct explanation. As already emphasized, the situation of the storyteller is different.

In his Preface to *The Portrait of a Lady*, Henry James recalls that in organizing his "ado" about Isabel Archer, having conceived the character, he asked, "And now what will she *do*?" and the reply came immediately, "Why, the first thing she will do will be to come to Europe." He did not have to infer, guess, or wait upon observation and evidence; he *knew*. He knew because he had thus decided. He so decided, no doubt, for a variety of artistic reasons; to develop his conception of a certain character in relation to others, against a particular background, in accordance with his plot. His aim was to produce a particular, perhaps a unique, story; a self-contained system having its own internal coherence. There is certainly a sense in which every work of fiction is a law unto itself. Nevertheless, I think there is a general notion which governs these constructions though its application may give very different results. This is the Aristotelian notion which is usually translated "probability" but which I prefer to call "artistic plausibility." This is not an ideal phrase but it is preferable to "probability" which suggests an evidential relation between premisses and conclusion and "possibility" which suggests a restriction to logical conceivability which might exclude some rare, strange and fantastic works. It is, moreover, a notion which applies only to what is verbal. Though some comparable notion may apply to them, one does not normally talk of "plausible" pictures, statues and symphonies, but does talk of "plausible stories." A plausible story is one which convinces; which induces acceptance. But since the plausibility is artistic plausibility, the conviction induced will not be the belief appropriate to factual statement. Nevertheless, one drawback to the notion is that it may suggest that all fiction is, or should be, realistic or naturalistic. It is true that although fiction does not consist of statements about life and natural events, yet much fiction does take lived experience as a model for its own connections. Sometimes, as with Charlotte Brontë's novels, using autobiographical material. Such stories convince by being "lifelike." But by no means all fiction is thus naturalistic. Nor is a story allegedly founded on fact necessarily fictionally convincing. To repeat the Aristotelian tag, "a convincing impossibility is better than an unconvincing possibility." There is, in fact, a range of plausible connections in fiction, varying from the purest naturalism to the wildest fantasy. If any convinces then it is justified. Much should obviously be said about who is convinced and whether he is a reliable judge, but I can do little more here than indicate the type of connection which differentiates works of fiction from descriptions of fact. It is the task of the literary critic to analyze the different types of plausibility, exemplified by, e.g., *Emma, War and Peace, The Portrait of a Lady, Wuthering Heights, Moby Dick, Alice in Wonderland* and *Grimm's Fairy Stories*. And though, perhaps, no rules can be given for attaining any particular type of plausibility, yet it is sometimes possible to say what does or would make a work unplausible. A mixture of elements from different plausible systems would, e.g., have this result. It is quite plausible that Alice should change her size by drinking from magic bottles, but it would be absurd that Emma Woodhouse or Fanny Price should do so. Or, to make such an incident plausible, Jane Austen's novels would need to be very different. For it would have needed explanation in quite different terms from the conventions she uses. This also applies to more important plausibilities. Emma Woodhouse could not suddenly murder Miss Bates after the ball, or develop a Russian sense of sin, without either destroying the plausibility of the novel or bringing about a complete revolution in its shape, though these incidents are in themselves more likely than that which befell Alice. But such examples raise questions about fiction and fact; art and life which I cannot now discuss.

NOTES

1. Cf. also "Art and Imagination," *Proc. Aris. Soc.*, 1952–53, p. 219.
2. See earlier Symposium on "Imaginary Objects," *Proc. Aris. Soc.*, Supp. Vol. 12, 1933, by G. Ryle, R. B. Braithwaite and G. E. Moore.
3. *Loc. cit.*, G. Ryle, pp. 18–43.
4. *Ibid.*, p. 59.
5. *Loc. cit.*, p. 68.
6. *Treatise of Human Nature*, Bk. I, Pt. 3, Sec. 10.
7. Cf. Notes on *The Tempest* from *Lectures on Shakespeare*.
8. I understood Professor Moore to hold such a view in a discussion in 1952. I do not, however, claim his authority for this version. Nor do I know if he is still of the same opinion.
9. Cf. also Empson, *The Structure of Complex Words*, London, 1951, ch. 1.
10. *Loc. cit.*, p. 32.
11. Quoted by Logan Pearsall Smith. S.P.E. Tract XVII, 1924.
12. See also E. M. Forster, *Aspects of the Novel*, Chs. 3 and 4.

NARRATIVE FORMS

As Northrop Frye argues in "Specific Continuous Forms," the point of making generic distinctions is not merely to diminish the frustrations of cataloguing for librarians but to promote intelligent literary judgments based on an awareness of differences in kind among works of fiction. The prevalence of the novel in the twentieth century, for instance, tends to generate novelistic expectations in readers unaware that there are other species of fiction abroad which have their own conventions, techniques, and modes of presentation. To condemn a romance for lacking the kind of circumstantial realism one has come to expect in novels is like condemning a whale for being without horns. Thus Frye distinguishes four forms of fiction—novel, romance, anatomy, and confession—each with its characteristic structural, thematic, and character "interests," and then notes how individual fictional works may reflect these forms in varying combinations.

Austin Warren's essay on "The Nature and Modes of Narrative Fiction" is less concerned with plotting the boundaries of specific forms than with exploring the broad influence of the romantic and novelistic modes on fiction generally, especially as regards the treatment of plot, characterization, and setting. The romantic mode specializes in the fantastic, the radically transformed—reality seen through a prism—

whereas the novel has traditionally dealt with the realistic—life seen through a window in all its recognizable, undistorted familiarity. But whether as prism or as window, the artistic glass is always there to remind us of the separation of fiction from life, of how what we as readers "see" is organized and shaped by the lens of fictional technique.

Though it might seem that a generic approach to fiction sacrifices the individuality of specific works—*this* novel in all its uniqueness disappearing into the generalized blur of *the* novel—individual differences are perhaps best appreciated after a work's likenesses to others of its kind have been established. That is, one does not examine a specific fictional work merely in order to pin the label of short story, novel, satire, romance, or something else on it, any more than one is content to identify a particular man as a liberal, conservative, Democrat, Republican, professor, or student. But recognizing certain generic characteristics in either people or literary fictions is a useful preliminary to formulating more exact definitions of their individuality. Robert B. Heilman's treatment of Thomas Mann's *Felix Krull* as one of the "Variations on the Picaresque" is an example of the kind of illuminating analysis that may result from placing a work within a generic context.

Since the novel has become the dominant fictional form in modern times, it deserves—and has in critical practice received—considerable attention. The following section, devoted entirely to the novel, should therefore be read as a continuation of the analysis of generic forms presented here.

AUSTIN WARREN

The Nature and Modes of Narrative Fiction

Literary theory and criticism concerned with the novel are much inferior in both quantity and quality to theory and criticism of poetry.
The cause customarily assigned for this would be the antiquity of
poetry, the comparative recency of the novel. But the explanation
scarcely seems adequate. The novel as an art form is, as one can say
in German, a form of *Dichtung;* is, indeed, in its high form, the modern
descendant of the epic—with drama, one of the two great forms. The
reasons are rather, one thinks, the widespread association of the novel
with entertainment, amusement, and escape rather than serious art—
the confounding of the great novels, that is, with manufactures made
with a narrow aim at the market. The lingering American popular view,
disseminated by pedagogues, that the reading of nonfiction was instructive and meritorious, that of fiction, harmful or at best self-indulgent,
was not without implicit backing in the attitude toward the novel of
representative critics like Lowell and Arnold.

There is an opposite danger, however, of taking the novel seriously
in the wrong way, that is, as a document or case history, as—what for
its own purposes of illusion it sometimes professes to be—a confession,
a true story, a history of a life and its times. Literature must always be
interesting; it must always have a structure and an aesthetic purpose,
a total coherence and effect. It must, of course, stand in recognizable
relation to life, but the relations are very various: the life can be
heightened or burlesqued or antithesized; it is in any case a selection,
of a specifically purposive sort, from life. We have to have a knowledge
independent of literature in order to know what the relation of a specific work to "life" may be.

Aristotle described poetry (that is, epic and drama) as nearer to

From *Theory of Literature* by Austin Warren and René Wellek. Copyright
1942, 1947, 1949, © 1965 by Harcourt, Brace and World, Inc. Reprinted by
permission of the publishers.

philosophy than to history. The dictum seems to have permanent suggestiveness. There is factual truth, truth in specific detail of time and place—truth of history in the narrow sense. Then there is philosophic truth: conceptual, propositional, general. From the points of view of "history," so defined, and philosophy, imaginative literature is "fiction," a lie. The word "fiction" still preserves this old Platonic charge against literature, to which Philip Sidney and Dr. Johnson reply that literature never pretended to be real in that sense; [1] and still preserving this vestigial remnant of the old charge of deception, it can still irritate the earnest writer of novels, who knows well that fiction is less strange and more representative than truth.

Wilson Follet remarks admirably of Defoe's narrative of Mrs. Veal and Mrs. Bargrave that "Everything in the story is true except the whole of it. And mark how difficult Defoe makes it to question even that whole. The tale is told by a third woman of exactly the same stamp as the other two, a life-long friend of Mrs. Bargrave. . . ." [2]

Marianne Moore speaks of poetry as presenting

for inspection, imaginary gardens with real toads in them.

The reality of a work of fiction—i.e., its illusion of reality, its effect on the reader as a convincing reading of life—is not necessarily or primarily a reality of circumstance or detail or commonplace routine. By all of these standards, writers like Howells or Gottfried Keller put to shame the writers of *Oedipus Rex, Hamlet,* and *Moby Dick.* Verisimilitude in detail, is a means to illusion, but often used, as in *Gulliver's Travels,* as a decoy to entice the reader into some improbable or incredible situation which has "truth to reality" in some deeper than a circumstantial sense.

Realism and naturalism, whether in the drama or the novel, are literary or literary-philosophical movements, conventions, styles, like romanticism or surrealism. The distinction is not between reality and illusion, but between differing conceptions of reality, between differing modes of illusion. [3]

What is the relation of narrative fiction to life? The Classical or Neo-Classical answer would be that it presents the typical, the universal—the typical miser (Molière, Balzac), the typical faithless daughters (*Lear, Goriot*). But are not such class concepts for sociology? Or it would have been said that art ennobles or heightens or idealizes life. There is such a style of art, of course, but it is a style, not the essence of art; though all art, to be sure, by giving aesthetic distance, by shaping and articulating, makes that pleasant to contemplate which would be painful to experience or even, in life, to witness. Perhaps it might be said that a work of fiction offers a "case history"—an illustration or exemplification of some general pattern or syndrome. There are instances—in short stories like Cather's "Paul's Case" or "The Sculptor's Funeral"—which approach it. But the novelist offers less a case—a character or event—than a world. The great novelists all have such a world—recognizable as overlapping the empirical world but distinct in its self-coherent intelligibility. Sometimes it is a world which can be mapped out in some area of the globe—like Trollope's counties and cathedral towns, Hardy's Wessex; but sometimes—as with Poe—it is not: Poe's horrendous castles are not in Germany or Virginia but in the soul. Dickens' world can be identified with London; Kafka's with old Prague: but both worlds are so "projected," so creative and created and hereafter recognized in the empirical world as Dickens characters and Kafka situations that the identifications seem rather irrelevant.

Meredith, Conrad, Henry James, and Hardy have all, says Desmond McCarthy, "blown great comprehensive iridescent bubbles, in which the human beings they describe, though they have of course a recognizable resemblance to real people, only attain in that world their full reality." Imagine, McCarthy says, "a character moved from one imaginary world to another. If Pecksniff were transplanted into *The Golden Bowl* he would become extinct. . . . The unforgivable artistic fault in a novelist is failure to maintain consistency of tone." [4]

This world or *Kosmos* of a novelist this pattern or structure or organism, which includes plot, characters, setting, world-view, "tone"—is what we must scrutinize when we attempt to compare a novel with life or to judge, ethically or socially, a novelist's work. The truth to life, or "reality," is no more to be judged by the factual accuracy of this or that detail than the moral judgment is to be passed, as Boston censors pass it, on whether specific sexual or blasphemous words occur within a novel. The soundly critical appeal is to the whole fictional world in comparison with our own experienced and imagined world, commonly less integrated than that of the novelist. We are content to call a novelist great when his world, though not patterned or scaled like our own, is comprehensive of all the elements which we find necessary to catholic scope or, though narrow in scope, selects for inclusion the deep and central, and when the scale or hierarchy of elements seems to us such as a mature man can entertain.

In using the term "world," one is using a space term. But "narrative fiction"—or, better, a term like "story," calls our attention to time, and a sequence in time. "Story" comes from "history": the "Chronicles of Barsetshire." Literature is generally to be classed as a time-art (in distinction from painting and sculpture, space-arts); but in a very active way modern poetry (non-narrative poetry) seeks to escape its destiny —to become a contemplative stasis, a "self-reflexive" pattern; and as Joseph Frank has well shown, the modern art-novel (*Ulysses, Nightwood, Mrs. Dalloway*) has sought to organize itself poetically, i.e., "self-reflexively." [5] This calls our attention to an important cultural phenomenon: the old narrative, or story (epic or novel) happened in time—the traditional time-span for the epic was a year. In many great novels, men are born, grow up, and die; characters develop, change; even a whole society may be seen to change (*The Forsyte Saga, War and Peace*) or a family's cyclic progress and decline exhibited (*Buddenbrooks*). The novel, traditionally, has to take the time dimension seriously.

In the picaresque novel, the chronological sequence is all there is: this happened and then that. The adventures, each an incident, which might be an independent tale, are connected by the figure of the hero. A more philosophic novel adds to chronology the structure of causation. The novel shows a character deteriorating or improving in consequence of causes operating steadily over a period of time. Or in a closely contrived plot, something has happened in time: the situation at the end is very different from that at the opening.

To tell a story, one has to be concerned about the happening, not merely the outcome. There is or was a kind of reader who must look ahead to see how a story "comes out"; but one who reads only the "concluding chapter" of a nineteenth-century novel would be somebody incapable of interest in story, which is process—even though process toward an end. There are certainly philosophers and moralists like Emerson who cannot take novels seriously primarily, one thinks, because action—or external action—or action in time—seems to them unreal. They cannot see history as real: history is just an unrolling in time of more of the same; and the novel is fictitious history.

A word should be said about the word "narrative," which, as applied to fiction, should imply the contrast of enacted fiction, i.e., drama. A story, or fable, can be represented by mimes, or it can be narrated by a single teller, who will be the epic teller, or one of his successors. The epic poet uses the first person and can, like Milton, make that a lyric or auctorial first person. The nineteenth-century novelist, even though he did not write in the first person, used the epic privilege of comment and generalization—what we might call the "essayistic" (as distinct from lyric) first person. But the chief pattern of narrative is its inclusiveness: it intersperses scenes in dialogue (which might be acted) with summary accounts of what is happening.[6]

The two chief modes of narrative fiction have, in English, been called the "romance" and the "novel." In 1785, Clara Reeve distinguished them: "The Novel is a picture of real life and manners, and of the time in which it is written. The Romance, in lofty and elevated language, describes what never happened nor is likely to happen."[7] The novel is realistic; the romance is poetic or epic: we should now call it "mythic." Mrs. Radcliffe, Sir Walter Scott, Hawthorne are writers of "romance." Fanny Burney, Jane Austen, Anthony Trollope, George Gissing are novelists. The two types, which are polar, indicate the double descent of prose narrative: the novel develops from the lineage of non-fictitious narrative forms—the letter, the journal, the memoir or biography, the chronicle or history; it develops, so to speak, out of documents; stylistically, it stresses representative detail, "mimesis" in its narrow sense. The romance, on the other hand, the continuator of the epic and the medieval romance, may neglect verisimilitude of detail (the reproduction of individuated speech in dialogue, for example), addressing itself to a higher reality, a deeper psychology. "When a writer calls his work a Romance," writes Hawthorne, "it need hardly be observed that he wishes to claim a certain latitude both as to its fashion and its material. . . ." If such a romance be laid in past time, it is not in order to picture with minute accuracy that past time, but to secure, in Hawthorne's words elsewhere, "a sort of poetic . . . precinct, where actualities would not be . . . insisted upon. . . ."[8]

Analytical criticism of the novel has customarily distinguished three constituents, plot, characterization, and setting: the last, so readily symbolic, becomes, in some modern theories, "atmosphere" or "tone." It is needless to observe that each of these elements is determinant of the others. As Henry James asks in his essay, "The Art of Fiction," "What is character but the determination of incident? What is incident but the illustration of character?"

The narrative structure of play, tale, or novel has traditionally been called the "plot"; and probably the term should be retained. But then it must be taken in a sense wide enough to include Chekhov and Flaubert and Henry James as well as Hardy, Wilkie Collins, and Poe: it must not be restricted to mean a pattern of close intrigue like Godwin's *Caleb Williams*.[9] We shall speak rather of types of plots, of looser and of more intricate, of "romantic" plots and "realistic." In a time of literary transition, a novelist may feel compelled to provide two kinds, one of them out of an obsolescent mode. Hawthorne's novels after *The Scarlet Letter* offer, clumsily, an old-fashioned mystery plot, while their real plot is of a looser, more "realistic," variety. In his later novels, Dickens devotes much ingenuity to his mystery plots, which may or may not coincide with the novel's real center of interest. The last third of *Huck Finn*, obviously inferior to the rest, seems prompted by a mistaken sense of responsibility to provide some "plot." The real plot, however, has already been in successful progress: it is a mythic plot, the meeting on a raft and journey down a great river of four who have escaped, for various reasons, from conventional society. One of the oldest and most universal plots is that of the Journey, by land or water: *Huck Finn, Moby Dick, Pilgrim's Progress, Don Quixote, Pickwick Papers, The Grapes of Wrath.* It is customary to speak of all plots as involving conflict (man against nature, or man against other men, or man fighting with himself); but then, like plot, the term must be given much latitude. Conflict is "dramatic," suggests some matching of approximately equal forces, suggests action and counteraction. Yet there are plots which it seems more rational to speak of in terms of a single line or direction, as plots of the chase or the pursuit: *Caleb Williams, The Scarlet Letter, Crime and Punishment*, Kafka's *Trial*.

The plot (or narrative structure) is itself composed of smaller narrative structures (episodes, incidents). The larger and more inclusive literary structures (the tragedy, the epic, the novel) have developed, historically, from earlier, rudimentary forms like the joke, the saying, the anecdote, the letter; and the plot of a play or novel is a structure of structures. The Russian formalists, and German form-analysts like Dibelius, give the term "motive" (Fr., *motif*, Germ., *motiv*) to the ultimate plot-elements.[10] "Motive," as thus used by literary historians, is borrowed from the Finnish folklorists, who have analyzed fairy and folk tales into their parts.[11] Obvious examples from written literature will be mistaken identities (*The Comedy of Errors*); the marriage of youth and old age ("January and May") filial ingratitude to a father (*Lear, Père Goriot*); the search of a son for his father (*Ulysses*, and *The Odyssey*).[12]

What we call the "composition" of the novel is, by the Germans and Russians, called its "motivation." The term might well be adopted into English as valuable precisely for its double reference to structural or narrative composition and to the inner structure of psychological, social, or philosophical theory of why men behave as they do—some theory of causation, ultimately. Sir Walter Scott asserts early, that "the most marked distinction between a real and fictitious narrative [is] that the former, in reference to the remote causes of the events it relates, is obscure . . . whereas in the latter case it is a part of the author's duty to . . . account for everything." [13]

Composition or motivation (in the largest sense) will include narrative method: "Scale," "pace"; devices: the proportioning of scenes or drama to picture or straight narrative and of both to narrative summary or digest.

Motifs and devices have their period character. The Gothic romance has its own; the realistic novel, its. Dibelius repeatedly speaks of Dickens' "realism" as of the *Märchen*, not of the naturalistic novel, the devices being utilized to lead into old-fashioned melodramatic motifs: the man supposed dead who comes to life, or the child whose real paternity is finally established, or the mysterious benefactor who turns out to be a convict.[14]

In a work of literary art, the "motivation" must increase the "illusion of reality": that is, its aesthetic function. "Realistic" motivation is an artistic device. In art, seeming is even more important than being.

The Russian formalists distinguish the "fable," the temporal-causal sequence which, however it may be told, is the "story" or story-stuff, from the "sujet," which we might translate as "narrative structure." The "fable" is the sum of all the motifs, while the "sujet" is the artistically ordered presentation of the motifs (often quite different). Obvious instances involve temporal displacement: beginning *in medias res*, like the *Odyssey* or *Barnaby Rudge*; backward and forward movements, as in Faulkner's *Absalom, Absalom*. The "sujet" of Faulkner's *As I Lay Dying* involves the story being narrated in turn by the members of a family as they carry the mother's body to a distant graveyard. "Sujet" is plot as mediated through "point of view," "focus of narration." "Fable" is, so to speak, an abstraction from the "raw materials" of fiction (the author's experience, reading, etc.); the "sujet" is an abstraction from the "fable"; or, better, a sharper focusing of narrative vision.[15]

Fable-time is the total period spanned by the story. But "narrative" time corresponds to "sujet": it is reading-time, or "experienced time," which is controlled, of course, by the novelist, who passes over years in a few sentences but gives two long chapters to a dance or tea-party.[16]

The simplest form of characterization is naming. Each "appellation" is a kind of vivifying, animizing, individuating. The allegoric or quasi-allegoric name appears in eighteenth-century comedy: Fielding's Allworthy and Thwackum, Witwould, Mrs. Malaprop, Sir Benjamin Backbite, with their echo of Jonson, Bunyan, Spenser, and *Everyman*. But the subtler practice is a kind of onomatopoeic toning, at which novelists as alien as Dickens and Henry James, Balzac and Gogol, are alike adept: Pecksniff, Pumblechook, Rosa Dartle (dart; startle), Mr. and Miss Murdstone (murder + stony heart). Melville's Ahab and Ishmael show what can be done by literary—in this instance, Biblical—allusion as a form of characterizing economy.[17]

Modes of characterization are many. Older novelists like Scott introduce each of their major persons by a paragraph describing in detail the physical appearance and another analyzing the moral and psychological nature. But this form of block characterization may be reduced to an introductory label. Or the label may turn into a device of mimicry or pantomime—some mannerism, gesture, or saying, which, as in Dickens, recurs whenever the character reappears, serving as emblematic accompaniment. Mrs. Gummidge is "always thinking of the old un"; Uriah Heep has a word, "umble," and also a ritual gesture of the hands. Hawthorne sometimes characterizes by a literal emblem: Zenobia's red flower; Westervelt's brilliantly artificial teeth. The later James of *The Golden Bowl* has one character see another in symbolic terms.

There are static characterizations and dynamic or developmental. The latter seems particularly suited to the long novel like *War and Peace*, as it is obviously less suited to drama, with its confined narrative time. Drama (e.g., Ibsen) can gradually disclose how a character has become what it is; the novel can show the change occurring. "Flat" characterization (which commonly overlaps "static") presents a single trait, seen as the dominant or socially most obvious trait. It may be caricature or may be abstractive idealization. Classical drama (e.g., Racine) applies it to major characters. "Round" characterization, like "dynamic," requires space and emphasis; is obviously usable for characters focal for point of view or interest; hence is ordinarily combined with "flat" treatment of background figures—the "chorus."[18]

There is obviously some kind of connection between characterization (literary method) and characterology (theories of character, personality types). There are character-typologies, partly literary tradition, partly folk-anthropology, which are used by novelists. In nineteenth-century English and American fiction, one finds brunettes, male and female (Heathcliffe, Mr. Rochester; Becky Sharp; Maggie Tulliver; Zenobia, Miriam; Ligeia) and blondes (female instances—Amelia Sedley; Lucy Dean; Hilda, Priscilla, and Phoebe [Hawthorne]; Lady Rowena [Poe]). The blonde is the home-maker, unexciting but steady and sweet. The brunette—passionate, violent, mysterious, alluring, and untrustworthy—gathers up the characteristics of the Oriental, the Jewish, the Spanish, and the Italian as seen from the point of view of the "Anglo-Saxon." [19]

In the novel, as in the drama, we have something like a repertory company; the hero, the heroine, the villain, the "character actors" (or "humor characters," or comic relief). There are the juveniles and ingénues and the elderly (the father and mother, the maiden aunt, the duenna, or the nurse). The dramatic art of the Latin tradition (Plautus and Terence, the *commedia dell'arte,* Jonson, Molière) uses a strongly marked and traditional typology of *miles gloriosus,* miserly father, wily servant. But a great novelist like Dickens largely adopts and adapts the types of the eighteenth-century stage and novel; he initiates only two types—the helpless old and young, and the dreamers or fantasts (e.g., Tom Pinch, in *Chuzzlewit).*[20]

Whatever the ultimate social or anthropological basis for literary character-types such as the blonde heroine and the brunette, the affective patterns can both be made out from the novels without documentary aid, and they have, commonly, literary-historical ancestries and lines—like the *femme fatale* and the dark Satanic hero studied by Mario Praz in *The Romantic Agony.*[21]

Attention to setting—the literary element of description as distinguished from narration—would at first thought seem to differentiate "fiction" from drama; our second thought, however, would rather make it a matter of period. Detailed attention to setting, whether in drama or the novel, is Romantic or Realistic (i.e., nineteenth-century) rather than universal. In drama, the setting may be given verbally within the play (as in Shakespeare) or indicated by stage directions to scene designers and carpenters. Some "scenes" in Shakespeare are not to be placed, localized, at all.[22] But within the novel, also, description of the setting is to a high degree variable. Jane Austen, like Fielding and Smollett, rarely describes either interiors or exteriors. The earlier novels of James, written under the influence of Balzac, are detailed for both houses and landscapes; the later novels substitute for how scenes look some symbolic rendering of how they totally *feel.*

Romantic description aims at establishing and maintaining a mood: plot and characterization are to be dominated by tone, effect—Mrs. Radcliffe and Poe are instances. Naturalistic description is a seeming documentation, offered in the interest of illusion (Defoe, Swift, Zola).

Setting is environment; and environments, especially domestic interiors, may be viewed as metonymic, or metaphoric, expressions of character. A man's house is an extension of himself. Describe it and you have described him. Balzac's detailed specifications for the house of the miser Grandet or the Pension Vauquer are neither irrelevant nor wasteful.[23] These houses express their owners; they affect, as atmosphere, those others who must live in them. The petty-bourgeois horror of the Pension is the immediate provocation of Rastignac's reaction and in another sense Vautrin's, while it measures the degradation of Goriot and affords constant contrast with the grandeurs alternately described.

Setting may be the expression of a human will. It may, if it is a natural setting, be a projection of the will. Says the self-analyst Amiel, "A landscape is a state of mind." Between man and nature there are obvious correlatives, most intensely (but not exclusively) felt by the Romantics. A stormy, tempestuous hero rushes out into the storm. A sunny disposition likes sunlight.

Again, setting may be the massive determinant—environment viewed as physical or social causation, something over which the individual has little individual control. This setting may be Hardy's Egdon Heath or Lewis' Zenith. The great city (Paris, London, New York) is the most real of the characters in many a modern novel.

A story can be told through letters or journals. Or it can develop from anecdotes. The frame-story enclosing other stories is, historically, a bridge between anecdote and novel. In the *Decameron*, the stories are thematically grouped. In the *Canterbury Tales*, such grouping of themes (e.g., marriage) is brilliantly supplemented by the conception of characterization of teller through tale and of a set of characters with psychological and social tensions between them. The story-of-stories has a Romantic version as well: in Irving's *Tales of a Traveller* and Hoffmann's *Tales of the Serapion Brethren*. The Gothic novel, *Melmoth the Wanderer*, is a strange but undeniably effective group of separate tales united only loosely save by their common tone of horror.

Another device, currently out of practice, is the short story included within a novel (e.g., the "Man on the Hill's Tale" in *Tom Jones;* the "Confessions of a Beautiful Soul," in *Wilhelm Meister*). This can be seen as, on one level, the attempt to fill out the size of a work; on another, as the search for variety. Both ends seem better served in the Victorian three-decker novels, which keep two or three plot-sequences in alternate movement (on their revolving stage) and eventually show how they interlock—a compounding of plots already practiced by the Elizabethans, often brilliantly. Artistically handled, one plot parallels the other (in *Lear*) or serves as "comic relief" or parody and hence underlining of the other.

Telling a story in the first person (the *Ich-Erzählung*) is a method carefully to be weighed against others. Such a narrator must not, of course, be confounded with the author. The purpose and effect of narration in the first person vary. Sometimes the effect is to make the teller less sharp and "real" than other characters (*David Copperfield*). On the other hand, Moll Flanders and Huck Finn are central to their own stories. In "The House of Usher," Poe's first-person narration enables the reader to identify himself with Usher's neutral friend and to withdraw with him at the catastrophic finale; but the neurotic or psychotic central character tells his own story in "Ligeia," "Berenice," and "The Tell-Tale Heart": the narrator, with whom we cannot identify, is making a confession, characterizing himself by what he reports and how he reports it.

Interesting is the question of how the story purports to exist. Some tales are elaborately introduced (*Castle of Otranto, Turn of the Screw, Scarlet Letter*): the story proper is given several degrees of detachment from its author or the reader by being represented as told to A by B, or as a manuscript entrusted to A by B, who perhaps wrote down the life-tragedy of C. Poe's first-person narratives are sometimes, ostensibly, dramatic monologues ("Amontillado"), sometimes the written confession of a tormented soul, avowedly unburdening himself ("The Tell-Tale Heart"). Often the assumption is not clear: in "Ligeia," are we to think of the narrator as talking to himself, rehearsing his story to refresh his own sense of horror?

The central problem of narrative method concerns the relation of the author to his work. From a play, the author is absent; he has disappeared behind it. But the epic poet tells a story as a professional story-teller, including his own comments within the poem, and giving the narration proper (as distinct from dialogue) in his own style.

The novelist can similarly tell a story without laying claim to having witnessed or participated in what he narrates. He can write in the third person, as the "omniscient author." This is undoubtedly the traditional and "natural" mode of narration. The author is present, at the side of his work, like the lecturer whose exposition accompanies the lantern slides or the documentary film.

There are two ways of deviating from that mixed mode of epic narration: one, which may be called the romantic-ironic, deliberately magnifies the role of the narrator, delights in violating any possible illusion that this is "life" and not "art," emphasizes the written literary character of the book. The founder of the line is Sterne, especially in *Tristram Shandy;* he is followed by Jean Paul Richter and Tieck in Germany; by Veltman and Gogol in Russia. *Tristram* might be called a novel about novel-writing, as might Gide's *Les Faux-Monnayeurs* and its derivative, *Point Counterpoint.* Thackeray's much-censured management of *Vanity Fair*—his constant reminder that these characters are puppets he has manufactured—is doubtless a species of this literary irony: literature reminding itself that it is but literature.

The opposite goal for the novel is the "objective" or "dramatic" method, argued for and illustrated by Otto Ludwig in Germany, Flaubert and Maupassant in France, Henry James in England.[24] The exponents of this method, critics as well as artists, have sought to represent it as the only artistic method (a dogma which need not be accepted). It has been admirably expounded in Percy Lubbock's *Craft of Fiction,* a Poetics of the novel based on the practice and the theory of Henry James.

"Objective" is the better term to use, since "dramatic" might mean "dialogue" or "action, behavior" (in contrast to the inner world of thought and feeling); but, quite clearly, it was the drama, the theater, which instigated these movements. Otto Ludwig formed his theories on the basis chiefly of Dickens, whose devices of pantomime and characterization by stock phrase were borrowed from the older eighteenth-century comedy and melodrama. Instead of narrating, Dickens' impulse is always to *present,* in dialogue and pantomime; instead of telling us *about,* he *shows* us. Later modes of the novel learn from other and subtler theaters, as James did from that of Ibsen.[25]

The objective method must not be thought of as limited to dialogue and reported behavior (James' *The Awkward Age;* Hemingway's "The Killers"). Such limitation would bring it into direct, and unequal, rivalry with the theater. Its triumphs have been in the presentation of that psychic life which the theater can handle but awkwardly. Its essentials are the voluntary absence from the novel of the "omniscient novelist" and, instead, the presence of a controlled "point of view." James and Lubbock see the novel as giving us, in turn, "picture" and "drama," by which they mean some character's consciousness of what is going on (within and without) in distinction from a "scene," which is partly at least in dialogue and which presents, in some detail, an important episode or encounter.[26] The "picture" is as "objective" as the "drama," only it is the objective rendering of a specific subjectivity—that of one of the characters (Madame Bovary, or Strether), while the "drama" is the objective rendering of speech and behavior. This theory admits of a shift of "point of view" (e.g., from the Prince to the Princess in the second half of *The Golden Bowl*), provided it be systematic. It also admits the author's use of a character within the novel, not unlike the author, who is either telling the narrative to some friends (Marlow, in Conrad's *Youth*) or the consciousness through which all is seen (Strether, in *The Ambassadors*): the insistence is upon the self-consistent objectivity of the novel. If the author is to be present other than "in solution," it must be by reducing himself or his representative to the same size and status as the other characters.[27]

Integral to the objective method is presentation in time, the reader's living through the process with the characters. To some extent, "picture" and "drama" must always be supplemented by "summary" (the "five days elapse between Acts I and II" of the theater); but it should be minimal. The Victorian novel used to end with a chapter summarizing the subsequent careers, marriages, and deaths, of the principal characters; James, Howells, and their contemporaries put an end to this practice, which they viewed as an artistic blunder. According to objectivist theory, the author must never anticipate what lies ahead; he must enroll his chart, letting us see only a line at a time. Ramon Fernandez sets up a distinction between the *récit*, the narrative of what has already taken place, and is now being told, according to the laws of exposition and description, and the *roman*, or novel, which represents events taking place in time, according to the order of living production.[28]

A characteristic technical device of the objective novel is what the Germans call *"erlebte Rede,"* and the French *"le style indirect libre"* (Thibaudet) and *"le monologue intérieur"* (Dujardin); and in English, the phrase, "stream of consciousness," which goes back to William James, is the loose, inclusive correspondent.[29] Dujardin defines "interior monologue" as a device for the "direct introduction of the reader into the interior life of the character, without any interventions in the way of explanation or commentary on the part of the author . . ." and as "the expression of the most intimate thoughts, those which lie nearest the unconscious. . . ." In *The Ambassadors,* says Lubbock, James does not "tell the story of Strether's mind; he makes it tell itself, he dramatizes it." [30] The history of these devices, and of their adumbrations in all modern literatures, only begins to be studied: the Shakespearean soliloquy is one ancestor; Sterne, applying Locke on the free association of ideas, is another; the "internal analysis," i.e., the summarizing by the author of a character's movement of thought and feeling, is a third.[31]

NOTES

1. Sidney: "Now for the poet, he nothing affirmeth, and therefore never lieth."
2. Wilson Follett, *The Modern Novel,* New York, 1918, p. 29.
3. The reader's exhortation that the novelist "deal with life" is often "an exhortation to preserve certain conventions of nineteenth-century prose fiction": Kenneth Burke, *Counterstatement,* New York, 1931, p. 238; cf. also p. 182 and p. 219.
4. D. McCarthy, *Portraits,* London, 1931, pp. 75, 156.
5. J. Frank, "Spatial Form in Modern Literature," *Sewanee Review,* LIII (1945), pp. 221–40, 433–56. Reprinted in *Criticism* (Schorer, Miles, McKenzie), New York, 1948, pp. 379–92.
6. The first two chapters of *Pride and Prejudice* are almost exclusively dialogue, while the third chapter opens with narrative summary, then returns to the "scenic" method.
7. Clara Reeve, *Progress of Romance,* London, 1785.
8. Hawthorne, prefaces to *The House of the Seven Gables* and *The Marble Faun.*
9. Poe's "Philosophy of Composition" opens with a quotation from Dickens: "Are you aware that Godwin wrote his *Caleb Williams* backwards?" Earlier, in a review of *Barnaby Rudge,* Poe had cited Godwin's novel as a masterpiece of close plotting.
10. *Motif* is commonly used in English criticism; but A. H. Krappe, *Science of Folklore,* London, 1930, sensibly urges that we use the English *motive* instead of the French form, which in turn acquired *its* sense under the influence of the German *Motiv.*
11. *Cf.* Aarne-Thompson, *Types of the Folk-Tale,* Helsinki, 1928.
12. *Cf.* G. Polti, *Thirty-six Dramatic Situations,* New York, 1916; P. Van Tieghem, *La littérature comparée,* Paris, 1931, p. 87 ff.
13. Sir Walter Scott, quoted by S. L. Whitcomb, *Study of a Novel,* Boston, 1905, p. 6. Whitcomb calls *motivation* "a technical term to denote the causation of the plot-movement, especially in reference to its conscious artistic arrangement."
The opening sentence of *Pride and Prejudice* is a good example of "moti-

vation" explicitly (even parodically) stated: "It is a truth universally acknowledged, that a single man in possession of a good fortune must be in want of a wife."

14. Dibelius, *Dickens,* 2nd ed., Leipzig, 1926, p. 383.

15. We refer here especially to Tomashevsky's treatment of "Thermatology" in his *Teoriyu literaturu,* Leningrad, 1931.

16. *Cf.* the discussion of "tempo" in Carl Grabo's *Technique of the Novel,* New York, 1928, pp. 214–36, and "Zeit" in Petsch's *Wesen und Formen der Erzählkunst,* Halle, 1934, p. 92 ff.

17. *Cf.* E. Berend, "Die Namengebung bei Jean Paul," *PMLA,* LVII (1942), pp. 820–50; E. H. Gordon, "The Naming of Characters in the Works of Dickens," *University of Nebraska Studies in Language,* etc., 1917; also John Forster's *Life of Dickens,* Bk. IX, Ch. 7, citing lists of names from the novelist's memoranda.

Henry James talks out the naming of his characters in the memoranda printed at the end of his unfinished novels, *The Ivory Tower* and *The Sense of the Past* (both 1917). *Cf.* also James' *Notebooks* (ed. Matthiessen and Murdock), New York, 1947, pp. 7–8, and *passim.*

On Balzac's character-naming, *cf.* E. Faguet, *Balzac* (Eng. tr., London, 1914), p. 120; and on Gogol's, V. Nabokov's *Gogol,* New York, 1944, p. 85 ff.

18. Flat and round characterization: *cf.* E. M. Forster, *Aspects of the Novel,* London, 1927, pp. 103–4.

19. On the typology of English heroines, *cf.* R. P. Utter and G. B. Needham, *Pamela's Daughters,* New York, 1936. On the polarity of light and dark heroines, *cf.* F. Carpenter, "Puritans Preferred Blondes," *New England Quarterly,* IX (1936), pp. 253–72; Philip Rahv, "The Dark Lady of Salem," *Partisan Review,* VIII (1941), pp. 362–81.

20. Dibelius, *Dickens,* Leipzig, 1916.

21. Mario Praz, *The Romantic Agony,* London, 1933.

22. *Cf.* Arthur Sewell, "Place and Time in Shakespeare's Plays," *Studies in Philology,* XLII (1945), pp. 205–24.

23. *Cf.* P. Lubbock, *Craft of Fiction,* London, 1921, pp. 205–35.

24. Otto Ludwig, "Romanstudien," *Gesammelte Schriften,* VI (1891), p. 59 ff; Maupassant, Introduction to *Pierre et Jean* (1887); H. James, Prefaces to the New York Edition (collected as *The Art of the Novel,* New York, 1934). *Cf.* also Oskar Walzel's "Objektive Erzählung," in *Das Wortkunstwerk,* Leipzig, 1926, p. 182 ff., and J. W. Beach, *The Twentieth Century Novel,* New York, 1932 .

25. Ludwig, *op. cit.,* pp. 66–7: The structure of Dickens' novels is analogous to that of plays. "Seine Romane sind erzählte Dramen mit Zwischenmusik, *d.i.,* erzählter."

On James and Ibsen, *cf.* Francis Fergusson, "James' Idea of Dramatic Form," *Kenyon Review,* V (1943), pp. 495–507.

26. On "picture" and "scene," *cf.* James' *Art of the Novel,* pp. 298–300, 322–3.

27. *Ibid.,* pp. 320–1, 327–9. James attacks narration in the first person as well as the "mere muffled majesty of irresponsible 'authorship' " (the omniscient narrator).

28. R. Fernandez, "La méthode de Balzac: Le récit et l'esthétique du roman," *Messages*, Paris, 1926, p. 59 ff. (English tr., London, 1927, pp. 59–88).

29. Oskar Walzel, "Von 'erlebter Rede,'" *Das Wortkunstwerk*, Leipzig, 1926, p. 207 ff.; Albert Thibaudet, *Flaubert*, Paris, 1935, pp. 229–32; E. Dujardin, *Le monologue intérieur* . . . , Paris, 1931; William James, *Principles of Psychology*, New York, 1890, Vol. I, p. 243: chap. IX, in which the phrase appears, is called "The Stream of Thought."

30. Lubbock, *op. cit.*, p. 147. "When Strether's mind is dramatized, nothing is shown but the passing images that anybody might detect, looking down upon a mind grown visible" (*ibid.*, p. 162).

31. *Cf.* L. E. Bowling, "What Is the Stream of Consciousness Technique?" *PMLA*, LXV (1950), pp. 337–45, and Melvin Friedman, *Stream of Consciousness: A Study in Literary Method*, New Haven, 1955.

NORTHROP FRYE

Specific Continuous Forms

In assigning the term fiction to the genre of the written word, in which prose tends to become the predominating rhythm, we collide with the view that the real meaning of fiction is falsehood or unreality. Thus an autobiography coming into a library would be classified as non-fiction if the librarian believed the author, and as fiction if she thought he was lying. It is difficult to see what use such a distinction can be to a literary critic. Surely the word fiction, which, like poetry, means etymologically something made for its own sake, could be applied in criticism to any work of literary art in a radically continuous form, which almost always means a work of art in prose. Or, if that is too much to ask, at least some protest can be entered against the sloppy habit of identifying fiction with the one genuine form of fiction which we know as the novel.

Let us look at a few of the unclassified books lying on the boundary of "non-fiction" and "literature." Is *Tristram Shandy* a novel? Nearly everyone would say yes, in spite of its easygoing disregard of "story values." Is *Gulliver's Travels* a novel? Here most would demur, including the Dewey decimal system, which puts it under "Satire and Humor." But surely everyone would call it fiction, and if it is fiction, a distinction appears between fiction as a genus and the novel as a species of that genus. Shifting the ground to fiction, then, is *Sartor Resartus* fiction? If not, why not? If it is, is *The Anatomy of Melancholy* fiction? Is it a literary form or only a work of "non-fiction" written with "style"? Is Borrow's *Lavengro* fiction? Everyman's Library says yes; the World's Classics puts it under "Travel and Topography."

The literary historian who identifies fiction with the novel is greatly embarrassed by the length of time that the world managed to get along without the novel, and until he reaches his great deliverance in Defoe, his perspective is intolerably cramped. He is compelled to reduce Tudor fiction to a series of tentative essays in the novel form, which works well enough for Deloney but makes nonsense of Sidney. He postulates a great fictional gap in the seventeenth century which exactly covers the golden age of rhetorical prose. He finally discovers that the word novel, which up to about 1900 was still the name of a more or less recognizable form, has since expanded into a catchall term which can be applied to practically any prose book that is not "on" something. Clearly, this novel-centered view of prose fiction is a Ptolemaic perspective which is now too complicated to be any longer workable, and some more relative and Copernican view must take its place.

When we start to think seriously about the novel, not as fiction, but as a form of fiction, we feel that its characteristics, whatever they are, are such as make, say, Defoe, Fielding, Austen, and James central in its tradition, and Borrow, Peacock, Melville, and Emily Bronte somehow peripheral. This is not an estimate of merit: we may think *Moby Dick* "greater" than *The Egoist* and yet feel that Meredith's book is closer to being a typical novel. Fielding's conception of the novel as a comic epic in prose seems fundamental to the tradition he did so much to establish. In novels that we think of as typical, like those of Jane Austen, plot and dialogue are closely linked to the conventions of the comedy of manners. The conventions of *Wuthering Heights* are linked rather with the tale and the ballad. They seem to have more affinity with tragedy, and the tragic emotions of passion and fury, which would shatter the balance of tone in Jane Austen, can be safely accommodated here. So can the supernatural, or the suggestion of it, which is difficult to get into a novel. The shape of the plot is different: instead of manoeuvering around a central situation, as Jane Austen does, Emily Bronte tells her story with linear accents, and she seems to need the help of a narrator, who would be absurdly out of place in Jane Austen. Conventions so different justify us in regarding *Wuthering Heights* as a different form of prose fiction from the novel, a form which we shall here call the romance. Here again we have to use the same word in several different contexts, but romance seems on the whole better than tale, which appears to fit a somewhat shorter form.

The essential difference between novel and romance lies in the conception of characterization. The romancer does not attempt to create "real people" so much as stylized figures which expand into psychological archetypes. It is in the romance that we find Jung's libido, anima, and shadow reflected in the hero, heroine, and villain respectively. That is why the romance so often radiates a glow of subjective intensity that the novel lacks, and why a suggestion of allegory is constantly creeping in around its fringes. Certain elements of character are released in the romance which make it naturally a more revolutionary form than the novel. The novelist deals with personality, with characters wearing their *personae* or social masks. He needs the framework of a stable society, and many of our best novelists have been conventional to the verge of fussiness. The romancer deals with individuality, with characters *in vacuo* idealized by revery, and, however conservative he may be, something nihilistic and untamable is likely to keep breaking out of his pages.

The prose romance, then, is an independent form of fiction to be distinguished from the novel and extracted from the miscellaneous heap of prose works now covered by that term. Even in the other heap known as short stories one can isolate the tale form used by Poe, which bears the same relation to the full romance that the stories of Chekhov or Katherine Mansfield do to the novel. "Pure" examples of either form are never found; there is hardly any modern romance that could not be made out to be a novel, and vice versa. The forms of prose fiction are mixed, like racial strains in human beings, not separable like the sexes. In fact the popular demand in fiction is always for a mixed form, a romantic novel just romantic enough for the reader to project his libido on the hero and his anima on the heroine, and just novel enough to keep these projections in a familiar world. It may be asked, therefore, what is the use of making the above distinction, especially when, though undeveloped in criticism, it is by no means unrealized. It is no surprise to hear that Trollope wrote novels and William Morris romances.

The reason is that a great romancer should be examined in terms of the conventions he chose. William Morris should not be left on the side lines of prose fiction merely because the critic has not learned to take the romance form seriously. Nor, in view of what has been said about the revolutionary nature of the romance, should his choice of that form be regarded as an "escape" from his social attitude. If Scott has any claims to be a romancer, it is not good criticism to deal only with his defects as a novelist. The romantic qualities of *The Pilgrim's Progress,* too, its archetypal characterization and its revolutionary approach to religious experience, make it a well-rounded example of a literary form: it is not merely a book swallowed by English literature to get some religious bulk in its diet. Finally, when Hawthorne, in the preface to *The House of the Seven Gables,* insists that his story should be read as romance and not as novel, it is possible that he meant what he said, even though he indicates that the prestige of the rival form has induced the romancer to apologize for not using it.

Romance is older than the novel, a fact which has developed the historical illusion that it is something to be outgrown, a juvenile and undeveloped form. The social affinities of the romance, with its grave idealizing of heroism and purity, are with the aristocracy (for the apparent inconsistency of this with the revolutionary nature of the form just mentioned, see the introductory comment on the *mythos* of romance in the previous essay). It revived in the period we call Romantic as part of the Romantic tendency to archaic feudalism and a cult of the hero, or idealized libido. In England the romances of Scott and, in less degree, the Brontes, are part of a mysterious Northumbrian renaissance, a Romantic reaction against the new industrialism in the Midlands, which also produced the poetry of Wordsworth and Burns and the philosophy of Carlyle. It is not surprising, therefore, that an important theme in the more bourgeois novel should be the parody of the romance and its ideals. The tradition established by *Don Quixote* continues in a type of novel which looks at a romantic situation from its own point of view, so that the conventions of the two forms make up an ironic compound instead of a sentimental mixture. Examples range from *Northanger Abbey* to *Madame Bovary* and *Lord Jim.*

The tendency to allegory in the romance may be conscious, as in *The Pilgrim's Progress,* or unconscious, as in the very obvious sexual mythopoeia in William Morris. The romance, which deals with heroes, is intermediate between the novel, which deals with men, and the myth, which deals with gods. Prose romance first appears as a late development of Classical mythology, and the prose Sagas of Iceland follow close on the mythical Eddas. The novel tends rather to expand into a fictional approach to history. The soundness of Fielding's instinct in calling *Tom Jones* a history is confirmed by the general rule that the larger the scheme of a novel becomes, the more obviously its historical nature appears. As it is creative history, however, the novelist usually prefers his material in a plastic, or roughly contemporary state, and feels cramped by a fixed historical pattern. *Waverley* is dated about sixty years back from the time of writing and *Little Dorrit* about forty years, but the historical pattern is fixed in the romance and plastic in the novel, suggesting the general principle that most "historical novels" are romances. Similarly a novel becomes more romantic in its appeal when the life it reflects has passed away: thus the novels of Trollope were read primarily as romances during the Second World War. It is perhaps the link with history and a sense of temporal context that has confined the novel, in striking contrast to the world-wide romance, to the alliance of time and Western man.

Autobiography is another form which merges with the novel by a series of insensible gradations. Most autobiographies are inspired by a creative, and therefore fictional, impulse to select only those events and experiences in the writer's life that go to build up an integrated pattern. This pattern may be something larger than himself with which he has come to identify himself or simply the coherence of his character and attitudes. We may call this very important form of prose fiction the confession form, following St. Augustine, who appears to have invented it, and Rousseau, who established a modern type of it. The earlier tradition gave *Religio Medici, Grace Abounding,* and Newman's *Apologia* to English literature, besides the related but subtly different type of confession favored by the mystics.

Here again, as with the romance, there is some value in recognizing a distinct prose form in the confession. It gives several of our best prose works a definable place in fiction instead of keeping them in a vague limbo of books which are not quite literature because they are "thought," and not quite religion or philosophy because they are Examples of Prose Style. The confession, too, like the novel and the romance, has its own short form, the familiar essay and Montaigne's *livre de bonne foy* is a confession made up of essays in which only the continuous narrative of the longer form is missing. Montaigne's scheme is to the confession what a work of fiction made up of short stories, such as Joyce's *Dubliners* or Boccaccio's *Decameron,* is to the novel or romance.

After Rousseau—in fact in Rousseau—the confession flows into the novel, and the mixture produces the fictional autobiography, the *Künstler-roman,* and kindred types. There is no literary reason why the subject of a confession should always be the author himself, and dramatic confessions have been used in the novel at least since *Moll Flanders.* The "stream of consciousness" technique permits of a much more concentrated fusion of the two forms, but even here the characteristics peculiar to the confession form show up clearly. Nearly always some theoretical and intellectual interest in religion, politics, or art plays a leading role in the confession. It is his success in integrating his mind on such subjects that makes the author of a confession feel that his life is worth writing about. But this interest in ideas and theoretical statements is alien to the genius of the novel proper, where the technical problem is to dissolve all theory into personal relationships. In Jane Austen, to take a familiar instance, church, state, and culture are never examined except as social data, and Henry James has been described as having a mind so fine that no idea could violate it. The novelist who cannot get along without ideas, or has not the patience to digest them in the way that James did, instinctively resorts to what Mill calls a "mental history" of a single character. And when we find that a technical discussion of a theory of aesthetics forms the climax of Joyce's *Portrait,* we realize that what makes this possible is the presence in that novel of another tradition of prose fiction.

The novel tends to be extroverted and personal; its chief interest is in human character as it manifests itself in society. The romance tends to be introverted and personal: it also deals with characters, but in a more subjective way. (Subjective here refers to treatment, not subject-matter. The characters of romance are heroic and therefore inscrutable; the novelist is freer to enter his characters' minds because he is more objective.) The confession is also introverted, but intellectualized in content. Our next step is evidently to discover a fourth form of fiction which is extroverted and intellectual.

We remarked earlier that most people would call *Gulliver's Travels* fiction but not a novel. It must then be another form of fiction, as it certainly has a form, and we feel that we are turning from the novel to this form, whatever it is, when we turn from Rousseau's *Emile* to Voltaire's *Candide,* or from Butler's *The Way of All Flesh* to the Erewhon books, or from Huxley's *Point Counterpoint* to *Brave New World.* The form thus has its own traditions, and, as the examples of Butler and Huxley show, has preserved some integrity even under the ascendancy of the novel. Its existence is easy enough to demonstrate, and no one will challenge the statement that the literary ancestry of *Gulliver's Travels* and *Candide* runs through Rabelais and Erasmus to Lucian. But while much has been said about the style and thought of Rabelais, Swift, and Voltaire, very little has been made of them as craftsmen working in a specific medium, a point no one dealing with a novelist would ignore. Another great writer in this tradition, Huxley's master Peacock, has fared even worse, for, his form not being understood, a general impression has grown up that his status in the development of prose fiction is that of a slapdash eccentric. Actually, he is as exquisite and precise an artist in his medium as Jane Austen is in hers.

The form used by these authors is the Menippean satire, also more rarely called the Varronian satire, allegedly invented by a Greek cynic named Menippus. His works are lost, but he had two great disciples, the Greek Lucian and the Roman Varro, and the tradition of Varro, who has not survived either except in fragments, was carried on by Petronius and Apuleius. The Menippean satire appears to have developed out of verse satire through the practice of adding prose interludes, but we know it only as a prose form, though one of its recurrent features (seen in Peacock) is the use of incidental verse.

The Menippean satire deals less with people as such than with mental attitudes. Pedants, bigots, cranks, parvenus, virtuosi, enthusiasts, rapacious and incompetent professional men of all kinds, are handled in terms of their occupational approach to life as distinct from their social behavior. The Menippean satire thus resembles the confession in its ability to handle abstract ideas and theories and differs from the novel in its characterization, which is stylized rather than naturalistic, and presents people as mouthpieces of the ideas they represent. Here again no sharp boundary lines can or should be drawn, but if we compare a character in Jane Austen with a similar character in Peacock we can immediately feel the difference between the two forms. Squire Western belongs to the novel, but Thwackum and Square have Menippean blood in them. A constant theme in the tradition is the ridicule of the *philosophus gloriosus,* already discussed. The novelist sees evil and folly as social diseases, but the Menippean satirist sees them as diseases of the intellect, as a kind of maddened pedantry which the *philosophus gloriosus* at once symbolizes and defines.

Petronius, Apuleius, Rabelais, Swift, and Voltaire all use a loose-jointed narrative form often confused with the romance. It differs from the romance, however (though there is a strong admixture of romance in Rabelais), as it is not primarily concerned with the exploits of heroes, but relies on the free play of intellectual fancy and the kind of humorous observation that produces caricature. It differs also from the picaresque form, which has the novel's interest in the actual structure of society. At its most concentrated the Menippean satire presents us with a vision of the world in terms of a single intellectual pattern. The intellectual structure built up from the story makes for violent dislocations in the customary logic of narrative, though the appearance of carelessness that results reflects only the carelessness of the reader or his tendency to judge by a novel-centered conception of fiction.

The word "satire," in Roman and Renaissance times, meant either of two specific literary forms of that name, one (this one) prose and the other verse. Now it means a structural principle or attitude, what we have called a *mythos*. In the Menippean satires we have been discussing, the name of the form also applies to the attitude. As the name of an attitude, satire is, we have seen, a combination of fantasy and morality. But as the name of a form, the term satire, though confined to literature (for as a *mythos* it may appear in any art, a cartoon, for example), is more flexible, and can be either entirely fantastic or entirely moral. The Menippean adventure story may thus be pure fantasy, as it is in the literary fairy tale. The Alice books are perfect Menippean satires, and so is *The Water-Babies*, which has been influenced by Rabelais. The purely moral type is a serious vision of society as a single intellectual pattern, in other words a Utopia.

The short form of the Menippean satire is usually a dialogue or colloquy, in which the dramatic interest is in a conflict of ideas rather than of character. This is the favorite form of Erasmus, and is common in Voltaire. Here again the form is not invariably satiric in attitude, but shades off into more purely fanciful or moral discussions, like the *Imaginary Conversations* of Landor or the "dialogue of the dead." Sometimes this form expands to full length, and more than two speakers are used: the setting then is usually a *cena* or symposium, like the one that looms so large in Petronius. Plato, though much earlier in the field than Menippus, is a strong influence on this type, which stretches in an unbroken tradition down through those urbane and leisurely conversations which define the ideal courtier in Castiglione or the doctrine and discipline of angling in Walton. A modern development produces the country-house weekends in Peacock, Huxley, and their imitators in which the opinions and ideas and cultural interests expressed are as important as the love-making.

The novelist shows his exuberance either by an exhaustive analysis of human relationships, as in Henry James, or of social phenomena, as in Tolstoy. The Menippean satirist, dealing with intellectual themes and attitudes, shows his exuberance in intellectual ways, by piling up an enormous mass of erudition about his theme or in overwhelming his pedantic targets with an avalanche of their own jargon. A species, or rather sub-species, of the form is the kind of encyclopaedic farrago represented by Athenaeus' *Deipnosophists* and Macrobius' *Saturnalia*, where people sit at a banquet and pour out a vast mass of erudition on every subject that might conceivably come up in a conversation. The display of erudition had probably been associated with the Menippean tradition by Varro, who was enough of a polymath to make Quintilian, if not stare and gasp, at any rate call him *vir Romanorum eruditissimus*. The tendency to expand into an encyclopaedic farrago is clearly marked in Rabelais notably in the great catalogues of torcheculs and epithets of codpieces and methods of divination. The encyclopaedic compilations produced in the line of duty by Erasmus and Voltaire suggest that a magpie instinct to collect facts is not unrelated to the type of ability that has made them famous as artists. Flaubert's encyclopaedic approach to the construction of *Bouvard et Pecuchet* is quite comprehensible if we explain it as marking an affinity with the Menippean tradition.

This creative treatment of exhaustive erudition is the organizing principle of the greatest Menippean satire in English before Swift, Burton's *Anatomy of Melancholy*. Here human society is studied in terms of the intellectual pattern provided by the conception of melancholy, a symposium of books replaces dialogue, and the result is the most comprehensive survey of human life in one book that English literature had seen since Chaucer, one of Burton's favorite authors. We may note in passing the Utopia in his introduction and his "digressions," which when examined turn out to be scholarly distillations of Menippean forms: the digression of air, of the marvellous journey; the digression of spirits, of the ironic use of erudition; the digression of the miseries of scholars, of the satire on the *philosophus gloriosus*. The word "anatomy" in Burton's title means a dissection or analysis, and expresses very accurately the intellectualized approach of his form. We may as well adopt it as a convenient name to replace the cumbersome and in modern times rather misleading "Menippean satire."

The anatomy, of course, eventually begins to merge with the novel, producing various hybrids including the *roman à these* and novels in which the characters are symbols of social or other ideas, like the proletarian novels of the thirties in this century. It was Sterne, however, the disciple of Burton and Rabelais, who combined them with greatest success. *Tristram Shandy* may be, as was said at the beginning, a novel, but the digressing narrative, the catalogues, the stylizing of character along "humor" lines, the marvellous journey of the great nose, the symposium discussions, and the constant ridicule of philosophers and pedantic critics are all features that belong to the anatomy.

A clearer understanding of the form and traditions of the anatomy would make a good many elements in the history of literature come into focus. Boethius' *Consolation of Philosophy*, with its dialogue form, its verse interludes and its pervading tone of contemplative irony, is a pure anatomy, a fact of considerable importance for the understanding of its vast influence. *The Compleat Angler* is an anatomy because of its mixture of prose and verse, its rural *cena* setting, its dialogue form, its deipnosophistical interest in food, and its gentle Menippean raillery of a society which considers everything more important than fishing and yet has discovered very few better things to do. In nearly every period of literature there are many romances, confessions, and anatomies that are neglected only because the categories to which they belong are unrecognized. In the period between Sterne and Peacock, for example, we have, among romances, *Melmoth the Wanderer;* among confessions, Hogg's *Confessions of a Justified Sinner;* among anatomies, Southey's *Doctor,* Amory's *John Buncle,* and the *Noctes Ambrosianae.*

To sum up then: when we examine fiction from the point of view of form, we can see four chief strands binding it together, novel, confession, anatomy, and romance. The six possible combinations of these forms all exist, and we have shown how the novel has combined with each of the other three. Exclusive concentration on one form is rare: the early novels of George Eliot, for instance, are influenced by the romance, and the later ones by the anatomy. The romance-confession hybrid is found, naturally, in the autobiography of a romantic temperament, and is represented in English by the extroverted George Borrow and the introverted De Quincey. The romance-anatomy one we have noticed in Rabelais; a later example is *Moby Dick,* where the romantic theme of the wild hunt expands into an encyclopaedic anatomy of the whale. Confession and anatomy are united in *Sartor Resartus* and in some of Kierkegaard's strikingly original experiments in prose fiction form, including *Either/Or.* More comprehensive fictional schemes usually employ at least three forms: we can see strains of novel, romance, and confession in *Pamela,* of novel, romance, and anatomy in *Don Quixote,* of novel, confesssion, and anatomy in Proust, and of romance, confession, and anatomy in Apuleius.

I deliberately make this sound schematic in order to suggest the advantage of having a simple and logical explanation for the form of, say, *Moby Dick* or *Tristram Shandy.* The usual critical approach to the form of such works resembles that of the doctors in Brobdingnag, who after great wrangling finally pronounced Gulliver a *lusus naturae*. It is the anatomy in particular that has baffled critics, and there is hardly any fiction writer deeply influenced by it who has not been accused of disorderly conduct. The reader may be reminded here of Joyce, for describing Joyce's books as monstrous has become a nervous tic. I find "demogorgon," "behemoth," and "white elephant" in good critics; the bad ones could probably do much better. The care that Joyce took to organize *Ulysses* and *Finnegans Wake* amounted nearly to obsession, but as they are not organized on familiar principles of prose fiction, the impression of shapelessness remains. Let us try our formulas on him.

If a reader were asked to set down a list of things that had most impressed him about *Ulysses*, it might reasonably be somewhat as follows. First, the clarity with which the sights and sounds and smells of Dublin come to life, the rotundity of the character-drawing, and the naturalness of the dialogue. Second, the elaborate way that the story and characters are parodied by being set against archetypal heroic patterns, notably the one provided by the *Odyssey*. Third, the revelation of character and incident through the searching use of the stream-of-consciousness technique. Fourth, the constant tendency to be encyclopaedic and exhaustive both in technique and in subject matter, and to see both in highly intellectualized terms. It should not be too hard for us by now to see that these four points describe elements in the book which relate to the novel, romance, confession, and anatomy respectively. *Ulysses*, then, is a complete prose epic with all four forms employed in it, all of practically equal importance, and all essential to one another, so that the book is a unity and not an aggregate.

This unity is built up from an intricate scheme of parallel contrasts. The romantic archetypes of Hamlet and Ulysses are like remote stars in a literary heaven looking down quizzically on the shabby creatures of Dublin obediently intertwining themselves in the patterns set by their influences. In the "Cyclops" and "Circe" episodes particularly there is a continuous parody of realistic patterns by romantic ones which reminds us, though the irony leans in the opposite direction, of *Madame Bovary*. The relation of novel and confession techniques is similar; the author jumps into his characters' minds to follow their stream of consciousness, and out again to describe them externally. In the novel-anatomy combination, too, found in the "Ithaca" chapter, the sense of lurking antagonism between the personal and intellectual aspects of the scene accounts for much of its pathos. The same principle of parallel contrast holds good for the other three combinations: of romance and confession in "Nausicaa" and "Penelope," of confession and anatomy in "Proteus" and "The Lotos-Eaters," of romance and anatomy (a rare and fitful combination) in "Sirens" and parts of "Circe."

In *Finnegans Wake* the unity of design goes far beyond this. The dingy story of the sodden HCE and his pinched wife is not contrasted with the archetypes of Tristram and the divine king: HCE is himself Tristram and the divine king. As the setting is a dream, no contrast is possible between confession and novel, between a stream of consciousness inside the mind and the appearances of other people outside it. Nor is the experiential world of the novel to be separated from the intelligible world of the anatomy. The forms we have been isolating in fiction, and which depend for their existence on the commonsense dichotomies of the daylight consciousness, vanish in *Finnegans Wake* into a fifth and quintessential form. This form is the one traditionally associated with scriptures and sacred books, and treats life in terms of the fall and awakening of the human soul and the creation and apocalypse of nature. The Bible is the definitive example of it; the Egyptian Book of the Dead and the Icelandic Prose Edda, both of which have left deep imprints on *Finnegans Wake,* also belong to it.

ROBERT B. HEILMAN

Felix Krull: Variations on Picaresque

There is a sense in which it is not surprising that Thomas Mann, having begun a picaresque story at the age of 36 and left it unfinished when the special demands of its style became burdensome, should never be able to dismiss it wholly from his mind, should at the age of 68 debate with himself whether to take up again the tale of a rogue or to begin work on the great Faustus theme, should in the eighth decade of his life return to the "artistic jest," as he once called it, and at 79 publish a continuation which was still not a conclusion, and should plan to go on from there. This persistent attachment to the story of Felix Krull is understandable if we remember Mann's tendency not to forget themes that had once got into his imagination, his delight in facing new technical problems, his zest in the unexpected or the daring, and, of course, that sense of the playful and the comic which we may lose sight of when, as may happen to the philosophic novelist, adulation focuses only on the portentously vatic.

Yet that Mann, after *Magic Mountain*, the Joseph series, and *Dr. Faustus* should at 80 be going on with an apparently trivial tale—think of Shakespeare after the tragedies returning, say, to *Taming of the Shrew*—will, somehow, evoke a question. And surely the basis of the question is the fact that the picaresque tradition is a relatively thin and discontinuous one, with few great works and fewer great practitioners. On the whole it seems meant for the writer, like the Byron of *Don Juan*, who will not or cannot encompass experience in its densities. If it be argued that *The Transposed Heads* and *The Holy Sinner* raise the same problem, or else eliminate the problem entirely by showing that Mann periodically tried a jocular hand at slight and slender forms, the answer must be that *The Transposed Heads* and *The Holy*

Sinner, however far they go or do not go in themselves, nevertheless belong to the realm of fable, fairy tale, and fantasy where all depths are possible; while *Felix Krull* is in a mode that is not only "realistic" but deliberately limited in its realistic scope.

II

In picaresque a "rogue" is "hero," and we may define rogue as one who lives by his wits. The word *rogue* suggests such other words as *scamp* and *rascal,* the family of terms by which we designate the person who lives partly, though not threateningly, outside communal standards of responsibility. It is, of course, part of his way of life to simulate insideness; when he achieves a partial insideness, not by a specially designed facade, but by aspects of personality that elicit a spontaneous warmth of response, he is likely to be called "lovable rogue"—a term that, though it suggests some actual paradoxes of human make-up, is likely to denote a sentimental stereotype. "Lives by his wits," popular phrase though it is, has substantial defining value. For one thing, it suggests the wit that characteristically belongs to the picaro—the instant readiness of mind, made evident in repartee, manipulation of ideas, or extemporization of apt words or actions. More important, it states affirmatively his central modus vivendi, and thus it simultaneously implies the lopping off of those elements of personality characteristically lacking in the picaro. Living by wits implies knowledge of "the world," a sharp insight into responses that may be played upon advantageously, a mastery of the techniques of playing upon them, the ready appraisal of life by what Charlotte Bronte might have called "the organ of computation"—in a word, the apparatus of a "lightning calculator." Since in the life of "wits" certain functions of the mind dominate, this life also means a diminution, if not total elimination, of emotional depths and moral concern. The rogue is without conscience or superego or the inhibitions created by the community's sense of right and wrong; not so much that he is the enemy of these or falls short of an expectable standard by which we judge him, as that he lives in another world from them. He lives outside the "ordinary" feelings of the community: his hypertrophy of practical intelligence replaces a full emotional development. Not that the picaro is entirely "heartless" or without feelings; it is aesthetically necessary that he be not a monster. His self-love gives him some link to the rest of mankind; he can fear; he may have transient fidelities. But if he is afraid, his fear does not deepen into terror. He may experience disgust, but not horror. He is likely to be well endowed with sex, but he hardly experiences passion or serious jealousy, and least of all love. He may find people difficult, objectionable, or annoyingly skeptical, but he does not hate.

The key is shallowness, which in this case is to be seen not as a defect but as a fact, like the size of feet, and understood to have both advantages and disadvantages; in shallowness lies the clue not only to the degree but also to the direction of his feelings. Ordinarily, rather than earning an emotional identity by experiencing a complex of rejections, acceptances, and modifications, he simply takes over available patterns of feeling, and these are most likely to be conventional or orthodox (in the presence of the articulate, energetic off-center sexuality of Diane Philibert, Felix Krull sounds almost like a proper young man). In their different ways, Jack Wilton and Moll Flanders are unprincipled conservatives, who automatically identify with lords or dominant classes; a Communist picaro, though a private entrepreneur in his roguery, would be Marxist in feeling. As a wearer of old school ties the rogue is still the shallow man, responsible for nothing and free to act as unconservatively as he pleases, for instance, to pick the pockets of his tie-brothers. If the picaro tries unpicaresquely to discover an individual order of feeling, his shallowness leads him into a foamily sentimental outsiderism (if this is not a redundancy) in which we can see resemblances, at a great distance, to bohemians, Robin Hoods, etc.

In looking at the man who lives by his wits, we do not use words such as *villain, revenge, cunning, malice, bitterness,* or *trouble-maker*, for those imply a profundity of feeling or an intensity of commitment foreign to this kind of schemer. Words like *crook* or *scoundrel* vary with context and intonation; they may denote either a picaro or a serious attacker of the moral order. *Criminal* seems to me not to belong to the vocabulary of picaresque, though I say this with some diffidence, since the word is used by good critics of Mann, and even by Mann himself, to apply to the Krull-world. True, criminal and picaro both break laws, and there are other subtler affiliations which we must observe later. But *criminal* implies earnestness, the will to disturb, seize, and violate; deliberateness or "engagedness" in an attack on the will of others or on the public order; ruthlessness; illness. *Picaro,* on the other hand, implies flippancy; harassments rather than serious attacks; the trick-or-treat prankster; seduction rather than rape; the securing of and playing upon the victim's consent; a relish of the game as such; in Dantean terms, less the perversion of right feeling than a non-function of right feeling. Let us say that both are "psychopathic personalities," one with a distorted soul, the other with a rudimentary one. The picaro is the literary equivalent of that familiar abnormal type that must use talents, which are often extraordinary, not for murder but for masquerade; who must take by trick what he could earn by effort; who must dazzle rather than seek respect; to whom the world is a theatre rather than a school; who by spectacular fakery can get by as a physician or even surgeon, but who would never take a medical degree. Though many variations, degrees of development, and overlappings are possible, the criminal has kinship with Iago, the picaro with Falstaff.

So much for the rogue as such; now for the rogue as "hero." The picaresque writer has the interesting technical problem of securing, for an extra-legal operator, "sympathy" and even "identification." He can do this by giving the picaro certain generally admired qualities— good nature, charm, an ironical view of himself. Or he can do it, as in *Lazarillo de Tormes* and *Guzman de Alfarache* and initially in *Moll Flanders,* by making the rogue somewhat a creature of necessity, mal-treated by others and by circumstances; though here the scent of the "problem" story, the bouquet of pathos, and the perfume of the senti-mental threaten the true picaresque mode. A sounder method is nega-tive: giving no place, or at least no prominence, to other characters who, by being larger or nobler people and thus having a stronger claim on our "right feelings," might usurp the sympathy due the picaro. One way of "protecting" the picaro is to endow representatives of right feeling and "right thinking," if these get into the story, with disagree-able personal traits—pretentiousness, complacency, and so on. But in this method the danger is that the work may slide into satire, which, though it may have a role in picaresque, is, as a mode, a different thing, generically related to melodrama and therefore calling upon another area of aesthetic responsiveness. Though neither picaresque nor satire is essentially unstable, either one may, if the tone is not skillfully con-trolled, lapse into the other. Sinclair Lewis's Elmer Gantry, intended as an object of satire, is treated with so little depth and thrust into such a frenzy of misdeeds that the moral critique is somehow transformed into a tale of adventures inviting a relish of successful rascality. Becky Sharp, conversely, is transmuted from picaresque heroine to object of satire: this happens when sympathy for her piquant gamesmanship is allowed to shift to her victims, who are shown fully enough to draw us in on their side (Rawdon as father, for instance). For the most important method in picaresque is to keep the victims out of sight, lest they threaten our alliance with the rogue (thus we never see the candy-store owner that Felix robs). Or the victims can deserve what they get, through graspingness, or foolish pride, or a gullibility which is an affront to all good sense—the area in which satire may transiently enter picaresque. Or most subtly the writer can, as I believe Mann does, convey a sense of the positive satisfaction accruing to the "victim" in his experiences with the rogue. Here analysis of picaresque would take us close to the general realm of that singular victim—dupe, seducee, or even murderee—who must unknowingly convey his unknown readiness to the trickster or evildoer who will fulfil him.

The rogue-hero determines not only the treatment of other characters but also the scene and structure. Such a hero precludes extensive analysis of a situation: while retention of sympathy for him means a cursory treatment of other characters, his own shallowness forestalls prolonged study of his own nature. Instead of depth and rigor we have speed and multiplicity: since without "character" a story cannot indefinitely be spun out of one set of circumstances, one situation must soon be replaced by another; and since living by wits alone is not conducive to long residence, one scene normally gives way to another without much delay. Picaresque is naturally cinematic and episodic. However, the familiar use of *picaresque* as if its basic meaning were *episodic* is quite inaccurate, for, while it is virtually impossible to be picaresque without being episodic, it is entirely possible to be episodic without being picaresque, as in *Joseph Andrews*. Though in criticism *episodic* has usually a pejorative sense, nonetheless the continual change of scene inherent in picaresque has compensations: the form is made for the travelogue-novel. Mann may well have had this sense of the picaresque, for Felix Krull loved "the world" and was evidently intended to explore a good deal of it. In the end the potential of the episodic travelogue-fiction depends on the endowments of the world-tourist. The man who lives by his wits can have any amount of wits the author chooses, any amount of descriptive and analytical intelligence; he can be a brilliant mirror of life in the world. Often Mann confers upon Krull the gifts of his own recording and exploring, even of his searching, mind; indeed, even a measure of his creative imagination. Among his exploits in this book he must indeed have enjoyed making the charlatan something of a philosopher, the masquerader an exemplar of his own industrious, even cataloguing, encyclopedism.

III

The form which cuts off the larger dimensions of human reality appeals by affording a relief from responsibility. For the reader it bans scruple and passion, offering aesthetic pleasure freed of the moral concern or emotional trials that are, in whatever way, a part of the aesthetic pleasure of "great" fiction. The writer of picaresque enjoys, apparently, freedom from the most severe imaginative demands; his mind can roam like a picaro, commenting where and as he will. He need reconcile the free flow of observation and opinion with only slight demands of structure and with the most easily obtainable consistencies of character. Mann can have a free hand here without our impugning his sense of form as we are inclined to do in his other novels.

But since picaresque is not the only fictional holiday from the full self, we must seek its uniqueness in another function. This, I suggest, is the catharsis of rascality—catharsis, certainly not as purification; perhaps as elimination; but primarily in the sense that it gives free "play" to certain human impulses. Or we might shift to the opposite metaphor and say that it permits these impulses to "work," and even, if one should want to argue for that end-result, to "work off." (The end-result, the psychic and moral residue of aesthetic experience, is outside the scope of this paper.) Through the picaresque hero a seamy side of man, the tricksy side, has a fling—that persistently present, though conscientiously kept under, side, where there lurks a universal impulse to escape the shadows of guilt and to put things over on others or the world, to be nimble of foot, and hand, and head. One need not be a wit to feel the charm of living by wits: in the rogue world every deed is a repartee of action. The reader put off by the gay libertinism may find a comparable satisfaction in the "success story," for Algeresque is really picaresque transposed into another key: a fragmented personality still gets the booty, but now he is an insider operating by the latest edicts of the central rules committee. Since now there are no reckonings, Algeresque is a much more misleading imaginative exercise.

In picaresque another quality has a fling, the quality which I will call the "instinct for episodes." The very episodic structure which, as we have seen, derives from the nature of the picaresque hero, shows us something about the aesthetic functioning of the form: it appeals to a longing to reduce the muddled continuum of life to episodes manageable by cleverness alone. And here we run into counter-impulses called into play by an apparently simple literary genre: for that control of life by ingenuity which is offered by picaresque is secured by a reduction of reality, and that reduction itself implies a yielding, a going-under. For the "instinct for episodes" means a secret inclination to discontinuity, to hit-and-run raids on life, the impulse to shun the long and exacting unity, to live instead by episodes. If this "instinct" for the episodic becomes dominant, that is, gets out of balance with counter-forces in our psychic equipment, it produces the "episodic character": he may find, within the norms of society, a way of life marked by many breaks and shifts, each perhaps eliciting a momentary burst of energy; or, outside the lines of conventional esteem, become a rolling stone, a gypsy or a "floater," or find some other style of "life by episodes."

At this point the orbit of the picaresque comes fairly close to another attribute of Everyman that is less likely to be recognizable because it is more held out of sight and rendered inoperative—namely, a certain vague proneness to degradation (perhaps a variant of the death wish). This appears normally in an impulse to relax the guards that give form to life or even in a taste for polite humiliation that is not restricted to eccentrics; radically in the life of the *clochard* or "bum" or in pursuits of a psycho-pathological sort; even sentimentally in certain flattering disguises—for instance, when dirtiness appears to its possessor to be an incisive critique of the falsities that may accompany cleanliness. But in what is necessarily a very oblique tapping of this element in the psyche, picaresque could very easily slide over into scatology or satire or a simplistic cynicism.

Finally, though I have argued that rogue and criminal must be distinguished, it may be profitable to consider the rogue a kind of denatured or sterile criminal, for we could then understand picaresque as releasing even the radically rebellious impulses. Since the conscious rebel finds all the direct voices he needs, the liberating picaro would speak only for those who in ordinary consciousness would take for granted their own unreserved sympathy with legal and moral order. The criminal, as it were devitalized in the picaro, could evoke the responses of the "good man" like an expressionistic symbol that passes through consciousness to engage other non-conscious powers. An exponent of catharsis doctrines might argue, from the tolerance of the picaro, for an analogous permissiveness of criminality by the social order generally, a "consent" through need, a letting-go to be followed by the imposition of penalties which are also a self-punishment. The analogy doubles us back again to fiction: in picaresque the non-moral holiday always comes to an end; the picaro is reformed or is jailed; and in the aesthetic experience the rascal after his play-period retreats within the citizen.

The operating hypothesis of picaro as residual criminal (true outlaw passion neutralised, as in the making of a serum) has another utility. The man who lives by his wits has usually a vigorous instinctive life; he somewhat paradoxically combines natural man and the sophisticated schemer. In this he is cousin, in however attenuated form, to some of the great embodiments of evil in literature: Goneril and Iago: the union of animal passion and exorbitant craft of mind.

IV

Though living by wits suggests immediately sleight-of-hand and verbal skill, it should also suggest the older meaning of *wit*, that is, mind or intelligence in a general sense. For the picaro is in his way a creature of "mind"; his family tree is that of Ulysses rather than that of Prometheus or Hercules or Roland or Romeo. The picaresque experience is in one sense an exercise of mind, really a reveling in the mind as conqueror, a relishing of power through purely mental rather than physical or political or social means. The picaresque hero, a solitary victor with weapons of intelligence, corresponds to a desire in Everyman, a desire essential enough to insure, even in an anti-intellectualist atmosphere, endemic dreams of mastery by brain-power, e.g., "control of nature." When, in ruminating about the picaresque mode, I first thought of the picaro as an imaginative representation of the instrumental intelligence, I felt immediately that there must be another artistic version of the dream of power—a version in which the impulse was not transposed into terms of playful rascality or seen in the intermittent flash of episodes, with the habitual picaresque flight closing off the full potential of energy in the idea only partly tapped by the fractional rogue-figure. In the other version, the theme would have to be, not living by wits alone, but living by brains alone, an earnest, total commitment to the exercise of power through the operations of mind. To complete the formulation was to identify the imaginative form of it: the Faustus myth. And to spot this cousinship, these divergent developments from a common starting-point, was also to see further into the contrasting aesthetic experiences of picaresque and tragedy:

in the picaresque, the free tasting of private power, easily summoned and applied as occasion came; in the Faustian, living in power while discovering the consequences of acquiring and regularly wielding it; in the former, indulging some of the self but happily cut off from the parts whence self-awareness and guilt would come; in the latter, being thrust by the fable of total self-indulgence into the depths of self where total knowledge is the final burden.

At this point I came across Mann's *Die Enstehung des Doktor Faustus,* and in it his account of his hesitating, after the completion of *Joseph* in 1943, between two possible subjects for his next work. It now seemed extraordinarily significant, more than a simple uncertainty between unconnected alternatives, that his choice lay between the Faustus theme and a continuation, after many years, of the Krull story. Then comes his climax: he reread the Krull materials—"with singular result," namely, "insight into the inner relation of the Faust-material with it (depending upon the solitariness-motif, here tragic-mystical, there humorous-criminal); . . ." In this exploration of the picaresque it seems to me worthwhile to record these independent conclusions, very close despite the difference of emphasis, on the affinity, illuminating as I hope it is, between the picaresque theme and the great tragic theme, or at least between the Mann versions of the two. One cannot note the bond without wondering whether Mann, in giving Krull the name Felix, of the meaning of which much is made, happened to recall that the Latin adjectives *felix* and *faustus* are synonyms. And one remembers, inevitably, the theory that in Hamlet and Falstaff a common theme is explored in different styles.

In all the literature that deals with the wit-conducted life there is, ultimately, ambiguity. Perhaps only detective stories naively exploit the passion for the mind's control of existence. Tragedy and picaresque set this passion in play; yet, though tragedy endows it with all the dignity of which it is capable in the completely presented human being, and picaresque lives by exercizing the human delight in this control, both are penetrated by a sense of the failure of mind alone. Oedipus finds mysteries he cannot solve by taking thought, Faustus learns the destructive price of power by knowledge. Picaresque heroes, at their best almost infinitely clever, nonetheless fall prey to sex, covetousness, prodigality, carelessness, vanity, in a word, to the irrationalities of human nature, and to accidents, the irrationalities of circumstance.

V

Within the limits of picaresque a novelist can do little or much. As one would expect of the writer who saw in Felix Krull a version of the Faustian solitary, Mann used his form very richly. Compare Simenon, also of international fame: his non-detective fictions have a great air of searching the soul, but in the end we have only psychological mechanisms and banalities; whereas Mann, with the air of one intent only on a literary gambol, convinces us that more is going on than meets the eye—which is precisely what does not happen in most picaresque. Not that he does not observe the basic conventions of his form: Felix's career falls into episodes, and we know that the law was to puncture his felicity. Yet the episodes are developed with unusual fullness, they have certain dramatic interconnections, and Felix periodically finds in one experience a reminder of something earlier, a linking image or concept or feeling; in these ways the book moves toward a unity that itself suggests complications beyond the picaresque. Felix's fall is long postponed; the moral guardian always hovering fretfully over traditional picaresque is less present; and in this increase in picaresque "purity" we sense an original amplification of the rogue tale. Felix's own intelligent perceptiveness drives us to seek the intentions behind the mask. We find, too, a sense of character that goes beyond picaresque habits: Susanna Kuckuck, for instance, is in several ways quite reminiscent of Aglaya Yepanchin in Dostoievski's *Idiot*.

A stylistic mode of enrichment is self-evident—a grandioseness that is a parodic reminder of serious autobiography. So it is not surprising to find Mann describing the "fantastic intellectual charm in the burlesque idea of taking a much loved tradition—self-portraiture in the Goethe manner, the introspective 'Confessions' of the born aristocrat—and transferring it to the criminal sphere." That Mann found an immediate stimulus in the memoirs of a living confidence man makes an enlightening parallel between him and Fielding. Fielding found in the life of the criminal Jonathan Wild the genesis of a fiction ironically employing traditional ideas of greatness; Mann found in the autobiography of Georges Manolescu the genesis of a fiction ironically employing the traditional manner of great autobiography. But whereas Fielding was at heart an angry homilist who fell into laborious irony, Mann's method is akin to that of Joyce: placing the heroic and the contemporary in an ambiguous juxtaposition marked more by ironic interplay than by satirical undermining.

In amplifying picaresque Mann took another Joycean tack. Felix is not an isolated Mann character but is another figure in the study of rascality with which Mann was infatuated; Felix has some kinship with Joseph. Mann says that he wrote the Joseph story because of an interest in "the eternally-human, eternally-recurring, timeless, . . . the mythical." It is clear, I think, that the Krull story was taking on a mythical dimension, and that in some way it would have continued the Joseph theme. Joseph is many things, Mann says, "but then he perceptibly slides into a Hermes part, the part of the mundane and skillful business man and the intelligent profit producer among the gods, . . ." It is fascinating to see how Hermes persisted in Mann's imagination, for Hermes comes into the Krull story as the patron deity of Felix as thief, and his name is repeatedly mentioned. Indeed, it is not only by being a thief that Felix is a Hermes-figure: he is identified with luck, travel, theft and trickery, priapism, eloquence, and the arts—over all of which Hermes presided. Mann was clearly infusing into picaresque something of the mythic that absorbed him; indeed, we might say that he was constructing "the picaresque myth."

Goethe had noted the possibilities in the Joseph materials, Goethe was the model and rival in the use of the Faust materials, Goethe was, if not exactly the target, at least the figure that contributed some of the meaning to the amiable joke in *Felix Krull*. There is at least a little complication in Mann's attitude to Goethe; beside the *"imitatio Goethe,"* as it has been called, there is a sly impulse to twitch up the prima donna's skirts in front of the audience—not to expose but to get a laugh from dignity undone. Mann says that *Felix Krull* represents "my attitude toward tradition, which is at once kindly and destructive" (elsewhere, "sympathetic and detached"). How true, we feel. But another meaning intrudes here: since Mann "identifies" with Goethe and tradition, the words "kindly and destructive" also imply something of his attitude to himself. Indeed, in the same sentence from which I have just quoted, Mann says that *Felix Krull* "may be the most personal" thing he has done. These words written in 1930 have a peculiar applicability to the whole work, the fragments already written and the major additions of almost twenty-five years later: Mann's most daring exploitation of picaresque is to model the hero partly on himself. In *Felix Krull* are his own fantastically jocular *Dichtung und Wahrheit* and *Wilhelm Meister* (Wilhelm's son, incidentally, was named Felix).

Nor is it too hard, keeping in mind the necessary reservations, to conceive of *Felix Krull* as autobiographic. Critics often allude to the elements of self-portraiture in Mann's works, and Mann himself speaks of an artistic work as "a realization . . . of our individuality," even as "the sole and painful way we have of getting the particular experience." But if, even after Mann himself says, "A work must have long roots in my life, . . ." Mann-as-picaro seems inherently improbable, we can at least note the parallels between the Krull story and the Mann story as Mann himself traces it in *A Sketch of My Life*. Mann reports that he was an indifferent student, given up by the school, but condescending to his fellows, becoming a young man of "indolence, bad civic conscience, and the sure and certain feeling of latent powers." Felix hated school, played truant skillfully, and always felt superior to others. The elder Mann died when Thomas was 15, the elder Krull committed suicide when Felix was 18. Mann says that the family business had not been going well, the Krull business had gone bankrupt. Thomas went to Munich and worked in an insurance office directed by a friend of his father, Felix went to Paris and took up a hotel job secured for him by a family friend. Thomas hated the army (his "determination to free myself was prompt, deadly and in the event irresistible"), developed an ankle inflammation in which there appears to have been at least a psychosomatic ingredient, and thus through medical connections secured a discharge after three months. To Felix, military service was an "unpleasant problem" that "weighed heavy on my heart"; his godfather "did not have any sort of connection with army doctors" (as Mann's family did); but he succeeded in having himself declared unfit by faking an epileptic attack. While working in the insurance office, Thomas "secretly . . . wrote my first tale"; from his secret life, of course, sprang his career. While working at the hotel, Felix had also his secret life as "gentleman"—the beginning of his basic way of life. An untried author, Mann persuaded the hesitant Fischer firm to take *Buddenbrooks* on his terms, and this was good for both. Felix, a novice thief, persuaded a receiver-of-stolen-goods to give him something like his own price, and both profited. It is most difficult not to see the autobiographic in Felix's comments on the expatriate's feelings about his native land—his tendency to sentimentalize it, to give it an undue authority, "especially when one's homeland has behaved unkindly, unjustly, and obtusely toward one," and eventually to "yield to the temptation" to return and "show himself to its narrow view in all the glitter he has gained abroad," and "with mixed anxiety and derision in his heart," to "feast upon its astonishment—just as, in due course, I shall report of myself."

And so on. Beyond the discovery of factual parallels, which I suspect could be carried into greater detail, the most interesting quarry for
the biographer would be the oblique self-revelation by the author.
What, for instance, is to be made of the fact that Felix's Lisbon friends,
his tutors in diverse ways, are in one striking way reminiscent of Mann's
parents: the husband is German, and the wife Portuguese? The difficulty arises when Felix makes love to the wife (as well as her daughter), but this difficulty is no greater than that of dismissing the German-
Portuguese marriage as a coincidence, since Mann was not the writer
to stumble into such patent resemblances of fable to life. Though biographical interpretation is not my object, it might be helpful to work
from Henry Hatfield's proposal that *Buddenbrooks* is "a sort of reck-
oning with the father image by the young man who has broken with
family tradition" and treat Senhora Kuckuck's passionate embrace of
Felix as an establishment of Thomas in the maternal approval, whether
the mother symbolize the family tradition or the artistic impulse sometimes said to have been transmitted to Thomas through his mother.
But this would be only part of it. What of Kuckuck, whose name
fittingly suggests both "cuckold" and "rote," and who embodies something of Mann's own encyclopedism? Again, Felix is an alter ego for
the Marquis of Venosta, who is also something of a Mann-figure: just
as Mann's long visit to Italy was the symbolic break with family tradition, so Venosta breaks with, or at least resists, his family by *not* taking
the grand tour planned for him. Mann here reverses the family history
in much the same way as he does in transmuting the splendid funeral
of his father into the paltry rites for Felix's father. The Marquis (the
insider who wants to get out) and Felix (the outsider who wants to
get in) are in part opposing sides of Mann, complementing each other
somewhat as do Serenus Zeitblom and Adrian Leverkühn, the contrasting masks of the author of *Dr. Faustus,* that sober twin of *Felix Krull.*

If we look for "oblique self-revelation," we must face the tantalizing
question of Mann's motive in rendering some phases of private history
in picaresque, of the "secret connections," as Mann himself puts it,
that "must lead from it [a work of his] to earliest childhood dreams, if
I am to consider myself entitled to it, if I am to believe in the legitimacy
of what I am doing." For one thing, picaresque would be the least
expectable mode of autobiographic fiction; it would permit surprise,
it would be new and daring, it would be ironic and vastly playful—all
ends that Mann valued. It would disarm the audience, and, as an anti-
dote to self-love, it would be an extraordinary means of securing

detachment, of providing a wonderful distance and even freedom. The most convincing guess about Mann's leaving *Felix Krull* long unfinished would rely on his remark that *The Magic Mountain* could not have been written ten years earlier, since for the work he needed certain experiences which had "to ripen within him." Surely this would be true for *Felix Krull,* in which the severely limited view of man would be possible to an artist of profound perceptions only when long experience would make possible a curbing of his total vision, and of which the comically disillusioned perspective, held serenely rather than with querulous cynicism, is possible only to an artist of the mature assurance conferred by long personal and professional growth. Through such control he might give voice to self-criticism or guilt, perhaps effect a catharsis. If, as Hatfield says, "Werther and Aschenbach die in order that their creators may live," it may be that Felix had to live on in order that his creator might live with himself. Might not the disillusioned artist large enough to include himself in his own disillusionment say, "How like a rogue's life mine looks!" Within the capacious irony of the rogue's tale there lies, we may conjecture, humility: partly an oblique confession, partly an assumption of Everyman's rascality, a discovery of the heart masterfully transfigured into an urbane jest.

VI

In his remarkable expansion of picaresque Mann, ever "novarum rerum cupidus," as he put it, altered tradition most strikingly by making *Felix Krull* "the story of an artist." This interpretation by Mann is not inconsistent with the other readings that I think the book requires—with the Hermes-myth suggested by the textual evidence, with the Goethe-parody that delighted Mann, and with the variation on autobiography that it is difficult not to infer. And if the picaro is, as I define him, one who lives by his wits, this definition also reflects much of the artist's professional modus vivendi—his skill, ingenuity, working with head rather than body, with individual artifice rather than group planning.

Mann's public wrestling with the problem of artist vs. bürger has shaped a large body of criticism. In the *Krull* chapters long available for study Mann's view of the artist strikes critics as denigratory. Though this view is open to argument, I wish less to debate than to distinguish two critical problems, both legitimate: one concerns the relation of a given work to the history of the writer's opinions on a given subject; the other concerns the kind of illumination of the theme by the unique work. The former problem belongs to biography; the latter, on which I want to work, to literary analysis. The assumption here is that the author is less recording an attitude, which may change tomorrow, than he is exploring a theme in the terms provided by the chosen form. This does not deny that he is recording an attitude, but it proposes that what is said is more than an attitude, and less impermanent. We might argue that *Felix Krull* says, "The artist is only a picaro," or, conversely, "The picaro is really an artist." The problem, however, is less one of contending for the deflation of one character, or the exaltation of the other, than of seeing what steady light is shed by the insistent pursuit of the analogy.

Mann's statement that Felix is an artist-figure is documented by many aspects of the story that need only be quickly mentioned: Felix's love of and skill in make-believe, costuming, and acting; his precocity and sensitivity; his flight from school to dreams; his sense of audience, whether he is staging scenes or doing daily jobs; his identification of himself with the "artists" at the circus; his taking on diverse roles with such ease that priest and soldier would claim him, and a whore thinks him "predestined for the service of love." Mann's technique is no less striking but goes deeper when he raises a serious problem of the artist. Early in the book Schimmelpreester complains that though they admire talent people never want to accept the "oddities that are always associated with it, and perhaps are essential to it," and shortly afterwards Felix himself is shocked when, after being charmed by a talented actor, he meets him without benefit of make-up and finds his face repulsive and his back covered by "horrible pustules." For the theme of the discrepancy between artist as artist and artist as person, the picaresque is an ingenious choice, for the hero's rascalities are a vivid comic symbol for all the "oddities" that accompany talent. Mann never forgets the duality of the artist, but, with characteristic novelty, he fuses two perspectives of the duality: the maculate man behind the charm of art, or, conversely—and more emphatically—the specialized conscience behind the consciencelessness in ordinary life.

This novelty is a key to the book, which Mann surely wrote with the love of novelty to which he refers more than once. For him the subject was old, but the method a total innovation. Early in the book Felix uses the words, "as one should see everything—that is, with a fresh eye undimmed by habit," and near the end he elaborates: "One should always try to see everything, even the most commonplace, the most completely matter of fact, with new, astonished eyes as though for the first time. In this way it wins back its power to amaze, which has faded into matter-of-factness, and the world remains fresh."

Take the traditional view of the artist as lonely, isolated, outside the community. This can become a romantic or sentimental truism. But exhibit this solitariness in the man who lives by his wits, outside the ordinary responsibilities and reciprocities, who never settles down but always travels, and it begins to take fresh outlines in a hard, un-touched-up light. Show this solitariness as at once instinctive and finicky, calculated and prudential, vain and protective, the aloofness of a rascal who in his felt superiority schemes against the world. Com-bine an almost racketeering toughness with a constant aesthetic aware-ness. Paint the picaro despising the majority, fearing that if "[I] spent myself in a loose sociability—I should literally do violence to some secret part of my nature," separating himself from the circus crowd and feeling that he belongs to the "profession" of "entertainer and illusionist." To picture loneliness without sloppy clichés, let the picaro study the circus "artists," have him ask, "Are they really human at all?", have him deny that they can love, lest the lions revolt and the acrobats "pitch headlong toward the ground into disgrace and death." Have the Marquis of Venosta tell the picaro: "You always hold something back. . . . You seem to me the type who is more loved than loving." Here are the outsider and his essential unresponsiveness, but also the devo-tion evoked by art and the artist.

Yet this solitary astonishingly seeks not pure contemplation but power, power in the very world withdrawn from. True to the picaro type, Felix is a lover and pursuer of things found only in the world—material things, physical comforts, society and high places; he even has a "natural instinct for good form." The solitary as man of the world—an inconsistency? Mann faces right into this, maneuvering his comic tale toward the inherent contradictoriness of all serious things. Felix says at one time that his basic "withdrawal from the world" can go "amiably hand in hand with an eager delight in the world"; at another time that "My basic attitude toward the world and society can only be called inconsistent." What we see in the dramatic action is the paradox that withdrawnness is often an attribute of the power-holder, that art must succeed in the world, that the artist is despite himself a strange mar-riage of bohemian and bourgeois.

How freshen up the fact that as technician the artist works through the concrete, that unlike the hermit he must cling to the immediately perceived and felt surfaces of life? Again make him a lover of the world, of all palpable and visible reality; make him an amorous observer and recorder of sensory surfaces, an embodiment of visual and olfactory and tactile passions. Let him stare into shop windows and lust after pastries and jewels, carpets and clothing; let him exclaim, ". . . the enticing, educational aspects of the world, . . . O scenes of the beautiful world!"

To fulfill himself as artist he must possess that world, take what he can as he can. But of course. How give life to a copy-book maxim for the aspiring writer? Let Felix be a thief—of bonbons, jewelry, money; even of the life and family history of another, at once ornamenting it and himself and so delighting an audience. The "ruthlessness" of the artist as artist appears with equal originality when Felix sharply rebuffs "honest Stanko" by refusing to join in a projected robbery, since he "was not born to be anybody's accomplice." Mann refines upon the artist's acquisition of materials in the two "robberies" from Diane Philibert: in the first, with a minimum of active effort, Felix takes what chance has offered; in the second, he takes what she offers herself; in each case what he gets is used shrewdly, not thrown away prodigally. When Diane insists that he "steal" from her for her own singular pleasure, in effect she is the individual begging the artist, "Use me."

In a well-known sense the artist must "love" all people, for hate leads only to polemics. So let the artist appear as the picaro Don Juan: let Felix love Genovefa the maid; Rosza the prostitute; Diane Philibert the bluestocking writer; both Senhora Kuckuck and her daughter Zouzou—old and young, arrogant aristocrat and "prickly" Puritan. Then a double reverse: let each bed-affair be a growth, a learning, even a symbolic statement. Let the prostitute be praised for giving her lover "refinement . . . *through* love." Let Diane, in that wonderful erotic scene in the hotel, embody at once the ambivalence of parental and sexual relations, a Jocasta candidly seeking youth (richer far than Cocteau's querulous neurotic), the "intellect [that] longs for the delights of the non-intellect," "spirit" yearning to glorify "beauty" and to be at one with the elemental, a highbrow humanity romantically possessing, in an "eternal instant," through the ageless art of which the ingenious youth is a symbol, the potency and completion not offered in everyday life. Let Zouzou, a remarkable character, be no less than a character, but attach to her the chill odor of literalist common sense, scientific reductionism and Puritan squeamishness: art must woo even this, striving to release its underlying, though incomplete, inclination to be at one with art. Thus Felix breaks inevitably into the home where "order, reason, and intelligent planning prevail"—breaks in, not to court but to seduce, for with none of them can he live after they have served him, and he them.

Felix does not merely use others; he gratifies them. From beginning to end he never loses the intent to give pleasure or the pleasure of giving it. Mann's view of art is Horatian, but here again he is entirely original. Don't show Felix as an insipid allegory of benevolent sweetness, but let him be seen blissfully inhaling applause for successful costumings, mimings, masquerades; report with satisfaction how much everyone likes him, even when he despises them; boast of the extraordinary pleasure he gives in sexual intercourse; have charm, not the Grandisonian kind, but the kind that charms men out of jobs and money, and women out of their clothes; please people not only by courtesy and attentiveness, but by funny stories, an "agreeable voice," a beautifying pronunciation of names, by flattery, and even pimping. But combine all this with indispensable self-restraint: like a Machiavellian prince, Felix must use all means that serve his end but cannot deviate into private self-indulgence. Excessive sexuality "impoverishes our capacity to charm, since only he who desires is amiable and not he who is satiated." But the art of pleasing is at once narcissistic and altruistic: ". . . I loved myself—in a way that is really socially useful, self-love turned outward as amiability." No sonorousness here of "self-respect" or "integrity." Yet what is dramatized is a stern, demanding, anti-romantic view of the artist, disavowing the crabbed hermit who writes or paints only to gratify himself, contemptuous of an unresponsive public.

Mann paints the artist as non-moral man; then he completes the story-teller's "double twist" by painting the morality of the non-moral man. If the artist always "shapes himself to please," nevertheless playing to the public on its own terms will not do; again Mann might have come from a reading of Horace to write that "a performance . . . had to be masterly if it was not to be ridiculous." Not only must art "work": it must have a kind of excellence which is found in what it communicates beyond itself; Felix has contempt for "every deception which fails to have a higher truth at its root and is simply a barefaced lie." In this we do not see him as either smirking or self-deceptive, any more than we do when he keeps emphasizing the necessity of "discipline." He has a sense of vocation, and he talks repeatedly of avoiding the cul-de-sac, the "shortcut to happiness." He rejects the love of wealthy Eleanor Twentyman and that of Lord Strathbogie, who by bribery would possess the artist personally, for he "rebelled against a form of reality that was simply handed to me and was in addition sloppy" in favor of a life "dependent . . . only on imagination." "The way" is virtually a basic metaphor with him, and his "reason" calls masquerading as Venosta a "bypath" and a "dangerous road." But he is won by the "charm of the adventure, an adventure that would call upon all my talents"—a response to a challenge that Mann as artist might have used of himself; besides, he feels a connection between this great disguise and his boyhood costumings and games of imagination, so that we are to see here not a detour but the main line of vocation.

But let us suppose that to serve his sense of excellence the artist must have something else besides Horatian learning and discipline and studiousness to please, that is, the *je ne sais quoi*, the mysterious spark, the non-rational gift of Ion—how give it a new, untrite phrasing? Let a worldly priest and a lustful woman independently praise Felix for an "agreeable quality of . . . voice," and an army doctor attribute to him "astounding hyperacuity of hearing." Let him assert that what he did, in acting an epileptic fit, "happened as though without my co-operation . . . to my own momentary amazement." Let him show "natural adroitness" in hotel work, know a waiter's skills "by instinct," make an impressive report on unseen architectural beauties, and show an "amazing and mysterious" gift for languages, chattering in virtually unknown tongues with an "almost ecstatic feeling of being possessed by a foreign spirit." Let him burst into a highly articulate rhapsody on love and "swear" that "it just came to me," that he was "inspired." Let him plunge recklessly into tennis, a new game to him, and through sheer daring and bravado balance his "hopeless errors" by "occasionally performing feats of pure genius"—the doctrine of "inspiration" in joking understatement.

Besides the fine comic representation of inherited ideas about art—the morality of vocation, the union of imagination and discipline, snatching a grace beyond the reach of art—there are exciting inquiries and speculations. More than once Mann grapples piquantly with the sensations of imaginative life. When the "starry-eyed" Kuckuck talks

of cosmic space and time, Felix has a "feeling of significance and vast-
ness"; Kuckuck's tale of origins produces a "feeling of expansion that
almost burst the limits of my nature." This strange excitement Felix
goes on to declare "identical with" what as a child he called "The
Great Joy," a "secret formula" of vague meaning but "soon endowed
with an intoxicating breadth of significance." He had first mentioned
an "incomparable expansion of my whole being" in describing the robbery of the candy store ("the carrying over of my dream treasure into
my waking life"), and this in turn he identified with a "nameless
sensation," "a yoking of emotions and fancies" which he called "The
Great Joy." Though this is in some way connected with sex also, he
insists that the sex act is only "the grosser part" of The Great Joy.
Mann suggests links among childhood imaginings, theft, sex, and new
knowledge. Whatever the center of the ultimately undefined association—mysterious transformation, initiation, creation—what is unmistakable is the groping for the symbolic continuity among diverse
experiences.

The finding of links, the quest of oneness, is an insistent theme,
announced plainly or given imaginative, even strange and puzzling,
forms. If art is "universal," the artist is a unifier; he has something in
common with all. Felix is to travel, it appears, to many countries; he
is a master of many tongues; but our attention is more caught by the
fact that, although his active maleness is not questioned, he has a
delicate attractiveness that puts him aesthetically between the two
sexes ("And I was," he says, an "extraordinary being in between"), so
that he excites homosexual impulses in the hotel owner and other men
and infatuates Lord Strathbogie—a bold symbolic way of attributing to
the great artist the human inclusiveness that lies behind the universality of his work. If Felix is equally attractive to all, he himself feels a
singular attraction, not to one person or even to a succession of persons,
but to pairs of persons, to what he regularly calls the "double image";
this appears first in a brother and sister whom he sees on the balcony
of a Frankfort hotel and who strangely excite his imagination; then in
the mother and daughter Kuckuck, who remind him of the Frankfort
pair, and near the end Felix tells us of a Lisbon toreador who was to
reappear later in his life "as part of a double image." It would be
unfair to the spirit of Mann to see in Felix's fascination with doubles,
given fantastic form in his simultaneous wooing of mother and daughter, anything less than a double meaning: say, the sexual overlapping

of apparently discrete experiences, as well as the artist's need to be at one with, to win, men and women, old and young; or possibly a reflection of the artist's own duality. But overlying all other meanings is the quest of oneness; in the kinship of different beings is a clue to unity. In Felix's mind the mother-daughter pair are imaginatively allied with the brother-sister pair, and he ultimately concludes that in the "double" of which he dreams there is "a significant whole blessedly embracing what is beguilingly human in both sexes." The "esemplastic" quality of Felix's imagination, striving to put two things into one, the "significant whole," or at least to discover unifying analogies, carries him even outside the "beguilingly human." In Kuckuck's lectures he is aware of the impulse to find unity in vast reaches of natural history; he hears that "men and animals are closely related," that man and nature are analogous, that in "playfully crossing the line from one domain into another" (organic and inorganic) nature "was trying to teach us that she was one," and that "All's well when Being and Well-Being are in some measure reconciled." When he praises love to Zouzou, Felix argues climactically that the kiss is "the pledge of that marvelous release from separateness" and that love always tries to "raise it [closeness] to the actual oneness of two lives, ..." The story moves toward more paradoxical intimations of unity when the aristocratic Senhora Kuckuck, who a little later will accept Felix as lover, undergoes a mounting passional excitement as the bull is fought and killed at the *corrida*. Felix glances "from her surging breast to the living statue of man and animal" and concludes: ". . . more and more the stern and elemental passion of this woman seemed to me one with the game of blood below." In the "game of blood" life, death, and art have a strange nexus; and in the same game, what is more, the professor traces links between Christian beliefs and practices and those of a rival blood-worship cult in which the god lived both in the bull who was sacrificed and in the man who killed him—a teaching that joined believers "in life and in death; and its mystery consisted in the quality and identity of slayer and slain, axe and victim, arrow and target."

What *Felix Krull* dramatizes is the working of a Joycean artist, if not finally putting all things into one, at least pursuing with fascination all the subterranean connections that reduce the multiplicity of the phenomenal world. The artist as artist does many things, but universality is his need, and unity his obsession. Such is the oneness ironically concealed behind the narrative disunity of the picaresque, the acquisitive and amatory episodes of the mobile rogue; these are the wonderfully original design for that part of the old *ars poetica* traditionally assigned to the *poeta*.

VII

The story was to end conventionally: the picaresque hero exposed and jailed. A romantic might argue that this would be society's inevitable rejection of the artist, a positivist that society eventually got its feet on the ground and rejected illusion; but both of these would be foreign to Mann, above all to the Mann of this book. It is safer to guess, I think, that imprisonment would have been a symbol of some failure of Felix's own—perhaps too great a fondness for "high life" in the "man of the world," a decline from that use and mastery of the world which are legitimately his into an unpermissible worldliness, such as tasteless pandering, being corrupted by material things, choosing local glory instead of moving on alone—or perhaps a nobler failure, an attempting of that ordinary humanity, of those personal devotions, which at the circus Felix theorized might mean the destruction of the artist. Or there is another possibility, and a more tempting one, that even within the confines of rogue comedy Mann might have explored another kind of flaw, such as vainglory and pride: for Mann did see Krull as a counterpart of Faustus, and one can imagine this audacious experimenter attempting a comic and yet not unheroic version of another artist who undertook too much. At one time Felix believed he "had improved upon nature, realized a dream," and with "strange and dreamlike satisfaction" he rested from his "creative task."

Here we have to look at the raison d'etre of the confidence man, who is distinguished among outlaws in that he requires the consent of his victims. Though we must not discount entirely the profit motive in the victims, it would account only in small part for confidence men, since there are better—i.e., safer or more intoxicating, as the individual's nerves require—ways of seeking gain. What we must postulate, I am convinced, is a basic need to confide, to show faith, to yield belief: in a word, a debased religious feeling (one would expect confidence men to flourish in skeptical ages.) Here is a distant secular echo of *credo quia impossible*, or, as a practicing Christian put it to an outsider hesitantly sticking a toe into Jordan, "I believe because I want to." We must also theorize that, whatever the eventual disillusionment and outraged outcries, the relation with the confidence man (the ritualistic exchanging of wallets, which is just what Venosta and Felix literally do) exists because the actions that constitute it are in some way satisfying or fulfilling in themselves. Now traditionally the writer of picaresque puts us on the side of the "con man" or "false god"; and this enjoyment of power becomes aesthetically possible because, as we have seen, the victims are not shown. But a greater writer of picaresque, who understood all the implications of "confidence," would surely mediate between the man of wits and those who believed in him, between the man of wits who not only took but in some way gave, and the faithful who not only were taken in but in some way fulfilled. Now is not this precisely what Mann does in *Felix Krull?* We see Felix energetically striving for, and eliciting, confidence; but whatever his ends, we also see his believing followers in some way rewarded or satisfied, finding, whatever the discrepancy between appearance and reality in Felix, a physical or psychic fulfillment—all the people for whom he works, Diane Philibert the novelist, the Marquis of Venosta, Luxembourg ambassador and Portuguese king, lecturing professor, and, on the evidence of an unfinished story, presumably his wife and daughter whom Felix strives to seduce. We see less victims than seekers and finders, tricked, yes, but served.

Now if the picaro is also thought of as artist, this theory of the confidence man is plainly relevant. Like the confidence man in real life and the picaro in fiction, the artist must win assent or confidence; the former must find the will to believe, the latter a comparable state of mind—namely, the willing suspension of disbelief. How boldly Mann puts it as he has Felix describe an audience's response to a skillful actor: "What unanimity in agreeing to let oneself be deceived! Here quite clearly there is in operation a general human need, implanted by God himself in human nature, . . ." Picaro and artist serve this need analogously, and for the "deceived" there is clear profit. When the actor left the stage, Felix reports, "shoulders slumped, and virtue seemed to go out of the audience." "Confidence man" and "audience" supply a need for each other: what happens between them is, in Mann's words, "a mutual fulfillment." What is here put theoretically is expressed dramatically in all the episodes of Felix's life.

In the foreground, we see an analogy between picaro-victim and artist-audience; and in the background, if my analysis is sound, a third relationship analogical to these two—that of deity and mankind. Does Mann, in all his kindly-ironic speculations on the need for belief and the fulfillment of believers, bring these ultimate terms into play? I believe that in part he does. When, in a childhood feat of imitative artistry, Felix delights his audience, he is called "an angel child and an amazing little devil." The casual terms of praise suggest the "inspiration" in which Felix always believes, and on another occasion this is emphatically construed as non-celestial; as an artist in epilepsy Felix suggests that he must have been under "a satanic influence and impulse"—a theory to which he devotes a half-page discussion that is a joke and yet not a joke. The intimation of the more-than-human comes in most strongly in the account of Andromache, the circus artist. Was she "really human," he asks several times. He "worshipped" her, the crowd "worshipped her"; their "lust for her was transformed into awe"; she was a "solemn angel," the vision of whom was "painful and uplifting at once." Though man was closer to the animals, she "was a chaste body, untainted by humanity, and stood much closer to the angels." This thoughtful contemplation of the circus divinities, with whom Felix identifies himself, seems entirely earnest, uncolored by the deadpan ambiguities so characteristic of the book. The tongue-in-cheek treatment of the more-than-human appears with greatest verve when Diane Philibert pours forth raptures as Felix undresses and joins her in bed: ". . . catch sight of the god . . . *prêt pour la chapelle* . . . your divine limbs . . . The holy breast . . . you angel of love . . . you young devil." Her "intellect longs for . . . the divinely stupid, it kneels before it, it prays to it, . . ." For her, "the divine, the masterpiece of creation" is Hermes, *"le dieu voleur,"* and thus she confers upon Felix a new identity that he never quite forgets. To him, Kuckuck praises Hermes as "an elegant deity" whose brain-cell fabric "must have assumed especially artful forms."

Thus in a jest, and on one occasion less gamesomely, Mann gently pushes the picaro-artist a little way toward the analogous divinity-figure. And there, perhaps, he would have dropped it. But a tempting possibility comes to mind: suppose the rogue attempted the ultimate deception, the confidence man got too much confidence, the artist set out to provide fulfillments beyond the reach of art? Suppose the master-builder aspired to too great heights in his "creative task," or the herald of the gods mistook himself for Apollo or Zeus? This might have been the climax of "picaresque tragedy"; it would have been entirely consistent with the complex terms of the story as far as Mann has taken it; as a "kindly-destructive" reflection on the religion of art, it would have been of a piece with the philosophical jesting of the work; and the jail where we know Felix was to land would have been the right purgatory for a hero whom, despite some divinity in the dimensions, the author was determined to hold in a fresh picaresque perspective.

"Only the episodic," Mann has Kuckuck say to Felix, "only what possessed a beginning and end, was interesting and worthy of sympathy because transitoriness had given it a soul." Mann has taken a standard episodic form, one very likely to be tedious, and discovered in it a soul: not an allegory, but, beyond its outer liveliness, an inner continuity and vivacity that encourage speculation about its generic form and about the artfulness of its fabric.

THE NOVEL

Despite its predecessors in medieval and Elizabethan romance, epic, and other forms of narrative fiction, the English novel became a mature and distinguishable form only in the eighteenth century, concurrently with what Ian Watt describes as the rise of a particular brand of individualism. The intricate social contacts of a Moll Flanders and Tom Jones or the birth of a Tristram Shandy, which would have received satiric treatment in Sidney, then become suitable subjects for serious fiction, however ironic their author's attitudes toward them are. Watt finds one of the first themes of the novel to be book-keeping, or social gains and losses, and corresponding shifts in manners, style of communication, and politics. In his reading of Defoe's *Robinson Crusoe*, the new money plot makes use of the old travel and adventure story, domesticating its romance elements so that the hero's travels gain him not a place in a knightly caste but "fortune": "profit is Crusoe's only vocation, and the whole world is his territory."

However, since the novel charts internal as well as social life and its bargaining processes, economic problems are never entirely separable from psychology, and the two together are much more complex than either separately. The novel is ideally suited to register their *impact* on each other and it does so almost from the beginning. In the eighteenth century novels, characters usually gain as much as they lose from their social negotiations, and their inner states are therefore not an issue (though morality may well be). After Romanticism has re-evaluated the subjective world and found society generally constrictive and often contaminating, it is natural for the novel to shift its ground. In G. Armour Craig's view of several nineteenth-century novels, the social matrix of the hero's life *compromises* his private vision. Though the same can sometimes be said of other heroes from Don Quixote to Herzog, the novels that Craig discusses place an exceptionally high premium on individual integrity and find its relations to the exterior world problematic.

Michel Brutor's account of the novel's evolution likewise concerns the dynamics of the individual and the group, but Butor interweaves with this basic notion several generic distinctions, primarily between feudal epic (whose hero stands for and organizes the values of his society), the picaresque novel, and other novels whose heroes belong to a concealed hierarchy. As opposed to the visible social order of feudal narrative, which can be represented in pageantry and heroic paradigms, the inner and partly concealed society of the novel must be explored and unfolded. The rise of an individual is keyed to the discovery of a social architecture whose implicit laws form some of the connective links of the novel's structure. Since any social architecture contains its own special values—its terms of praise and dispraise, its emotions and innuendoes which outsiders do not fully understand, and its coupling (or syntax) of events—Butor's concept of the novel implies stylistic as well as generic distinctions. The styles of a given novel may range from the special idiom of the rogue to the solidified vocabulary of the established hero. At other times a withdrawn and isolated hero may fail to communicate despite a common language, and the novel then becomes a disjunctive form probing the remoteness of each member of the society.

Traditionally, the novel reflects the natural as well as the social and psychological worlds, and the hero's alienation from nature is potentially another source of disjunction. Non-human objects and settings may participate directly in the action or comment on it indirectly, as in Thomas Hardy nature both symbolizes human feeling and is a thing-in-itself, indecipherable and indifferent to the hero's life. On the grounds that objects are merely isolated surfaces, Alain Robbe-Grillet argues against such symbolic functions of nature and its close involvement in humanistic concerns: objects in fiction should mask no metaphoric connection among themselves and evidence no sympathy or antipathy for characters as they do in old myths. Since tightly constructed works can tolerate only a minimum of unrelatedness, this position means that they can be given only a minimum of attention beyond a demonstration of their irrelevance. In generic terms, what Robbe-Grillet calls for essentially is a distinct division between *romance* and the novel.

Leslie Fiedler reminds us that the novel has another concern besides its natural, social, and psychological subjects, namely its audience. Without an audience of a certain kind it cannot survive, and the present decline of the reading public argues a rather quick end of "that fat, solid commodity invented by the bourgeoisie for ends of commerce and culture climbing." Recurrent predictions of its demise such as this testify to the novel's exceptionally close ties to its environment and to its relatively short history, which has not given it an opportunity to function in a variety of conditions. However, that history is by no means simple, nor does it point to a particular time schedule of changes. Seen as one phase of an evolving set of narrative modes (that probably began when the first caveman, showing off for the first audience, adorned his account of recent hunting exploits with hints of divine favor or persecution), the novel will perhaps appear ready not so much for burial as for transmigration. It may move further and further away from the old myths as Robbe-Grillet desires, or it may pass through further experiments such as the past two decades have produced in abundance. Only one thing is relatively certain: as older forms of narrative were vital to its birth and development, the novel in turn will be relevant to what follows and no less implicated in its social surroundings.

IAN WATT

Robinson Crusoe, Individualism and the Novel

The novel's serious concern with the daily lives of ordinary people
seems to depend upon two important general conditions: the society
must value every individual highly enough to consider him the proper
subject of its serious literature; and there must be enough variety of
belief and action among ordinary people for a detailed account of them
to be of interest to other ordinary people, the readers of novels. It is
probable that neither of these conditions for the existence of the novel
obtained very widely until fairly recently, because they both depend on
the rise of a society characterised by that vast complex of interdepend-
ent factors denoted by the term "individualism."

Even the word is recent, dating only from the middle of the nineteenth century. In all ages, no doubt, and in all societies, some people
have been "individualists" in the sense that they were egocentric,
unique or conspicuously independent of current opinions and habits;
but the concept of individualism involves much more than this. It
posits a whole society mainly governed by the idea of every individual's intrinsic independence both from other individuals and from that
multifarious allegiance to past modes of thought and action denoted by
the word "tradition"—a force that is always social, not individual. The
existence of such a society, in turn, obviously depends on a special type
of economic and political organisation and on an appropriate ideology;
more specifically, on an economic and political organisation which
allows its members a very wide range of choices in their actions, and
on an ideology primarily based, not on the tradition of the past, but
on the autonomy of the individual, irrespective of his particular social
status or personal capacity. It is generally agreed that modern society
is uniquely individualist in these respects, and that of the many his-

From *The Rise of the Novel,* 1957. Reprinted by permission of the University of California Press.

130

torical causes for its emergence two are of supreme importance—the rise of modern industrial capitalism and the spread of Protestantism, especially in its Calvinist or Puritan forms.

I

Capitalism brought a great increase of economic specialisation; and this, combined with a less rigid and homogeneous social structure, and a less absolutist and more democratic political system, enormously increased the individual's freedom of choice. For those fully exposed to the new economic order, the effective entity on which social arrangements were now based was no longer the family, nor the church, nor the guild, nor the township, nor any other collective unit, but the individual: he alone was primarily responsible for determining his own economic, social, political and religious roles.

It is very difficult to say when this change of orientation began to affect society as a whole—probably not until the nineteenth century. But the movement certainly began much earlier. In the sixteenth century the Reformation and the rise of national states decisively challenged the substantial social homogeneity of mediaeval Christendom, and, in the famous words of Maitland, "for the first time, the Absolute State faced the Absolute Individual." Outside the political and religious sphere, however, change was slow, and it is likely that it was not until the further development of industrial capitalism, especially in England and in the Low Countries, that a mainly individualist social and economic structure came into being and started to affect a considerable part, although by no means a majority, of the total population.

It is, at least, generally agreed that the foundations of the new order were laid in the period immediately following the Glorious Revolution of 1689. The commercial and industrial classes, who were the prime agents in bringing about the individualist social order, had achieved greater political and economic power; and this power was already being reflected in the domain of literature. The middle classes of the towns, we have seen, were becoming much more important in the reading public; and at the same time literature began to view trade, commerce and industry with favour. This was a rather new development. Earlier writers, Spenser, Shakespeare, Donne, Ben Jonson and Dryden, for example, had tended to support the traditional economic and social order and had attacked many of the symptoms of emergent individualism. By the beginning of the eighteenth century, however,

Addison, Steele and Defoe were somewhat ostentatiously setting the seal of literary approval on the heroes of economic individualism.

The new orientation was equally evident in the philosophical domain. The great English empiricists of the seventeenth century were as vigorously individualist in their political and ethical thought as in their epistemology. Bacon hoped to make a really new start in social theory by applying his inductive method to an accumulation of factual data about a great number of particular individuals; [1] Hobbes, also feeling that he was dealing with a subject that had not been properly approached before, based his political and ethical theory on the fundamentally egocentric psychological constitution of the individual; [2] while in his *Two Treatises of Government* (1690) Locke constructed the class system of political thought based on the indefeasibility of individual rights, as against the more traditional ones of Church, Family or King. That these thinkers should have been the political and psychological vanguard of nascent individualism, as well as the pioneers of its theory of knowledge, suggests how closely linked their reorientations were both in themselves and in relation to the innovations of the novel. For, just as there is a basic congruity between the non-realist nature of the literary forms of the Greeks, their intensely social, or civic, moral outlook, and their philosophical preference for the universal, so the modern novel is closely allied on the one hand to the realist epistemology of the modern period, and on the other to the individualism of its social structure. In the literary, the philosophical and the social spheres alike the classical focus on the ideal, the universal and the corporate has shifted completely, and the modern field of vision is mainly occupied by the discrete particular, the directly apprehended sensum, and the autonomous individual.

Defoe, whose philosophical outlook has much in common with that of the English empiricists of the seventeenth century, expressed the diverse elements of individualism more completely than any previous writer, and his work offers a unique demonstration of the connection between individualism in its many forms and the rise of the novel. This connection is shown particularly clearly and comprehensively in his first novel, *Robinson Crusoe*.

II

Robinson Crusoe has been very appropriately used by many economic theorists as their illustration of *homo economicus*. Just as "the body politic" was the symbol of the communal way of thought typical of previous societies, so "economic man" symbolised the new outlook of individualism in its economic aspect. Adam Smith has been charged with the invention; actually, the concept is much older, but it is natural that it should have come to the fore as an abstraction expressing the individualism of the economic system as a whole only when the individualism of that system itself had reached an advanced stage of development.

That Robinson Crusoe, like Defoe's other main characters, Moll Flanders, Roxana, Colonel Jacque and Captain Singleton, is an embodiment of economic individualism hardly needs demonstration. All Defoe's heroes pursue money, which he characteristically called "the general denominating article in the world"; [3] and they pursue it very methodically according to the profit and loss book-keeping which Max Weber considered to be the distinctive technical feature of modern capitalism.[4] Defoe's heroes, we observe, have no need to learn this technique; whatever the circumstances of their birth and education, they have it in their blood, and keep us more fully informed of their present stocks of money and commodities than any other characters in fiction. Crusoe's book-keeping conscience, indeed, has established an effective priority over his other thoughts and emotions; when his Lisbon steward offers him 160 moidores to alleviate his momentary difficulties on return, Crusoe relates: "I could hardly refrain from tears while he spoke; in short, I took 100 of the moidores, and called for a pen and ink to give him a receipt for them." [5]

Book-keeping is but one aspect of a central theme in the modern social order. Our civilisation as a whole is based on individual contractual relationships, as opposed to the unwritten, traditional and collective relationships of previous societies; and the idea of contract played an important part in the theoretical development of political individualism. It had featured prominently in the fight against the Stuarts, and it was enshrined in Locke's political system. Locke, indeed, thought that contractual relationships were binding even in the state of nature; [6] Crusoe, we notice, acts like a good Lockean—when others arrive on the island he forces them to accept his dominion with written contracts acknowledging his absolute power (even though we have previously been told that he has run out of ink).[7]

But the primacy of the economic motive, and an innate reverence for book-keeping and the law of contract are by no means the only matters in which Robinson Crusoe is a symbol of the processes associated with the rise of economic individualism. The hypostasis of the economic motive logically entails a devaluation of other modes of thought, feeling and action: the various forms of traditional group relationship, the family, the guild, the village, the sense of nationality—all are weakened, and so, too, are the competing claims of non-economic individual achievement and enjoyment, ranging from spiritual salvation to the pleasures of recreation.[8]

This inclusive reordering of the components of human society tends to occur wherever industrial capitalism becomes the dominant force in the economic structure,[9] and it naturally became evident particularly early in England. By the middle of the eighteenth century, indeed, it had already become something of a commonplace. Goldsmith, for instance, thus described the concomitants of England's vaunted freedom in *The Traveller* (1764):

> That independence Britons prize too high,
> Keeps man from man, and breaks the social tie;
> The self-dependent lordlings stand alone,
> All claims that bind and sweeten life unknown;
> Here by the bonds of nature feebly held,
> Minds combat minds, repelling and repell'd . . .
>   Nor this the worst. As nature's ties decay,
> As duty, love, and honour fail to sway,
> Fictitious bonds, the bonds of wealth and law,
> Still gather strength, and force unwilling awe.[10]

Unlike Goldsmith, Defoe was not a professed enemy of the new order—quite the reverse; nevertheless there is much in *Robinson Crusoe* that bears out Goldsmith's picture, as can be seen in Defoe's treatment of such group relationships as the family or the nation.

For the most part, Defoe's heroes either have no family, like Moll Flanders, Colonel Jacque and Captain Singleton, or leave it at an early age never to return, like Roxana and Robinson Crusoe. Not too much importance can be attached to this fact, since adventure stories demand the absence of conventional social ties. Still, in *Robinson Crusoe* at least, the hero has a home and family, and leaves them for the classic reason of *homo economicus*—that it is necessary to better his economic condition. "Something fatal in that propension of nature" calls him to the sea and adventure, and against "settling to business" in the station to which he is born—"the upper station of low life"; and this despite the panegyric which his father makes of that condition. Later he sees this lack of "confined desires," this dissatisfaction with "the state wherein God and Nature has placed" him, as his "original sin." [11] At the time, however, the argument between his parents and himself is a debate, not about filial duty or religion, but about whether going or staying is likely to be the most advantageous course materially: both sides accept the economic argument as primary. And, of course,, Crusoe actually gains by his "original sin," and becomes richer than his father was.

Crusoe's "original sin" is really the dynamic tendency of capitalism itself, whose aim is never merely to maintain the *status quo*, but to transform it incessantly. Leaving home, improving on the lot one was born to, is a vital feature of the individualist pattern of life. It may be regarded as the economic and social embodiment of the "uneasiness" which Locke had made the centre of his system of motivation,[12] an uneasiness whose existence was, in the very opposite outlook of Pascal, the index of the enduring misery of mortal man. "All the unhappiness of men arises from one single fact, that they cannot stay quietly in their own room" Pascal had written.[13] Defoe's hero is far from agreeing. Even when he is old, Crusoe tells us how: ". . . nothing else offering, and finding that really stirring about and trading, the profit being so great, and, as I may say, certain, had more pleasure in it, and more satisfaction to the mind, than sitting still, which, to me especially, was the unhappiest part of life." [14] So, in the *Farther Adventures*, Crusoe sets out on yet another lucrative Odyssey.

The fundamental tendency of economic individualism, then, prevents Crusoe from paying much heed to the ties of family, whether as a son or a husband. This is in direct contradiction to the great stress which Defoe lays on the social and religious importance of the family in his didactic works such as the *Family Instructor;* but his novels reflect not theory but practice, and they accord these ties a very minor, and on the whole obstructive, role.

Rational scrutiny of one's own economic interest may lead one to be as little bound by national as by family ties. Defoe certainly valued individuals and countries alike primarily on their economic merits. Thus one of his most patriotic utterances takes the characteristic form of claiming that his compatriots have a greater productive output per hour than the workmen of any other country.[15] Crusoe, we notice, whom Walter de la Mare has justly called Defoe's Elective Affinity,[16] shows xenophobia mainly where the economic virtues are absent. When they are present—as in the Spanish Governor, a French papist priest, a faithful Portuguese factor—his praise is unstinted. On the other hand, he condemns many Englishmen, such as his English settlers on the island, for their lack of industry. Crusoe, one feels, is not bound to his country by sentimental ties, any more than to his family; he is satisfied by people, whatever their nationality, who are good to do business with; and he feels, like Moll Flanders, that "with money in the pocket one is at home anywhere." [17]

What might at first appear to place *Robinson Crusoe* in the somewhat special category of "Travel and Adventure" does not, then, altogether do so. The plot's reliance on travel does tend to allot *Robinson Crusoe* a somewhat peripheral position in the novel's line of development, since it removes the hero from his usual setting in a stable and cohesive pattern of social relations. But Crusoe is not a mere footloose adventurer, and his travels, like his freedom from social ties, are merely somewhat extreme cases of tendencies that are normal in modern society as a whole, since, by making the pursuit of gain a primary motive, economic individualism has much increased the mobility of the individual. More specifically, Robinson Crusoe's career is based, as modern scholarship has shown, [18] on some of the innumerable volumes which recounted the exploits of those voyagers who had done so much in the sixteenth century to assist the development of capitalism by providing the gold, slaves and tropical products on which trade expansion depended; and who had continued the process in the seventeenth century by developing the colonies and world markets on which the future progress of capitalism depended.

Defoe's plot, then, expresses some of the most important tendencies of the life of his time, and it is this which sets his hero apart from most of the travellers in literature. Robinson Crusoe is not, like Autolycus, a commercial traveller rooted in an extended but still familiar locality; nor is he, like Ulysses, an unwilling voyager trying to get back to his family and his native land: profit is Crusoe's only vocation, and the whole world is his territory.

The primacy of individual economic advantage has tended to diminish the importance of personal as well as group relationships, and especially of those based on sex; for sex, as Weber pointed out, [19] being one of the strongest non-rational factors in human life, is one of the strongest potential menaces to the individual's rational pursuit of economic ends, and it has therefore, as we shall see, been placed under particularly strong controls in the ideology of industrial capitalism.

Romantic love has certainly had no greater antagonist among the novelists than Defoe. Even sexual satisfaction—where he speaks of it—tends to be minimised; he protested in *The Review*, for example, that "the Trifle called Pleasure in it" was "not worth the Repentance."[20] As to marriage, his attitude is complicated by the fact that economic and moral virtue in the male is no guarantee of a profitable matrimonial investment: on his colony "as it often happens in the world (what the wise ends of God's Providence are in such a disposition of things I cannot say), the two honest fellows had the two worst wives, and the three reprobates, that were scarce worth hanging . . . had three clever, diligent, careful and ingenious wives."[21] His puzzled parenthesis bears eloquent testimony to the seriousness with which he views this flaw in the rationality of Providence.

It is not surprising, therefore, that love plays little part in Crusoe's own life, and that even the temptations of sex are excluded from the scene of his greatest triumphs, the island. When Crusoe does notice the lack of "society" there, he prays for the solace of company, but we observe that what he desires is a male slave.[22] Then, with Friday, he enjoys an idyll without benefit of woman—a revolutionary departure from the traditional expectations aroused by desert islands from the *Odyssey* to the *New Yorker*.

When eventually Crusoe returns to civilisation, sex is still strictly subordinated to business. Only when his financial position has been fully secured by a further voyage does he marry; and all he tells us of this supreme human adventure is that it was "not either to my disadvantage or dissatisfaction." This, the birth of three children, and his wife's death, however, comprise only the early part of a sentence, which ends with plans for a further voyage.[23]

Women have only one important role to play, and that is economic. When Crusoe's colonists draw lots for five women, we are gleefully informed that:

> He that drew to choose first . . . took her that was reckoned the homeliest and eldest of the five, which made mirth enough among the rest . . . but the fellow considered better than any of them, that it was application and business that they were to expect assistance in as much as anything else; and she proved the best wife of all the parcel.[24]

"The best wife of all the parcel." The language of commerce here reminds us that Dickens once decided on the basis of Defoe's treatment of women that he must have been "a precious dry and disagreeable article himself." [25]

The same devaluation of non-economic factors can be seen in Crusoe's other personal relationships. He treats them all in terms of their commodity value. The clearest case is that of Xury, the Moorish boy who helped him to escape from slavery and on another occasion offered to prove his devotion by sacrificing his own life. Crusoe very properly resolves "to love him ever after" and promises "to make him a great man." But when chance leads them to the Portuguese Captain, who offers Crusoe sixty pieces of eight—twice Judas's figure—he cannot resist the bargain, and sells Xury into slavery. He has momentary scruples, it is true, but they are cheaply satisfied by securing a promise from the new owner to "set him free in ten years if he turn Christian." Remorse later supervenes, but only when the tasks of his island life make manpower more valuable to him than money. [26]

Crusoe's relations with Man Friday are similarly egocentric. He does not ask him his name, but gives him one. Even in language—the medium whereby human beings may achieve something more than animal relationships with each other, as Crusoe himself wrote in his *Serious Reflections* [27]—Crusoe is a strict utilitarian. "I likewise taught him to say Yes and No," [28] he tells us; but Friday still speaks pidgin English at the end of their long association, as Defoe's contemporary critic Charles Gildon pointed out. [29]

Yet Crusoe regards the relationship as ideal. He is "as perfectly and completely happy if any such thing as complete happiness can be found in a sublunary state." [30] A functional silence, broken only by an occasional "No, Friday," or an abject "Yes, Master," is the golden music of Crusoe's *île joyeuse*. It seems that man's social nature, his need for friendship and understanding, is wholly satisfied by the righteous bestowal or grateful receipt, of benevolent but not undemanding patronage. It is true that later, as with Xury, Crusoe promises himself "to do something considerable" for his servant, "if he outlive me." Fortunately, no such sacrifice is called for, as Friday dies at sea, to be rewarded only by a brief word of obituary compassion. [31]

Emotional ties, then, and personal relationships generally, play a very minor part in *Robinson Crusoe*, except when they are focussed on economic matters. For instance, after Crusoe has left, it is only when his faithful old agent in Lisbon reveals that he is now a very rich man that we get any emotional climax: "I turned pale and grew sick; and had not the old man run and fetched me a cordial, I believe the sudden surprise of joy had overset nature, and I had died upon the spot." [32] Only money—fortune in its modern sense—is a proper cause of deep feeling; and friendship is accorded only to those who can safely be entrusted with Crusoe's economic interests.

Sitting still, we saw, was "the unhappiest part of life" to Robinson Crusoe; leisure pursuits are almost as bad. In this he resembles his author, who seems to have made as few concessions to such distractions as anyone. The fewness of Defoe's literary friendships has been commented on, and he is perhaps a unique example of a great writer who was very little interested in literature, and says nothing of interest about it as literature. [33]

In his blindness to aesthetic experience Crusoe is Defoe's peer. We can say of him as Marx said of his archetypal capitalist: "enjoyment is subordinated to capital, and the individual who enjoys to the individual who capitalises." [34] Some of the French versions of *Robinson Crusoe* make him address hymns of praise to nature, beginning "Oh Nature!" [35] Defoe did not. The natural scene on the island appeals not for adoration, but for exploitation; wherever Crusoe looks his acres cry out so loud for improvement that he has no leisure to observe that they also compose a landscape.

Of course, in a wintry way, Crusoe has his pleasures. If he does not, like Selkirk, [36] dance with his goats, he at least plays with them, and with his parrot and his cats; but his deepest satisfactions come from surveying his stock of goods: "I had everything so ready at my hand," he says, "that it was a great pleasure to me to see all my goods in such order, and especially to find my stock of all necessaries so great." [37]

If Robinson Crusoe's character depends very largely on the psychological and social orientations of economic individualism, the appeal of his adventures to the reader seems mainly to derive from the effects of another important concomitant of modern capitalism, economic specialisation.

The division of labour has done much to make the novel possible: partly because the more specialised the social and economic structure, the greater the number of significant differences of character, attitude and experience in contemporary life which the novelist can portray, and which are of interest to his readers; partly because, by increasing the amount of leisure, economic specialisation provides the kind of mass audience with which the novel is associated; and partly because this specialisation creates particular needs in that audience which the novel satisfies. Such, at least, was the general view of T. H. Green: "In the progressive division of labour, while we become more useful as citizens, we seem to lose our completeness as men . . . the perfect organisation of modern society removes the excitement of adventure and the occasion for independent effort. There is less of human interest to touch us within our calling. . . ." "The alleviation" of this situation, Green concluded, "is to be found in the newspaper and the novel." [38]

It is very likely that the lack of variety and stimulation in the daily task as a result of economic specialisation is largely responsible for the unique dependence of the individual in our culture upon the substitute experiences provided by the printing press, particularly in the forms of journalism and the novel. *Robinson Crusoe*, however, is a much more direct illustration of Green's thesis, since much of its appeal obviously depends on the quality of the "occasions for independent effort" in the economic realm which it offers Defoe's hero, efforts which the reader can share vicariously. The appeal of these efforts is surely a measure of the depth of the deprivations involved by economic specialisation, deprivations whose far-reaching nature is suggested by the way our civilisation has reintroduced some of the basic economic processes as therapeutic recreations: in gardening, home-weaving, pottery, camping, woodwork and keeping pets, we can all participate in the character-forming satisfactions which circumstances force on Defoe's hero; and like him, demonstrate what we would not otherwise know, that "by making the most rational judgment of things, every man may be in time master of every mechanic art." [39]

Defoe was certainly aware of how the increasing economic specialisation which was a feature of the life of his time had made most of the "mechanic arts" alien to the experience of his readers. When Crusoe makes bread, for instance, he reflects that " 'Tis a little wonderful and what I believe few people have thought much upon, viz., the strange multitude of little things necessary in the providing, procuring, curing, dressing, making and finishing this one article of bread." [40] Defoe's description goes on for seven pages, pages that would have been of little interest to people in mediaeval or Tudor society, who saw this and other basic economic processes going on daily in their own households. But by the early eighteenth century, as Kalm reported, most women did not "bake, because there is a baker in every parish or village," [41] and Defoe could therefore expect his readers to be interested in the very detailed descriptions of the economic life which comprise such an important and memorable part of his narrative.

Robinson Crusoe, of course, does not deal with the actual economic life of Defoe's own time and place. It would be somewhat contrary to the facts of economic life under the division of labour to show the average individual's manual labour as interesting or inspiring; to take Adam Smith's famous example of the division of labour in *The Wealth of Nations,*[42] the man who performs one of the many separate operations in the manufacture of a pin is unlikely to find his task as absorbing and interesting as Crusoe does. So Defoe sets back the economic clock, and takes his hero to a primitive environment, where labour can be presented as varied and inspiring, and where it has the further significant difference from the pin-maker's at home that there is an absolute equivalence between individual effort and individual reward. This was the final change from contemporary economic conditions which was necessary to enable Defoe to give narrative expression to the ideological counterpart of the Division of Labour, the Dignity of Labour.

The creed of the dignity of labour is not wholly modern: in classical times the Cynics and Stoics had opposed the denigration of manual labour which is a necessary part of slave-owning society's scale of values; and later, Christianity, originally associated mainly with slaves and the poor, had done much to remove the odium on manual labour. The idea, however, was only fully developed in the modern period, presumably because its compensatory affirmation became the more necessary as the development of economic specialisation made manual labour more stultifying; and the creed itself is closely associated with the advent of Protestantism. Calvinism in particular tended to make its adherents forget the idea that labour was God's punishment for Adam's disobedience, by emphasising the very different idea that untiring stewardship of the material gifts of God was a paramount religious and ethical obligation.[43]

The quality of Crusoe's stewardship cannot be doubted; he allows himself little time for rest, and even the advent of new manpower— Friday's—is a signal, not for relaxation, but for expanded production. Defoe clearly belongs to the tradition of Ascetic Protestantism. He had written much that sounds like the formulations of Weber, Troeltsch and Tawney; in Dickory Cronke's aphorism, for example: "When you find yourself sleepy in a morning, rouse yourself, and consider that you are born to business, and that in doing good in your generation, you answer your character and act like a man." [44] He had even—with a certain sophistic obtuseness—propounded the view that the pursuit of economic utility was quite literally an imitation of Christ: "Usefulness being the great pleasure, and justly deem'd by all good men the truest and noblest end of life, in which men come nearest to the character of our B. Saviour, who went about doing good." [45]

Defoe's attitude here exhibits a confusion of religious and material values to which the Puritan gospel of the dignity of labour was peculiarly liable: once the highest spiritual values had been attached to the performance of the daily task, the next step was for the autonomous individual to regard his achievements as a quasi-divine mastering of the environment. It is likely that this secularisation of the Calvinist conception of stewardship was of considerable importance for the rise of the novel. *Robinson Crusoe* is certainly the first novel in the sense that it is the first fictional narrative in which an ordinary person's daily activities are the centre of continuous literary attention. These activities, it is true, are not seen in a wholly secular light; but later novelists could continue Defoe's serious concern with man's worldly doings without placing them in a religious framework. It is therefore likely that the Puritan conception of the dignity of labour helped to bring into being the novel's general premise that the individual's daily life is of sufficient importance and interest to be the proper subject of literature.

III

Economic individualism explains much of Crusoe's character; economic specialisation and its associated ideology help to account for the appeal of his adventures; but it is Puritan individualism which controls his spiritual being.

Troeltsch has claimed that "the really permanent attainment of individualism was due to a religious, and not a secular movement, to the Reformation and not the Renaissance." [46] It is neither feasible nor profitable to attempt to establish priorities in such matters, but it is certainly true that if there is one element which all forms of Protestantism have in common it is the replacement of the rule of the Church as the mediator between man and God by another view of religion in which it is the individual who is entrusted with the primary responsibility for his own spiritual direction. Two aspects of this new Protestant emphasis—the tendency to increase consciousness of the self as a spiritual entity, and the tendency to a kind of democratisation of the moral and social outlook—are particularly important both to *Robinson Crusoe* and to the development of the presuppositions on which the formal realism of the novel is based.

The idea of religious self-scrutiny as an important duty for each individual is, of course, much older than Protestantism; it derives from the individualist and subjective emphasis of primitive Christianity, and finds its supreme expression in St. Augustine's *Confessions*. But it is generally agreed that it was Calvin, in the sixteenth century, who re-established and systematised this earlier pattern of purposive spiritual introspection, and made it the supreme religious ritual for the layman as well as for the priest: every good Puritan conducted a continual scrutiny of his inner man for evidence of his own place in the divine plot of election and reprobation.

This "internalisation of conscience" is everywhere manifested in Calvinism. In New England, it has been said, "almost every literate Puritan kept some sort of journal"; [47] and, in England, *Grace Abounding* is the great monument of a way of life which Bunyan shared with the other members of his sect,[48] the Baptists, who were, with one or two minor additions and subtractions, orthodox Calvinists. In later generations the introspective habit remained even where religious conviction weakened, and there resulted the three greatest autobiographical confessions of the modern period, those of Pepys, Rousseau and Boswell, all of whom were brought up under the Calvinist discipline; their fascination with self-analysis, and indeed their extreme egocentricity, are character traits which they shared both with later Calvinism in general [49] and with Defoe's heroes.

The importance of this subjective and individualist spiritual pattern to Defoe's work, and to the rise of the novel, is very evident. *Robinson Crusoe* initiates that aspect of the novel's treatment of experience which rivals the confessional autobiography and outdoes other literary forms in bringing us close to the inward moral being of the individual; and it achieves this closeness to the inner life of the protagonist by using as formal basis the autobiographical memoir which was the most immediate and widespread literary expression of the introspective tendency of Puritanism in general.

Defoe himself, of course, was born and bred a Puritan. His father was a Dissenter, perhaps a Baptist, more probably a Presbyterian, in any case a Calvinist; and he sent his son to a dissenting academy, probably intending him for the ministry. Defoe's own religious beliefs changed a good deal, and he expressed in his writings the whole gamut of doctrines, from intransigent predestinarianism to rational deism, which Puritanism held during its varied course of development; nevertheless, there is no doubt that Defoe remained and was generally considered to be a Dissenter, and that much of the outlook revealed in his novels is distinctively Puritan.

There is nothing to suggest that Robinson Crusoe was intended to be a Dissenter. On the other hand, the note of his religious reflections is often Puritan in character—their tenor has been seen by one theologian as very close to the Presbyterian Shorter Catechism of the 1648 Westminster Assembly.[50] Crusoe certainly exhibits frequent signs of Bibliolatry: he quotes some twenty verses of the Bible in the first part of Robinson Crusoe alone, besides making many briefer references; and he sometimes seeks divine guidance by opening the Bible at random. But the most significant aspect of his spiritual life is his tendency to rigorous moral and religious self-examination. Each of his actions is followed by a passage of reflection in which Crusoe ponders over the problem of how it reveals the intentions of divine providence. If the corn sprouts, it is surely a divine miracle "so directed for my sustenance"; if he has a bout of fever "a leisurely review of the miseries of death" [51] eventually convinces him that he deserves reprobation for neglecting to show his gratitude for God's mercies to him. The modern reader no doubt tends to pay little attention to these parts of the narrative; but Crusoe and his author showed their point of view very clearly by allotting the spiritual realm as much importance as the practical, both in space and emphasis. It would therefore appear that what are probably the vestigial remnants of the Calvinist introspective discipline helped to provide us for the first time in the history of fiction with a hero whose day-by-day mental and moral life is fully shared by the reader.

This crucial literary advance was not, of course, brought about by the introspective tendency of Puritanism alone. As we have seen, the gospel of work had a similar effect in giving the individual's daily economic task almost as much importance as his daily spiritual self-examination; and the parallel effects of both these tendencies were supplemented by another closely related tendency in Puritanism.

If God had given the individual prime responsibility for his own spiritual destiny, it followed that he must have made this possible by signifying his intentions to the individual in the events of his daily life.

The Puritan therefore tended to see every item in his personal experience as potentially rich in moral and spiritual meaning; and Defoe's
hero is acting according to this tradition when he tries to interpret so
many of the mundane events of the narrative as divine pointers which
may help him to find his own place in the eternal scheme of redemption
and reprobation.

In that scheme, of course, all souls had equal chances, and it therefore followed that the individual had as full an opportunity of showing
his spiritual qualities in the ordinary conduct of life as in its rarer and
more dramatic exigencies. This was one reason for the general Puritan
tendency towards the democratisation of the moral and social scale,
and it was assisted by several other factors. There were, for instance,
many social, moral and political reasons why the Puritans should be
hostile to the aristocratic scale of values; nor could they fail to dis-
approve of its literary expression in the traditional heroes of romance,
extrovert conquerors whose victories are won, not in the spirit or in
the counting-house but on the battlefield and in the boudoir. It is at all
events clear that Puritanism brought about a fundamental and in a
sense democratic orientation in the social and literary outlook of its
adherents, an orientation which was described by Milton's lines in
Paradise Lost: "To know / That which before us lies in daily life / Is
the prime wisdom," [52] and which evoked one of Defoe's most eloquent
pieces of writing, an essay in *Applebee's Journal* (1722) on the funeral
of Marlborough. The essay's peroration begins:

> What then is the work of life? What the business of great men,
> that pass the stage of the world in seeming triumph as these
> men, we call heroes, have done? Is it to grow great in the
> mouth of fame, and take up many pages in history? Alas! that
> is no more than making a tale for the reading of posterity, till
> it turns into fable and romance. Is it to furnish subject to the
> poets, and live in their immortal rhymes, as they call them?
> That is, in short, no more than to be hereafter turned into
> ballad and song, and be sung by old women to quiet children;
> or, at the corner of a street, to gather crowds in aid of the
> pickpocket and the whore. Or is their business rather to add
> virtue and piety to their glory, which alone will pass them into
> Eternity, and make them truly immortal? What is glory with-
> out virtue? A great man without religion is no more than a
> great beast without a soul.

Then Defoe modulates into something more like the narrowly ethical evaluation of merit which was to be one of the legacies of Puritanism to the middle-class code: "What is honour without merit? And what can be called true merit, but that which makes a person a good man, as well as a great man." [53]

Neither Crusoe, nor indeed any of Defoe's heroes, it must be admitted, are conspicuous by these standards of virtue, religion, merit and goodness; and, of course, Defoe did not intend them to be so. But these standards do represent the moral plane on which Defoe's novels exist, and by which his heroes must be judged: the ethical scale has been so internalised and democratised that, unlike the scale of achievement common in epic or romance, it is relevant to the lives and actions of ordinary people. In this Defoe's heroes are typical of the later characters of the novel: Robinson Crusoe, Moll Flanders and even Colonel Jacque never think of glory or honour; they have their being on the moral plane of day-to-day living more completely than those of previous narratives, and their thoughts and actions only exhibit an ordinary, a democratic goodness and badness. Robinson Crusoe, for instance, is Defoe's most heroic character, but there is nothing unusual about his personality or the way he faces his strange experiences; as Coleridge pointed out, he is essentially "the universal representative, the person, for whom every reader could substitute himself . . . nothing is done, thought, suffered, or desired, but what every man can imagine himself doing, thinking, feeling, or wishing for." [54]

Defoe's presentation of Robinson Crusoe as the "universal representative" is intimately connected with the egalitarian tendency of Puritanism in yet another way. For not only did this tendency make the way the individual faced every problem of everyday life a matter of deep and continuing spiritual concern; it also encouraged a literary outlook which was suited to describing such problems with the most detailed fidelity.

In *Mimesis*, a brilliant panorama of realistic representation in literature from Homer to Virginia Woolf, Erich Auerbach has demonstrated the general connection between the Christian view of man and the serious literary portrayal of ordinary people and of common life. The classical theory of genres had reflected the social and philosophical orientation of Greece and Rome: tragedy described the heroic vicissitudes of people better than ourselves in appropriately elevated language, whereas the domain of everyday reality belonged to comedy which was supposed to portray people "inferior to ourselves" in an appropriately "low" style. Christian literature, however, reflecting a very different social and philosophical outlook, had no place for this *Stiltrennung* or segregation of styles according to the class status of the subject-matter. The gospel narratives treated the doings of humble people with the utmost seriousness and on occasion, indeed, with sublimity; later, this tradition was continued in many of the medieval literary forms, from the lives of the saints to the miracle plays; and it eventually found its greatest expression in Dante's *Divina Commedia*.[55]

The classicising tendencies of the Renaissance and the Counter-Reformation, however, re-established the old doctrine of genre, and indeed elaborated it to an extent that would certainly have surprised Aristotle. The supreme example of this elaboration is found in French literature of the seventeenth century, and especially in tragedy; not only was the unremitting use of a fully codified *style noble* prescribed, but even the objects and actions of everyday life were banished from the stage.

In Protestant countries, however, the *Stiltrennung* never achieved such authority, especially in England where neoclassicism was confronted by the example of Shakespeare and that characteristic mingling of the tragic and comic modes which was part of his legacy from the Middle Ages. Nevertheless, in one important respect even Shakespeare followed the *Stiltrennung*: his treatment of low and rustic characters is very similar to that of the protagonists of the neo-classical tradition from Ben Jonson to Dryden, and there is nothing egalitarian about it. It is very significant that the main exceptions to this derogatory attitude are found in the works of Puritan writers. In Adam, Milton created the first epic hero who is essentially a "universal representative"; Bunyan, seeing all souls as equal before God, accorded the humble and their lives a much more serious and sympathetic attention than they received in the other literature of his period; while the works of Defoe are the supreme illustration in the novel of the connection between the democratic individualism of Puritanism and the objective representation of the world of everyday reality and all those who inhabit it.

There is a great difference, however, between Bunyan and Defoe, a difference which suggests why it is Defoe, rather than Bunyan, who is often considered to be our first novelist. In the earlier fiction of the Puritan movement—in such works as Arthur Dent's *Plain Man's Pathway to Heaven,* or the stories of Bunyan and his Baptist *confrère* Benjamin Keach—we have many elements of the novel: simple language, realistic descriptions of persons and places, and a serious presentation of the moral problems of ordinary individuals. But the significance of the characters and their actions largely depends upon a transcendental scheme of things: to say that the persons are allegorical is to say that their earthly reality is not the main object of the writer, but rather that he hopes to make us see through them a larger and unseen reality beyond time and place.

In Defoe's novels, on the other hand, although religious concerns are present they have no such priority of status: indeed the heritage of Puritanism is demonstrably too weak to supply a continuous and controlling pattern for the hero's experience. If, for example, we turn to the actual effect of Crusoe's religion on his behaviour, we find that it has curiously little. Defoe often suggests that an incident is an act of Divine providence or retribution, but this interpretation is rarely supported by the facts of the story. To take the crucial instance: if Crusoe's original sin was filial disobedience—leaving home in the first place— it is certain that no real retribution follows, since he does very well out of it; and later he often sets out for further journeys without any fear that he may be flouting Providence. This indeed comes very near to the "neglect" of the "Cautious, warning and instruction . . . Providence" which Crusoe called a "kind of Practical Atheism" in his *Serious Reflections*.[56] Where Providence is bringing blessings—as, for instance, when he finds the grains of corn and rise—things are different: Crusoe need only accept. But the trilogy as a whole certainly suggests that any of the less co-operative interventions of Providence can safely be neglected.

Marx sourly noted this somewhat gratuitous character of Crusoe's religious life. "Of his prayers we take no account, since they are a source of pleasure to him, and he looks on them as so much recreation." [57] He would have been pleased to find that Gildon thought that the "religious and useful reflections" were "in reality . . . put in . . . to swell the bulk of Defoe's treatise to a five-shilling book." [58] Both Marx and Gildon were right in drawing attention to the discontinuity between the religious aspects of the book and its action: but their explanations do Defoe some injustice. His spiritual intentions were probably quite sincere, but they have the weakness of all "Sunday religion" and manifest themselves in somewhat unconvincing periodical tributes to the transcendent at times when a respite from real action and practical intellectual effort is allowed or enforced. Such, certainly, is Crusoe's religion, and we feel that it is in the last analysis the result of an unresolved and probably unconscious conflict in Defoe himself. He lived fully in the sphere of practical and utilitarian action, and could be wholly true to his being when he described this aspect of Robinson Crusoe's life. But his religious upbringing forced him from time to time to hand over a brilliant piece of narrative by a star-reporter to a distant colleague on the religious page who could be relied on to supply suitable spiritual commentaries quickly out of stock. Puritanism made the editorial policy unalterable; but it was usually satisfied by a purely formal adherence. In this, too, Defoe is typical of the development of Puritanism; in the phrase of H. W. Schneider, "beliefs seldom become doubts; they become ritual." [59] Otherworldly concerns do not provide the essential themes of Defoe's novels: but they do punctuate the narrative with comminatory codas that demonstrate a lifetime of somewhat mechanical practice.

NOTES

1. *Advancement of Learning*, Bk. II, especially ch. 22, sect. xvi and ch. 23, sect. xiv.
2. *Elements of Law*, Pt. I, ch. 13, sect. iii.
3. *Review*, III (1706), No. 3.
4. *The Theory of Social and Economic Organisation*, trans. Henderson and Parsons (New York, 1947), pp. 186–202.
5. *The Life and Strange Surprising Adventures of Robinson Crusoe*, ed. Aitken (London, 1902), p. 316.
6. Second treatise, "Essay concerning . . . Civil Government," sect. 14.
7. *Life*, pp. 277, 147.
8. See Max Weber, *The Protestant Ethic and the Spirit of Capitalism*, trans. Parsons (London, 1930), pp. 59–76; *Social and Economic Organisation*, pp. 341–354.
9. See, for example, Robert Redfield, *Folk Culture of Yucatan* (Chicago, 1941), pp. 338–369.
10. ll. 339–352.
11. *Life*, pp. 2–6, 216.
12. *Human Understanding*, Bk. II, ch. 21, sects. xxxi-lx.
13. *Pensées*, No. 139.
14. *Farther Adventures of Robinson Crusoe*, ed. Aitken (London, 1902), p. 214.
15. *A Plan of the English Commerce* (Oxford, 1928), pp. 28, 31–32.
16. *Desert Islands and Robinson Crusoe* (London, 1930), p. 7.
17. *Moll Flanders*, ed. Aitken (London, 1902), I, 186.
18. See especially A. W. Secord, *Studies in the Narrative Method of Defoe* (Urbana, 1924).

19. Weber, *Essays in Sociology,* trans. Gerth and Mills (New York, 1946), p. 350.
20. I (1705), No. 92.
21. *Farther Adventures,* p. 78.
22. *Life,* pp. 208–210, 225.
23. *Life,* p. 341.
24. *Farther Adventures,* p. 77.
25. John Forster, *Life of Charles Dickens,* revised Ley (London, 1928), p. 611 n.
26. *Life,* pp. 27, 34–36, 164.
27. *Serious Reflections during the Life and Surprising Adventures of Robinson Crusoe,* ed. Aitken (London, 1902), p. 66.
28. *Life,* p. 229.
29. *Robinson Crusoe Examin'd and Criticis'd,* ed. Dottin (London and Paris, 1923), pp. 70, 78, 118.
30. *Life,* pp. 245–246.
31. *Farther Adventures,* pp. 133, 177–180.
32. *Life,* p. 318.
33. See James R. Sutherland, *Defoe* (London, 1937), p. 25; W. Gückel and E. Günther, "D. Defoes und. J. Swifts Belesenheit und literarische Kritik," *Palaestra,* CIL (1925).
34. My translation from *Notes on Philosophy and Political Economy,* in *Oeuvres Philosophiques,* ed. Molitor (Paris, 1937), VI, 69.
35. See William-Edward Mann, *Robinson Crusoë en France* (Paris, 1916), p. 102.
36. See Appendix, *Serious Reflections,* ed. Aitken, p. 322.
37. *Life,* p. 75.
38. "Estimate of the Value and Influence of Works of Fiction in Modern Times," *Works,* ed. Nettleship, III, 40.
39. *Life,* p. 74.
40. *Life,* p. 130.
41. *Account of His Visit to England,* p. 326.
42. Bk. I, ch. 1.
43. See Ernest Troeltsch, *Social Teaching of the Christian Churches,* trans. Wyon (London, 1931), I, 119; II, 589; Tawney, *Religion and the Rise of Capitalism* (London, 1948), pp. 197–270).
44. *The Dumb Philosopher* (1719), ed. Scott (London, 1841), p. 21.
45. *The Case of Protestant Dissenters in Carolina,* 1706, p. 5.
46. *Social Teaching,* I, 328.
47. Perry Miller and Thomas H. Johnson, *The Puritans* (New York, 1938), p. 461.
48. See William York Tindall, *John Bunyan: Mechanick Preacher* (New York, 1934), pp. 23–41.
49. Troeltsch, *Social Teaching,* II, 590.
50. James Moffat, "The Religion of Robinson Crusoe," *Contemporary Review,* CXV (1919), 669.
51. *Life,* I, 85, 99.
52. VIII, 192–194.
53. *Cit.* W. Lee, *Daniel Defoe* (London, 1869), III, 29–30.

54. *Works,* ed. Potter, p. 419.
55. *Mimesis: The Representation of Reality in Western Literature,* trans. Trask (Princeton, 1953), especially pp. 41–49, 72–73, 148–173, 184–202, 312–320, 387, 431–433, 466, 491. I translate *stil-trennung,* from the German edition (Bern, 1946), "segregation of styles," as slightly more specific than Mr. Trask's "separation of styles." The two succeeding paragraphs continue to summarise from *Mimesis,* except for what is said about Puritanism.
56. P. 191.
57. *Capital* (New York, 1906), p. 88.
58. *Robinson Crusoe Examin'd,* ed. Dottin, pp. 110–111.
59. *The Puritan Mind* (New York, 1930), p. 98. A close analogy to Crusoe's gloomy spiritual self-accusations which have so little effect upon his actions, is provided by the rituals described in Perry Miller, "Declension in a Bible Commonwealth," *Proc. Amer. Antiquarian Soc.,* LI (1941), 37–94.

G. ARMOUR CRAIG

The Unpoetic Compromise: On the Relation between Private Vision and Social Order in Nineteenth-Century English Fiction

The heroine of Charlotte Brontë's *Jane Eyre,* ending one large episode of her life and about to begin another, stands at the window of her room at Lowood School. She looks out beyond the garden:

> . . . there was the hilly horizon. My eye passed all other objects to rest on those most remote, the blue peaks: it was those I longed to surmount; all within their boundary of rock and heath seemed prison-ground, exile limits.[1]

Jane Eyre's position and attitude are familiar to readers of nineteenth-century English fiction. We may recall that Becky Sharp also dreamed of freedom in her room at Miss Pinkerton's Academy: "She had a little room in the garret, where the maids heard her walking and sobbing at night; but it was with rage and not with grief" (p. 15). We may remember that Dorothea Brooke, preparing herself for the judicious proposal of Mr. Casaubon, "pondered the vision that had arisen before her of a possible future to which she looked forward with trembling hope" while she "absorbed into the intensity of her mood, the solemn glory of the afternoon with its long swathes of light between far-off rows of limes, whose shadows touched each other." Like Jane Eyre and many another heroine, Dorothea is "a nature altogether ardent . . . hemmed in by a social life" which seems "a labyrinth of petty courses"; and like other young seekers, "the thing which seemed to her best, she wanted to justify by the completest knowledge" (pp. 22, 24). Much

From *Society and Self in the Novel,* edited by Mark Schorer. Copyright 1955 by Columbia University Press. Reprinted by permission of the publisher.

later, Jude Fawley climbs the workmen's ladder to the roof of the barn and sees or thinks he sees the far-off lights of Christminster, and he resolves someday to reach the "city of light" (p. 25). Or there is Esther Summerson, waking on her first morning at Bleak House: she had arrived in darkness, and she looks out her window to see the strange world turn visible in friendly morning light. "As the prospect gradually revealed itself, and disclosed the scene over which the wind had wandered in the dark, like my memory over my life, I had a pleasure in discovering the unknown objects that had been around me in my sleep." Esther's vision of "dark places . . . all melted away" is an anticipation of the adventure before her (pp. 84–85).

A large anthology of such passages might be compiled. The beholder of lights, shadows, and distant regions is almost invariably an orphan, is usually a young woman, and is always on the brink of a new social relation. In some of the worst novels as well as in the best, from a high place and in solitude the heroine looks out on the world, and in her vision we see her difference from those around her. Milly Theale, in *The Wings of the Dove*, is first presented to us in a higher situation and with a wider range of vision than any other heroine can sustain. She looks down on "the kingdoms of the earth" from an Alpine promontory, and we see her there through the eyes of Susan Stringham, who breathlessly debates the alternatives implied by such a view. She concludes that Milly's attitude is a large affirmation: it bespeaks not some "horrible hidden obsession" but "a state of uplifted and unlimited possession that had nothing to gain from violence" (pp. 138–139). For Mrs. Stringham, Milly is "the real thing, the romantic life itself" (p. 120); and so she must be for the reader, who first encounters her in this Jamesian elaboration of what may almost be called a convention. By her solitary elevation the heroine is distinguished from the world around her. Her difference may be simple hostility or partial acquiescence, or it may be a relation that only pages and pages of dialogue and action can express. But the interest of the reader is in how the difference will turn out. He looks forward to what George Eliot calls "the outcome" of the "nature" set off before him.

That our interest in such "outcomes" is of limited importance, we do not readily grant. For most of us, as for Henry James, the novel is "a direct impression of life," and it is difficult to imagine the register of any impression richer or fuller than this. Yet respectable men, beginning perhaps with Plato, have found the preoccupations of the novel-reader dangerously narrow. The philosopher T. H. Green in 1862 said,

Novel-reading aggravates two of the worst maladies of modern times, self-consciousness and want of reverence. . . . Scarcely understanding what is meant by "divine indifference" as to the fate of individual existences in the evolution of God's plan, we weary heaven with complaints that we find the world contrary, or that we cannot satisfy ourselves with a theory of life.[2]

Such lamentation may well be the occupational disease of the novel-reader, for "divine indifference" towards the fate of the characters before him is just what he cannot attain. And a sense of the contrariness of the world, even of the inadequacy of theories of life, will often be our response to the pages before us. Green goes on to say that the events of a novel cannot be subordinated to "ideas," nor can they be simple "phenomena to excite curiosity." The reader cannot be detached and neutral: if he reads a novel at all, its events must become "misfortunes or blessings to excite sentiment." Green believed that such sentiment dies hard; the habitual reader of novels must come to think "his personal joys and sorrows of interest to angels and men"; the world becomes for him not "a theater for the display of God's glory and the unknown might of man," but "merely an organism for affecting himself with pains and pleasures." "Thus regarded," Green concludes, "it must needs lose its claim on his reverence, for it is narrowed to the limits of his own consciousness." [3]

With all its negations, this description is not easy to improve. Although it looks at the novel in its unredeemed state of mere literature and sees it as something less than myth or fable, it describes the novel in relation to an interested reader rather than an abstract concept. The novel so considered does indeed describe events as "misfortunes or blessings to excite sentiment," and it cannot but limit the world of its events to the reader's own consciousness. And while it may or may not be true that all novel readers go on reading long after their books have been closed, Green lived at a time when great twenty-part stories were providing thousands with irresistible ways of imagining their own lives, and only the strong-minded man can refuse to see himself as the center of an absorbing tale. But what Green's criticism implies, and the limitation he attacks, is a necessary "this-sidedness" in the world of fiction. The most a novel can present to its readers is a social world. Jane Eyre does not see the blue peaks and dream of becoming a mountain-climber, nor is Esther Summerson about to take up the study of optics. The "outcomes" we anticipate will involve their "natures" with others, and as we read of their relations with others, society will emerge for us not as seen from some supra-social position or as adapted to some presocial end, but as a felt relation—as a relation experienced from within. The novelist's world, however obvious it may be to say so, does not contain the evolution of God's plan or the unknown might of man. As a world discovered while we read, it can be no more than an organism affecting us with known pleasure and pain, and its relations can go no higher than the limits of a single consciousness. Whatever larger purposes he may glimpse in other situations, it is a truth universally acknowledged that a single man in possession of a good novel must be in want of society.

But precisely because their worlds are limited to the grasp of the single consciousness, the novels of the last century yield some surprising observations when we approach them through our interest in the outcome of private visions. They can show us how large the single consciousness must be when it achieves a sense of society, and they can show us the distinctions it must contain if the difference between the dreamer and the world is to be preserved. They can show us, in brief, just how much variety the mere social mind can support. No novel is more relevant to such an approach than *Jane Eyre*. The success of this work a literary historian must find too good to be true; it is the novel he must have invented if he had not found so many readers captured by it. For no heroine dreams more often or more successfully than the heroine of this strange romance.

After she has escaped from the "prison-ground" of Lowood to become governess at Thornfield, Jane's visions enlarge and become more frequent. Ofter, she tells us, she climbed to the attic of the big house and there "looked out afar over sequestered field and hill, and along dim sky-line," longing for "a power of vision which might overpass that limit." Whenever she was "restless" in the confines of her womanly duties she went to this high place and there, "safe in the silence and solitude," listened with her "inward ear" to "a tale that was never ended —a tale my imagination created, and narrated continuously; quickened with all of incident, life, fire, feeling, that I desired and had not in my actual existence" (p. 116). The heroine of this vague inner narrative is of course Jane herself, but as the grammar of these fragments will have indicated, Jane Eyre is also the narrator of that larger history in which these recurring visions constitute an episode of indefinite length. We begin to suspect that the outcome of this heroine's visions cannot but be in her favor, and our suspicions are soon justified.

Jane Eyre moves towards her unnamed goal beyond the skyline by a highly secular version of those "gradations of glory" (p. 60) which Helen Burns believed in beyond this life. The first glorious gradation is of course Jane's elevation by her master's proposal of marriage. Mr. Rochester is ardent but candid: "You—you strange—you almost unearthly thing! I love as my own flesh. You—poor and obscure, and small and plain as you are—I entreat to accept me as a husband" (p. 275). Such a consummation Jane properly characterizes as she accepts it: "to imagine such a lot befalling me is a fairy tale—a daydream" (p. 280). So far the tale told by her imagination has come true, and so far the sentimental reader sighs in an ecstasy of satisfaction.

But Jane soon ascends another gradation. On her wedding day it is revealed that Rochester is already married. He grimly conducts the party back from the church to Thornfield, and there in the very attic where Jane was wont to dream—where indeed sometimes her dreams were interrupted by eerie laughter—shows them the secret of the manor: a grovelling madwoman whom he must keep locked up. It is clear that morally at least Jane has risen a little over her master: she has plotted no bigamy, she is no deceiver. And after Rochester's explanations and protestations of love, she confirms her superiority by refusing to fly with him to the south of France as his mistress. She reflects, it is true, that such a liaison would put her in the social position of Rochester's former mistresses. But it is also true that she refuses his proposal because it is irreligious. In her depression after the discovery of the bestial wife, Jane says, "One idea only still throbbed life-like within me—a remembrance of God" (p. 321). In her infatuation during the courtship, Rochester had come to stand between her and "every thought of religion": "I could not, in those days, see God for his creature: of whom I had made an idol" (p. 297). But now religion is the only resource: "I will keep the law given by God; sanctioned by man," she declares (p. 344), and then runs away from Thornfield.

At the end of her flight Jane is befriended by the Rivers family, but she overwhelmingly returns their kindness when she learns she is their cousin and heiress of their uncle's handsome estate. She shares the inheritance with them and is for the first time in her career equal in money and the power of property to those around her, while the reader takes satisfaction in observing that this reward comes after the exercise of virtue. Yet Jane is not therefore better than all around her, for she owes her power to the righteousness of the brother, St. John Rivers, who is, appropriately, a most devout young clergyman. He has discovered Jane's name and parentage and has arranged that she should receive the bequest. But her moral stature is sufficient for St. John, for he asks her to marry him and go with him to India as a missionary. And with her refusal, or at least her evasion, of this proposal, Jane ascends the next gradation of glory.

For St. John's proposal is made from the highest motives. He has judged Jane carefully and finds her sufficient for the duties he asks her to share. "A missionary's wife you must—shall be. . . . I claim you —not for my pleasure, but for my Sovereign's service." Of his own role he is certain: "I am the servant of an infallible master . . . my captain is the All-perfect." And he is certain of hers: "God and nature intended you for a missionary's wife." When Jane offers to go with him not as his wife but as a sister and fellow-laborer, St. John is even more emphatic: "Do you think God will be satisfied with half an oblation? Will he accept a mutilated sacrifice?" There can be no compromise: "consider my offer: and do not forget that if you reject it, it is not me you deny, but God" (pp. 437, 438, 442, 446). The full, official, and authentic representative of religion, the embodiment of the power through which Jane has risen above the importuning of Mr. Rochester, has spoken. It is hardly conceivable that our heroine should rise above his claim.

But rise she does, when one midnight a little later St. John renews his suit. Jane is wavering: "Religion called—Angels beckoned—God commanded—life rolled together like a scroll. . . ." But in one of the great moments of Victorian literature her struggle suddenly ends. Her heart stands still "to an inexpressible feeling" which rouses her senses "as if their utmost activity hitherto had been but torpor." She hears her name called three times: "Jane! Jane! Jane!" but by a voice that comes from nowhere—"I had heard it—where or whence, for ever impossible to know." But it is a human voice—"a known, loved, well-remembered voice, that of Edward Fairfax Rochester." It speaks "in pain and woe, wildly, eerily, urgently," and Jane answers promptly: "I am coming! Wait for me! Oh, I will come," and adds very sensibly, "Where are you?" (pp. 456-58).

Two consequences of this unearthly conversation must be noticed. One is immediate. St. John, whose condition we can only imagine, is brushed aside. "It was *my* time to assume ascendancy. *My* powers were in play and in force." Jane orders him to leave and he obeys at once; he is in fact finished. The origin of the voice cannot be known, but it has demolished the claims of the servant of the All-perfect.

The second consequence is more startling. Leaving her cousins, Jane discovers Rochester living in a far-off manor in deep woods. She learns that Thornfield has been burned down, set on fire by the maniac in the attic, and that in trying to save her Rochester has been blinded and has lost his left hand. By Jane's return to him he is almost precisely as astonished as she had been by his proposal of marriage, and they seem at last equals by the reversals of their fortunes. For then, some ten chapters back, just before he had asked her to marry him, Jane had passionately exclaimed against the social difference between them: "If God had gifted me with some beauty and much wealth, I should have made it as hard for you to leave me, as it is now for me to leave you" (p. 274). But now, at the end of the story, these differences have disappeared, for the character of Jane's beauty is at least irrelevant and she is rich. Moreover the moral equality Jane had claimed on the earlier occasion seems fully established now. Then, she had cried: "Do you think, because I am poor, obscure, plain, and little, I am soulless and heartless? I have as much soul as you—and full as much heart!" (p. 274). We have seen her assert this fullness of heart in defiance of Rochester's wishes, but now, at their reunion, Rochester seems her equal in this respect also. For he tells her how he has begun "only of late" to see "the hand of God" in his doom. He has begun to experience "remorse, repentance," and has risen so far towards Jane's moral rank that he has even begun to pray. He proceeds to relate a particularly vehement prayer he offered not four nights since—yes, near midnight on Monday. Alone, weary and desolate, he prayed that he might be taken from the torments of his life. "That I merited all I endured, I acknowledged—that I could scarcely endure more, I pleaded; and the alpha and omega of my heart's wishes broke involuntarily from my lips in the words—'Jane! Jane! Jane!'" (pp. 487–88). He tells further how he heard Jane's reply, and concludes his remarkable recital by offering still another prayer, in which he begs his "Redeemer" to give him strength to lead henceforth a purer life. He puts out his hand to be led, and we may imagine with what mighty crescendo of some heavenly Victorian Wurlitzer, is taken home by Jane, his "prop and guide."

But before they depart, Jane addresses a confidential observation to the only listener who can share it:

> Reader, it was on Monday night—near midnight—that I too had received the mysterious summons: . . . I listened to Mr. Rochester's narrative; but made no disclosure in return. The

coincidence struck me as too awful and inexplicable to be communicated or discussed (p. 488).

But the reason she offers for her silence stands oddly beside Mr. Rochester's account of his repentance and conversion: "If I told anything," she says, "my tale would be such as must necessarily make a profound impression on the mind of my hearer; and that mind, yet from its suffering too prone to gloom, needed not the deeper shade of the supernatural." She ends her address to the reader with a paraphrase of the Virgin's response to the tidings of the shepherds: "I kept these things then, and pondered them in my heart." The final gradation has been achieved; Jane stands alone in glory. Rochester may have risen to the moral level from which she once refused him, but she has overpassed even this peak.

To imagine a different consequence here is to see how impossible it is for Jane to be anyone's equal. We might rewrite the address to the reader as a confession to Rochester: "I too, O Edward, I too!" Such a disclosure in return ought to produce the happiest union of equals before God, though what kind of God is perhaps hard to say. But that Jane makes no such disclosure, despite the confusion of "gloom" and "shade" with Rochester's new religious state, is the most consistent stroke in the book. Back in the speech before Rochester's proposal of marriage, when Jane protests her moral equality while granting her social inferiority, she winds up her declaration with an explanation of its rhetoric: "I am not talking to you now through the medium of custom, conventionalities, or even of mortal flesh:—it is my spirit that addresses your spirit; just as if both had passed through the grave, and we stood at God's feet, equal—as we are" (p. 274). That such an exchange of spiritual addresses should eventually occur in this novel is indeed "too awful and inexplicable to be communicated or discussed." For whatever anyone else may know, Jane Eyre, who is both heroine and narrator, must know better. And by her dramatic overwhelming of St. John, Jane has overpassed the religious grounds on which Rochester now claims equality with her. Jane's own "heart," the private morality of her "soul," has carried her higher than the grounds of Rochester's conversion. The movement of her vision towards realization is so rapacious that no terms are left in which to account for it; certainly there were no terms beyond religion for a writer such as Charlotte Brontë. Her heroine has narrated herself into silence, and the novel must end.

In every relationship Jane rises from inferiority to superiority. Her inferiority is expressed again and again as imprisonment; her superiority appears as the narrative confirmation of her rightness in resisting imprisonment. For resisting the gross attack of John Reed and for asserting an unpalatable version of the Reed family's behavior towards her, Jane is imprisoned in the Red Room at Gateshead. After imprisonment she so far ascends as to dispute Mrs. Reed's account of her to the infamous Mr. Brocklehurst: "*You* are deceitful," she insists (p. 36). Later she returns to Gateshead, accomplished, successful, and above all *right*: her version of the Reed children has been borne out, and Mrs. Reed on her deathbed confesses that she has been deceitful, first in not carrying out the wishes of her dead husband with respect to Jane and later in lying to the uncle who has been seeking Jane to leave her his fortune. The night after Rochester's dreadful wife is exposed, Jane dreams of the Red Room, and next day, as Rochester begs her to become his mistress, she feels another kind of imprisonment: "I was experiencing an ordeal: a hand of fiery iron grasped my vitals" (p. 342). From this prison she rises on the wings of religious principle only to enter a new one. For when St. John for the last time urges her to be his missionary bride, Jane reports: "My iron shroud contracted round me: persuasion advanced with slow step" (p. 440). Earlier she speaks of St. John's influence on her as a contraction of her "liberty of mind." But her triumph over St. John makes her superior not only to the version of her nature that he insists on; it also makes her superior to the highest equality anyone can conceive of in this little world of gentle-folk, parsons, governesses, servants, teachers, and manufacturers—equality before the throne of God. The movement of this novel is literally transcendence with a vengeance.

It will long since have appeared that this recurring ascent is expressed symbolically, and few novels of the period are so thoroughly articulated in images. The sexual symbols are so frequent and crude that the novel might be subtitled The Red and The Black. The destruction of Rochester's strong hand and volcanic eyes, which has been called, no doubt rightly, a castration symbol,[4] is monstrously prepared for in the paraphrase of a passage from the Sermon on the Mount with which Jane decides what she must do after learning that Rochester is married: "No; you shall tear yourself away, none shall help you; you shall yourself, pluck out your right eye: yourself cut off your right hand: your heart shall be the victim; and you, the priest, to transfix it" (p. 322). The subterranean sadism is all too rich, and the imagery is sometimes so gross that the reader must laugh if he does not close his eyes and skip. Perhaps the grimmest joke in the book is the compliment offered to Jane by both St. John and Rochester: "You delight in sacrifice." [5]

But these underground horrors are not the subject of Jane Eyre, inevitable though they may be as the vehicle, and relevant as they may be to all we know and infer about the life of its author. They are inevitable because there is no difference between the mind that knows the world of this novel and the mind that seeks to know it in terms of a private vision. In such a structure it becomes more and more difficult to distinguish between behavior and motive, and the narrative finally succumbs so completely to the motive that no irony is possible. But the horrors of its real subject are enough, for this novel like any other is about the mind and society, and the action of this novel is the triumph of the mind's version of society. When her story ends Jane has reduced not only the initially overpowering differences of rank; she has reduced to the shape of her own vision the power that, for Charlotte Brontë at least, supports all differences of rank. As he begins his last prayer to his "Redeemer," Rochester tells Jane that when she returned he feared she might not be "real" but might be "silence and annihilation." Perhaps Rochester is the prophet after all.

To eradicate the social difference between an orphan-governess and a gentleman might well involve the convulsion of a supra-Christian power. There can be no doubt, however, that the reduction of the world to the terms of a single vision, no matter how moral its content or how sanctified its motives, is attended by the most dreadful violence. The power of the "I" of this novel is secret, undisclosable, absolute. There are no terms to explain its dominance, because no terms can appear which are not under its dominance. The violence with which it simplifies the differences labeled "inferior," "poorer," "richer," "better," or "higher," the killing and maiming and blinding which are the consequences of its dialectic, tell us as clearly as fiction can that even fantasy must subdue a real world. Jane Eyre's vision masters her world, but the price of her mastery is absolute isolation. When she knows her world completely she is out of it by the most rigorous necessity. I know no other work that so effectively demonstrates the demon of the absolute.

From this ruinous monolith, however, we may make some useful observations of other nineteenth-century novels. We can look back to the enormous sanity of Jane Austen's Emma, to a heroine who also enjoys some literary visions of the world about her. But the difference between *Jane Eyre* and *Emma* is nowhere so clear as in the two sentences in which they are most similar. At the crisis of Emma's career the narrator says: "Seldom, very seldom does complete truth belong to any human disclosure; seldom can it happen that something is not a little disguised, or a little mistaken . . ." (p. 384). It is not a matter of "a coincidence . . . too awful and inexplicable to be communicated or discussed": the terms which have brought about Emma's shattering "coincidence" are the same terms with which she will adjust her vision. Or we can look forward to the pathos which the narrator of *Middlemarch* finds in the necessary blindness of all our perceptions of others: "If we had a keen vision and feeling of all ordinary human life, it would be like hearing the grass grow and the squirrel's heart beat, and we should die of that roar which lies on the other side of silence" (p. 207).

But perhaps the most illuminating comparison may be made between *Jane Eyre* and *Bleak House*, for the latter, though one novel, has two narratives. The first narrative, in the conventional third person, connects for us at the outset the world of London and Chancery with the world of Fashion. The thick fog of the end of Michaelmas Term covers both: it reaches from the bored Lady Dedlock to the corrupted ground of a neglected city churchyard. Although no one can penetrate the fog of Chancery and no one can connect the ramifications of the great case of Jarndyce and Jarndyce, yet under the fog and darkness connections are constantly made. The impersonal narrator asks:

> What connexion can there be, between the place in Lincoln-shire, the house in town, . . . and the whereabouts of Jo the outlaw with the broom, who had that distant ray of light upon him when he swept the churchyard steps? What connexion can there have been between many people in the innumerable histories of this world, who, from opposite sides of great gulfs, have nevertheless been very curiously brought together? (p. 202).

And in his narrative such questions are answered. Jo the crossing-sweeper brings a mysterious lady to see the grave of the nameless law-writer whose hand Lady Dedlock has recognized. Lady Dedlock and the dead man are brought together across great gulfs by the curiosity of Tulkinghorn, the lawyer. And Esther Summerson is connected with

Lady Dedlock by the curiosity of Mr. Guppy, the sentimental clerk with the authoritarian parent. Even Grandfather Smallweed connects Esther with Lady Dedlock in his curious association with The Reverend and Mrs. Chadband.

The second narrative, that of Esther Summerson, is in the first person, and it opens with the assertion: "I know I am not clever" (p. 13). The connections made in the third-person narrative are incomprehensible to Esther. She cannot understand the stigma which is her aunt's sole contribution to her education: "Your mother, Esther, was your disgrace, and you are hers" (p. 16). She is the subject of investigations and concealments described in the third-person narrative, but she is apart from them. But though she is not clever, Esther is good, and by her direct, inarticulate humanity she crosses some gulfs. When Mrs. Pardgiggle's bristling inquisition succeeds only in setting up an "iron barrier" between her message of grace and the poor brickmakers of St. Albans, Esther, weeping compassion, shares the sorrows of Jenny, the mistreated mother. When Jo the crossing-sweeper comes in his sickness to the brickmakers', having been "moved on" and "chivvied" by Inspector Bucket, Mr. Chadband, Mrs. Snagsby, and other seekers of connection, Esther cannot know that he is surprised and frightened by her because she resembles the lady he has taken to see the "berryin ground." But she can take Jo to Bleak House and give him medicine and care. She risks disease, as that believer in the harmonious fitness of things, Harold Skimpole, will not. And from Charley, her maid, who nurses Jo and whom she in turn nurses, Esther takes the fever. Its effects change her face.

The judicious reader, if he will, may see Esther's disease and disfigurement as an illustration of a large theme first adumbrated in *Dombey and Son*. There, in a solemn declamation on the origin of evil, Dickens proposes an analogy: "men of science," he says, report that from the "polluted air" of the slums of cities there rise "noxious particles" which if they were visible would appear "lowering in a dense black cloud . . . and rolling slowly on to corrupt the better portions of a town." "But," says the prophetic voice, "if the moral pestilence that rises with them, and in the eternal laws of outraged Nature, is inseparable from them, could be made discernible too, how terrible the revelation! Then we should see depravity, impiety, drunkenness, theft, murder, and a long train of nameless sins against the natural affections and repulsions of mankind, . . . creeping on, to blight the innocent and spread contagion among the pure" (pp. 600–601). Esther's fever of course has its origin in the "polluted air" of the worst part of the city; though the "noxious particles" of its "corruption" are invisible, we can trace their movement. Jo has come from Tom-all-Alone's, the decaying property at issue in the great Chancery suit. And Jo has also come from the pestilential churchyard where Esther's nameless father is buried. The course of the physical pestilence, from the churchyard to Jo to Charley to Esther, is clear. But the "moral pestilence," the "creeping on" of literally "nameless sins" that "blight the innocent," is not so easily discernible. Perhaps the apt illustration is the dwindling away of Richard Carstone, who succumbs to the wasting fever of Chancery. But the causes of Richard's corruption are described in the third-person narrative; only its piteous effects are wept over by Esther. And the blight of Richard of course involves no typhoid or cholera literally rising from the wastelands of the city.

There is no necessity, it is true, that the theme announced in *Dombey* should be expressed in *Bleak House*. Yet to notice its partial appositeness to the account of Esther's illness is to notice also how removed she is from even the connections and inseparabilities decreed by "outraged Nature." In her illness Esther becomes temporarily blind, and if we read her distress as the outcome of the moral stigma announced by her aunt we shall be puzzled by its aftermath. For the fever so transforms her face that no one henceforth can connect her with Lady Dedlock. Indeed, after her illness, Esther meets her long-lost mother at Chesney Wold, and it is difficult to imagine a more self-effacing response to Lady Dedlock's revelation: Esther says, "I felt, through all my tumult of emotion, a burst of gratitude to the providence of God that I was so changed as that I could never disgrace her by any trace of likeness; so that nobody could ever now look at me, and look at her, and remotely think of any near tie between us" (p. 467). Esther's world is impenetrable to those who look for "ties" near or remote. Next day, after thinking in vain upon the story her mother has told—"I could not disentangle all that was about me"—Esther meets her friend and fellow-ward, Ada, for the first time since her transformation. "Ah, my angel girl! the old dear look, all love, all kindness, all affection. Nothing else in it—no, nothing, nothing!" (p. 474). Esther is safe in her world of goodness and affection.

Between the narrative of Esther and the narrative in which Krook, the parody of the Lord Chancellor, spontaneously combusts in his rag-and-bottle shop surrounded by secrets he cannot decipher, the gulf is greater than can be bridged by any connection. Dickens has cast

Esther's narrative in the past tense; the third-person narrative is all in the present tense. Krook's charred remains are discovered before our eyes; the savor of his decomposition presently fills the neighborhood and mingles with the fog. Esther, moreover, as an independent narrator, is never a character in the impersonal narrative: she appears there but once and by report only, when Jo on his deathbed tells Mr. Snagsby that "the lady as wos and yit as warn't the t'other lady" has come to visit him (p. 593). Mr. Jarndyce, who alone rivals Esther in goodness, also appears but once in the third-person narrative, again virtually by report and at Jo's deathbed. Skimpole, the Pardiggles and Jellybys—all the grotesques of charity and goodwill—appear only in Esther's narrative. She never meets Sir Leicester Dedlock, though early in her narrative she innocently encounters Krook, and near the end she is puzzled to see Grandfather Smallweed. It is perhaps irrelevant to systematize the division of roles between the two narratives, and Dickens occasionally attributes to Esther an observation inappropriate for her.[6] But it is as clear as grammar and structure can make it that the voice of the impersonal narrator cannot appear in Esther's narrative, and the converse, I think, holds as well.

The difference between the two narratives is most nearly removed in the episode of Lady Dedlock's flight. Threatened by Tulkinghorn, who knows her secret, Lady Dedlock disappears. The search for her is conducted by Inspector Bucket, who, along with Alan Woodcourt, the doctor, seems to be the new social mind capable of any connection. The search is narrated by Esther, to whom the pausing and speeding, the dashing out of London and the doubling back, are bewildering. The pursuit ends at the entrance to the churchyard: "a dreadful spot in which the night was very slowly stirring; but where I could see heaps of dishonoured graves and stones, hemmed in by filthy houses, with a few dull lights in their windows, and on these walls a thick humidity broke out like a disease." Here are the pestilential darkness and miasma kept constantly before us in the third-person narrative. And here too, we may expect, is the gradual lifting of the night, that clearing of the prospect, in which Esther takes pleasure as her first morning dawns at Bleak House. Here, if anywhere, in the faintly stirring night, and before her father's grave, Esther will make the great connection. For at the entrance to the cemetery, "drenched in the fearful wet of such a place," is a woman lying. "I saw before me, lying on the step, the mother of the dead child. She lay there, with one arm around a bar of the iron gate, and seeming to embrace it." Esther thinks the woman is

Jenny, the poor brickmaker's wife whose dead child she covered with her own handkerchief. Bucket tries to suggest to her another connection; he tells her that Lady Dedlock changed clothes with Jenny, and that Jenny went on to mislead the pursuers. But Esther cannot understand him: "They changed clothes at the cottage. I could repeat the words in my mind, and I knew what they meant of themselves; but I attached no meaning to them in any other connexion." She sees Woodcourt restrain Bucket, a look of compassion on his face. "But my understanding for all this was gone." She has seen "a distressed, unsheltered, senseless creature," and goes to her. "I passed on to the gate, and stooped down. I lifted the heavy head, put the long dank hair aside, and turned the face. And it was my mother cold and dead" (pp. 746–47). Esther, at last, has seen everything.

But just here is the end of Chapter 59 of *Bleak House*. Chapter 60 begins, "I proceed to other passages of my narrative." And after a sentence or two about the consolation "from the goodness all about me," Esther moves on to the account of her own little Bleak House in the north with Alan Woodcourt, to the hilarious collapse of the great lawsuit, to the sad exit of Richard Carstone, and to the last delicious assurance: "I know that my dearest little pets are very pretty, and that my darling is very beautiful, and that my husband is very handsome, and that my guardian has the brightest and most benevolent face that was ever seen; and that they can very well do without much beauty in me— even supposing—" Some readers may wince at so rosy a sunset, but it is the proper last word for Esther.

For it is as clear as the blank space of a chapter division that the great connection is not to be made in her gentle language. As she approaches the figure on the step, her terms are consistent: "my understanding for all this was gone"; "I could repeat the words in my mind . . . but I attached no meaning to them in any other connexion." She not only cannot understand the change of clothes and the erratic journey through the night; there are also no words in her narrative to express the meaning of her final discovery. It may be that Esther is herself in a sense "the dead child" and that her recognition of the fallen woman as "the mother of the dead child" is some very fine writing indeed. Yet to say so is to insist by her symbolic death upon the remoteness of Esther from the ties that would bind the severed halves of this enormous book. The two narratives are as separate as their grammar, and if the separation is a flaw, it seems to me a flaw which only a great writer could have committed. It is sometimes a sign of genius not to follow ideas to their conclusions, not to bring them all into harmony,[7] and the genius of Dickens here is his recognition that while two narratives are necessary they are not combinable. The voice that would articulate both is far on the other side of silence.

The sermon on moral and physical pestilence in *Dombey and Son* is concluded by an apostrophe: "Oh for a good spirit who would take the housetops off . . . and show a Christian people what dark shapes issue from admidst their homes . . . For only one night's view of the pale phantoms rising . . . from the thick and sullen air where Vice and Fever propagate together, raining down tremendous social retributions. . . . Bright and blest the morning that should rise on such a night . . ." (p. 601). However angelic she may be, Esther Summerson has no such dimensions as these. The "bright, blest morning" rises on her own night, not on that of all London and all society. The reader may know in the critical scene that the humid graveyard contains both her father and her mother, but he will have to strain a little to see that Vice and Fever have rained down their retribution here. Lady Dedlock dies of exposure, but whether in necessary compensation for the sins of her youth or in pathetic wastefulness of innocence, we do not know. We know only that Esther is good, is kind, and runs to the figure on the stones precisely because she does not understand. She does not know the world in terms of poverty or vice or degradation; she knows, what the Mrs. Pardiggles and Lord Chancellors do not, only Jenny, the mother of the dead child.

The goodness of this "I" cannot engulf the world of *Bleak House;* it cannot dissipate the fog or dry up the pestilence of the city. On the one hand, spontaneous combustion: the evils of society will explode of themselves if no Angel comes to expose them. This is no doubt a naïve faith, and certainly Dickens has his troubles with it. But on the other hand, goodness, sympathy, love, affection, the satisfactions of the private vision. It is their staying on the other hand that is so impressive here. Though he may have hoped for the self-destruction of the institutions he condemned, Dickens was neither so foolish nor so cruel as to conceive of the end of the world in a blood-bath of love and kindness. The voice of "outraged Nature" or of the spirit above the housetops must speak in tones louder than those of a not very clever "I." In *Bleak House* Dickens rejected the ruthless shape of fantasy for the unpoetic compromise of two parallel and unmeeting narrative lines. It would require the style of Henry James and a heroine as loftily placed as Milly Theale to bring them together. But this is another and a longer story.

NOTES

1. *Jane Eyre*, p. 89. The page numbers cited are those of the Modern Library (1950) reprint; for other works the page numbers cited are as follows: W. M. Thackeray, *Vanity Fair*, Modern Library (1950) reprint; George Eliot, *Middlemarch*, The World's Classics (1947) reprint; Thomas Hardy, *Jude the Obscure*, Modern Library (1923) reprint; Charles Dickens, *Bleak House*, Everyman's Library (1954) reprint; Henry James, *The Wings of the Dove*, Modern Library (1937) reprint; Charles Dickens, *Dombey and Son*, Everyman's Library (1946) reprint; Jane Austen, *Emma*, The World's Classics (1950) reprint.
2. *The Works of Thomas Hill Green*, ed. R. L. Nettleship (3 vols., London, 1911), III, 37, 38. The essay is entitled "An Estimate of the Value and Influence of Works of Fiction in Modern Times."
3. *Ibid.*, pp. 38, 39.
4. See Richard Chase, "The Brontës: A Centennial Observance," *Kenyon Review*, IX (1947), 495; reprinted in William Van O'Connor, Forms of Modern Fiction (Minneapolis, 1948), p. 108.
5. This is Rochester's version (p. 486). St. John says that in Jane he "recognized a soul that revelled in the flame and excitement of sacrifice" (p. 439).
6. Cf. Edgar Johnson, *Charles Dickens: His Tragedy and Triumph* (2 vols., New York, 1952), II, 766–67.
7. As observed in a comment on the difference between Engels and Marx: "Marx as Writer," *The* [London] *Times Literary Supplement*, 8 September 1950, p. 558.

MICHEL BUTOR

Thoughts on the Novel: The Individual & the Group

It is often suggested that the novel, in the modern post-Cervantes sense of the word, differs from the epic in that the latter relates the adventures of a group, the former those of an individual. But since Balzac, at any rate, it has become evident that the novel in its higher forms aspires to override this distinction, and to relate through the medium of individual adventures the movement of an entire society, of which it is itself only a detail, a significant point; for the totality which we call society, properly understood, consists not only of men but of all sorts of material and cultural objects. I should like therefore to try and elucidate not only the relation between the individual and the group within the novelist's story, but correlatively the effect of his work on such relations within the social setting in which it appears.

The medieval epic, the *chanson de geste*, belongs to a society of the old régime, strongly and clearly hierarchised with its feudal nobility. Within the body of individuals composing it there exists a clearly defined section, evident to all and known by all, which wields authority. Those who are not members of this group are "obscure," known only to their close acquaintance, whereas the noble is recognised and respected as such by everyone in his own country and neighbouring countries. The noble's authority rests on his fame; he is that part of our province which is well known to the outside world, and through which, therefore, people of other lands are made aware of our presence. Without him we should relapse into obscurity and be of no account. We should then be forced to belong to a different noble, to join up with another province; we should no longer be able to distinguish ourselves from it.

From *Encounter*, Vol. xx, No. 6, June 1963. Reprinted by permission of the publisher and author.

The hierarchy of the old régime is therefore not only political, it is above all semantic. Relationships of force and authority are subsidiary to a relationship of representation; the noble is the name. Of course mere force and violence cannot confer nobility. If a particularly stalwart peasant murders his young lord in some remote spot, he is not therefore acknowledged as the lord's successor by his fellows. His act was simply an absurd crime. In order for force to be adequately displayed it needs a setting: the field of battle (or the tournament), some setting which will allow it to become language.

In the battlefield, indeed, the warrior who strikes the hardest blows can help those around him; he will be the head of a small body which will break up if he is killed. To say that so-and-so is standing fast implies that the group of his companions is standing fast too. They will therefore be known by his name. When he speaks in his own name he is speaking in theirs too, for it is the same. There is no way of distinguishing them from the rest as a unit, save through him. Shakespeare calls Cleopatra "Egypt," the King of France "France," the Duke of Kent "Kent." In the relation between the suzerain and his vassals, the name acts as a connecting link: when people speak of the King of France, the word France refers to people and possessions, but inversely, when they speak of France's people and possessions, the word France refers to the king. It is thus quite legitimate that in such a context the history of a country should be the history of that country's kings, the story of a war the exploits of great captains.

As soon as a noble's name is uttered, we are immediately aware of all that it refers to: the land and its habitants, his liegemen, and all we know about them, immediately appear as a background against which the name stands out in full brilliance. But also, whatever stands out against such a background, whatever becomes illustrious, whatever can be identified and acquires renown promotes the segregation of the whole. The light which the individual projects on to himself is reflected on those who surround him. The difference which he proclaims is not confined to himself as an individual; it differentiates the group for the first time. The creation of a new noble implies the recognition of a new province.

Becoming thus the name of a new region, it involves everything to which it previously referred, particularly the family which it served to designate. We are still familiar with this phenomenon to-day: within a large family, to distinguish the sub-groups, the name of the nearest or best-known member is used: grandparents, uncles, aunts and cousins will ask for news of the Henrys or the Charleses, or how things are going at Madeleine's or Geneviève's. The hero who acquires renown confers his own distinction on his wife and children too. While others' families remain unknown, his becomes famous. The whole cell moves into the foreground.

Thus the whole of society is reconstructed in each man's consciousness, and in order that this may go on, it is indispensable that any display of power within a setting of nobility and truth should correspond to the giving of a name, that every good soldier should be ennobled, and moreover that the possession of a name should be counterbalanced by the possibility of displaying physical power, and *"une valeur,"* if not in war, then at least in a tournament or, as a last resort, in a duel. Failing which, it is no longer clear why these particular people should bear these names. The noble must consequently maintain the renown of his name. His life, his exploits must unceasingly foster the metaphorical bonds which connect him with what he represents.

Clearly, the role that the Epic is to play in the equilibrium of such a society is indispensable. Except in times of crisis or of glory, it keeps alive the awareness of what enabled one particular family to become the name of a whole body of people. If for too long a period the representative of a province, the duke, count or earl, has failed to get himself talked about in the neighbouring regions, the whole of his people will be forgotten too. If his vassals no longer have cause to talk of him amongst themselves, they will cease to put their trust in him, and will inevitably start looking for someone else better fitted to represent them. But when present exploits are lacking, former ones can replace them—and indeed, provided the narrator's language acquires sufficient substance and his words are well strung together in recognisable form, so much the better, for some bygone exploit (which at its time was indistinguishable from a hundred others) will become, thanks to the poet who takes it as his theme, the examplar of such exploits, the most famous, the one by which all present deeds are judged. So a family which has lost much of its glory will regain it to a considerable extent in the songs of its minstrel.

So at times when the feudal organisation is in danger of dissolution through the incapacity of certain nobles, the epic may save a whole family from the obscurity that threatens to overwhelm it, and a whole nation from the chaos and inevitable war which would follow from such a decline. The *Gerusalemme Liberata* is a last effort of genius to try and restore to noble families the lustre they were rapidly losing.

But even in Tasso's time the classic themes of the epic were no longer adequate, for they bore no relation to what, in actual fact, can make a man known or bring him power. The physical or moral qualities of an individual no longer enable him to organise a group around him in battle, because the art of war has grown so complicated. So many instruments are now interposed between the arm and the wound, that the bravest man is always at the mercy of a bullet or cannon-ball fired from afar by an invisible foe who may be an utter coward and weakling. Single combat—that central episode in the wars and *chansons de geste* of medieval times, their point of highest significance, their moment of truth—no longer has any meaning. Henceforward fighting takes place in confusion and obscurity. All the traditional exploits are out of date, and, it is no longer possible to acquire or maintain a name in this way. Nobility, with all the advantages appertaining to it, begins to appear more and more as something unjust, although perhaps necessary; the impression is gaining ground that those who are in the best places are not the best people, that their position is due only to chance, to something arbitrary which is hopefully thought of as supernatural. Now, and not before, as we know, the theory of Divine Right takes shape.

These people can no longer make us known. They are not qualified in any way to do so, and moreover we can make ourselves known without their help. The development of learning and commerce has given us an awareness of the universe and of other nations and states, which is independent of the nobility. Formerly the best way to find out something about England was to see its King. If he was rich, that meant his country was rich; if his courtiers were numerous, that meant his country was well organised, and he was properly in contact with it. All these signs which were once so clear, and in which people still believed at the time of the Field of the Cloth of Gold, are now devoid of meaning. Everyone knows that there is no longer any relation between the jewels worn by sovereigns and the resources of their nations, that if Louis XIV is surrounded by a host of courtiers it is precisely because he chooses to to do without them in his contacts with his provinces. The king, consequently, is still in authority, but he is no longer representative.

The nobles have authority, but nobody knows why. Since nobility implies no quality, it must be a quality in itself. It becomes completely closed: nobody can possibly "become" a noble, you have to be "born" one. Don Quixote finds himself confronted with a closed nobility: the world he lives in offers him no way of winning fame. The lessons he learns from the romances of chivalry can only render him ridiculous. He calls himself Don Quixote de la Mancha, but he cannot get anyone else to call him so except in mockery.

But if nobility has nothing more to say, it is because there is another language and other representative people who must be spoken of, or who can speak for themselves. If I know that the King of England is no longer representative of his country, it is because I have met sailors and drapers who seem to me to represent it far more powerfully, to whom even nobles turn to-day.

The original novel-hero, then, is someone who emerges from the obscurity of the bourgeoisie or working class and climbs the social ladder without succeeding in becoming integrated into the nobility. He consorts with them; he is soon as well known as they are, or better. He is consequently a proof of the fact that the existing hierarchy of society is only a semblance. The fundamental theme of the 18th-century novel is that of the *parvenu*, the upstart, (Le Sage, Marivaux, Fielding); the narrator tells us how he has climbed so high, how he has managed to write the book that ladies are now reading. He is really far cleverer than all the nobles who have not had to do anything to attain their rank. By his rise, he proclaims that the accepted organisation of society has another hidden within it. The Epic showed us, at times when we were doubtful of it, that society really was organised as it appeared to be. The Novel, on the contrary, discloses a secret hierarchy in opposition to the accepted one. The noble no longer represents what he claims to represent; one might even say he no longer governs what he appears to govern. Even before the upstart had succeeded *sur le plan romanesque,* in asserting his triumph as a well-bred man, a man of good society, a man speaking the fine language once peculiar to the nobility, a strange sort of novel-hero had succeeded the noble hero of former times—the criminal, surrounded by a whole counter-aristocracy revealed to us by the picaresque novel. Thus "Lazarillo de Tormès" introduced the reader into a fascinating region, close at hand, an unknown mysterious world in which everything took on a different meaning. This man is supposed to obey that man; look closer, and you'll see that it's the other way about. The nobility once combined power and light; now it possesses only an undeserved light, and power is associated with darkness. While princes parade, unknown figures moving in the shadows, almost without anyone's knowledge, wield authority and power. It is to these that one must turn if one hopes to rise in the world, but it is better, of course, to say nothing about one's association with them. Only fiction can transmit the password. Such men are capable of levelling almost miraculously those obstacles that had seemed insurmountable.

The picaresque novel reveals to its reader the innards, *les dessous et les coulisses*, of society. We all know the royal court, now indeed a closed circle but one whose magnificent pageantry is famous far and wide; here is a court in reverse, in some respects more like what a court should be (and used to be) than the existing court. Can this ragged figure passing by, whom but for my novel-reading I should never have noticed, be in fact the chief of a veritable army? Does he possess treasures hidden in caves? Is he capable of those exploits that nobles can no longer perform and can he call forth from his companions that sort of loyalty that we meet with nowhere else nowadays? In that case, is this world of night and falsehood less false than the world of daylight? Can this be the last refuge of truth, the last place where an individual's qualities can be displayed?

When the *parvenu* gains access to the world of light and language, he does so as an individual whose family ties are stretched to breaking-point—the nobles (into whose sphere he has moved without being able to become one of them) are still set apart from him by their birth; but this is inevitably accompanied by a transformation in society's awareness of itself. The *parvenu* is proud of being read by ladies, but he writes above all for other potential upstarts. He encourages them, offers them his own example, shows them how to look for the real power-relations and social groupings that underlie accepted forms. He undeceives his reader, teaches him to be wary and to conspire. He substitutes the rough, secretive teaching of the brigand for the futile lessons of chivalric romances.

The theme of the secret society is a fundamental one in the novel, particularly in the nineteenth century. The novelist then first becomes aware that his work itself, by uncovering the shady side of things, destroying appearances and revealing secrets, is going to form the nucleus of an unobtrusive group, an association between readers, that he has introduced a new, positive and effective relationship into the midst of those which he has been exposing or offering as models. The allusion to some particular character or detail will enable them to recognise each other without the knowledge of outsiders, to distinguish themselves from non-readers, from the unaware and the uninitiated. It will give rise to a certain language, a grouping of conversations and affinities. Being common property, with common references, it will reveal to them what they have in common.

With Proust, this theme assumes a particularly striking form, since it is the nobility itself (once the best-known, indeed the only well-known part of society) which takes on this aspect. The link between the name of a person and the name of a region has definitely been overstretched, and so the aristocracy has become unknown to the man in the street. It is merely a memory. But extremely clear power-relations persist within it none the less. In actual fact, the pitiable old man whom we encounter as we did the ragged beggar a short while ago, has only to speak a word to dissipate the barrier that confronts us—not only within his own closed circle, but also (thanks to snobbery, and to the fascination that bygone glory still exerts over people who are extremely powerful to-day yet uncertain of their own value) over a whole social fringe that clings to it.

The aristocracy, thus inverted, is in contact with that *monde renversé*, that secret society *par excellence*, the world of homosexuals. Already in Balzac sexual inversion served as a metaphor for that overturning of the social hierarchy which is one of the novel's key moments: Vautrin is the Napoleon of jailbirds. With Proust, Charlus, prince of that secret society which the Faubourg Saint-Germain has become, is also Morel's slave.

It is very important that the novel itself should comprise a secret. The reader must not know at the beginning how it is to end. It must bring about a change in myself; I must have learnt, by the end, something which I did not previously know, that I had not guessed, that others cannot guess without having read it, and this finds particularly clear expression, as might be expected, in such popular forms as the detective story.

We see thus that individualism in the novel is only on the surface. The rise of an individual is one of the main themes of the classical novel, but it is impossible to describe this without at the same time describing the architecture of a social group, or more exactly without transforming the picture that this social group has of its own organisation, which sooner or later transforms that structure itself. The novel is the expression of a changing society; it soon becomes the expression of a society that is conscious of change.

The novels of the eighteenth century allowed us to move from one level to another within the social edifice without any sense of disturbing its order. Since only a few upstarts succeeded in climbing out of their place, the structure as a whole remained fairly stable. But soon the changes were to become so obvious that some account had to be given of them.

So long as the nobility (even uprooted) remains distinct and well-known, the novel can be constructed around an isolated individual who emerges from his original background to climb the social ladder without overturning it. His achievement, or his story, will add another panel to society's picture of itself, completing the first. And it is clearly in the interests of the nobility, of *"le beau monde,"* to insist on the isolation of the writer, or his protagonist. It is most fascinating: a ploughman's son, or a grocer's, comes into contact with dukes, and teaches dukes about ploughmen and grocers, but on condition that ploughmen, taken as a whole, will remain ploughmen, their allegiance to the nobility unchanged. The upstart will be a member of the household, of the *salon,* if he adopts its language, if he has acquired some polish, if he has assumed the manners, the culture which is recognised as a model, if he can take people in, if his humble origin is not too obvious. And the essential originality of his nature, the fact that he is an exception, must be corrected and toned down, according to a code against whose increasingly absurd and severe laws he will soon react violently. The ploughman's son must talk not as ploughmen do, but as dukes ought to. He will soon be the only witness to their language, a witness whose purity they will seek to guard. For the dukes themselves, to show their sophistication, will vulgarise their own talk, pepper their speech with the expressions of the populace.

The divorce between the nobility and its language, of which the upstart story-teller becomes aware as he first gains access to the latter, forces him to withdraw into himself. Where style is concerned, he finds the same contradiction between apparent power and real power. The nobles force him to speak a language they themselves have abandoned; they harry him for using expressions which betray his origin, but which they themselves, on the other hand, tend increasingly to use. Underneath the professed rule of a certain form of speech can gradually be discerned its very opposite. The true power lies elsewhere, in that region from which he has risen but from which he has carefully cut himself off, a region which is not yet ready to listen to him and is still unable to read. The support of the nobility has begun to fail him; it is collapsing and it has grown increasingly suspicious. He thus finds himself isolated in the midst of a crowd that does not yet understand him, deserted by an aristocracy that refuses to understand him.

The theme of the upstart gradually climbing up the social ladder, while remaining an outsider, was to be replaced, little by little, during the 19th century, by that of the individual, noble by nature, if not by birth, whose aristocratic spirit is contrasted with the ruined aristocracy. He feels lost as he confronts an opaque crowd, that massive obscure power which has no obvious representatives. As the biography of an individual has become the very type of the novel-form, he will envisage the crowd as a huge individual, but an individual who is necessarily incomplete, since one cannot speak to him, since he cannot answer with words—not a collective man, therefore, but a collective animal, not a common consciousness but a massive unconsciousness, incapable of reasoning and of all but the most elementary emotional reactions.

In the famous description of the Battle of Waterloo in the *Chartreuse de Parme*, it is clear that heroic and illustrious deeds are no longer possible, as they were a few years earlier in the revolutionary wars. Armies are now reduced to crowds passively obeying orders the reasons for which they cannot understand. And Fabrice, the spectator, who longed to win glory, is not even capable of distinguishing their hierarchy:

> A quarter of an hour later, from something said by a hussar beside him, Fabrice gathered that one of these generals was the celebrated Marshal Ney. He could not however, guess which of the four generals was Marshal Ney. . . .

Stendhal himself admirably indicates the distance dividing contemporary warfare, a clash between passive crowds led by unseen individuals, from the wars of chivalry:

> He had begun to think himself the intimate friend of all the soldiers amongst whom he had been galloping for the last few hours. He imagined between himself and them the noble friendship of Tasso's and Ariosto's heroes. . . .

A few moments later:

> He began to weep bitterly. One by one he discarded his fine
> dreams of chivalrous and sublime friendship, like that of the
> heroes of the *Gerusalemme Liberata*. . . .

Whereas in the world of the epic, language is current from end to
end of society, each noble in his domain being able to communicate
with the humblest member, and the conversation of nobles amongst
themselves establishing an uninterrupted flow of consciousness, here the
individual, of noble spirit but lost amid the crowd, is confronted with a
catastrophic cleavage. Everyone seems to be speaking the same language, and yet communication proves impossible between the novelist
(or his hero, withdrawn into himself) and that threatening mass. These
people with whom he cannot make contact, and yet who are, as he
clearly sees, at the origin of all power and hence the subject *par excellence* of his stories, will have to be described by him as if they were
animals, and soon as if they were objects. But this tendency of the
naturalistic novel towards total externality—which is, in fact, the crisis
of the individualist novel, the moment when its inadequacy is revealed
—is presently to make the novelist utterly incomprehensible to himself.
Forced to recognise that in spite of his differences he is one of these
people, he will be consumed, as it were, by the absolute detachment
of his attitude towards them. The remoteness he intends to maintain
with regard to whatever is not himself will soon penetrate his own personality. He will be in danger of emptying himself out, in a sort of fran-
tic flight.

As for "socialist realism," it may be said to consist of a simple juxtaposition of crowd behaviour with individual adventures, without succeeding in establishing any authentic middle term between these. It
remains at the level of a false epic, in which the organic link provided
by the nobility has been abolished while nothing has been found to
take its place. Whereas its purpose is to throw light on the activity of
a human group, it merely succeeds in showing us passive masses on
the one hand, individual adventures on the other, but deprived of any
true originality with respect to the setting in which they take place.
We skip from the biography of the indispensable leader to the behaviour of the crowd, whom he controls without being able to establish
any continuity between them. The only role that this sort of literature

can play is that of upholding the established hierarchy. In spite of all its efforts it fails to justify it clearly, as the inner link is missing; so this hierarchy is forced to control it constantly, whereas in the epic such control was quite unnecessary. The novelist of socialist realism is thus always, despite his good intentions, an individual lost in an alien crowd whose rulers mistrust him; the very fact that he consents to be controlled shows that he is aware of the maladjustment. The literature of socialist realism is a degraded epic, which has adopted certain methods from the novel but which is still awaiting its *Don Quixote*. Only a profound renewal of the structure of narrative can enable so grave a contradiction to be overcome, can consequently enable the novel to play, in those countries where socialist realism is current to-day, its true role as an advance guard of consciousness, to display its basic progressive activity. It is evident that all the great works of the past will give us precious suggestions in this quest.

It is essential that the story should grasp society as a whole, not from outside, like a crowd scanned from the point of view of an isolated individual, but from within, like something to which one belongs, and from which individuals, however original and outstanding they may be, will never be able to detach themselves completely.

All speech is primarily a dialogue, that is to say it cannot be the expression of an isolated individual. Any utterance implies a first and a second person. I am aware of what people are saying to each other before I know who they are, and the two poles confronting one another define themselves correlatively for me. The society to which I belong is a whole in which anyone can speak to anyone else, but this whole is divided up and organised into sub-sections. I don't speak to every member of it in the same way; there are certain words that some people don't know and won't understand, certain allusions, references, suggestions which will only function for others, those in particular who have read the same books as myself. It is thus that the existence of a novel will automatically determine a group of possible dialogues, its characters, its events being so many references and examples put at the disposal of those who have read it, directly or indirectly (*i.e.*, through reading a summary of it, hearing it spoken of, etc. . . .). It is easy to see that the "language" of an individual will be strictly determined by the different groups to which he belongs within society, and that the elements of diverse origin will be able to organise themselves and unite in original ways, sometimes so original that he may himself become his only possible interlocutor. If he fails to break down this wall, then his language will dissolve into its elements, or destroy the isolated individual through madness or suicide. But if, on the contrary, he succeeds in making himself understood, it is because the pattern of the group of which he is a characteristic example has become increasingly common; the synthesis or the invention which is realised through him is valid for others beside himself; it will gather together homologous individuals amongst whom he will institute a mode of communication, to whom he will give strength; it will organise an original group which can effect a profound transformation of the whole aspect of society and the whole of its language.

In the same way that on beginning geometry one considers lines as being made up of points, and that one is soon forced to reverse the process and to define a point as the intersection of two lines, so the novelist begins by imagining a group as the sum of its individuals, until the time when he is forced to admit that an individual can only be defined as the meeting-point between several groups.

If I begin a story by declaring that so-and-so is a ploughman's son, the two characters only appear to me in their relation to one another, and in their common situation within a social whole to which I myself belong, so huge that it has to be defined in space or in time. If I add that he is fair-haired, it is because he is thereby distinguished from other ploughmen's sons, or at least from other members of the whole group, and because this distinction is somehow important, since in the setting of my story it is either an advantage or a disadvantage to be fair-haired; if I say he was tall, it means taller than other people, or taller than ourselves, etc. . . . .

Individualism in the novel is only an illusion, but an illusion which has had grave consequences on the theory of the novel, and which we need to counteract to-day.

Let us go back to our earlier example: an 18th-century *parvenu*, whose father was a ploughman and who will end by consorting with a duke. Once he has reached the top, the words ploughman and duke still retain roughly the same meaning, the distance between the two conditions is still roughly the same. The hierarchy thus appears as an invariable factor, in relation to which the individual's position changes, while his personality is gradually enriched. But if we look closer we see that this invariability is merely an abstraction, and that more and more, as the number of upstarts increases, we are obliged to take into account the alteration that has occurred during the course of the story in the hierarchy itself; so that what changes is not merely the position of the individual upstart but that of all three individuals who served as reference marks. Let us call them A, B, C. I shall soon find it impossible to go on as if the distance between B and C remained constant. The story will no longer be that of A going from B to C, but the transformation of the figure ABC into A'B'C'.

Very special conditions will be needed, then if we are to follow the evolution of an individual step by step, just as very special conditions are needed in order to observe the behaviour of a crowd from outside. The general case is that of the joint evolution of various individuals within a social group that is being more or less rapidly transformed.

The linear form of novel structure is consequently replaced by a polyphonic structure. The 18th-century letter-novel already showed us a clear polyphony of individual adventures. All the great novels of the 19th century were to add to this a polyphony of social backgrounds. Each character exists only in his relations to what surrounds him: people and material (or cultural) objects. The concept of a ploughman had seemed an unchanging one; I can no longer use it to characterise my hero once and for all. Moreover, either the ploughman-father is not like other ploughmen and that is why his son enjoyed advancement, or else he is like other ploughmen, and in that case all ploughmen's sons can enjoy it too provided they encounter certain people, or certain circumstances, which then themselves become characteristic. In other words, it is the upstart's career which enlightens us as to his origin, and consequently his father's personality, or anyone else's only becomes known to us in relation to his own; this naturally takes place at different stages, and the individuals are distinguished gradually, with reference to a crowd which forms the background.

What is clear, and enlightening, is the pattern, either stable or shifting, within which I can insert myself *qua* reader, at one spot or another, considering things from one point of view or another. The individual in the novel can never be completely determined; there is always an opening for me to put myself in his place, or at least take up a position in relation to him.

But if one can take up a position at different points in a pattern, this being implicit in polyphonic writing, does it not follow that the reader's journey through it can be made in several ways? It is rare for the adventures of an individual to be so outstanding in relation to other people that his biography can be written in linear fashion, following its chronological order. Surely it is more usual for individuals to evolve in relation to one another during the same period of time. If sometimes there seems an unquestionably right order in which the adventures must be related, at other times there often seem to be several equally good solutions, so that the decision to tell one thing before another may actually seem an arbitrary one. Should not the transition from linear narrative to polyphonic narrative lead us in quest of mobile forms? We know that the advance of polyphonic thought in contemporary music has led composers to face the same question.

Let us imagine a correspondence between two people. If each of them waits until the other has answered to write in his turn, the letters can naturally be set out in chronological order. But if they write more often, each sending a letter a day, answering the letter of the day before, we shall have two series crossing one another, and it will prove extremely hard to find a justification every time for giving priority to one or other of the two contemporary documents. To isolate the two series would be a poor solution, since one would lose the important sequence formed by the letters of both correspondents. The document ought therefore to be arranged so that those which were written at the same time should come before the reader's eye simultaneously, for instance A's letter on the left-hand page facing B's on the right-hand page. Then we should have a coherent *mobile* in which the reader can vary his course, reading the double pages now in the usual order left/right, now reversing that order, now reading the series of right-hand pages or left-hand ones.

If we increase the number of correspondents, what was exceptional becomes the rule, and more and more letters will be coincident or intercalated. The study of the visual properties of that material object, a book, will enable wholly new solutions to be found for such problems. It will not only open up vast new prospects for the art of the novel but will put at the disposal of each one of us instruments with which to grasp the behaviour of the groups to which we belong.

ALAIN ROBBE-GRILLET

Old "Values" and the New Novel

> Tragedy is but a means of accepting human misfortune, of subsuming human misery, and therefore of justifying it as necessary, as a kind of wisdom or purification. To reject this salvage operation and to seek out technical means not to yield treasonably to it (for nothing is more insidious than tragedy) is in our time a necessary undertaking.   ROLAND BARTHES

Two years ago, in an article entitled "A Fresh Start for Fiction," I made an effort to define the direction which might be taken by a new and as yet hesitant spirit of research in fiction. One point which I took for granted was the complete rejection of the old myths of *profondeur*, or depth of meaning in objects. The almost unanimously violent reactions of critics, the objections raised by esteemed friends proved, however, that I had proceeded much too hastily. Aside from a few persons who were themselves engaged in similar artistic, literary, or philosophic endeavors, no one was willing to concede that such a position did not lead necessarily to a denial of man himself. It became apparent, in fact, that there existed a quite tenacious fidelity to those old "myths."

That writers as different as François Mauriac and André Rousseaux should, for example, agree in denouncing the exclusive description of *surfaces* as a gratuitous mutilation of the novelist's art, as a result of blindness on the part of a young literary revolutionary caught up in some sort of sterile despair, was not after all too surprising. More unexpected, and more disturbing, was the position—identical in many re-

From *Evergreen Review*, Vol. 3, No. 9 Summer 1959, translated by Bruce Morrissette. Copyright © 1959 by Grove Press, Inc. Reprinted by permission of Grove Press, Inc. A revised version of this essay was later published by Grove Press, Inc. in *For a New Novel* by Alain Robbe-Grillet.

spects—taken by certain materialistic critics who did not hesitate to rely, in judging my programme, on certain "values" dangerously similar to the traditional values of Christianity. (And yet one could scarcely accuse this group of religious bias!) In both camps the fundamental principle was the same: an unabandonable solidarity between the human spirit and the world. Art had to play its "natural," reassuring role of mediator; and I was condemned in the name of "humanity."

Besides, they said, I was being rather naïve in claiming to deny depth of meaning; my own novels, it appeared, were only interesting, or readable, to the extent—to what extent was a matter of argument—that they expressed such depths without my realizing it.

It is obvious that there is only a rather loose parallelism between the three works I have published to date and my theoretical views on the possible future of the novel. Surely everyone will agree that a two- or three-hundred page novel must necessarily be more complex than a ten page article, and that it is always easier to point out a new path than to follow it. It does not ensue, however, that a partial—or even complete—failure in such an effort must be construed as decisive proof that the direction itself was wrong.

Finally, it must be emphasized that Humanism—Christian or otherwise—characteristically strives to reach out for and salvage *everything*, including whatever may attempt to restrict it, or to challenge it in its entirety. This salvaging of the opposition is in fact one of the mainsprings of its action.

It is not that I insist on justifying myself at any cost; I am merely trying to clarify the issues. The various positions outlined above are extremely useful for this purpose. What I am attempting here is less to refute certain arguments than to define their true import, and to state precisely how and why I must differ. Polemics are always useless; but the opportunity to engage in real dialogue should be accepted. And if dialogue is impossible, we must know the reason why. In any case we are all, I believe, sufficiently interested in these problems to warrant further open discussion.

Is there not, first of all, something faintly fraudulent about this term "humanity" that is constantly being thrown up to us? If the word is not entirely devoid of meaning, just what does it signify?

Apparently those who use it constantly, who employ it as their single criterion for praise or blame, confuse (voluntarily, perhaps) the precise and strict consideration of man in his situation in the world—the phenomena of man's existence—with a certain anthropocentric atmosphere, vague yet all-encompassing, that confers on everything its so-called "meaning," that is, that sends out through the interior of everything a more or less crafty network of feelings and thoughts. By simplifying the position of these new inquisitors, we may summarize it in two sentences. If I say, "The world is mankind," I shall always obtain absolution; but if I say, "Things are things, and man is only man," I shall be immediately judged guilty of a crime against humanity.

The crime is to state that something exists in the world which is not mankind, which makes no signs to man, which has nothing in common with him. From their viewpoint, the crime lies especially in recognizing this separation, this distance, without making any effort to transcend or to sublimate it.

Let us try another approach. How can a work of art be "inhuman," or "anti-human"? How can they, in particular, accuse a novel of turning against or away from man when it follows from page to page each of his steps, describing only what he does, what he sees, or what he imagines? And let it be made clear at once that it is not the character in the novel who is under attack from the critics. In so far as he is a "character," an individual moved by torments and passions, no one will ever accuse *him* of being inhuman, even if he should be a sadistic psychopath and a criminal—rather the contrary, many would say.

But in the novel the eye of this man comes to rest on things with a hard insistence: he sees them, but refuses to make them part of him, refuses to enter into any conniving or doubtful relationship with them, refuses to ask anything of them or to feel towards them any agreement or disagreement whatsoever. He may even, by chance, make them a support for his passion, for the line of sight that he directs at the world. But his glance limits itself to taking precise measurements; and his passion, likewise, stops at the surface of objects, without trying to penetrate them, since there is nothing inside, and without pretending to address to them the least emotional appeal, since they would not answer.

To condemn in the name of "humanity" a novel that presents such a character is to adopt the viewpoint of Humanism, which decrees that it is not enough to depict man as *there*, where he is, but commands us to proclaim that man is everywhere. Under the pretext than man can have only a subjective knowledge of the world, Humanism chooses man as the justification of everything. Like a "soul bridge" erected between man and things, the vision of Humanism is, above all, a pledge of solidarity.

In the realm of literature this solidarity is expressed mainly through the systematic search for analogies, or for analogical relationships.

Metaphor, in fact, is never an innocent figure of speech. To say that time is "capricious" or a mountain "majestic," to speak of the "heart" of the forest, of a "pitiless" sun, of a village "crouching" in the hollow of a valley is, to some extent, to furnish information about the things themselves: forms, dimensions, situations, etc. But the choice of an analogical vocabulary, however simple, always goes beyond giving an account of purely physical data; and what is added cannot be attributed to literary concerns only. The height of the mountain takes on, regardless of the writer's intention, a moral value; the heat of the sun becomes the result of an implied volition. In almost all contemporary literature these anthropomorphic analogies are reiterated too insistently, too coherently, not to be regarded as clues to a whole metaphysical system.

One must conclude that the writers who use such terminology are more or less consciously setting up a constant *rapport* between the universe and the human being who inhabits it. Thus the feelings of man are made to appear to originate one by one from his contacts with the world, and to find in the world their natural correspondences, if not their fulfillment.

Metaphor, which is supposed to express only comparison without concealed meaning, always introduces in fact a subterranean communication, a movement of sympathy—or of antipathy—which is its true *raison d'être*. As far as comparison is concerned, metaphor is nearly always useless, adding nothing new to the description. What loss would the village suffer if it were merely "situated" in the hollow of the valley? The word "crouching" gives no additional information. It does, on the other hand, transport the reader (guided by the author) into the hypothetical soul of the village. If I accept the word "crouching" I am no longer merely a spectator; I become myself the village (for the duration of the phrase), and the hollow of the valley functions as a sort of pit in which I seek refuge.

Taking these adhesive possibilities of the metaphor as their stronghold, the defenders of metaphor will reply that it thus possesses the advantage of bringing out an element not previously felt. Becoming the village—they say—the reader will project himself into the situation of the village, and therefore understand it better. Similarly for the mountain: I will depict it better, they claim, by stating that it is majestic than by measuring the angle at which my sight must be lifted to judge its height. . . . And this is sometimes true; but such procedure always implies a more serious counterpart. It is precisely this participation that is dangerous, because it leads directly to the idea of a hidden unity.

In truth, one must add, this additional benefit in descriptive value is only an excuse: the true practitioners of the metaphor aim only at the idea of a non-descriptive communication. If they lacked the verb "crouch" they would not even mention the position of the village. The heights of the mountain would mean nothing to them if it did not offer the moral spectacle of "majesty." . . .

Everything is contaminated. Above all the novel, which is the primary domain in our days of the tragic spirit. From women in love who become nuns to policemen who become gangsters, including along the way tormented criminals, prostitutes with pure souls, righteous men constrained by their conscience to commit injustices, sadists motivated by love, lunatics led by logic, the typical "character" of the novel must be, above all else, a *double* being. The plot will be "human" to the degree that it is equivocally dual, and the whole novel will be regarded as "true" in so far as it contains contradictions.

It is easy to laugh at this; it is less easy to free oneself from the conditioning effects imposed by tragedy on our mental patterns. One can go so far as to state that rejecting the ideas of "nature" and predestination leads *directly* to tragedy. There is no significant piece of contemporary literature that does not express at the same time the affirmation of our freedom and the "tragic" principle of its abandonment.

At least two great novels, in recent decades, have presented us with two new forms of this fatal complicity, under the names of *absurdity* and *nausea*.

Albert Camus, everyone knows, has designated as *absurdity* the impassable abyss that stands between man and the world, between the aspirations of the human spirit and the incapacity of the world to satisfy them. The "absurd" is therefore, for him, neither in man nor in things, but in the impossibility of establishing between the two any *rapport* other than "strangeness."

Readers must have noticed, however, that the hero of *L'Etranger* (*The Stranger*) carries on with the world an obscure kind of connivance, composed of bitterness and fascination. The relationships between this and the objects around him are in no way innocent: "absurdity" constantly leads to disappointment, withdrawal, revolt. It would hardly be an exaggeration to argue that it is actually *things* that finally draw the protagonist into his criminal act: the sun, the sea, the dazzling sand, the glistening knife, the spring gushing from the rocks, the revolver. . . . And, as to be expected, the principal role, among these things, is played by Nature.

Nor is the novel written in as *neutral* or "cleansed" style as the first pages might lead us to believe. Instead, only objects already burdened with a flagrantly obvious human significance are neutralized, carefully, and for moral reasons (thus the mother's coffin, described minutely with respect to the form and depth of penetration of its screws). Together with this we discover, more and more as the moment of the murder approaches, the most revealing classical metaphors, referring directly to man, or implying his omnipresence. The countryside is "gorged with sunlight," the evening is "like a melancholy truce," the holes in the roadway reveal the "shining flesh" of the tar, the earth is "blood colored," the sunlight is a "dazzling rain," its reflection on a shell is a "sword of light," the day has "cast anchor in an ocean of boiling metal." . . . Without counting the "breathing" of the "lazy" waves, the "sleeping" promontory, the "panting" sea and the "cymbals" of the sun. . . .

The central scene of the novel is the perfect image of a painful solidarity. The implacable sun is always "the same," its reflection on the knife blade held by the Arab "touches" the hero's forehead and "grinds into" his eyes. His hand clenches the revolver; he wishes to "shake" the sun; he fires repeatedly, four times. "And it was like four sharp knocks that I had struck upon the door of misfortune."

Thus "absurdity" turns out to be a form of tragic Humanism. It is not a recognition of the separation between man and objects. It is a lovers' quarrel between them, which leads to a crime of passion. The world is accused of complicity in murder.

When Sartre writes (in his *Explication de L'Étranger*) that the Stranger "refuses anthropomorphism," he gives us, as proved by the above citations, an incomplete view of the work. Sartre has certainly noticed these passages, but prefers to think that Camus, "unfaithful to his principles, is creating poetry." Could one not say, rather, that these metaphors are the real "explication" of the novel? Camus does not refuse anthropomorphism, but uses it with great economy and subtlety, in order to give it greater weight.

All of which fits into the pattern, since the real object is, as Sartre admits, to show us (in Pascal's words) "the natural misery of our condition." . . .

LESLIE FIEDLER

The End of the Novel

And what is there for Burroughs to do with the novel in his present future, his anticipation of non-human times? Nothing, of course, but to destroy it; or rather, to make clear that it has already destroyed itself; for it is a form which realized itself in the mid-eighteenth century, precisely at the moment that men become conscious of their unconscious minds and resolved to redeem them. And it is hard to see how it can outlive the faith of the first novelists in the power of reason to know even the irrational. There are various ways to declare the death of the novel: to mock it while seeming to emulate it, like Nabokov, or John Barth; to reify it into a collection of objects like Robbe-Grillet; or to *explode* it, like William Burroughs, to leave only twisted fragments of experience and the miasma of death. The latter seems, alas, the American way; and it is certainly the way which has haunted Burroughs, whose recent work has been impregnated with the image of the Nova, the flare-up of an exploding planet, which blends into, on the one hand, the glare and terror of the atom bomb, and, on the other, the spatter and release of orgasm. "A new mythology," Burroughs comments, explaining this very image like the good sciencefictionist he is, "is possible in the space age."

But what form will emerge to embody that mythology? Surely nothing Burroughs himself has been able to contrive; for since he has been thrown back on his own largely mechanical and magical devices; since, that is to say, Ginsberg last put the semblance of a book together for him, he has seemed repetitious, dull, and long-winded. The nausea of the end has an intrinsic appeal as strong as that of pornography itself; but for a long time Burroughs has lived simply on the basis of that appeal. Only the belated discovery of his early work has given him now the reputation of a new and currently rewarding writer.

Perhaps, though, we do not have to believe Burroughs, who has a special stake in declaring the end of everything. Perhaps, after all, the novel still flourishes in the United States in forms too conventional to be noticed by those determined to pretend that we have still, or at last, an avant-garde. Are not many of our recent novels major efforts by major or immensely promising writers? Do we not have big books by James Baldwin and Philip Roth, Bernard Malamud, Robert Penn Warren and Mary McCarthy? Was there not a last book from Faulkner, as well as another by Nabokov, and even the twenty-years-promised-and-delayed magnum opus of Katherine Anne Porter? Indeed, in prospect, even those who know that fewer and fewer people buy novels these days, and who for a long time have had a prevision of the year in which every adult in the United States would write a novel which no one else would read—even such professional ironists have not been able to prevent a tremor of excitement from unsettling their tranquil sense of doom.

But how every one of these books (except the anti-novel of Nabokov) cheated our hopes: the Malamud slight and inconclusive; the Roth morally obtuse and ill-organized; the Baldwin shrill and unconvincing; the McCarthy intolerably "female" in the worst sense; the Porter appallingly obvious and dull. Surely there has never been so large a cluster of egregious flops in the span of a couple of years; and surely it is not merely that, for quite different reasons unconnected with each other or with the general cultural situation, so large a number of promising writers have betrayed not only their extravagant promises but even our quite modest expectations. Is there no relationship at all between so general a failure and the fact, reported by publishers and known to every writer, that at the moment, in our country of 180,000,000 people, a good first novel, prominently and favorably reviewed, may sell as few as 600 copies?

Yet any suggestion that the novel, after its brief two hundred years of existence, may be about to disappear, in the United States at least, lose its pre-eminence, its status as the reigning literary genre, is greeted by howls of dismay and hoots of contempt. Such predictions are received not with the pious lack of interest or mild concern common to literary statements, but with the sort of agitation more appropriate to a surmise that the United States may be approaching its final days as a significant power, or that the Church of Rome has outlived its last accommodation. To many earnest types I meet and read, forecasts of the death of the novel seem even *more* unnerving than comments on the death of the Republic or of God, the end of the family, or the overthrow of the male sex.

This must be, it occurs to me, because we cannot imagine anything after the novel that is still literature, cannot conceive of an alternative form which will provide all the satisfactions of the novel, including the exercise of those prestigeful skills we call "reading." Such a failure does not, I think, reflect the weakness of our imaginations, but rather our appreciation of the fact that the novel is the last narrative art-form invented, or capable of being invented, for *literates*. Beyond it, we sense, lie only those forms to which we who read cannot help condescending a little: comic books, movies, television, etc. Most of us find it personally upsetting to confess, even to ourselves, that the reigning narrative art of the not-so-distant future may well be one appropriate to a post-literate culture; and this despite our realization that it becomes more and more difficult to write what most people mean when they say a "book," a recognizable novel.

Still, we tell ourselves, there will always be the novels which have survived; even if no one ever writes another *Moby Dick*, someone will be around to read the first one. And surely it will have been preserved to be read by an interested élite, however marginal literacy may become. That novels like *Moby Dick* will survive, I cannot doubt; and it pleases me to envision a tiny few gathering in that world, perhaps half-secretly, to discuss with each other the remaining great books, the reading of which has become an art as learned and abstruse, and suspect, as deciphering hieroglyphics. Meanwhile everyone else will be acquiring only the simple skills required to follow the pidgin used in the subtitles of foreign movies or to consult the schedule of the day's television programs.

If the novel disappears, then, it will have disappeared for two quite different reasons: First because the artistic faith that sustained its writers is dead, and second because the audience-need it was invented to satisfy is being better satisfied otherwise. From the consumer's point of view, the novel came into existence at the paradoxical insistence of a hitherto illiterate middle-class audience that everyone be given the skills necessary for deciphering words on a page, and yet that no one be required to practice those skills against his will. The demand for the extension of literacy and the reservation of the right to reject literacy were thus bound up together from the first, and no literary form extant at the moment of their formulation seemed capable of satisfying both at once. What history required (and what those who stood in its vanguard were willing to pay for) was a new genre which made possible symbolic, or perhaps better, demonstration literacy. This represents a typical demand and a typical solution of the modern world, of mass industrial society, which has gone on to demand and get, along similar lines, demonstration trials (the Reichstag trial, the Moscow trials) and demonstration voting—either in the form of the two-party choice, much admired in the democracies, or of the single-party-plebiscite favored in totalitarian regimes.

From any traditional point of view, then, from the standpoint, say, of those still pledged in the eighteenth century to writing epics in verse, the novel seemed already anti-literature, even post-literature; that is, it appeared then precisely what we take television or comic books to be now. In the jargon of our own day, the novel represents the beginnings of popular culture, of that machine-made, mass-produced, mass-distributed *ersatz* which, unlike either traditional high art or folk art, *does not know its place;* since, while pretending to meet the formal standards of literature, it is actually engaged in smuggling into the republic of letters extra-literary satisfactions. It not merely instructs and delights and moves, but also embodies the myths of a society, serves as the scriptures of an underground religion; and these latter functions, unlike the former ones, depend not at all on any particular form, but can be indifferently discharged by stained-glass windows, comic strips, ballads, and movies.

Yet it is precisely this cultural *ambiguity* of the novel which made it for so long so popular on so many levels, at the same time creating those tensions and contradictions by virtue of which it is presently dying. From the first, there have been, certainly, two kinds of novel, not always clearly distinguished from each other (sometimes because of the blessed un-self-consciousness of their writers; sometimes because of their deviousness): the bestseller, ill-written and scriptural, and at home in the world of mass culture; and the art novel, a hybrid form into which men of talent and the highest ambitions have poured certain insights and perceptions no longer viable in traditional forms—including basic criticisms of mass culture itself. It is for this reason that the serious artist has had to *fight* for the attention of the audience which invented the genre he exploits and resents his attempt to use that genre against its own values and aspirations. But in modern times there has been no other audience.

The serious novelist has, then, tended simultaneously to woo and to war on the bourgeois world; which in turn has both wooed and warred on him by adapting to its own uses (i.e., by turning into stereotypes) the very devices he has used to mock it. Pornography, horror, the merciless documentation of the sordid which we call "naturalism," even the attack on mass culture itself, have been assimilated into mass culture; just as the favorite refuges of the artist, his bohemias and places of exile, have been transformed into tourist attractions; and his very vices, from tobacco to marijuana, have become country-club diversions.

The only unredeemable offense against middlebrow culture in the power of the novelist is to consider his work as absolute art: a form which aspires to the condition of poetry, and which refuses the weary reader any possibility of forgetting that he is reading *words,* dealing not with archetypes only, but with nuances of language, and the strategies of form. The perpetrators of that ultimate offense have already been immortalized in scandal; and the names of Proust, Mann, Joyce, and Kafka, for instance, stir still in some quarters the uneasy grimace and the embarrassed snicker. In the United States, however, there has never been an unequivocal avant-gardist among the novelists of first rank. What experimentalism there has been in our fiction has been imported and, at the moment of importation, accommodated to middlebrow demands. Think, for instance, of how the example of Joyce's *Portrait of the Artist as a Young Man* is modified in Thomas Wolfe's *Look Homeward, Angel.*

As early as the twenties, certain of our writers had learned from the example of the European avant-garde simply to do otherwise: Scott Fitzgerald, for instance, Glenway Wescott and, after a brief period of indecision, Kay Boyle. Others took longer to accommodate themselves, like Katherine Anne Porter, who only in the past few years has clearly exposed herself as having gone over to ladies'-magazine fiction; while Hemingway's and Faulkner's final apostasy to art is revealed only in their last works, and, especially, in the works of their followers. There is, in the American grain, an implicit anti-intellectualism, a contempt for mere art (of which Mark Twain is a chief source) which threatens always to turn our writers against their fellows and to deliver them into the hands of their enemies. However, so long as the counter-tendency to avant-gardism ran strong in the Western world in general, this native

American know-nothingism cast a valuable counterbalance, protecting our novelists against becoming academicians of the new.

There is now, however, nothing to stem a world-wide drift toward middlebrow art except the sterile and academic nostalgia for yesterday's avant-garde on the part of such European writers as Alain Robbe-Grillet. Everywhere else there are signs of a great revolt against the aspirations of the novel to art, a turning on the part of novelists themselves—without outside pressure—toward the mass audience. Included in this great middlebrow revolt are writers as different from each other as Yael Dayan in Israel, Françoise Sagan in France, Kingsley Amis and John Wain in England; and in America, Jack Kerouac, J. D. Salinger, Truman Capote, Herbert Gold, Vance Bourjaily, perhaps even Philip Roth.

Some of these writers, in America, at least, are harder to recognize as Philistines than, say, Irwin Shaw or James Gould Cozzens because, to begin with, they are younger, and because there attaches to them, for one reason or another, a certain avant-garde cachet. They are likely to appear in magazines, with avant-garde pretensions or an avant-garde past (the *Evergreen Review,* for instance, or *Partisan Review*); and they may even lead lives more like those once led by avant-garde artists than by most of the readers to whom they actually appeal. Moreover, they have failed to develop a new or notable Philistine style, writing, whether ill or well, in manners associated not so long ago with experimental writers of the first rank. And finally, they may not even know they write for the great audience, since, in fact, they often don't get its attention. Certain writers of the school of Saul Bellow (not including Bellow himself), Herbert Gold, for instance, could in this regard cry out in all truth, "How can I be as bad as the critics say I am, when I'm not even popular?"

The disconcerting fact suggested by such cases is this: at the moment when a considerable wave of semi-serious writers find themselves, deliberately or not, wooing the mass audience for the novel, that audience has begun to detach itself from the novel completely. After all, what does the largest sub-literate public need fiction for? What documentary realism once promised to give them in novel form, non-fiction provides more efficiently, more painlessly. And the mythical reassurances they have long sought in books (boy gets girl, good man kills bad, etc.) the non-literary arts of television and film provide more vividly and at less intellectual cost. At the same moment, those non-literary arts satisfy more fully, less hypocritically than the hybrid novel form ever could, the revulsion of the great audience from the very act of reading, their half-secret, shamefaced hatred of the literacy which once they had found it politically expedient to demand.

In the end, what the neo-middlebrow movements succeed in doing is not (as some exponents of that movement may fondly hope) to raise the level of the mass audience, but to substitute, for the former élite, a pseudo-élite conditioned to *kitsch*, corn, and self-congratulation. The rejection of literacy by the mass audience and the betrayal of standards by the semi-artist combine with the onslaught against the novel form by the exponents of the alteration of consciousness to doom that genre, or at least to make the possibility of that doom a leading item on the agenda of contemporary criticism. I, myself, though I practice the art of the novel ironically and desperately in a world which provides me no assurances about the nature, or even existence, of such an audience as I dream, am inclined to believe that the history of the genre is approaching its end.

I do not mean, of course, that I have lost faith in the survival of the art of fiction, for I cannot conceive a human situation in which stories are not somehow told, and I do not myself foresee the end of man. Perhaps narrative will not continue much longer to be entrusted to print and bound between hard covers. But this does not especially dismay me, since I have no special affection for the novel as such: that fat, solid commodity invented by the bourgeoisie for the ends of commerce and culture-climbing. There is always the screen, if the page proves no longer viable: the neighborhood movie, the drive-in, or the parlor television set. And I presume that if cinema eventually becomes a lost art, too, there will be some of us scratching pictographs on the walls of caves, or telling each other stories over bonfires made of the last historical romance hailed as the novel of the year in the last book review section of the last *New York Times*.

TECHNIQUE

In his *Poetics*, Aristotle claimed that literature satisfies two needs deeply rooted in human nature. An instinct for imitation makes us delight in the correspondences between literature and outside reality, and an instinct for harmony or order makes us delight in the internal correspondences established among all the diverse elements of a literary work. Simultaneously realistic and formalistic, literature is responsive to life itself, which in some degree it reflects, and to the demands of art that make it more than merely a reproduction of life. Even the most fantastic and abstractly formal fiction cannot dispense entirely with reality. Most of the essays in the previous section, in fact, stress the dependence of the novel on external social and economic conditions. On the other hand, even the most realistic fiction inevitably interprets and transforms reality. The essays in this section, therefore, focus on this transformative process, stressing technique as the literary middle-man between life and art.

Technique, however, is a somewhat indeterminate category which may refer to specific means of rendering experience in fiction, such as point of view, dramatization, or narrative, or can expand beyond the mechanics of craft to become synonymous with fictional form itself.

In "Technique as Discovery," Mark Schorer regards technique as the over-all organizing form to which all the elements of fiction become assimilated. Technique is not a kind of polish put on the created work but an integral aspect of the creative process, not a means by which preconceived content is translated into fiction but a transforming and informing agent that unites with content in the act of expressing it. Thus until content has gone through the alembic of technique, it is not fully discovered.

Schorer's conception of the formative effect of technique on content is given at least partial confirmation by the novelist Elizabeth Bowen when she observes that the writer comes to understand his characters "in the course of the actual writing of the novel." Indeed, the whole drift of her discussion is toward the primacy of purely literary considerations in fictional creation—plot, characterization, scene, dialogue, angle, and the ways in which all of these interact. The final determinant of what goes in and what stays out is the writer's indefinable but crucial sense of relevance, which means relevance not to "life" but to the literary demands of the work itself, "the inherent poetic truth that the novel states."

In the preface to *The Nigger of the Narcissus*, Joseph Conrad said that his primary object as a writer was to enable the reader to "see" his story as though it were enacted before him. Influenced by Conrad, Henry James, and others, Percy Lubbock is concerned with how that seeing is directed by the writer's control of point of view, perhaps the most pervasive and influential of the techniques at his disposal. If the reader is to see, the author must get out of his way, which means that in what Lubbock regards as the finest fiction the author must avoid narration in favor of dramatization; he must "show," not "tell about." As this is not always possible, however, the writer may substitute for himself as narrator a character who tells the story in the first-person; or, even if he adopts the third-person point of view, he may set up his verbal camera over the shoulder of one of the characters and imperceptibly move it backwards and forwards.

Commentary (telling), which is anathema to Lubbock—an unwarranted interruption of fictional illusion by the author—is given extended consideration by Wayne Booth, who distinguishes between its reliable and unreliable uses. The section presented here from his chapter on "reliable commentary" suggests how the awkwardness of smuggling certain information to the reader in purely dramatic form—by "showing" alone—can be effectively avoided through "telling" of the right sort. In "Telling as Showing," he points out that some of the vitality of a work like *Tom Jones,* which repeatedly employs commentary by the author, may arise from the reader's interest in the author as controlling consciousness not behind but in the forefront of a novel. In fact, the evolving relationship between author and reader may constitute a kind of subplot that complements and enriches the fictional experience.

In "The Functions of Stream of Consciousness," Robert Humphrey defines a technique in which the author not only gets himself out of the reader's visual way but gets his characters' conscious minds out of the way, too. The result is a purely objective presentation of subjectivity. What has seemed to some readers an over-preoccupation with technique in the interests of art actually derives, Humphrey notes, from the writer's desire to depict life accurately. The life so depicted is simply the unconscious and preconscious levels of mind rather than the external reality more traditionally dealt with.

MARK SCHORER

Technique as Discovery

Modern criticism, through its exacting scrutiny of literary texts, has demonstrated with finality that in art beauty and truth are indivisible and one. The Keatsian overtones of these terms are mitigated and an old dilemma solved if for beauty we substitute form, and for truth, content. We may, without risk of loss, narrow them even more, and speak of technique and subject matter. Modern criticism has shown us that to speak of content as such is not to speak of art at all, but of experience; and that it is only when we speak of the *achieved* content, the form of the work of art as a work of art, that we speak as critics. The difference between content, or experience, and achieved content, or art, is technique.

When we speak of technique, then, we speak of nearly everything. For technique is the means by which the writer's experience, which is his subject matter, compels him to attend to it; technique is the only means he has of discovering, exploring, developing his subject, of conveying its meaning, and, finally, of evaluating it. And surely it follows that certain techniques are sharper tools than others, and will discover more; that the writer capable of the most exacting technical scrutiny of his subject matter will produce works with the most satisfying content, works with thickness and resonance, works which reverberate, works with maximum meaning.

We are no longer able to regard as seriously intended criticism of poetry which does not assume these generalizations; but the case for fiction has not yet been established. The novel is still read as though its content has some value in itself, as though the subject matter of fiction has greater or lesser value in itself, and as though technique were not a primary but a supplementary element, capable perhaps of not unat-

From *Hudson Review*, Vol. I, No. 1, Spring 1948. Copyright 1948 by *Hudson Review*. Reprinted by permission.

tractive embellishments upon the surface of the subject, but hardly of its essence. Or technique is thought of in blunter terms than those which one associates with poetry, as such relatively obvious matters as the arrangement of events to create a plot; or, within plot, of suspense and climax; or as the means of revealing character motivation, relationship, and development; or as the use of point of view, but point of view as some nearly arbitrary device for the heightening of dramatic interest through the narrowing or broadening of perspective upon the material, rather than as a means toward the positive definition of theme. As for the resources of language, these, somehow, we almost never think of as a part of the technique of fiction—language as used to create a certain texture and tone which in themselves state and define themes and meanings; or language, the counters of our ordinary speech, as forced, through conscious manipulation, into all those larger meanings which our ordinary speech almost never intends. Technique in fiction, all this is a way of saying, we somehow continue to regard as merely a means to organizing material which is "given" rather than as the means of exploring and defining the values in an area of experience which, for the first time *then*, are being given.

Is fiction still regarded in this odd, divided way because it is really less tractable before the critical suppositions which now seem inevitable to poetry? Let us look at some examples: two well-known novels of the past, both by writers who may be described as "primitive," although their relative innocence of technique is of a different sort—Defoe's *Moll Flanders* and Emily Brontë's *Wuthering Heights;* and three well-known novels of this century—*Tono-Bungay,* by a writer who claimed to eschew technique; *Sons and Lovers,* by a novelist who, because his ideal of subject matter ("the poetry of the immediate present") led him at last into the fallacy of spontaneous and unchangeable composition, in effect eschewed technique; and *A Portrait of the Artist as a Young Man,* by a novelist whose practice made claims for the supremacy of technique beyond those made by anyone in the past or by anyone else in this century.

Technique in fiction is, of course, all those obvious forms of it which are usually taken to be the whole of it, and many others; but for the present purposes, let it be thought of in two respects particularly: the uses to which language, as language, is put to express the quality of the experience in question; and the uses of point of view not only as a mode of dramatic delimitation, but more particularly, of thematic definition. Technique is really what T. S. Eliot means by "convention"—any selection, structure, or distortion, any form or rhythm imposed upon the world of action; by means of which—it should be added—our apprehension of the world of action is enriched or renewed. In this sense, everything is technique which is not the lump of experience itself, and one cannot properly say that a writer has no technique or that he eschews technique, for, being a writer, he cannot do so. We can speak of good and bad technique, of adequate and inadequate, of technique which serves the novel's purpose, or disserves.

II

In the prefatory remarks to *Moll Flanders*, Defoe tells us that he is not writing fiction at all, but editing the journals of a woman of notorious character, and rather to instruct us in the necessities and the joys of virtue than to please us. We do not, of course, take these professions seriously, since nothing in the conduct of the narrative indicates that virtue is either more necessary or more enjoyable than vice. On the contrary, we discover that Moll turns virtuous only after a life of vice has enabled her to do so with security; yet it is precisely for this reason that Defoe's profession of didactic purpose has interest. For the actual morality which the novel enforces is the morality of any commercial culture, the belief that virtue pays—in worldly goods. It is morality somewhat less than skin deep, having no relation to motives arising from a sense of good and evil, least of all, of evil-*in*-good, but exclusively from the presence or absence of food, drink, linen, damask, silver, and time-pieces. It is the morality of measurement, and without in the least intending it, *Moll Flanders* is our classic revelation of the mercantile mind: the morality of measurement, which Defoe has completely neglected to measure. He fails not only to evaluate this material in his announced way, but to evaluate it at all. His announced purpose is, we admit, a pious humbug, and he meant us to read the book as a series of scandalous events; and thanks to his inexhaustible pleasure in excess and exaggeration, this element in the book continues to amuse us. Long before the book has been finished, however, this element has also become an absurdity; but not half the absurdity as that which Defoe did not intend at all—the notion that Moll could live a rich and full life of crime, and yet, repenting, emerge spotless in the end. The point is, of course, that she has no moral being, nor has the book any moral life. Everything is external. Everything can be weighed, measured, handled, paid for in gold, or expiated by a prison term. To this, the whole texture of the novel testifies: the bolts of goods, the inventories, the itemized accounts, the landlady's bills, the lists, the ledgers: all this, which taken together comprises what we call Defoe's method of circumstantial realism.

He did not come upon that method by any deliberation: it represents precisely his own world of value, the importance of external circumstance to Defoe. The point of view of Moll is indistinguishable from the point of view of her creator. We discover the meaning of the novel (at unnecessary length, without economy, without emphasis, with almost none of the distortions or the advantages of art) in spite of Defoe, not because of him. Thus the book is not the true chronicle of a disreputable female, but the true allegory of an impoverished soul —the author's; not an anatomy of the criminal class, but of the middle class. And we read it as an unintended comic revelation of self and of a social mode. Because he had no adequate resources of technique to separate himself from his material, thereby to discover and to define the meanings of his material, his contribution is not to fiction but to the history of fiction, and to social history.

The situation in *Wuthering Heights* is at once somewhat the same and yet very different. Here, too, the whole novel turns upon itself, but this time to its estimable advantage; here, too, is a revelation of what is perhaps the author's secret world of value, but this time, through what may be an accident of technique, the revelation is meaningfully accomplished. Emily Brontë may merely have stumbled upon the perspectives which define the form and the theme of her book. Whether she knew from the outset, or even at the end, what she was doing, we may doubt; but what she did and did superbly we can see.

We can assume, without at all becoming involved in the author's life but merely from the tone of somnambulistic excess which is generated by the writing itself, that this world of monstrous passion, of dark and gigantic emotional and nervous energy, is for the author, or was in the first place, a world of ideal value; and that the book sets out to persuade us of the moral significance of such unmoral passion. We are, I think, expected, in the first place, to take at their own valuation these demonic beings, Heathcliff and Cathy: as special creatures, set apart from the cloddish world about them by their heightened capacity for feeling, set apart, even, from the ordinary objects of human passion as, in their transcendental, sexless relationship, they identify themselves with an uncompromising landscape and cosmic force. Yet this is absurd, as much of the detail that surrounds it ("Other dogs lurked in other recesses") is absurd. The novelist Emily Brontë had to discover these absurdities to the girl Emily; her technique had to evaluate them for what they were, so that we are persuaded that it is not Emily who is mistaken in her estimate of her characters, but they who are mistaken in their estimate of themselves. The theme of the moral magnificence of unmoral passion is an impossible theme to sustain, and what interests us is that it was device—and this time, mere, mechanical device—which taught Emily Brontë that, the needs of her temperament to the contrary, all personal longing and reverie to the contrary, perhaps—that this was indeed not at all what her material must mean as art. Technique objectifies.

To lay before us the full character of this passion, to show us how it first comes into being and then comes to dominate the world about it and the life that follows upon it, Emily Brontë gives her material a broad scope in time, lets it, in fact, cut across three generations. And to manage material which is so extensive, she must find a means of narration, points of view, which can encompass that material, and, in her somewhat crude concept of motive, justify its telling. So she chooses a foppish traveller who stumbles into this world of passionate violence, a traveller representing the thin and conventional emotional life of the far world of fashion, who wishes to hear the tale: and for her teller she chooses, almost inevitably, the old family retainer who knows everything, a character as conventional as the other, but this one representing not the conventions of fashion, but the conventions of the humblest moralism. What has happened is, first, that she has chosen as her narrative perspective those very elements, conventional emotion and conventional morality, which her hero and heroine are meant to transcend with such spectacular magnificence; and second, that she has permitted this perspective to operate throughout a long period of time, And these two elements compel the novelist to see what her unmoral passions come to. Moral magnificence? Not at all; rather, a devastating spectacle of human waste; ashes. For the time of the novel is carried on long enough to show Heathcliff at last an emptied man, burned out by his fever ragings, exhausted and will-less, his passion meaningless at last. And it goes even a little further, to Lockwood, the fop, in the graveyard, sententiously contemplating headstones. Thus in the end the triumph is all on the side of the cloddish world, which survives.

Perhaps not all on that side. For, like Densher at the end of *The Wings of the Dove*, we say, and surely Hareton and the second Cathy say, "We shall never be again as we were!" But there is more point in observing that a certain body of materials, a girl's romantic daydreams, have, through the most conventional devices of fiction, been pushed beyond their inception in fancy to their meanings, their conception as a written book—that they, that is, are not at all as they were.

III

Technique alone objectifies the materials of art; hence technique alone evaluates those materials. This is the axiom which demonstrates itself so devastatingly whenever a writer declares, under the urgent sense of the importance of his materials (whether these are autobiography, or social ideas, or personal passions)—whenever such a writer declares that he cannot linger with technical refinements. That art will not tolerate such a writer H. G. Wells handsomely proves. His enormous literary energy included no respect for the techniques of his medium, and his medium takes its revenge upon his bumptiousness. "I have never taken any very great pains about writing. I am outside the hierarchy of conscious and deliberate writers altogether. I am the absolute antithesis of Mr. James Joyce. . . . Long ago, living in close conversational proximity to Henry James, Joseph Conrad, and Mr. Ford Madox Hueffer, I escaped from under their immense artistic preoccupations by calling myself a journalist." Precisely. And he escaped—he disappeared—from literature into the annals of an era.

Yet what confidence! "Literature," Wells said, "is not jewelry, it has quite other aims than perfection, and the more one thinks of 'how it is done' the less one gets it done. These critical indulgences lead along a fatal path, away from every natural interest towards a preposterous emptiness of technical effort, a monstrous egotism of artistry, of which the later work of Henry James is the monumental warning. 'It,' the subject, the thing or the thought, has long since disappeared in these amazing works; nothing remains but the way it has been 'manipulated.' " Seldom has a literary theorist been so totally wrong; for what we learn as James grows for us and Wells disappears, is that without what he calls "manipulation," there is no "it," no "subject" in art. There is again only social history.

The virtue of the modern novelist—from James and Conrad down—is not only that he pays so much attention to his medium, but that, when he pays most, he discovers through it a new subject matter, and a greater one. Under the "immense artistic preoccupations" of James and Conrad and Joyce, the form of the novel changed, and with the technical change, analogous changes took place in substance, in point of view, in the whole conception of fiction. And the final lesson of the modern novel is that technique is not the secondary thing that it seems to Wells, some external machination, a mechanical affair, but a deep and primary operation; not only that technique *contains* intellectual and moral implications, but that it *discovers* them. For a writer like Wells, who wished to give us the intellectual and the moral history of our times, the lesson is a hard one: it tells us that the order of intellect and the order of morality do not exist at all, in art, except as they are organized in the order of art.

Wells's ambitions were very large. "Before we have done, we will have all life within the scope of the novel." But that is where life already is, within the scope of the novel; where it needs to be brought is into novels. In Wells we have all the important topics in life, but no good novels. He was not asking too much of art, or asking that it include more than it happily can; he was not asking anything of it—as art, which is all that it can give, and that is everything.

A novel like *Tono-Bungay*, generally thought to be Wells's best, is therefore instructive. "I want to tell—*myself*," says George, the hero, "and my impressions of the thing as a whole"—the thing as a whole being the collapse of traditional British institutions in the twentieth century. George "tells himself" in terms of three stages in his life which have rough equivalents in modern British social history, and this is, to be sure, a plan, a framework; but it is the framework of Wells's abstract thinking, not of his craftsmanship, and the primary demand which one makes of such a book as this, that means be discovered whereby the dimensions of the hero contain the experiences he re-counts, is never met. The novelist flounders through a series of literary imitations—from an early Dickensian episode, through a kind of Shavian interlude, through a Conradian episode, to a Jules Verne vision at the end. The significant failure is in that end, and in the way that it defeats not only the entire social analysis of the bulk of the novel, but Wells's own ends as a thinker. For at last George finds a purpose in science. "I decided that in power and knowledge lay the salvation of my life, the secret that would fill my need; that to these things I would give myself."

But science, power and knowledge, are summed up at last in a destroyer. As far as one can tell Wells intends no irony, although he may here have come upon the essence of the major irony in modern history. The novel ends in a kind of meditative rhapsody which denies every value that the book had been aiming toward. For of all the kinds of social waste which Wells has been describing, this is the most inclusive, the final waste. Thus he gives us in the end not a novel, but a hypothesis; not an individual destiny, but a theory of the future; and not his theory of the future, but a nihilistic vision quite opposite from everything that he meant to represent. With a minimum of attention to the virtues of technique, Wells might still not have written a good novel; but he would at any rate have established a point of view and a tone which would have told us what he meant.

To say what one means in art is never easy, and the more intimately one is implicated in one's material, the more difficult it is. If, besides, one commits fiction to a therapeutic function which is to be operative not on the audience but on the author, declaring, as D. H. Lawrence did, that "One sheds one's sicknesses in books, repeats and presents again one's emotions to be master of them," the difficulty is vast. It is an acceptable theory only with the qualification that technique, which objectifies, is under no other circumstances so imperative. For merely to repeat one's emotions, merely to look into one's heart and write, is also merely to repeat the round of emotional bondage. If our books are to be exercises in self-analysis, then technique must—and alone can— take the place of the absent analyst.

Lawrence, in the relatively late Introduction to his *Collected Poems*, made that distinction of the amateur between his "real" poems and his "composed" poems, between the poems which expressed his demon directly and created their own form "willy-nilly," and the poems which, through the hocus pocus of technique, he spuriously put together and could, if necessary, revise. His belief in a "poetry of the immediate present," poetry in which nothing is fixed, static, or final, where all is shimmeriness and impermanence and vitalistic essence, arose from this mistaken notion of technique. And from this notion, an unsympathetic critic like D. S. Savage can construct a case which shows Lawrence driven "concurrently to the dissolution of personality and the dissolution of art." The argument suggests that Lawrence's early, crucial novel, *Sons and Lovers*, is another example of meanings confused by an impatience with technical resources.

The novel has two themes: the crippling effects of a mother's love on the emotional development of her son; and the "split" between kinds of love, physical and spiritual, which the son develops, the kinds represented by two young women, Clara and Miriam. The two themes should, of course, work together, the second being, actually, the result of the first: this "split" is the "crippling." So one would expect to see the novel developed, and so Lawrence, in his famous letter to Edward Garnett, where he says that Paul is left at the end with the "drift towards death," apparently thought he had developed it. Yet in the last few sentences of the novel, Paul rejects his desire for extinction and turns towards "the faintly humming, glowing town," to life—as nothing in his previous history persuades us that he could unfalteringly do.

The discrepancy suggests that the book may reveal certain confusions between intention and performance.

The first of these is the contradiction between Lawrence's explicit characterizations of the mother and father and his tonal evaluations of them. It is a problem not only of style (of the contradiction between expressed moral epithets and the more general texture of the prose which applies to them) but of point of view. Morel and Lawrence are never separated, which is a way of saying that Lawrence maintains for himself in this book the confused attitude of his character. The mother is a "proud, *honorable* soul," but the father has a "small, *mean* head." This is the sustained contrast; the epithets are characteristic of the whole; and they represent half of Lawrence's feelings. But what is the other half? Which of these characters is given his real sympathy—the hard, self-righteous, aggressive, demanding mother who comes through to us, or the simple, direct, gentle, downright, fumbling, ruined father? There are two attitudes here. Lawrence (and Morel) loves his mother, but he also hates her for compelling his love; and he hates his father with the true Freudian jealousy, but he also loves him for what he is in himself, and he sympathizes more deeply with him because his wholeness has been destroyed by the mother's domination, just as his, Lawrence-Morel's, has been.

This is a psychological tension which disrupts the form of the novel and obscures its meaning, because neither the contradiction in style nor the confusion in point of view is made to right itself. Lawrence is merely repeating his emotions, and he avoids an austerer technical scrutiny of his material because it would compel him to master them. He would not let the artist be stronger than the man.

The result is that, at the same time that the book condemns the mother, it justifies her; at the same time that it shows Paul's failure, it offers rationalizations which place the failure elsewhere. The handling of the girl, Miriam, if viewed closely, is pathetic in what it signifies for Lawrence, both as man and artist. For Miriam is made the mother's scape-goat, and in a different way from the way that she was in life.

The central section of the novel is shot through with alternate state-ments as to the source of the difficulty: Paul is unable to love Miriam wholly, and Miriam can love only his spirit. The contradictions appear sometimes within single paragraphs, and the point of view is never adequately objectified and sustained to tell us which is true. The ma-terial is never seen as material; the writer is caught in it exactly as firmly as he was caught in his experience of it. "That's how women are with me," said Paul. "They want me like mad, but they don't want to belong to me." So he might have said, and believed it; but at the end of the novel, Lawrence is still saying that, and himself believing it.

For the full history of this technical failure, one must read *Sons and Lovers* carefully and then learn the history of the manuscript from the book called *D. H. Lawrence: A Personal Record*, by one E. T., who was Miriam in life. The basic situation is clear enough. The first theme —the crippling effects of the mother's love—is developed right through to the end; and then suddenly, in the last few sentences, turns on itself, and Paul gives himself to life, not death. But all the way through, the insidious rationalizations of the second theme have crept in to destroy the artistic coherence of the work. A "split" would occur in Paul; but as the split is treated, it is superimposed upon rather than developed in support of the first theme. It is a rationalization made from it. If Miriam is made to insist on spiritual love, the meaning and the power of theme one are reduced; yet Paul's weakness is disguised. Lawrence could not separate the investigating analyst, who must be objective, from Lawrence, the subject of the book; and the sickness was not healed, the emotion not mastered, the novel not perfected. All this, and the character of a whole career, would have been altered if Law-rence had allowed his technique to discover the fullest meaning of his subject.

A Portrait of the Artist as a Young Man, like *Tono-Bungay* and *Sons and Lovers*, is autobiographical, but unlike these it analyzes its mate-rial rigorously, and it defines the value and the quality of its experience not by appended comment or moral epithet, but by the texture of the style. The theme of *A Portrait*, a young artist's alienation from his en-vironment, is explored and evaluated through three different styles and methods as Stephen Dedalus moves from childhood through boyhood into maturity. The opening pages are written in something like the stream of consciousness of *Ulysses*, as the environment impinges di-rectly on the consciousness of the infant and the child, a strange, open-ing world which the mind does not yet subject to questioning, selection, or judgment. But this style changes very soon, as the boy begins to explore his surroundings, and as his sensuous experience of the world is enlarged, it takes on heavier and heavier rhythms and a fuller and fuller body of sensuous detail, until it reaches a crescendo of romantic opulence in the emotional climaxes which mark Stephen's rejection of domestic and religious values. Then gradually the style subsides into the austerer intellectuality of the final sections, as he defines to himself the outlines of the artistic task which is to usurp his maturity.

A highly self-conscious use of style and method defines the quality of experience in each of these sections, and, it is worth pointing out in connection with the third and concluding section, the style and method evaluate the experience. What has happened to Stephen is, of course, a progressive alienation from the life around him as he progressed in his initiation into it, and by the end of the novel, the alienation is complete. The final portion of the novel, fascinating as it may be for the developing aesthetic creed of Stephen-Joyce, is peculiarly bare. The life experience was not bare, as we know from *Stephen Hero;* but Joyce is forcing technique to comment. In essence, Stephen's alienation is a denial of the human environment; it is a loss; and the austere discourse of the final section, abstract and almost wholly without sensuous detail or strong rhythm, tells us of that loss. It is a loss so great that the texture of the notation-like prose here suggests that the end is really all an illusion, that when Stephen tells us and himself that he is going forth to forge in the smithy of his soul the uncreated conscience of his race, we are to infer from the very quality of the icy, abstract void he now inhabits, the implausibility of his aim. For *Ulysses* does not create the conscience of the race; it creates our consciousness.

In the very last two or three paragraphs of the novel, the style changes once more, reverts from the bare, notative kind to the romantic prose of Stephen's adolescence. "Away! Away! The spell of arms and voices; the white arms of roads, their promise of close embraces and the black arms of tall ships that stand against the moon, their tale of distant nations. They are held out to say: We are alone—come." Might one not say that the austere ambition is founded on adolescent longing? That the excessive intellectual severity of one style is the counterpart of the excessive lyric relaxation of the other? And that the final passage of *A Portrait* punctuates the illusory nature of the whole ambition?

For *Ulysses* does not create a conscience. Stephen, in *Ulysses,* is a little older, and gripped now by guilt, but he is still the cold young man divorced from the human no less than the institutional environ-ment. The environment of urban life finds a separate embodiment in the character of Bloom, and Bloom is as lost as Stephen, though touch-ingly groping for moorings. Each of the two is weakened by his inabil-ity to reach out, or to do more than reach out to the other. Here, then, is the theme again, more fully stated, as it were in counterpoint.

But if Stephen is not much older, Joyce is. He is older as an artist not only because he can create and lavish his Godlike pity on a Leopold Bloom, but also because he knows now what both Stephen and Bloom mean, and *how much*, through the most brilliant technical operation ever made in fiction, they can be made to mean. Thus *Ulysses*, through the imaginative force which its techniques direct, is like a pattern of concentric circles, with the immediate human situation at its center, this passing on and out to the whole dilemma of modern life, this passing on and out beyond that to a vision of the cosmos, and this to the myth-ical limits of our experience. If we read *Ulysses* with more satisfaction than any other novel of this century, it is because its author held an attitude toward technique and the technical scrutiny of subject matter which enabled him to order, within a single work and with superb coherence, the greatest amount of our experience.

IV

In the United States during the last twenty-five years, we have had many big novels but few good ones. A writer like James T. Farrell apparently assumes that by endless redundancy in the description of the surface of American Life, he will somehow write a book with the scope of *Ulysses*. Thomas Wolfe apparently assumed that by the mere disgorging of the raw material of his experience he would give us at last our epic. But except in a physical sense, these men have hardly written novels at all.

The books of Thomas Wolfe were, of course, journals, and the primary role of his publisher in transforming these journals into the semblance of novels is notorious. For the crucial act of the artist, the unique act which is composition, a sympathetic editorial blue pencil and scissors were substituted. The result has excited many people, especially the young, and the ostensibly critical have observed the prodigal talent with the wish that it might have been controlled. Talent there was, if one means by talent inexhaustible verbal energy, excessive response to personal experience, and a great capacity for auditory imitativeness, yet all of this has nothing to do with the novelistic quality of the written result; until the talent is controlled, the material organized, the content achieved, there is simply the man and his life. It remains to be demonstrated that Wolfe's conversations were any less interesting as novels than his books, which is to say that his books are without interest as novels. As with Lawrence, our response to the books is determined, not by their qualities as novels but by our response to him and his qualities as a temperament.

This is another way of saying that Thomas Wolfe never really knew what he was writing *about*. Of Time and the River is merely a euphemism for Of a Man and his Ego. It is possible that had his conception of himself and of art included an adequate respect for technique and the capacity to pursue it, Wolfe would have written a great novel on his true subject—the dilemma of romantic genius; it was his true subject, but it remains his undiscovered subject, it is the subject which *we* must dig out for him, because he himself had neither the lamp nor the pick to find it in and mine it out of the labyrinths of his experience. Like Emily Brontë, Wolfe needed a point of view beyond his own which would separate his material and its effect.

With Farrell, the situation is opposite. He knows quite well what his subject is and what he wishes to tell us about it, but he hardly needs the novel to do so. It is significant that in sheer clumsiness of style, no living writer exceeds him, for his prose is asked to perform no service beyond communication of the most rudimentary kind of fact. For his ambitions, the style of the newspaper and the lens of the documentary camera would be quite adequate, yet consider the diminution which Leopold Bloom, for example, would suffer, if he were to be viewed from these, the technical perspectives of James Farrell. Under the eye of this technique, the material does not yield up enough; indeed, it shrinks.

More and more writers in this century have felt that naturalism as a method imposes on them strictures which prevent them from exploring through all the resources of technique the full amplifications of their subjects, and that thus it seriously limits the possible breadth of aesthetic meaning and response. James Farrell is almost unique in the complacency with which he submits to the blunt techniques of naturalism; and his fiction is correspondingly repetitive and flat.

That naturalism had a sociological and disciplinary value in the nineteenth century is obvious; it enabled the novel to grasp materials and make analyses which had eluded it in the past, and to grasp them boldly; but even then it did not tell us enough of what, in Virginia Woolf's phrase, is "really real," nor did it provide the means to the maximum of reality coherently contained. Even the Flaubertian ideal of objectivity seems, today, an unnecessarily limited view of objectivity, for as almost every good writer of this century shows us, it is quite as possible to be objective about subjective states as it is to be objective about the circumstantial surfaces of life. Dublin, in *Ulysses*, is a moral setting: not only a city portrayed in the naturalistic fashion of Dickens' London, but also a map of the modern psyche with its oblique and baffled purposes. The second level of reality in no way invalidates the first, and a writer like Joyce shows us that, if the artist truly respects his medium, he can be objective about both at once. What we need in fiction is a devoted fidelity to every technique which will help us to discover and to evaluate our subject matter, and more than that, to discover the amplifications of meaning of which our subject matter is capable.

Most modern novelists have felt this demand upon them. André Gide allowed one of his artist-heroes to make an observation which considerably resembles an observation we have quoted from Wells. "My novel hasn't got a subject. . . . Let's say, if you prefer it, it hasn't got *one* subject. . . . 'A slice of life,' the naturalist school said. The great defect of that school is that it always cuts its slice in the same direction; in time, lengthwise. Why not in breadth? Or in depth? As for me I should like not to cut at all. Please understand; I should like to put everything into my novel." Wells, with his equally large blob of potential material, did not know how to cut it to the novel's taste; Gide cut, of course—in every possible direction. Gide and others. And those "cuts" are all the new techniques which modern fiction has given us. None, perhaps, is more important than that inheritance from French symbolism which Huxley, in the glittering wake of Gide, called "the musicalization of fiction." Conrad anticipated both when he wrote that the novel "must strenuously aspire to the plasticity of sculpture, to the colour of painting, and to the magic suggestiveness of music—which is the art of arts," and when he said of that early but wonderful piece of symbolist fiction, *Heart of Darkness*, "It was like another art altogether. That sombre theme had to be given a sinister resonance, a tonality of its own, a continued vibration that, I hoped, would hang in the air and dwell on the ear after the last note had been struck." The analogy with music, except as a metaphor, is inexact, and except as it points to techniques which fiction can employ as fiction, not very useful to our sense of craftsmanship. It has had an approximate exactness in only one work, Joyce's final effort, and an effort unique in literary history, *Finnegans Wake*, and here, of course, those readers willing to approach the "ideal" effort Joyce demands, discovering an inexhaustible wealth and scope, are most forcibly reminded of the primary importance of technique to subject, and of their indivisibility.

The techniques of naturalism inevitably curtail subject and often leave it in its original area, that of undefined social experience. Those of our writers who, stemming from this tradition, yet, at their best, achieve a novelistic definition of social experience—writers like the occasional Sherwood Anderson, William Carlos Williams, the occasional Erskine Caldwell, Nathanael West, and Ira Wolfert in *Tucker's People*, have done so by pressing naturalism far beyond itself, into positively gothic distortions. The structural machinations of Dos Passos and the lyrical interruptions of Steinbeck are the desperate maneuvers of men committed to a method of whose limitations they despair. They are our symbolists *manqués*, who end as allegorists.

Our most accomplished novels leave no such impression of desperate and intentional struggle, yet their precise technique and their determination to make their prose work in the service of their subjects have been the measure of their accomplishment. Hemingway's *The Sun Also Rises* and Wescott's *The Pilgrim Hawk* are works of art not because they may be measured by some external, neo-classic notion of form, but because their forms are so exactly equivalent with their subjects, and because the evaluation of their subjects exists in their styles.

Hemingway has recently said that his contribution to younger writers lay in a certain necessary purification of the language; but the claim has doubtful value. The contribution of his prose was to his subject, and the terseness of style for which his early work is justly celebrated is no more valuable, as an end in itself, than the baroque involutedness of Faulkner's prose, or the cold elegance of Wescott's. Hemingway's early subject, the exhaustion of value, was perfectly investigated and invested by his bare style, and in story after story, no meaning at all is to be inferred from the fiction except as the style itself suggests that there is no meaning in life. This style, more than that, was the perfect technical substitute for the conventional commentator; it expresses and it measures that peculiar morality of the stiff lip which Hemingway borrowed from athletes. It is an instructive lesson, furthermore, to observe how the style breaks down when Hemingway moves into the less congenial subject matter of social affirmation: how the style breaks down, the effect of verbal economy as mute suffering is lost, the personality of the writer, no longer protected by the objectification of an adequate technique, begins its offensive intrusion, and the entire structural integrity slackens. Inversely, in the stories and the early novels, the technique was the perfect embodiment of the subject and it gave that subject its astonishing largeness of effect and of meaning.

One should correct Buffon and say that style is the subject. In Wescott's *Pilgrim Hawk*, a novel which bewildered its many friendly critics by the apparent absence of subject, the subject, the story, is again in the style itself. This novel, which is a triumph of the sustained point of view, is only bewildering if we try to make a story out of the narrator's observations upon others; but if we read his observations as oblique and unrecognized observations upon himself the story emerges with perfect coherence, and it reverberates with meaning, is as suited to continuing reflection as the greatest lyrics.

The rewards of such respect for the medium as the early Hemingway and the occasional Wescott have shown may be observed in every good writer we have. The involutions of Faulkner's style are the perfect equivalent of his involved structures, and the two together are the perfect representation of the moral labyrinths he explores, and of the ruined world which his novels repeatedly invoke and in which these labyrinths exist. The cultivated sensuosity of Katherine Anne Porter's style has charm in itself, of course, but no more than with these others does it have aesthetic value in itself; its values lie in the subtle means by which sensuous details become symbols, and in the way that the symbols provide a network which is the story, and which at the same time provides the writer and us with a refined moral insight by means of which to test it. When we put such writers against a writer like William Saroyan, whose respect is reserved for his own temperament, we are appalled by the stylistic irresponsibility we find in him, and by the almost total absence of theme, or defined subject matter, and the abundance of unwarranted feeling. Such a writer inevitably becomes a sentimentalist because he has no means by which to measure his emotion. Technique, at last, is measure.

These writers, from Defoe to Porter, are of unequal and very different talent, and technique and talent are, of course, after a point, two different things. What Joyce gives us in one direction, Lawrence, for all his imperfections as a technician, gives us in another, even though it is not usually the direction of art. Only in some of his stories and in a few of his poems, where the demands of technique are less sustained and the subject matter is not autobiographical, Lawrence, in a different way from Joyce, comes to the same aesthetic fulfilment. Emily Brontë, with what was perhaps her intuitive grasp of the need to establish a tension between her subject matter and her perspective upon it, achieves a similar fulfillment; and, curiously, in the same way and certainly by intuition alone, Hemingway's early work makes a moving splendor from nothingness.

And yet, whatever one must allow to talent and forgive in technique, one risks no generalization in saying that modern fiction at its best has been peculiarly conscious of itself and of its tools. The technique of modern fiction, at once greedy and fastidious, achieves as its subject matter not some singleness, some topic or thesis, but the whole of the modern consciousness. It discovers the complexity of the modern spirit, the difficulty of personal morality, and the fact of evil—all the untractable elements under the surface which a technique of the surface alone can not approach. It shows us—in Conrad's words, from *Victory*—that we all live in an "age in which we are camped like bewildered travellers in a garish, unrestful hotel," and while it puts its hard light on our environment, it penetrates, with its sharp weapons, the depths of our bewilderment. These are not two things, but only an adequate technique can show them as one. In a realist like Farrell, we have the environment only, which we know from the newspapers; in a subjectivist like Wolfe, we have the bewilderment only, which we record in our own diaries and letters. But the true novelist gives them to us together, and thereby increases the effect of each, and reveals each in its full significance.

Elizabeth Bowen, writing of Lawrence, said of modern fiction, "We want the naturalistic surface, but with a kind of internal burning. In Lawrence every bush burns." But the bush burns brighter in some places than in others, and it burns brightest when a passionate private vision finds its objectification in exacting technical search. If the vision finds no such objectification, as in Wolfe and Saroyan, there is a burning without a bush. In our committed realists, who deny the resources of art for the sake of life, whose technique forgives both innocence and slovenliness—in Defoe and Wells and Farrell, there is a bush but it does not burn. There, at first glance, the bush is only a bush; and then, when we look again, we see that, really, the thing is dead.

ELIZABETH BOWEN

Notes on Writing a Novel

PLOT—*Essential. The Pre-Essential*

Plot might seem to be a matter of choice. It is not. The particular plot is something the novelist is driven to. It is what is left after the whittling-away of alternatives. The novelist is confronted, at a moment (or at what appears to be the moment: actually its extension may be indefinite) by the impossibility of saying what is to be said in any other way.

He is forced towards his plot. By what? By the "what is to be said." What is "what is to be said?" A mass of subjective matter that has accumulated—impressions received, feelings about experience, distorted results of ordinary observation, and something else—*x*. This matter is *extra* matter. It is superfluous to the non-writing life of the writer. It is luggage left in the hall between two journeys, as opposed to the perpetual furniture of rooms. It is destined to be elsewhere. It cannot move till its destination is known. Plot is the knowing of destination.

Plot is diction. Action of language, language of action.

Plot is story. It is also "a story" in the nursery sense = lie. The novel lies, in saying that something happened that did not. It must, therefore, contain uncontradictable truth, to warrant the original lie.

Story involves action. Action towards an end not to be foreseen (by the reader) but also towards an end which, having *been* reached, must be seen to have been from the start inevitable.

Action by whom? The Characters (see CHARACTERS). Action in view of what, and because of what? The "what is to be said."

What about the idea that the function of action is to *express* the characters? This is wrong. The characters are there to provide the

From *Collected Impressions* by Elizabeth Bowen. Published 1950 by Alfred A. Knopf, Inc. Reprinted by permission.

action. Each is created, and must only be so created, as to give his or her action (or rather, contributory part in the novel's action) verisimilitude.

What about the idea that plot should be ingenious, complicated— a display of ingenuity remarkable enough to command attention? If more than such a display, what? Tension, or mystification towards tension, are good for emphasis. For their own sakes, bad.

Plot must further the novel towards its object. What object? The non-poetic statement of a poetic truth.

Have not all poetic truths been already stated? The essence of a poetic truth is that no statement of it can be final.

Plot, story, is in itself un-poetic. At best it can only be not anti-poetic. It cannot claim a single poetic licence. It must be reasoned—onward from the moment when its non-otherness, its only-possibleness has become apparent. Novelist must always have one foot, sheer circumstantiality, to stand on, whatever the other foot may be doing. (N.B.—Much to be learnt from story-telling to children. Much to be learnt from the detective story—especially non-irrelevance. [See RELEVANCE])

Flaubert's *"Il faut intéresser."* Stress on manner of telling: keep in mind, "I will a tale *unfold.*" Interest of watching silk handkerchief drawn from a conjuror's watch.

Plot must not cease to move forward. (See ADVANCE.) The *actual* speed of the movement must be even. *Apparent* variations in speed are good, necessary, but there must be no actual variations in speed. To obtain those apparent variations is part of the illusion-task of the novel. Variations in texture can be made to give the effect of variations in speed. Why are *apparent* variations in speed necessary? (a) For emphasis. (b) For non-resistance, or "give," to the nervous time-variations of the reader. Why is *actual* evenness, non-variation, of speed necessary? For the sake of internal evenness for its own sake. Perfection of evenness = perfection of control. The evenness of the speed should be the evenness inseparable from tautness. The tautness of the taut string is equal (or even) all along and at any part of the string's length.

CHARACTERS

Are the characters, then, to be constructed to formula—the formula pre-decided by the plot? Are they to be drawn, cut out, jointed, wired, in order to be manipulated for the plot?

No. There is no question as to whether this would be right or wrong.

It would be impossible. One cannot "make" characters, only mario-nettes. The manipulated movement of the marionette is not the "action" necessary for plot. Characterless action is not action at all, in the plot sense. It is the indivisibility of the act from the actor, and the inevita-bility of *that* act on the part of *that* actor, that gives action veri-similitude. Without that, action is without force or reason. Forceless, reasonless action disrupts plot. The term "creation of character" (or characters) is misleading. Characters pre-exist. They are *found*. They reveal themselves slowly to the novelist's perception—as might fellow-travellers seated opposite one in a very dimly-lit railway carriage.

The novelist's perceptions of his characters take place *in the course of the actual writing of the novel*. To an extent, the novelist is in the same position as his reader. But his perceptions should be always just in advance.

The ideal way of presenting character is to invite perception.

In what do the characters pre-exist? I should say, in the mass of matter (see PLOT) that had accumulated before the inception of the novel.

(*N.B.*—The unanswerability of the question, from an outsider: "Are the characters in your novel invented, or are they from real life?" Obvi-ously, neither is true. The outsider's notion of "real life" and the nov-elist's are hopelessly apart.)

How, then, is the pre-existing character—with its own inner spring of action, its contrarieties—to be made to play a preassigned rôle? In relation to character, or characters, once these have been contem-plated, *plot* must at once seem over-rigid, arbitrary?

What about the statement (in relation to PLOT) that "each character is created in order, and only in order, that he or she may supply the required action?" To begin with, strike out "created." Better, the char-acter is *recognized* (by the novelist) by the signs he or she gives of unique capacity to act in a certain way, which "certain way" fulfills a need of the plot.

The character is there (in the novel) for the sake of the action he or she is to contribute to the plot. Yes. But also, he or she exists *outside* the action being contributed to the plot.

Without that existence of the character outside the (necessarily lim-ited) action, the action itself would be invalid.

Action is the simplification (for story purposes) of complexity. For each one act, there are an x number of rejected alternatives. It is the palpable presence of the alternatives that gives action interest. Therefore, in each of the characters, while he or she is acting, the play and pull of alternatives must be felt. It is in being seen to be capable of alternatives that the character becomes, for the reader, valid.

Roughly, the action of a character should be unpredictable before it has been shown, inevitable when it has been shown. In the first half of a novel, the unpredictability should be the more striking. In the second half, the inevitably should be the more striking.

(Most exceptions to this are, however, masterpiece-novels. In *War and Peace, L'Education Sentimentale* and *Le Recherche du Temps Perdu*, unpredictability dominates up to the end.)

The character's prominence in the novel (pre-decided by the plot) decides the character's range—of alternatives. The novelist must allot (to the point of rationing) psychological space. The "hero," "heroine" and "villain" (if any) are, by agreement, allowed most range. They are entitled, for the portrayal of their alternatives, to time and space. Placing the characters in receding order to their importance to the plot, the number of their alternatives may be seen to diminish. What E. M. Forster has called the "flat" character has no alternatives at all.

The ideal novel is without "flat" characters.

Characters must *materialize*—i.e., must have a palpable physical reality. They must be not only see-able (visualizable); they must be to be felt. Power to give physical reality is probably a matter of the extent and nature of the novelist's physical sensibility, or susceptibility. In the main, English novelists are weak in this, as compared to French and Russians. Why?

Hopelessness of categoric "description." Why? Because this is static. Physical personality belongs to action: cannot be separated from it. Pictures must be in movement. Eyes, hands, stature, etc., must appear, and only appear, *in play*. Reaction to physical personality is part of action—love, or sexual passages, only more marked application of this general rule.

(Conrad an example of strong, non-sexual use of physical personality.)

The materialization (in the above sense) of the character for the novelist must be instantaneous. It happens. No effort of will—and obviously no effort of intellect—can induce it. The novelist can *use* a character that has not yet materialized. But the unmaterialized character represents an enemy pocket in an area that has been otherwise cleared. This cannot go on for long. It produces a halt in plot.

When the materialization *has* happened, the chapters written before it happened will almost certainly have to be recast. From the plot point of view, they will be found invalid.

Also, it is essential that for the reader the materialization of the character should begin early. I say begin, because for the *reader* it may, without harm, be gradual.

Is it from this failure, or tendency to fail, in materialization that the English novelist depends so much on engaging emotional sympathy for his characters?

Ruling sympathy out, a novel must contain at least one *magnetic* character. At least one character capable of keying the reader up, as though he (the reader) were in the presence of someone he is in love with. This is not a rule of salesmanship but a pre-essential of *interest*. The character must do to the reader what he has done to the novelist—magnetize towards himself perceptions, sense-impressions, desires.

The unfortunate case is, where the character has, obviously, acted magnetically upon the author, but fails to do so upon the reader.

There must be combustion. Plot depends for its movement on internal combustion.

Physically, characters are almost always copies, or composite copies. Traits, gestures, etc., are searched for in, and assembled from, the novelist's memory. Or, a picture, a photograph or the cinema screen may be drawn on. Nothing physical can be *invented*. (Invented physique stigmatizes the inferior novel.) Proust (in last volume) speaks of this assemblage of traits. Though much may be lifted from a specific person in "real life," no person in "real life" could supply everything (physical) necessary for the character in the novel. No such person could have just that exact degree of physical intensity required for the character.

Greatness of characters is the measure of the unconscious greatness of the novelist's vision. They are "true" in so far as he is occupied with poetic truth. Their degrees in realness show the degrees of his concentration.

SCENE—*Is a derivative of Plot. Gives actuality to Plot*

Nothing can happen nowhere. The locale of the happening always colours the happening, and often, to a degree, shapes it.

Plot having pre-decided what is to happen, scene, scenes, must be so found, so chosen, as to give the happening the desired force.

Scene, being physical, is, like the physical traits of the characters, generally a copy, or a composite copy. It, too, is assembled—out of memories which, in the first place, may have had no rational connection with one another. Again, pictures, photographs, the screen are sources of supply. Also dreams.

Almost anything drawn from "real life"—house, town, room, park, landscape—will almost certainly be found to require *some* distortion for the purposes of the plot. Remote memories, already distorted by the imagination, are most useful for the purposes of scene. Unfamiliar or once-seen places yield more than do familiar, often-seen places.

Wholly invented scene is as unsatisfactory (thin) as wholly invented physique for a character.

Scene, much more than character, is inside the novelist's conscious power. More than any other constituent of the novel, it makes him conscious *of* his power.

This can be dangerous. The weak novelist is always, compensatorily, scene-minded. (Jane Austen's economy of scene-painting, and her abstentions from it in what might be expected contexts, could in itself be proof of her mastery of the novel.)

Scene is only justified in the novel where it can be shown, or at least felt, to act upon action or character. In fact, where it has dramatic use.

Where not intended for dramatic use, scene is a sheer slower-down. Its staticness is a dead weight. It cannot make part of the plot's movement by being shown *in play*. (Thunderstorms, the sea, landscape flying past car or railway-carriage windows are not scene but happenings.)

The deadeningness of straight and prolonged "description" is as apparent with regard to scene as it is with regard to character. Scene must be evoked. For its details relevance (see RELEVANCE) is essential. Scene must, like the characters, not fail to materialize. In this it follows the same law—instantaneous for the novelist, gradual for the reader.

In "setting a scene" the novelist directs, or attempts to direct, the reader's visual imagination. He must allow for the fact that the reader's memories will not correspond with his own. Or, at least, not at all far along the way.

DIALOGUE—*Must* (1) Further Plot. (2) Express Character

Should not on any account be a vehicle for ideas for their own sake. Ideas only permissible where they provide a key to the character who expresses them.

Dialogue requires more art than does any other constituent of the novel. Art in the *celare artem* sense. Art in the trickery, self-justifying distortion sense. Why? Because dialogue must appear realistic without being so. Actual realism—the lifting, as it were, of passages from a stenographer's take-town of a "real life" conversation—would be disruptive. Of what? Of the illusion of the novel. In "real life" everything is diluted; in the novel everything is condensed.

What are the realistic qualities to be imitated (or faked) in novel dialogue?—Spontaneity. Artless or hit-or-miss arrival at words used. Ambiguity (speaker not sure, himself, what he means). Effect of choking (as in engine): more to be said than can come through. Irrelevance. Allusiveness. Erraticness: unpredictable course. Repercussion.

What must novel dialogue, behind mask of these faked realistic qualities, really be and do? It must be pointed, intentional, relevant. It must crystallize situation. It must express character. It must advance plot.

During dialogue, the characters confront one another. The confrontation is in itself an occasion. Each one of these occasions, throughout the novel, is unique. Since the last confrontation, something has changed, advanced. What is being said is the effect of something that has happened; at the same time, what is being said *is in itself something happening*, which will in turn, leave its effect.

Dialogue is the ideal means of showing what is between the characters. It crystallizes relationships. It *should*, ideally, so be effective as to make analysis of explanation of the relationships between the characters unnecessary.

Short of a small range of physical acts—a fight, murder, love-making—dialogue is the most vigorous and visible inter-action of which characters in a novel are capable. Speech is what the characters *do to each other*.

Dialogue provides means for the psychological materialization of the characters. It should short-circuit description of mental traits. Every sentence in dialogue should be descriptive of the character who is speaking. Idiom, tempo, and shape of each spoken sentence should be calculated by novelist, towards this descriptive end.

Dialogue is the first case of the novelist's need for notation from real life. Remarks or turns of phrase indicatory of class, age, degree of intellectual pretension, *idées reçues*, nature and strength of governing fantasy, sexual temperament, persecution-sense or acumen (fortuitous arrival at general or poetic truth) should be collected. (*N.B.*—Proust, example of this semi-conscious notation and putting to use of it.)

All the above, from *class to acumen,* may already have been established, with regard to each character, by a direct statement by the novelist to the reader. It is still, however, the business of dialogue to show these factors, or qualities, in play.

There must be present in dialogue—*i.e.,* in each sentence spoken by each character—*either* (a) calculation, or (b) involuntary self-revelation.

Each piece of dialogue *must* be "something happening." Dialogue *may* justify its presence by being "illustrative"—but this secondary use of it must be watched closely, challenged. Illustrativeness can be stretched too far. Like straight description, it then becomes static, a dead weight—halting the movement of the plot. The "amusing" for its *own* sake, should above all be censored. So should infatuation with any idiom.

The functional use of dialogue for the plot must be the first thing in the novelist's mind. Where functional usefulness cannot be established, dialogue must be left out.

What is this functional use? That of a bridge.

Dialogue is the thin bridge which must, from time to time, carry the entire weight of the novel. Two things to be kept in mind—(a) the bridge is there to permit *advance,* (b) the bridge must be strong enough for the weight.

Failure in any one piece of dialogue is a loss, at once to the continuity and the comprehensibility of the novel.

Characters should, on the whole, be under rather than over articulate. What they *intend* to say should be more evident, more striking (because of its greater inner importance to the plot) than what they arrive at *saying.*

ANGLE

The question of angle comes up twice over in the novel.

Angle has two senses—(a) visual, (b) moral.

(a) *Visual Angle.*—This has been much discussed—particularly I think by Henry James. Where is the camera-eye to be located? (1) In the breast or brow of *one* of the characters? This is, of course, simplifying and integrating. But it imposes on the novel the limitations of the "I"—whether the first person is explicitly used or not. Also, with regard to any matter that the specific character does not (cannot) know, it involves the novelist in long cumbrous passages of cogitation, speculation and guesses. *E.g.*—of any character other than the specific (or virtual) "I" it must always be "he appeared to feel," "he could be seen to see," rather than "he felt," "he saw." (2) In the breast or brow of a succession of characters? This is better. It *must,* if used, involve very careful, considered division of the characters, by the novelist, in the *seeing* and the *seen.* Certain characters gain in importance and magnetism by being only *seen:* this makes them more romantic, fatal-seeming, sinister. In fact, no character in which these qualities are, for the plot, essential should be allowed to enter the *seeing* class. (3) In the breast or brow of omniscient story-teller (the novelist)? This, though appearing naïve, would appear best. The novelist should retain right of entry, at will, into any of the characters: their memories, sensations and thought-processes should remain his, to requisition for appropriate use. What conditions "appropriateness"? The demands of the plot. Even so, the novelist must not lose sight of point made above—the gain in necessary effect, for some characters, of their remaining *seen*—their remaining closed, apparently, even to the omniscience of the novelist.

The cinema, with its actual camera-work, is interesting study for the novelist. In a good film, the camera's movement, angle and distance have all worked towards one thing—the fullest possible realization of the director's idea, the completest possible surrounding of the subject. Any trick is justified if it adds a statement. With both film and novel, plot is the pre-imperative. The novelist's relation to the novel is that of the director's relation to the film. The cinema, cinema-going has no doubt built up in novelists a great authoritarianism. This seems to me good.

(b) *Moral Angle.*—This too often means, pre-assumptions—social, political, sexual, national, aesthetic, and so on. These may all exist, sunk at different depths, in the same novelist. Their existence cannot fail to be palpable; and their nature determines, more than anything else, the sympatheticness or antipatheticness of a given novel to a given circle of readers.

Pre-assumptions are bad. They limit the novel to a given circle of readers. They cause the novel to act immorally *on* that given circle. (The lady asking the librarian for a "nice" novel to take home is, virtually, asking for a novel whose pre-assumptions will be identical with her own.) Outside the given circle, a novel's pre-assumptions must invalidate it for all other readers. The increasingly bad smell of most pre-assumptions probably accounts for the growing prestige of the detective story: the detective story works on the single, and universally acceptable, pre-assumption that an act of violence is anti-social, and that the doer, in the name of injured society, must be traced.

Great novelists write without pre-assumption. They write from outside their own nationality, class or sex.

To write thus should be the ambition of any novelist who wishes to state poetic truth.

Does this mean he must have no angle, no moral view-point? No, surely. Without these, he would be (a) incapable of maintaining the *conviction* necessary for the novel; (b) incapable of *lighting* the characters, who to be seen at all must necessarily be seen in a moral light.

From what source, then, must the conviction come? and from *what* morality is to come the light to be cast on the characters?

The conviction must come from certainty of the validity of the truth the novel is to present. The "moral light" has not, actually, a moral source; it is moral (morally powerful) according to the strength of its power of revelation. Revelation of what? The virtuousness of the action of the character. What is virtue in action? Truth in action. Truth by what ruling, in relation to what? Truth by the ruling of, and in relation to, the inherent poetic truth that the novel states.

The presence, and action, of the poetic truth is the motive (or motor) morality of the novel.

The direction of the action of the poetic truth provides—in fact, *is*— the moral angle of the novel. If he remains with that truth in view, the novelist has no option as to his angle.

The action, or continuous line of action, of a character is "bad" in so far as it runs counter to, resists, or attempts to deny, the action of the poetic truth. It is predisposition towards such action that constitutes "badness" in a character.

"Good" action, or "goodness" in the character, from predisposition towards such action, is movement along with, expressive of and contributory to, the action of the poetic truth.

If the novelist's moral angle is (a) decided by recognition of the poetic truth, and (b) maintained by the necessity of stating the truth by showing the truth's action, it will be, as it should be, impersonal. It will be, and (from the "interest" point of view) will be able to stand being, pure of pre-assumptions—national, social, sexual, etc.

(*N.B.*—"Humour" is the weak point in the front against pre-assumptions. Almost all English humour shows social (sometimes, now, backed by political) pre-assumptions. (Extreme cases—that the lower, or employed, classes are quaint or funny—that aristocrats, served by butlers, are absurd. (National pre-assumptions show in treatment of foreigners.)

ADVANCE

It has been said that plot must advance; that the underlying (or inner) speed of the advance must be even. How is this arrived at?

(1) Obviously, first, by the succession, the succeedingness, of events or happenings. It is to be remembered that *everything* put on record at all—an image, a word spoken, an interior movement of thought or feeling on the part of a character—is an event or happening. These proceed out of one another, give birth to one another, in a continuity that must be (a) obvious, (b) unbroken.

(2) Every happening cannot be described, stated. The reader must be made to feel that what has not been described or stated has, none the less, happened. How? By the showing of subsequent events or happenings whose source *could* only have been in what has not actually been stated. Tuesday is Tuesday by virtue of being the day following Monday. The stated Tuesday must be shown as a derivative of the unstated Monday.

(3) For the sake of emphasis, time must be falsified. But the novelist's consciousness of the subjective, arbitrary and emotional nature of the falsification should be evident to the reader. Against this falsification—in fact, increasing the force of its effect by contrast—a clock should be heard always impassively ticking away at the same speed. The passage of time, and its demarcation, should be a factor in plot. The either concentration or even or uneven spacing-out of events along time is important.

The statement "Ten years had passed," or the statement "It was now the next day"—each of these is an event.

(4) Characters most of all promote, by showing, the advance of the plot. How? By the advances, from act to act, in their action. By their showing (by emotional or physical changes) the effects both of action and of the passage of time. The diminution of the character's alternatives shows (because it is the work of) advance—by the end of a novel the character's alternatives, many at the beginning, have been reduced to almost none. In the novel, everything happens either *to* or *because* of one of the characters. By the end of the novel, the character has, like the silk worm at work on the cocoon, spun itself out.

Completed action is marked by the exhaustion (from one point of view) of the character. Throughout the novel, each character is expending potentiality. This expense of potentiality must be felt.

(5) Scene promotes, or contributes to, advance by its freshness. Generically, it is fresh, striking, from being unlike the scene before. It is the new "here and now." Once a scene ceases to offer freshness, it is a point-blank enemy to advance. Frequent change of scene *not* being an imperative of the novels—in fact, many novels by choice, and by wise choice, limiting themselves severely in this matter—how is there to continue to be freshness? By means of ever-differing presentation. Differing because of what? Season of year, time of day, effects of a happening (*e.g.*, with house, rise or fall in family fortunes, an arrival, a departure, a death), beholding character's mood. At the first presentation, the *scene* has freshness; afterwards, the freshness must be in the *presentation*. The same scene can, by means of a series of presentations, each having freshness, be made to ripen, mature, to actually advance. The *static* properties in scene can be good for advance when so stressed as to show advance by contrast—advance on the part of the characters. Striking "unchangingness" gives useful emphasis to change. Change should not be a factor, at once, in *both* scene and character; either unchanged character should see, or be seen against, changed scene, or changed character should see, or be seen, against unchanged scene. *Two* changes obviously cancel each other out, and would cancel each other's contribution to the advance of plot.

RELEVANCE

Relevance—the question of it—is the headache of novel writing.

As has been said, the model for relevance is the well-constructed detective story: nothing is "in" that does not tell. But the detective story is, or would appear to be, simplified by having *fact* as its kernel. The detective story makes towards concrete truth; the novel makes towards abstract truth.

With the detective story, the question "relevant to *what?*" can be answered by the intelligence. With the novel, the same question must constantly, and in every context, be referred to the intuition. The intelligence, in a subsequent check over, may detect, but cannot itself put right, blunders, lapses or false starts on the part of the intuition.

In the notes on Plot, Character, Scene and Dialogue, everything has

come to turn, by the end, on relevance. It is seen that all other rele-
vances are subsidiary to the relevance of the plot—*i.e.*, the relevance to
itself that the plot demands. It is as contributory, in fact relevant, to
plot that character, scene and dialogue are examined. To be perfectly
contributory, these three must be perfectly relevant. If character, scene
or dialogue has been weakened by anything irrelevant *to itself,* it can
only be imperfectly relevant—which must mean, to a degree disruptive
—to the plot.

The main hope for character (for each character) is that it should
be magnetic—*i.e.*, that it should *attract* its parts. This living propensity
of the character to assemble itself, to integrate itself, to make itself in
order to *be* itself will not, obviously, be resisted by the novelist. The
magnetic, or magnetizing, character can be trusted as to what is relevant to *itself.* The trouble comes when what is relevant to the character
is found to be not relevant to the plot. At this point, the novelist must
adjudicate. It is possible that the character may be right; it is possible
that there may be some flaw in the novelist's sense of what is relevant
to the plot.

Again, the character may, in fact must, decide one half of the question of relevance in dialogue. The character attracts to itself the right,
in fact the only possible, idiom, tempo and phraseology for *that* particular character in speech. In so far as dialogue is *illustrative,* the
character's, or characters', pull on it must not be resisted.

But in so far as dialogue must be "something happening"—part of
action, a means of advancing plot—the other half of the question of
dialogue relevance comes up. Here, the pull from the characters may
conflict with the pull from the plot. Here again the novelist must adjudicate. The recasting and recasting of dialogue that is so often necessary is, probably, the search for ideal compromise.

Relevance in scene is more straightforward. Chiefly, the novelist
must control his infatuation with his own visual power. *No* non-contrib-
utory image, must be the rule. Contributory to what? To the mood of
the "now," the mood that either projects or reflects action. It is a good
main rule that objects—chairs, trees, glasses, mountains, cushions—
introduced into the novel should be stage-properties, necessary for
"business." It will be also recalled that the well-set stage shows many
objects *not* actually necessary for "business," but that these have a right
to place by being descriptive—explanatory. In a play, the absence of the
narrating voice makes it necessary to establish the class, period and

general psychology of the characters by means of objects that can be seen. In the novel, such putting of objects to a descriptive (explanatory) use is excellent—alternative to the narrator's voice.

In scene then, relevance demands either usefulness for action or else explanatory power in what is shown. There is no doubt that with some writers (Balzac, sometimes Arnold Bennett) categoricalness, in the presentation of scene, is effective. The aim is, usually, to suggest, by multiplication and exactitude of detail, either a scene's material oppressiveness or its intrinsic authority. But in general, for the purposes of most novelists, the number of objects genuinely necessary for explanation will be found to be very small.

Irrelevance, in any part, is a cloud and a drag on, a weakener of, the novel. It dilutes meaning. Relevance crystallizes meaning.

The novelist's—any writer's—object is, to whittle down his meaning to the exactest and finest possible point. What, of course, is fatal is when he does not know what he does mean: he has no point to sharpen.

Much irrelevance is introduced into novels by the writer's vague hope that at least some of this *may* turn out to be revelant, after all. A good deal of what might be called provisional writing goes to the first drafts of first chapters of most novels. At a point in the novel's progress, relevance becomes clearer. The provisional chapters are then recast.

The most striking fault in work by young or beginning novelists submitted for criticism, is irrelevance—due either to infatuation or indecision. To direct such an author's attention to the imperative of relevance is certainly the most useful—and possibly the only—help that can be given.

PERCY LUBBOCK

Point of View

The whole intricate question of method, in the craft of fiction, I take
to be governed by the question of the point of view—the question of the
relation in which the narrator stands to the story. He tells it as *he* sees
it, in the first place; the reader faces the story-teller and listens, and
the story may be told so vivaciously that the presence of the minstrel
is forgotten, and the scene becomes visible, peopled with the characters
of the tale. It may be so, it very often is so for a time. But it is not so
always, and the story-teller himself grows conscious of a misgiving. If
the spell is weakened at any moment, the listener is recalled from the
scene to the mere author before him, and the story rests only upon the
author's direct assertion. Is it not possible, then, to introduce another
point of view, to set up a fresh narrator to bear the brunt of the reader's
scrutiny? If the story-teller is *in* the story himself, the author is dramatized; his assertions gain in weight, for they are backed by the presence
of the narrator in the pictured scene. It is advantage scored; the author
has shifted his responsibility, and it now falls where the reader can see
and measure it; the arbitrary quality which may at any time be de-
tected in the author's voice is disguised in the voice of his spokesman.
Nothing is now imported into the story from without; it is self-contained, it has no associations with anyone beyond its circle.

Such is the first step towards dramatization, and in very many a story
it may be enough. The spokesman is there, in recognizable relation with
this matter; no question of his authority can arise. But now a difficulty
may be started by the nature of the tale that he tells. If he has nothing
to do but to relate what he has seen, what anyone might have seen in
his position, his account will serve very well; there is no need for more.
Let him unfold his chronicle as it appears in his memory. But if he is

From *The Craft of Fiction*. Copyright 1921 by Percy Lubbock; renewed
1949. Reprinted by permission of the Viking Press and Jonathan Cape, Ltd.

himself the subject of his story, if the story involves a searching exploration of his own consciousness, an account in his own words, after the fact, is not by any means the best imaginable. Far better it would be to see him while his mind is actually at work in the agitation, whatever it may be, which is to make the book. The matter would then be objective and visible to the reader, instead of reaching him in the form of a report at second hand. But how to manage this without falling back upon the author and *his* report, which has already been tried and for good reasons, as it seemed, abandoned? It is managed by a kind of repetition of the same stroke, a further shift of the point of view. The spectator, the listener, the reader, is now himself to be placed at the angle of vision; not an account or a report, more or less convincing, is to be offered him, but a direct sight of the matter itself, while it is passing. Nobody expounds or explains; the story is enacted by its look and behaviour at particular moments. By the first stroke the narrator was brought into the book and set before the reader; but the action appeared only in his narrative. Now the action is there, proceeding while the pages are turned; the narrator is forestalled, he is watched while the story is in the making. Such is the progress of the writer of fiction towards drama; such is his method of evading the drawbacks of a mere reporter and assuming the advantages, as far as possible, of a dramatist. How far he may choose to push the process in his book— that is a matter to be decided by the subject; it entirely depends upon the kind of effect that the theme demands. It may respond to all the dramatization it can get, it may give all that it has to give for less. The subject dictates the method.

And now let the process be reversed, let us start with the purely dramatic subject, the story that will tell itself in perfect rightness, unaided, to the eye of the reader. This story never deviates from a strictly scenic form; one occasion or episode follows another, with no interruption for any reflective summary of events. Necessarily it must be so, for it is only while the episode is proceeding that no question of a narrator can arise; when the scene closes the play ceases till the opening of the next. To glance upon the story from a height and to give a general impression of its course—this is at once to remove the point of view from the reader and to set up a new one somewhere else; the method is no longer consistent, no longer purely dramatic. And the dramatic story is not only scenic, it is also limited to so much as the ear can hear and the eye see. In rigid drama of this kind there is naturally no admission of the reader into the private mind of any of the characters; their thoughts and motives are transmuted into action. A subject wrought to this pitch of objectivity is no doubt given weight and compactness and authority in the highest degree; it is like a piece of modelling, standing in clear space, casting its shadow. It is the most finished form that fiction can take.

But evidently it is not a form to which fiction can aspire in general. It implies many sacrifices, and these will easily seem to be more than the subject can usefully make. It is out of the question, of course, wherever the main burden of the story lies within some particular consciousness, in the study of a soul, the growth of a character, the changing history of a temperament; there the subject would be needlessly crossed and strangled by dramatization pushed to its limit. It is out of the question, again, wherever the story is too big, too comprehensive, too widely ranging, to be treated scenically, with no opportunity for general and panoramic survey; it has been discovered, indeed, that even a story of this kind *may* fall into a long succession of definite scenes, under some hands, but it has also appeared that in doing so it incurs unnecessary disabilities, and will likely suffer. These stories, therefore, which will not naturally accommodate themselves to the reader's point of view, and the reader's alone, we regard as rather pictorial than dramatic—meaning that they call for some narrator, somebody who *knows,* to contemplate the facts and create an impression of them. Whether it is the omniscient author or a man in the book, he must gather up his experience, compose a vision of it as it exists in his mind, and lay *that* before the reader. It is the reflection of an experience; and though there may be all imaginable diversity of treatment within the limits of the reflection, such is its essential character. In a pictorial book the principle of the structure involves a point of view which is not the reader's.

It is open to the pictorial book, however, to use a method in its picture-making that is really no other than the method of drama. It is somebody's experience, we say, that is to be reported, the general effect that many things have left upon a certain mind; it is a fusion of innumerable elements, the deposit of a lapse of time. The straightforward way to render it would be for the narrator—the author or his selected creature—to view the past retrospectively and discourse upon it, to recall and meditate and summarize. That is picture-making in its natural form, using its own method. But exactly as in drama the subject is distributed among the characters and enacted by them, so in picture the effect may be entrusted to the elements, the reactions of the moment, and *performed* by these. The mind of the narrator becomes the stage, his voice is no longer heard. His voice *is* heard so long as there is narrative of any sort, whether he is speaking in person or is reported obliquely; his voice is heard, because in either case the language and the intonation are his, the direct expression of his experience. In the drama of his mind there is no personal voice, for there is no narrator; the point of view becomes the reader's once more. The shapes of thought in the man's mind tell their own story. And that is the art of picture-making when it uses the dramatic method.

But it cannot always do so. Constantly it must be necessary to offer the reader a summary of facts, an impression of a train of events, that can only be given as somebody's narration. Suppose it were required to render the general effect of a certain year in a man's life, a year that has filled his mind with a swarm of many memories. Looking into his consciousness after the year has gone, we might find much there that would indicate the nature of the year's events without any word on his part; the flickers and flashes of thought from moment to moment might indeed tell us much. But we shall need an account from him too, no doubt; too much has happened in a year to be wholly acted, as I call it, in the movement of the man's thought. He must narrate—he must make, that is to say, a picture of the events as he sees them, glancing back. Now if he speaks in the first person there can, of course, be no uncertainty in the point of view; he has his fixed position, he cannot leave it. His description will represent the face that the facts in their sequence turned towards *him;* the field of vision is defined with perfect distinctness, and his story cannot stray outside it. The reader, then, may be said to watch a reflection of the facts in a mirror of which the edge is nowhere in doubt; it is rounded by the bounds of the narrator's own personal experience.

This limitation may have a convenience and a value in the story, it may contribute to the effect. But it need not be forfeited, it is clear, if the first person is changed to the third. The author may use the man's field of vision and keep as faithfully within it as though the man were speaking for himself. In that case he retains this advantage and adds to it another, one that is likely to be very much greater. For now, while the point of view is still fixed in space, still assigned to the man in the book, it is free in *time;* there no longer stretches, between the narrator and the events of which he speaks, a certain tract of time, across which the past must appear in a more or less distant perspective. All the variety obtainable by a shifting relation to the story in time is thus in the author's hand; the safe serenity of a far retrospect, the promising or threatening urgency of the present, every gradation between the two, can be drawn into the whole effect of the book, and all of it without any change of the seeing eye. It is a liberty that may help the story indefinitely, raising this matter into strong relief, throwing that other back into vaguer shade.

And next, still keeping mainly and ostensibly to the same point of view, the author has the chance of using a much greater latitude than he need appear to use. The seeing eye is with somebody in the book, but its vision is reinforced; the picture contains more, becomes richer and fuller, because it is the author's as well as his creature's, both at once. Nobody notices, but in fact there are now two brains behind that eye; and one of them is the author's, who adopts and shares the *position* of his creature, and at the same time supplements his wit. If you analyse the picture that is now presented, you find that it is not all the work of the personage whose vision the author has adopted. There are touches in it that go beyond any sensation of his, and indicate that some one else is looking over his shoulder—seeing things from the same angle, but seeing more, bringing another mind to bear upon the scene. It is an easy and natural extension of the personage's power of observation. The impression of the scene may be deepened as much as need be; it is not confined to the scope of one mind, and yet there is no blurring of the focus by a double point of view. And thus what I have called the sound of the narrator's voice (it is impossible to avoid this mixture of metaphors) is less insistent in oblique narration, even while it seems to be following the very same argument that it would in direct, because another voice is speedily mixed and blended with it.

So this is another resource upon which the author may draw according to his need; sometimes it will be indispensable, and generally, I suppose, it will be useful. It means that he keeps a certain hold upon the narrator *as an object;* the sentient character in the story, round whom it is grouped, is not utterly subjective, completely given over to the business of seeing and feeling on behalf of the reader. It is a considerable point; for it helps to meet one of the great difficulties in the story which is carefully aligned towards a single consciousness and consistently so viewed. In that story the man or woman who acts as the vessel of sensation is always in danger of seeming a light, uncertain weight compared with the other people in the book—simply because the other people are objective images, plainly outlined, while the seer in the midst is precluded from that advantage, and must see without being directly seen. He, who doubtless ought to bulk in the story more massively than any one, tends to remain the least recognizable of the company, and even to dissolve in a kind of impalpable blur. By his method (which I am supposing to have been adopted in full strictness) the author is of course forbidden to look this central figure in the face, to describe and discuss him; the light cannot be turned upon him immediately. And very often we see the method becoming an embarrassment to the author in consequence, and the devices by which he tries to mitigate it, and to secure some reflected sight of the seer, may even be tiresomely obvious. But the resource of which I speak is of a finer sort.

It gives to the author the power of imperceptibly edging away from the seer, leaving his consciousness, ceasing to use his eyes—though still without substituting the eyes of another. To revert for a moment to the story told in the first person, it is plain that in that case the narrator has no such liberty; his own consciousness must always lie open; the part that he plays in the story can never appear in the same terms, on the same plane, as that of the other people. Though he is not visible in the story to the reader, as the others are, he is at every moment *nearer* than they, in his capacity of the seeing eye, the channel of vision; nor can he put off his function, he must continue steadily to see and to report. But when the author is reporting *him* there is a margin of freedom. The author has not so completely identified himself, as narrator, with his hero that he can give him no objective weight whatever. If necessary he can allow him something of the value of a detached and phenomenal personage, like the rest of the company in the story, and that without violating the principle of his method. He cannot make his hero actually visible—there the method is uncompromising; he cannot step forward, leaving the man's point of view, and picture him from without. But he can place the man at the same distance from the reader as the other people, he can almost lend him the same effect, he can make of him a dramatic actor upon the scene.

And how? Merely by closing (when it suits him) the open consciousness of the seer—which he can do without any look of awkwardness or violence, since it conflicts in no way with the rule of the method. That rule only required that the author, having decided to share the point of view of his character, should not proceed to set up another of his own; it did not debar him from allowing his hero's act of vision to lapse, his function as the sentient creature in the story to be intermitted. The hero (I call him so for convenience—he may, of course, be quite a subordinate onlooker in the story) can at any moment become impenetrable, a human being whose thought is sealed from us; and it may seem a small matter, but in fact it has the result that he drops into the plane of the people whom he has hitherto been seeing and judging. Hitherto subjective, communicative in solitude, he has been in a category apart from them; but now he may mingle with the rest, engage in talk with them, and his presence and his talk are no more to the fore than theirs. As soon as some description or discussion of them is required, then, of course, the seer must resume his part and unseal his mind; but meanwhile, though the reader gets no direct view of him, still he is there in the dialogue with the rest, his speech (like theirs) issues from a hidden mind and has the same dramatic value. It is enough, very likely, to harden our image of him, to give precision to his form, to save him from dissipation into that luminous blur of which I spoke just now. For the author it is a resource to be welcomed on that account, and not on that account alone.

For besides the greater definition that the seer acquires, thus detached from us at times and relegated to the plane of his companions, there is much benefit for the subject of the story. In the tale that is quite openly and nakedly somebody's narrative there is this inherent weakness, that a scene of true drama is impossible. In true drama nobody *reports* the scene; it *appears*, it is constituted by the aspect of the occasion and the talk and the conduct of the people. When one of the people who took part in it sets out to report the scene, there is at once a mixture and a confusion of effects; for his own contribution to the scene has a different quality from the rest, cannot have the same crispness and freshness, cannot strike in with a new or unexpected note. This weakness may be well disguised, and like everything else in the whole craft it may become a positive and right effect in a particular story, for a particular purpose; it is always there, however, and it means that the full and unmixed effect of drama is denied to the story that is rigidly told from the point of view of one of the actors. But when that point of view is held in the manner I have described, when it is open to the author to withdraw from it silently and to leave the actor to play his part, true drama—or something so like it that it passes for true drama—is always possible; all the figures of the scene are together in it, one no nearer than another. Nothing is wanting save only that direct, unequivocal sight of the hero which the method does indeed absolutely forbid.

Finally there is the old, immemorial, unguarded, unsuspicious way of telling a story, where the author entertains the reader, the minstrel draws his audience round him, the listeners rely upon his word. The voice is then confessedly and alone the author's; he imposes no limitation upon his freedom to tell what he pleases and to regard his matter from a point of view that is solely his own. And if there is anyone who can proceed in this fashion without appearing to lose the least of the advantages of a more cautious style, for him the minstrel's licence is proper and appropriate; there is no more to be said. But we have yet to discover him; and it is not very presumptuous in a critic, as things are, to declare that a story will never yield its best to a writer who takes the easiest way with it. He curtails his privileges and chooses a a narrower method, and immediately the story responds; its better condition is too notable to be forgotten, when once it has caught the attention of a reader. The advantages that it gains are not nameless, indefinable graces, pleasing to a critic but impossible to fix in words; they are solid, we can describe and recount them. And I can only conclude that if the novel is still as full of energy as it seems to be, and is not a form of imaginative art that, having seen the best of its day, is preparing to give place to some other, the novelist will not be willing to miss the inexhaustible opportunity that lies in its treatment. The easy way is no way at all; the only way is that by which the most is made of the story to be told, and the most was never made of any story except by a choice and disciplined method.

WAYNE BOOTH

The Uses of Reliable Commentary

It is not surprising that critics have been tempted to discuss commentary—and usually to condemn it—as if it were a single thing which can be judged simply according to our general views of the novel. But it should prove worthwhile to abandon such a priori judgments and to look into some good novels to discover the effects commentary has, in fact, been used to achieve. Afterward we may still find ourselves saying that though authors have used commentary for such-and-such purposes, we wish that they had not. But at the very least we should be in a position to decide with some precision whether any of the particular achievements of the author's voice have been worth the sacrifice of whatever general qualities we hold dear.

PROVIDING THE FACTS, PICTURE, OR SUMMARY

The most obvious task for a commentator is to tell the reader about facts that he could not easily learn otherwise. There are many kinds of facts, of course, and they can be "told" in an unlimited number of ways. Stage setting, explanation of the meaning of an action, summary of thought processes or of events too insignificant to merit being dramatized, description of physical events and details whenever such description cannot spring naturally from a character—these all occur in many different forms.

As Chaucer begins his tale of Criseyde's woes, he disposes of the fall of Troy in seven lines of summary exactly suited to the needs of his story:

> But how this town com to destruccion

> Ne falleth naught to purpos me to telle;
> For it were here a long disgression
> Fro my matere, and yow to long to dwelle.
> But the Troian gestes, as they felle,
> In Omer, or in Dares, or in Dite,
> Whoso that kan may rede hem as they write.

The "Chaucer" who here reminds us that we are reading one tale among many, that he is selecting his materials in our own interest, and that if we want *other* stories we can go to Homer and other authors for them, accompanies us intimately throughout *Troilus and Criseyde*. Whatever is not directly pertinent to his purposes, he summarizes.

> And if I hadde ytaken for to write
> The armes of this ilke worthi man,
> Than wolde ich of his batailles endite;
> But for that I to writen first bigan
> Of his love, I have seyd as I kan.—
> His worthi dedes, whoso list him heere,
> Rede Dares, he kan telle hem alle ifeere.[1]

He never lets us forget his presence, yet his presence cannot be said to detract from the tale he tells. He *tells* us a good deal about those aspects of the tale which, though necessary, are not entitled to the heightening that would come if they were dramatized. And yet the over-all effect is to make us feel that we have been given a better story, more carefully worked, than would have been possible if he had simply served up his materials raw.

The great narrators have always managed to find some way to make such summary interesting, as Fielding does with his ironic invitation for us to fill in the gaps in *Tom Jones*. He gives the reader, he says, "an opportunity of employing that wonderful sagacity, of which he is master, by filling up these vacant spaces of time with his own conjectures." Since he is assured that most of his readers are "upper graduates in criticism," he leaves them "a space of twelve years" in which to apply their skills (Book III, chap. i).

The provision of this kind of summary is only one of dozens of distinguishable techniques for providing facts, most of which—perhaps fortunately—have never been named. What, for example, are we to call the device of narrating by footnotes? In Marcel Aymé's *Le chemin des écoliers* (1946) the author occasionally provides in footnotes information that lies beyond the range of his characters. During the German occupation of France, Michaud watches four German soldiers "performing their tourist duties" in front of the Sacré-Cœur. He envies them, momentarily, their carefree existence. Suddenly we are given a footnote, telling us that the four soldiers were named Arnold, Eisenhart, Heinecken, and Schulz. "The first one was killed on the Russian front. The second one, wounded in the Crimea, returned home with both legs missing and was poisoned by his wife." And so on, until Schulz, the last, is described as torn to bits by an angry mob of Parisians at the time of the liberation. This factual intrusion commenting sardonically on Michaud's envy is brief, clean, effective, and entirely appropriate to the work in which it appears. If we try to think of an equally concise way to provide this ironic juxtaposition of the hero's envy with their disastrous future, we see that it simply could not be done by anyone but the omniscient author speaking in his own person. It need not be done in a footnote, of course, although the outlandish artifice of a footnote is in this case the simplest way of showing that these facts, while necessary to the story, are strictly side issues; the characters described cannot possibly become important to the story later on. The only ready alternative would be a dramatized interpolation, shifting us forward to four episodes, swiftly giving the future of the four soldiers. But to do so would not only take much more space, it would imply importance and thus muddy the pattern of expectations for the reader.

This is simply one colorful recent example of the most common and most useful service that direct telling can perform. In the same way the author may provide a bit of summary between scenes, summary that could be provided by none of the characters. Or he may give facts about one character that no other character could know. "Ray saw Leopold thinking: Oh yes, an Englishman! (It should be clear that Ray looked like any of these tall Englishmen who . . .)." Thus Elizabeth Bowen's narrator enters *The House in Paris* (1935) to give us a description of Ray which Ray could *almost* achieve himself but which, coming from the author, is more useful since more certain; it is untainted with doubt about whether he is in fact giving an unbiased report.

When we remember the many cumbersome "mirror-views" in modern fiction—"What he saw in the mirror was a man of middle-height"— we see how much trouble the desire to dramatize such descriptive detail can cause. Some situations do, indeed, lend themselves to this kind of pseudodrama, particularly when what is seen in the mirror, and the fact of the character's long, self-absorbed gaze, are themselves clues to help us grasp his nature. But even when the mirror is thus truly functional, more concentrated information can often be given by maintaining a reliable narrator's voice independent of the character's subjective vision. "Though the sleepy, short-sighted countenance and rather bald head reflected in the looking-glass were of such an insignificant type that at first sight they would certainly not have attracted particular attention in any one, yet the owner of the countenance was satisfied with all that he saw in the looking-glass." Thus Dostoevski, in *The Double* (1846), writing before point of view had been much troubled about, makes his opening description largely dramatic and at the same time uses his own commentary to betray his character's egotism. By taking an omniscient position he can do in four lines what any other method would require far more to do. Anyone who tries to translate the passage into a completely objective portrayal of Golyadkin's own thoughts without losing any of the effect, including the clarity, will see how much he has sacrificed.

A major function of indisputable fact is the control of dramatic irony. The simplest form is a straight description, as in several of the above examples, of how one character misinterprets another's unspoken thoughts or motives. "After she got to be a big girl," the narrator of Faulkner's *Light in August* tells us, Lena would "ask her father to stop the wagon at the edge of town and she would get down and walk. She would not tell her father why she wanted to walk instead of riding. He thought that it was because of the smooth streets, the sidewalks. But it was because she believed that the people who saw her . . . would believe that she lived in the town too." The fact of the misinterpretation is something only the omniscient narrator could know, since it is made up of the father's private judgment and the daughter's private motive; yet the scene would be pointless as a clue to Lena's character unless the misjudgment were made clear to us.

More obvious effects are achieved by explicitly controlling the reader's expectations, insuring that he will not travel burdened with the false hopes and fears held by the characters. Some sophisticated readers object strenuously to self-evident manipulations of this kind, yet half the fun of many novels depends on them. Even the "effaced" James found it appropriate in *The Ambassadors* (1903) to heighten our anticipations by saying such things as, "This was the very beginning with him of a condition as to which, later on, as will be seen, he found cause to pull himself up. . . ." [2]

James was the first to formulate clearly the aesthetic problem presented by bald factual summary. He did not, except in *The Awkward Age* (1899), attempt to do away with summary entirely. But he became more and more determined to find a way to make summary itself dramatic—whether as description, narration, or moral and psychological evaluation.

The details of his effort to keep "it all within my hero's compass," [3] to push all summary back into the minds of the characters, are so important that they must be discussed at length later on. No one has ever resisted with more intelligence and integrity the temptations to unassimilated information that beset every novelist. We need only look at any one of thousands of "informative" novels written before and since his time to realize the importance of his effort to make everything count. The travelogues inserted by Balzac (for example, *Les chouans* [1829]), Madame de Staël (for example, *Corinne* [1807]), and Dickens (for example, *Martin Chuzzlewit* [1843–44]), to say nothing of many modern regional novelists, are only an extreme form of a blight that can be found everywhere, from novels that are really only disguised gossip about army life or penthouse life or life in Greenwich Village to novels that do little more than catalogue the unfortunate contents of one type of mind.

But we can accept James's importance without agreeing with Lubbock that James's solution to the problem of summary exacts no price. "The novelist, more free than the playwright, could of course *tell* us, if he chose, what lurks behind this agitated spirit [Strether in *The Ambassadors*]; he could step forward and explain the restless appearance of the man's thought. But if he prefers the dramatic way, admittedly the more effective, there is nothing to prevent him from taking it." [4] By following the Jamesian way the novelist surrenders none of his freedom. "That liberty . . . of standing above the story and taking a broad view of many things, of transcending the limits of the immediate scene—nothing of this is sacrificed by the author's steady advance in the direction of drama. The man's mind has become visible, phenomenal, dramatic; but in acting its part it still lends us eyes, is still an opportunity of extended vision" (p. 149).

But there is, after all, a sacrifice. When the novelist chooses to deliver his facts and summaries as though from the mind of one of his characters, he is in danger of surrendering precisely "that liberty of transcending the limits of the immediate scene"—particularly the limits of that character he has chosen as his mouthpiece. The consequences of this sacrifice will run thematically throughout Part III of this book. For the present, it is enough to say that a fact, when it has been given to us by the author or his unequivocal spokesman, is a very different thing from the same "fact" when given to us by a fallible character in the story. When a character speaks realistically, within the drama, the convention of absolute reliability has been destroyed, and while the gains for some fictional purposes are undeniable, the costs are undeniable too.

Whenever a fact, whenever a narrative summary, whenever a description must, or even might, serve as a clue to our interpretation of the character who provides it, it may very well lose some of its standing as fact, summary or description. Prufrock's notion of the evening sky as etherized patient is no longer fact or description at all, if what the reader requires is knowledge about the real weather. As unreliability increases, there obviously can come a point at which such transformed information ceases to be useful even in characterization of minds, unless the author retains some method of showing what the facts are from which the speaker's interpretations characteristically diverge.

What Caliban sees of Prospero in Browning's poem can tell us all we need to know about Caliban only because we know about Prospero from another source. All of our pleasure in the irony would be lost— though there might be compensations of another kind—if we had to spend our time puzzling whether Browning's and Caliban's views are identical.

There can be no dramatic irony, by definition, unless the author and audience can somehow share knowledge which the characters do not hold. Though reliable narration is by no means the only way of conveying to the audience the facts on which dramatic irony is based, it is a useful way, and in some works, works in which no one but the author can conceivably know what needs to be known, it may be indispensable. In much of the great comic fiction, for example, our amusement depends on the author's telling us in advance that the characters' troubles are temporary and their concern ridiculously exaggerated. Anyone who doubts the value of this kind of rhetoric should imagine himself trying to narrate *Tom Jones* without the author's voice to remind his readers that things are not as bad for Tom as they look, or *Great Expectations* without the voice of the mature Pip to heighten, on the one hand, our sense of the younger Pip's moral decline and to preserve, on the other, our sympathy for him as he goes down and our certainty that he will again rise. But dramatic irony can be equally important in more serious works. Could we ever really prefer a reading of *The Great Gatsby* cleansed of the knowledge given us in the opening? "When I came back from the East last autumn," Nick tells us, "I felt that I wanted the world to be in uniform and at a sort of moral attention forever. . . . Only Gatsby . . . was exempt from my reaction—Gatsby, who represented everything for which I have an unaffected scorn. . . . There was something gorgeous about him . . . an extraordinary gift for hope, a romantic readiness such as I have never found in any other person and which it is not likely I shall ever find again. No—Gatsby turned out all right at the end; it is what preyed on Gatsby, what foul dust floated in the wake of his dreams that temporarily closed out my interest in the abortive sorrows and short-winded elations of men." After reading this, we know a good deal that no one in the story will know as it progresses. The younger Nick as a "lucid reflector" in the James manner would be an unreliable witness to the events. As it is, the older Nick provides thoroughly reliable guidance.

"Sing, goddess, the anger of Peleus' son Achilleus / and its devastation, which put pains thousandfold upon the Achaians / . . ."—yes, *that* is the order of causation in *this* work; we know where we stand from this point on, despite the great number of lesser ambiguities. To purge the *Iliad* of this absolutism would be to destroy it. Whenever the demands of concision or clarity or dramatic irony of the most emphatic kind are more important than making the story seem to be telling itself, or giving an air of the puzzling ambiguities of life, the author will seek those devices which can maintain facts as facts and reliable judgments as reliable judgments. . . .

NOTES

1. Book V, ll. 1765–71.
2. New York, 1930, p. 80.
3. Preface to *The Ambassadors*, in *The Art of the Novel*, ed. R. P. Blackmur (New York, 1947), p. 317.
4. *The Craft of Fiction* (London, 1921), pp. 157–58.

WAYNE BOOTH

Telling as Showing: Dramatized Narrators, Reliable and Unreliable

RELIABLE NARRATORS AS DRAMATIZED SPOKESMEN
FOR THE IMPLIED AUTHOR

What is the context into which Fielding's narrator intrudes, at the end of *Joseph Andrews*, to say of Fanny, "How, reader, shall I give thee an adequate idea of this lovely young creature! . . . to comprehend her entirely, conceive youth, health, bloom, beauty, neatness, and innocence, in her bridal bed; conceive all these in their utmost perfection, and you may place the charming Fanny's picture before your eyes"? His earlier comments obviously provide part of the context. But if this is so, how does this new context, itself made up of "intrusions," relate to the whole story? And what of that still larger context, the author's and reader's experience with previous fiction?

Obviously the notion of function with which we have been working so far must be enlarged. Though commentary has served in the ways outlined above, and though no other device could have served most of them as well, it is also true that to look at these functions is only a first step in explaining the power of the great commentators. In *Don Quixote,* for example, our delight in the comments by various narrators obviously is not fully explained by showing that such commentary serves to heighten the effect of the knight's adventures. Though Cid Hamete Benengeli's farewell to his pen parallels in comic style Don Quixote's farewell to his books and to life itself, such a parallel fails to explain the full delight of the passage. "Here shalt thou remain, hung upon this rack by this brass wire. I know not if thou beest well cut or not, O pen of mine, but here thou shalt live for long ages to come, unless some presumptuous and scoundrelly historians should take thee down to profane thee. . . . For me alone Don Quixote was born and I for him; it was for him to act, for me to write, and we two are one in spite of that Tordesillesque pretender who had, and may have, the audacity to write with a coarse and ill-trimmed ostrich quill of the deeds of my valiant knight. . . ." [1]

The effect here is made up of many elements. There is pleasure in mere ornament: the history of intruding narrators is full of sheer overflowing narrative exuberance, as if the story itself, good as it is, did not provide adequate scope for the author's genius. There is parody of previous fiction: the laying down of swords, flutes, horns, and other romantic objects was part of the tradition ridiculed in *Don Quixote*. But quite obviously the most important quality here is something else entirely: the narrator has made of himself a dramatized character to whom we react as we react to other characters.

Narrators like Cid Hamete, who can speak for the norms on which the action is based, can become companions and guides quite distinct from the wonders they have to show. Our admiration or affection or sympathy or fascination or awe—no two of these narrators affect us in precisely the same way—is more intense just because it has been made personal; the telling is itself a dramatic rendering of a relationship with the author's "second self" which in strictly impersonal fiction is often less lively because only implicit.

There has been very little critical discussion of this relationship. But it is not hard to find confessions to its effect. At the beginning of *The Catcher in the Rye* (1951), J. D. Salinger's adolescent hero says, "What really knocks me out is a book that, when you're all done reading it, you wish the author that wrote it was a terrific friend of yours and you could call him up on the phone whenever you felt like it." Many more mature readers have found themselves feeling the same way. Even Henry James, in spite of his mistrust of the author's voice, cannot resist the appeal of a great loquacious author like Fielding. After describing the deficiencies of Tom Jones's mind and the partial compensation of his vitality, James says, "Besides which his author—*he* handsomely possessed of a mind—has such an amplitude of reflexion for him and round him that we see him through the mellow air of Fielding's fine old moralism, fine old humour and fine old style, which somehow enlarge, make every one and every thing important." [2]

It may be extreme to call this relationship one of identification, as do Paul Goodman and H. W. Leggett,[3] but there are times when we do surrender ourselves to the great authors and allow our judgments to merge completely with theirs. Our surrender need not be dramatized by giving open voice to the narrator, but it is in its service that many comments find their major justification. Much commentary that seems excessive if judged by narrow standards of function is wholly defensible when seen as contributing to our sense of traveling with a trustworthy companion, an author who is sincerely battling to do justice to his materials. George Eliot, for example, involves us constantly in her battle to deal with the truth, even at the expense of beauty or pleasure. " 'This Rector of Broxton is little better than a pagan!' I hear one of my readers exclaim. 'How much more edifying it would have been if you had made him give Arthur some truly spiritual advice! You might have put into his mouth the most beautiful things—quite as good as reading a sermon.' " The story of *Adam Bede* (1859) stops for several pages while she gives her answer to "my fair critic." "Certainly I could, if I held it the highest vocation of the novelist to represent things as they never have been and never will be." But her "strongest effort is to avoid any such arbitrary picture, and to give a faithful account of men and things as they have mirrored themselves in my mind." Even if the mirror is "defective," she feels herself "as much bound to tell you as precisely as I can what that reflection is, as if I were in the witness-box narrating my experience on oath." Out of context such talk may sound overdone, even boastful. But in context it can be convincing. "So I am content to tell my simple story, without trying to make things seem better than they were; dreading nothing, indeed, but falsity, which, in spite of one's best efforts, there is reason to dread. Falsehood is so easy, truth so difficult." [4] Obviously, one effect of this passage is to remind us that the Rector *is* more convincing than an idealized portrait would be. But a more important effect is to involve us on the side of the honest, perceptive, perhaps somewhat inept, but certainly uncompromising author in the almost overwhelming effort to avoid falsehood.

Even the most clumsily worded intrusion can redeem itself by conveying this sense of how deeply the narrator cares about what he is doing. The graceless conclusion of Melville's *Billy Budd*, for example, serves to remind us of the author's very real problems and thus to make us forgive every seeming fault. "The symmetry of form attainable in pure fiction cannot so readily be achieved in a narration essentially having less to do with fable than with fact. Truth uncompromisingly told will always have its ragged edges. . . . Though properly the story ends with his life something in way of sequel will not be amiss. Three brief chapters will suffice" (p. 274, chap. xxix).

Dostoevski is frequently masterful in making his narration seem to be a part of the battle. When he says that he does "not feel very competent" to the tremendous task before him, the effect is never to make us doubt his competence. His tendency to identify himself and his weaknesses with his hero's is especially effective. In *The Double* there is a fine satirical passage about the futility of the author's desire to portray the glorious world into which his hero desires, with equal futility, to rise.[5]

"FIELDING" IN "TOM JONES"

It is frustrating to try to deal critically with such effects, because they can in no way be demonstrated to the reader who has not experienced them. No amount of quotation, no amount of plot summary, can possibly show how fully the implied author's character dominates our reactions to the whole. About all we can do is to look closely at one work, *Tom Jones,* analyzing in static terms what in any successful reading is as sequential and dynamic as the action itself.

Though the dramatized Fielding does serve to pull together many parts of *Tom Jones* that might otherwise seem disconnected, and though he serves dozens of other functions, from the standpoint of strict function he goes too far: much of his commentary relates to nothing but the reader and himself. If we really want to defend the book as art, we must somehow account for these "extraneous" elements. It is not difficult to do so, however, once we think of the effect of our intimacy on our attitude toward the book as a whole. If we read straight through all of the seemingly gratuitous appearances by the narrator, leaving out the story of Tom, we discover a running account of growing intimacy between the narrator and the reader, an account with a kind of plot of its own and a separate denouement. In the prefatory chapter to his final volume, the narrator makes this denouement explicit, suggesting a distinct interest in the "story" of his relationship with the reader. This interest certainly requires some explanation if we wish to claim that *Tom Jones* is a unified work of art and not half-novel, half-essay.

> We are now, reader, arrived at the last stage of our long journey. As we have, therefore, travelled together through so

many pages, let us behave to one another like fellow-travellers in a stagecoach, who have passed several days in the company of each other; and who, notwithstanding any bickerings or little animosities which may have occurred on the road, generally make all up at last, and mount, for the last time, into their vehicle with cheerfulness and good-humour.

The farewell goes on for several paragraphs, and at times the bantering tone of much of the work is entirely abandoned. "And now, my friend, I take this opportunity (as I shall have no other) of heartily wishing thee well. If I have been an entertaining companion to thee, I promise thee it is what I have desired. If in anything I have offended, it was really without any intention."

It may be extravagant to use the term "subplot" for the story of our relationship with this narrator. Certainly the narrator's "life" and Tom Jones's life are much less closely parallel than we expect in most plots and subplots. In *Lear*, Gloucester's fate parallels and reinforces Lear's. In *Tom Jones*, the "plot" of our relationship with Fielding-as-narrator has no similarity to the story of Tom. There is no complication, not even any sequence except for the gradually increasing familiarity and intimacy leading to farewell. And much of what we admire or enjoy in the narrator is in most respects quite different from what we like or enjoy in his hero.

Yet somehow a genuine harmony of the two dramatized elements is produced. It is from the narrator's norms that Tom departs when he gets himself into trouble, yet Tom is always in harmony with his most important norms. Not only does he reassure us constantly that Tom's heart is always in the right place, his presence reassures us of both the moral and the literary rightness of Tom's existence. As we move through the novel under his guidance, watching Tom sink to the depths, losing, as it appears, Allworthy's protection, Sophia's love, and his own shaky hold on decency, we experience for him what R. S. Crane has called the "comic analogue of fear." [6] And our growing intimacy with Fielding's dramatic version of himself produces a kind of comic analogue of the true believer's reliance on a benign providence in real life. It is not just that he promises a happy ending. In a fictional world that offers no single character who is both wise and good—even Allworthy, though all worthy, is no model of perspicacity—the author is always there on his platform to remind us, through his wisdom and benevolence, of what human life ought to be and might be. What is more, his self-portrait is of a life enriched by a vast knowledge of literary culture and of a mind of great creative power—qualities which could never be so fully conveyed through simply exercising them without comment on the dramatic materials of Tom's story.

For the reader who becomes too much aware of the author's claim to superlative virtues, the effect may fail. He may seem merely to be posing. For the reader with his mind on the main business, however, the narrator becomes a rich and provocative chorus. It is his wisdom and learning and benevolence that permeate the world of the book, set its comic tone between the extremes of sentimental indulgence and scornful indignation, and in a sense redeem Tom's world of hypocrites and fools.

One can imagine, perhaps, a higher standard of virtue, wisdom, or learning than the narrator's. But for most of us he succeeds in being the highest possible in his world—and, at least for the nonce, in ours. He is not trying to write for any other world, but for *this* one he strikes the precise medium between too much and too little piety, benevolence, learning, and worldly wisdom. When he draws to the end of his farewell, then, at a time when we know we are to lose him, and uses terms which inevitably move us across the barrier to death itself, we find, lying beneath our amusement at his playful mode of farewell, something of the same feeling we have when we lose a close friend, a friend who has given us a gift which we can never repay. The gift he leaves—his book—is himself, precisely himself. The author has created this self as he has written the book. The book and the friend are one. "For however short the period may be of my own performances, they will most probably outlive their own infirm author, and the weakly productions of his abusive contemporaries." Was Fielding literally infirm as he wrote that sentence? It matters not in the least. It is not Fielding we care about, but the narrator created to speak in his name. . . .

NOTES

1. Samuel Putnam translation (New York, 1949).
2. Preface to *The Princess Casamassima*, p. 68.
3. "In novels we identify with the omniscient narrator" (Goodman, *Structure of Literature* [Chicago, 1954], p. 153). "It is indeed true that the reader of

fiction identifies himself with the author of a story rather than with the characters of the story" (H. W. Leggett, *The Idea in Fiction* [London, 1934], p. 188).

4. *Adam Bede*, Book II, chap. xvii, "In Which the Story Pauses a Little."

5. *The Short Novels of Dostoievsky*, trans. Constance Garnett (New York, 1945), chap. iv, p. 501.

6. *Critics and Criticism*, ed. R. S. Crane (Chicago, 1952), p. 637.

ROBERT HUMPHREY

The Functions of Stream of Consciousness

> The discovery that memories, thoughts, and feelings exist outside the primary consciousness is the most important step forward that has occurred in psychology since I have been a student of that science. WILLIAM JAMES

Stream of consciousness is one of the delusive terms which writers and critics use. It is delusive because it sounds concrete and yet it is used as variously—and vaguely—as "romanticism," "symbolism," and "surrealism." We never know whether it is being used to designate the bird of technique or the beast of genre—and we are startled to find the creature designated is most often a monstrous combination of the two. The purpose of this study is to examine the term and its literary implications.

STREAM OF CONSCIOUSNESS DEFINED

Stream of consciousness is properly a phrase for psychologists. William James coined it.[1] The phrase is most clearly useful when it is applied to mental processes, for as a rhetorical locution it becomes doubly metaphorical; that is, the word "consciousness" as well as the word "stream" is figurative, hence, both are less precise and less stable. If, then, the term stream of consciousness (I shall use it since it is already established as a literary label) is reserved for indicating an approach to the presentation of *psychological* aspects of character in fiction, it can be used with some precision. This reservation I shall make, and it is the basis from which the contradicting and often mean-

From *Stream of Consciousness in the Modern Novel*, 1962. Reprinted by permission of the University of California Press.

ingless commentary on the stream-of-consciousness novel can be resolved.[2]

The stream-of-consciousness novel is identified most quickly by its subject matter. This, rather than its techniques, its purposes, or its themes, distinguishes it. Hence, the novels that are said to use the stream-of-consciousness *technique* to a considerable degree prove, upon analysis, to be novels which have as their essential subject matter the consciousness of one or more characters; that is, the depicted consciousness serves as a screen on which the material in these novels is presented.

"Consciousness" should not be confused with words which denote more restricted mental activities, such as "intelligence" or "memory." The justifiably irate comments of the psychology scholars deplore the layman's use of the term. One of these scholars writes: "It has been said that no philosophical term is at once so popular and so devoid of standard meaning as *consciousness;* and the layman's usage of the term has been credited with begging as many metaphysical questions as will probably be the privilege of any single word." [3] The area which we are to examine here is an important one in which this confusion has been amassed. Since our study will concern persons who are laymen in psychology, it is necessary that we proceed with the "layman's usage." Naturally, the stream-of-consciousness writers have not defined their label. We readers who have stamped it on them must try to do it.

Consciousness indicates the entire area of mental attention, from preconsciousness on through the levels of the mind up to and including the highest one of rational, communicable awareness.[4] This last area is the one with which almost all psychological fiction is concerned. Stream-of-consciousness fiction differs from all other psychological fiction precisely in that it is concerned with those levels that are more inchoate than rational verbalization—those levels on the margin of attention.

So far as stream-of-consciousness fiction is concerned, it is pointless to try to make definite categories of the many levels of consciousness. Such attempts demand the answers to serious metaphysical questions, and they put serious questions about the stream-of-consciousness writers' concepts of psychology and their aesthetic intentions—questions which the epistemologists, the psychologists, and the literary historians have not yet answered satisfactorily. It is desirable for an analysis of stream-of-consciousness fiction to assume that there are levels of consciousness from the lowest one just above oblivion to the highest one which is represented by verbal (or other formal) communication. "Low" and "high" simply indicate degrees of the rationally ordered. The adjectives "dim" and "bright" could be used just as well to indicate these degrees. There are, however, two levels of consciousness which can be rather simply distinguished: the "speech level" and the "prespeech level." There is a point at which they overlap, but otherwise the distinction is quite clear. The prespeech level, which is the concern of most of the literature under consideration in this study, involves no communicative basis as does the speech level (whether spoken or written). This is its salient distinguishing characteristic. In short, the prespeech levels of consciousness are not censored, rationally controlled, or logically ordered. By "consciousness," then, I shall mean the whole area of mental processes, including especially the prespeech levels. The term "psyche" I shall use as a synonym for "consciousness," and at times, even the word "mind" will serve as another synonym. These synonyms, although they are handicapped by the various evocative qualities they possess, are convenient to use because they lend themselves well to the forming of adjectives and adverbs.

Hence, "consciousness" must not be confused with "intelligence" or "memory" or any other such limiting term. Henry James has written novels which reveal psychological processes in which a single point of view is maintained so that the entire novel is presented through the intelligence of a character. But these, since they do not deal at all with prespeech levels of consciousness, are not what I have defined as stream-of-consciousness novels. Marcel Proust has written a modern classic which is often cited as an example of stream-of-consciousness fiction,[5] but *A la recherche du temps perdu* is concerned only with the reminiscent aspect of consciousness. Proust was deliberately recapturing the past for the purposes of communication; hence he did not write a stream-of-consciousness novel. Let us think of consciousness as being in the form of an iceberg—the whole iceberg and not just the relatively small surface portion. Stream-of-consciousness fiction is, to follow this comparison, greatly concerned with what lies below the surface.

With such a concept of consciousness, we may define stream-of-consciousness fiction as a type of fiction in which the basic emphasis is placed on exploration of the prespeech levels of consciousness for the purpose, primarily, of revealing the psychic being of the characters.

When some of the novels which fall into this classification are considered, it becomes immediately apparent that the techniques by which the subjects are controlled and the characters are presented are palpably different from one novel to the next. Indeed, there is no stream-of-consciousness technique. Instead, there are several quite different techniques which are used to present stream of consciousness.

THE SELF-CONSCIOUS MIND

It is not an uncommon misconception that many modern novels, and particularly the ones that are generally labeled stream of consciousness, rely greatly upon private symbols to represent private confusions. The misconception comes primarily from considering whatever is "internal" or "subjective" in characterization as arrant fantasy, or, at best, as psychoanalytical.[6] Serious misreadings and unsound evaluations result from this initial misunderstanding, particularly in discussion of major twentieth-century novels. I refer to such subjective fiction as *Ulysses, Mrs. Dalloway, To the Lighthouse,* and *The Sound and the Fury.* These novels may very well be within a category we can label stream of consciousness, so long as we know what we are talking about. The evidence reveals that we never do—or never have done so.

It is meaningless to label all of the novels stream of consciousness that are generally named as such, unless we mean by that phrase simply "inner awareness." The expression of this quality is what they have in common. It is, however, apparent that that is not what has been meant when they have been so labeled and forced to share the same categorical niche. It is not what William James meant when he coined the term. James was formulating psychological theory and he had discovered that "memories, thoughts, and feelings exist outside the primary consciousness" and, further, that they appear to one, not as a chain, but as a stream, a flow.[7] Whoever, then, first applied the phrase to the novel did so correctly only if he was thinking of a *method* of representing inner awareness. What has actually happened is that *monologue intérieur* was clumsily translated into English. But it is palpably true that the methods of the novels in which this device is used are different, and that there are dozens of other novels which use internal monologue which no one would seriously classify as stream of consciousness. Such are, for example, *Moby Dick, Les Faux-monnayeurs,* and *Of Time and the River.* Stream of consciousness, then, is not a synonym for *monologue intérieur.* It is not a term to name a particular method or technique; although it probably was used originally in literary criticism for that purpose. One can safely conjecture that such a loose and fanciful term was a radiant buoy to well-meaning critics who had lost their bearings. The natural, and historically accurate, association of the term with psychology, along with the overwhelming psychoanalytical trend of twentieth-century thought, has resulted in giving all novels that could be loosely associated with the loose phrase "stream of consciousness" a marked Viennese accent.

The word "stream" need not concern us immediately, for representation of the flow of consciousness is, provided one is convinced that consciousness flows, entirely a matter of technique. The approach to take is to consider the word "consciousness" and to attempt to formulate what, to the various writers, is the ultimate significance of what consciousness contains. It is, in short, a psychological and a philosophical question. Stream-of-consciousness literature is psychological literature, but it must be studied at the level on which psychology mingles with epistemology. Immediately the question confronts us: What does consciousness contain? Then, too, what does it contain so far as philosophy and psychology have investigated it *and* what does it contain so far as the novelists in question have represented it? These may be mutually exclusive questions; they are certainly different ones. But the concern here is not with psychological theory; it is with novelistic subject matter. The question for this study is a phenomenological one: What does consciousness contain in the sense of what has it contained so far as the consciousness of the novelists have experienced it? Any answer must respect the possible range of a creative writer's sensitivity and imagination. No answer needs proving beyond the gesture of saying: There it is in Virginia Woolf; there it is in James Joyce. It should be remembered that, first, we are attempting to clarify a literary term; and second, we are trying to determine how fictional art is enriched by the depiction of inner states.

The attempt to create human consciousness in fiction is a modern attempt to analyze human nature. Most of us will be convinced, now, that it can be the starting point of that most important of all intellectual functions. We have, for example, Henry James's word for it that "experience is never limited, and it is never complete." He continues in the same context to point to the "chamber of consciousness" as the chamber of experience.[8] Consciousness, then, is *where* we are aware of human experience. And this is enough for the novelist. He, collectively, leaves nothing out: sensations and memories, feelings and conceptions, fancies and imaginations—and those very unphilosophic, but consistently unavoidable phenomena we call intuitions, visions, and insights. These last terms, which usually embarrass the epistomologist, unlike the immediately preceding series, are not always included under the label "mental life." Precisely for this reason it is important to point them up here. Human "knowledge" which comes not from "mental" activity but from "spiritual" life is a concern of novelists, if not of psychologists. Knowledge, then, as a category of consciousness must include intuition, vision, and sometimes even the occult, so far as twentieth-century writers are concerned.

Thus, we may, on inductive grounds, conclude that the realm of life with which stream-of-consciousness literature is concerned is mental and spiritual experience—both the whatness and the howness of it. The whatness includes the categories of mental experiences: sensations, memories, imaginations, conceptions, and intuitions. The howness includes the symbolizations, the feelings, and the processes of association. It is often impossible to separate the what from the how. Is, for example, memory a part of mental content or is it a mental process? Such fine distinctions, of course, are not the concern of novelists as novelists. Their object, if they are writing stream of consciousness, is to enlarge fictional art by depicting the inner states of their characters.

The problem of character depiction is central to stream-of-consciousness fiction. The great advantage, and consequently the best justification of this type of novel, rests on its potentialities for presenting character more accurately and more realistically. There is the example of the *roman expérimental* behind James Joyce, Virginia Woolf, and Dorothy Richardson, and though a little farther removed, behind William Faulkner. But there is a difference, and it is a tremendous one, between Zola and Dreiser, say, two novelists who attempted a kind of laboratory method in fiction, and the stream-of-consciousness writers. It is indicated chiefly in the difference in subject matter—which is, for the earlier novelists, motive and action (external man) and for the later ones, psychic existence and functioning (internal man). The difference is also revealed in the psychological and philosophical thinking in back of this. Psychologically it is the distinction between behavioristic concepts and psychoanalytical ones; philosophically, it is that between a broad materialism and a generalized existentialism. Combined, it is the difference between being concerned about what one does and being concerned about what one is.

I do not offer a Freudian or Existential brief for stream-of-consciousness literature. All of its authors doubtless were familiar, more or less, with psychoanalytical theories and with the twentieth-century recrudescence of personalism and were directly or indirectly influenced by them. Even more certain can we be that these writers were influenced by the broader concepts of a "new psychology" and a "new philosophy" —a nebulous label for all postbehavioristic and non-positivistic thinking, including any philosophy or psychology which emphasized man's inner mental and emotional life (e.g., Gestalt psychology, psychoanalytical psychology, Bergsonian ideas of *durée* and the *élan vital,* religious mysticism, much symbolic logic, Christian existentialism, etc.). It is this background which led to the great difference between Zola's subject matter and Joyce's; between Balzac's and Dorothy Richardson's. Yet as novelists all of these writers were concerned with the problem of characterization. There is naturalism in character depiction found in the work of both the late and the early of the above novelists, but there is a contrast and it is determined by the difference in psychological focusing. In short, the stream-of-consciousness novelists were, like the naturalists, trying to depict life accurately; but unlike the naturalists, the life they were concerned with was the individual's psychic life.

In examining the chief stream-of-consciousness writers in order to discover their diverse evaluations of inner awareness, we need to keep in mind two important questions: What can be accomplished by presenting character as it exists pyschically? How is fictional art enriched by the depiction of inner states? The direction of the following discussion will be toward answering these questions.

IMPRESSIONS AND VISIONS

Unlike most originators of artistic genres, the twentieth-century pioneer in stream of consciousness remains the least well-known of the important stream-of-consciousness writers. It is the price a writer pays, even an experimental writer, for engendering monotony. Readers may justifiably neglect Dorothy Richardson, but no one who would understand the development of twentieth-century fiction can. With a great debt to Henry James and Joseph Conrad, she invented the fictional depiction of the flow of consciousness. Sometimes she is brilliant; always she is sensitive to the subtleties of mental functioning; but finally, she becomes lost in the overflow—a formless, unending deluge of realistic detail.

It is difficult to grasp Dorothy Richardson's aims. She gives this account of them herself in the brilliant foreword to *Pilgrimage:*

. . . the present writer, proposing at this moment to write a novel and looking around for a contemporary pattern, was faced with the choice between following one of her regiments and attempting to produce a feminine equivalent of the current masculine realism. Choosing the latter alternative, she presently set aside, at the bidding of a dissatisfaction that revealed its nature without cause, a considerable mass of manuscript. Aware, as she wrote, of the gradual falling away of the preoccupations that for a while had dictated the briskly moving script, and of the substitution, for these inspiring preoccupations, *of a stranger in the form of contemplated reality having for the first time in her experience its own say, and apparently justifying those who acclaim writing as the surest means of discovering the truth about one's own thoughts* and beliefs, she had been at the same time increasingly tormented, not only by the failure, of this now so independently assertive reality, adequately to appear within the text, but by its revelation, whencesoever focused, of a hundred faces, any one of which, the moment it was entrapped within the close mesh of direct statement, summoned its fellows to disqualify it.[9]

The italics are mine and the words they emphasize reveal just what a reader gets from *Pilgrimage*. It is a psychical autobiography, which means that it is almost impossible for a reader to be empathic toward it or to understand the importance of its implications. It is difficult to see either a microcosm or an exemplum here. There is a certain amount of universal interest possible in looking in on how a fairly sensitive but greatly limited mind functions and in discovering how it classifies and rejects; and there is even an interest in discovering what a great amount of dullness a mind encounters in the world—but such an interest is not likely to last throughout twelve volumes. The one possibility left for Dorothy Richardson was to reveal some of the mysteries of psychic life, to depict it as an area from which something of the external world could be explained. But this she does not do. She does not investigate the world of consciousness on a level that is deep enough.

Two interpretations of *Pilgrimage* have suggested a thematic significance in the work: John Cowper Powys, Dorothy Richardson's most persuasive admirer, justifies her novel because it is a presentation of the feminine view of life, which he is convinced is a worth-while thing in itself, necessary to supplement the masculine picture of things.[10] Dorothy Richardson herself evidently believed this also. She says, we recall, that she began writing in order "to produce a feminine equivalent of the current masculine realism." Unfortunately, the dichotomy between the feminine and masculine viewpoints is too tenuous, if not wholly inadequate, for any degree of profundity. Granted a possible over-all difference between these two classes of attitudes, still the basic problems and situations of life (hence of art) are neither masculine nor feminine, but simply human. One might as well propose that Faulkner writes in order to present a psychotic equivalent of the current sane realism! Faulkner has, certainly, advantages, which we shall consider presently, in presenting life from an abnormal person's point of view—and likewise there are certain values inherent in the presentation of life from a feminine point of view—but these values cannot be realized in a vacuum. An adequate purpose is not found in presenting these viewpoints merely for the sake of novelty. It is hardly justified, at least, for important literature. Another critic, Joseph Warren Beach, thinks of *Pilgrimage* as a quest story. He believes the point of the novel lies in Miriam's continuous search for a symbolic "little coloured garden," and again that she is on a pilgrimage "to some elusive shrine, glimpsed here and there and lost to view." This theory is easily credible, and it gives an important justification to the novel; but as Beach intimates, how digressive, how vague, and how long! [11]

Dorothy Richardson deserves more credit as a pioneer in novelistic method than as a successful creator of fiction. There are indications that the pioneering fever was the conscious impetus, for the opening chapters of *Pilgrimage* were "written to the accompaniment of a sense of being upon a fresh pathway, an adventure so searching and, sometimes, so joyous as to produce a longing for participation." [12] By "participation" Dorothy Richardson meant "readers"; but I suspect she will always be rather bland hors d'oeuvres for the reading public. However, another kind of participation came. Dorothy Richardson recognizes this, too, in her foreword: "The lonely track, meanwhile, had turned out to be a populous highway. Amongst those who had simultaneously entered it, two figures stood out. One a woman mounted upon a magnificently caparisoned charger, the other a man walking, with eyes devoutly closed, weaving as he went a rich garment of new words wherewith to clothe the antique dark material of his engrossment." The woman we take to be Virginia Woolf; the man, who is described more aptly, is certainly James Joyce. There is little difficulty in determining why either of these writers used stream-of-consciousness methods.

Virginia Woolf speaks eloquently as a critic herself, and the key to her purposes is in her critical writing. Less eloquently, though authoritatively, are her purposes spoken by a number of other critics, partly because she gives them the key and partly because she lucidly reveals in her novels what she is about. Since Virginia Woolf's accomplishments have been so thoroughly analyzed,[13] it is necessary here only to summarize in order to provide a direct answer to the question which is in front of us: For what purpose does this writer use stream of consciousness?

Let us answer the question at once and show afterward why we have come to the answer. Virginia Woolf wanted to formulate the possibilities and processes of inner realization of truth—a truth she reckoned to be inexpressible; hence only on a level of the mind that is not expressed could she find this process of realization functioning. At least this is true with her three stream-of-consciousness novels. The first two of these, *Mrs. Dalloway* and *To the Lighthouse,* can be considered together, since they illustrate in only slightly different ways the same achievement. *The Waves* marks a different approach.

Clarissa Dalloway, Mrs. Ramsay, and Lily Briscoe all have moments of vision. Not that they are disciplined mystics who have prepared themselves for this, but their creator believed that the important thing in human life is the search the individual constantly has for meaning and identification. The fulfillment of her characters is therefore achieved when Virginia Woolf feels they are ready to receive the vision. The novels are a record of their preparations for the final insight. The preparations are in the form of fleeting insights into other characters and syntheses of present and past private symbols.

We know from Virginia Woolf's essays that she believed the important thing for the artist to express is his private vision of reality, of what life, subjectively, is. She thought that the search for reality is not a matter of dramatic external action. "Examine an ordinary mind on an ordinary day," she says, and again: "Life is . . . a luminous halo, a semi-transparent envelope surrounding us from the beginning of consciousness to the end. Is it not the task of the novelists to convey this varying, this unknown and uncircumscribed spirit . . . ?"[14] Thus the search, thought Virginia Woolf, is a psychic activity, and it is the preoccupation (it surrounds us) of most human beings. The only thing is that most human beings are not aware of this psychic activity, so deep down is it in their consciousness. This is one of the reasons Virginia Woolf chose characters who are extraordinarily sensitive, whose psyches would at least occasionally be occupied with this search. And it is, above all, the reason that she chose the stream-of-consciousness medium for her most mature presentation of this theme.

Analogically, we may call the Virginia Woolf of these two stream-of-consciousness novels a mystic. She is a mystic in that she is interested in the search her characters make for unification. The climax of *Mrs. Dalloway* suggests the mystic's search for cosmic identification. And what, in the novel, is more nearly the mystic's vision of light than Lily Briscoe's crucial attainment of vision in *To the Lighthouse?* It is because this novelist is building up to the moments of illumination that her method is one of presenting psychic impressions. She selects these impressions as stages toward arriving at a vision. It is not the undifferentiated trivia that impinge on consciousness which interest her; it is the illusive event that is meaningful and that carries the germ of the final insight.

The Waves is a different kind of accomplishment. In this novel there is no mystical quest after identity and subjective essence; it is a presentation of the purest psychological analysis in literature. Not, let it be noted, of psychoanalysis. Spontaneous psychic life is presented in this novel. The achievement is the tracing of the growth of psychic lives. The method is as much the presentation of uncensored observations by the characters of each other as it is of the characters' own psychological make-up. Indeed, the two are the same thing in this "X-ray of intuition," as Bernard Blackstone labels it.

The psychic anatomy here is not a bare analysis, however. It is full of the impressionist's sensitivity to color, sound, and shapes as Virginia Woolf's earlier novels are. The formal soliloquies are close to poetry in their concentrated quality, their dependence on rhythms, and their exact diction. This work is the most eloquent of this eloquent novelist's fiction. It is also the most uncommunicative, for here Virginia Woolf's private sense of the significant is confined to characters who remain only individuals and never compose into universal symbols. Reality is the aim and it is achieved, but the rich symbolic significance of the characters of the two earlier stream-of-consciousness novels is lacking. As much as we may admire and enjoy this work, we are almost bound to agree with David Daiches that it is overloaded with technique.

SATIRES AND IRONIES

A person much more often charged with such artistic trammeling is

James Joyce. In creative productions the ends justify the means, and Joyce has contributed hugely to a revitalized fiction. What the ends of *Ulysses* finally are, I do not expect to determine. The many volumes which have been written to explain Joyce's purposes threaten the cursory appraisal; but I should like at least to suggest one important achievement of Joyce's in *Ulysses* which is central to his whole purpose and which is greatly dependent on stream-of-consciousness techniques. This is the marvelous degree of objectivity which he achieves. Joyce, more than any other novelist, gains what Joseph Warren Beach terms "dramatic immediacy." In *A Portrait of the Artist as a Young Man*, Joyce, in the guise of Stephen, states his theory of the evolution of artistic form when he maintains that "the personality of the artist, at first a cry or a cadence or a mood and then a fluid and lambent narrative, finally refines itself out of existence, impersonalizes itself, so to speak. The esthetic image in the dramatic form is life purified in and projected from the human imagination. The mystery of esthetic like that of material creation is accomplished. The artist, like the God of the creation, remains within or behind or beyond or above his handiwork, invisible, refined out of existence, indifferent, paring his fingernails." [15] The author is almost "refined out of existence" in *Ulysses*. Why does Joyce place such an important emphasis on ridding his work of signs of its author? As a feat in itself it would be nothing more than an interesting tour de force. The effect of this great accomplishment is to make the reader feel he is in direct contact with the life represented in the book. It is a method for doing what Joyce wanted to do, and that is to present life as it actually is, without prejudice or direct evaluations. It is, then, the goal of the realist and the naturalist. The thoughts and actions of the characters are there, as if they were created by an invisible, indifferent creator. We must accept them, because they exist.

If Joyce's accomplishment is, then, that of the most successful of realists, what is his aim? What view of life can he communicate by impersonalizing his creation through presenting the direct interior monologues of his characters? The answer is this—and it is from this basis that a future evaluation of *Ulysses* must start: for Joyce, existence is a comedy and man is to be satirized, gently not bitterly, for his incongruous and pitiful central role in it. The objective distance of the author, working as it chiefly does in *Ulysses* on the level of man's daydreams and mental delusions, shows the smallness of man, the great disparity between his ideals and his actualities, and the prosaicness of most of the things he considers special. Joyce's methods point to this: the *Odyssey* pattern is a means for equating the heroic and the ordinary, and the undifferentiated internal monologue is a means for equating the trivial and the profound. Life is depicted by Joyce so minutely that there is no room for any values to stand out. Joyce presents life with its shortcomings and its inherent contradictions, and the result is satire. Only within stream of consciousness could the necessary objectivity be attained for making it all convincingly realistic; for the pathos is in the fact that *man* thinks he is special and heroic, not that *Joyce* thinks he is pitiful.

Joyce is a writer of comedy and of satiric comedy at that. He is not a jokester or a funny man. The novel is not as a whole, in any sense, a hoax: the overtones are too far-reaching; there is too credible a concept of man's psychic life presented. It is obvious, however, that *Ulysses* is, fundamentally, a satirical comment on modern man's life. Joyce could never have shown this convincingly with any subject other than man's life on the level of consciousness, where the ideal can be reached for, even by the everyman Leopold Bloom, whose very next act or thought will show how far he actually is from it.[16]

The only other writer who utilizes effectively this natural advantage for satire in depiction of psyche is William Faulkner. But there is a difference. Faulkner, although he makes wide use of comic materials, is not a writer of comedy, not even of divine comedy. Faulkner's satires of circumstance are, like those of the Hardy of *Jude the Obscure* and the poems, irrevocably tragic. And they are more profound than Joyce's. One way to explain this is to consider Faulkner as a stream-of-consciousness writer who combines the views of life of Woolf with those of Joyce. Faulkner's views are not the same in either case; but the cast is similar in both. His characters search for insight, and their search is fundamentally ironic.

Since relatively little study has been published on Faulkner, it is necessary to consider his accomplishment more thoroughly than we have those of the other writers. It is tempting to go afield in doing this, but we shall try to focus on answering that question which underlies the present study: Why does Faulkner choose to deal with psychic processes in *The Sound and the Fury* and *As I Lay Dying?* One commentator has it that Faulkner, in the former novel, which we shall consider first, was trying to depict the Freudian idea of dream mechanism and consequently was dealing with unconscious manifestations of libido activity.[17] This certainly, if valid, would automatically put the novel in the stream-of-consciousness genre—if, that is, it could produce a work of art at all. Another writer decides that since the date of the Benjy episode is an Easter Sunday, Benjy is a Christ symbol, etc., which puts the novel I don't know where.[18] These interpretations may be discarded because they involve the heresies of dehumanization, which Faulkner must hate more than anything else. Three much more convincing and sensible critics agree on the basic proposition that all of Faulkner's work can be interpreted on a basis of broad myth and related symbolism. The principle of this interpretation is that Faulkner's entire work is a dramatization, in terms of myth, of the social conflict between the sense of ethical responsibilities in traditional humanism and the amorality of modern naturalism (animalism) in Faulkner, in the South, and by extension, I suppose, universally.[19]

If we begin with this principle as a basis for interpretation of *The Sound and the Fury*, we can understand that the novel is another chapter in the history of the collapse of the humanism of the Sartoris (here Compson) family in a world of the animalism of the Snopeses. The chief character symbol of the Sartoris-Compson code is Quentin III, who commits suicide; the symbol of the Snopes code is Jason IV (actually a Sartoris-Compson), who collapses most completely in that he embraces Snopesism. The other characters represent symbolically stages in degeneracy of, and escape from, the Sartoris-Compson code: Benjy by inherited idiocy; Candace by sexual promiscuity; Mr. Compson by rhetoric and liquor; Mrs. Compson by invalidism; Maury by liquor and laziness. The main conflict then is focused on Quentin and Jason, protagonists respectively of Sections II and III of the novel. But Section I has Benjy as the center of things. The reason for this is that Benjy, with an idiot's mind, is able to present the necessary exposition in not only its simplest tragic terms, but also in terms of symbols, which because they are from an idiot's mind are conveniently general in their meaning and are therefore flexible. It must be remembered, too, that Faulkner saw idiocy as a possible way for a Sartoris-Compson to escape the ethical rigor of a code that depends on exertion of intellect and will. Benjy's role, then, is both to reflect an aspect of Compson degeneracy and to introduce the terms of the main conflict with the simple, forceful symbols available to an idiot.

This conflict is centered on Quentin. Thus the central episode of the novel, which concerns him, is the crucial one. Quentin is determined to preserve the Sartoris-Compson traditions of humanism—in terms of the honor of the Compsons. His obsession is with his sister Candace, who has given in to Snopesism sexually; but Quentin must not accept the fact of her promiscuity, for to him, her honor is a symbol of the dying honor of the Compsons. He convinces himself that he is the violator of Candace's chastity. This conviction is finally without effect because no one else believes him. Eventually Quentin has to accept his defeat and recognition of the Compson defeat. Unable to stand this, he, too, escapes—by suicide.

Faulkner's method puts the struggle in terms of Quentin's psychic conflict, for it is on a prespeech level of mental life that his actual defeat comes—his consciousness defeats him. He can escape everything (he goes to Harvard and he is a gentleman) except his knowledge of the truth. He even attempts to escape his consciousness of the factual world (he takes the hands off his watch; he attempts a substitute for his sister with the little Italian girl), but the only way to do this is by death. In an important sense, then, it is Quentin's consciousness that is his antagonist.

It is almost enough to submit that the advantages of the stream-of-consciousness method for this novel are explained by the central role consciousness itself plays in it. However, we might suggest here the advantages stream-of-consciousness fiction has in presenting symbols as substitutes for rationally formulated ideas. This can be illustrated in both the Benjy and Quentin sections of the novel. The two kinds of mental aberration represented reveal themselves naturally in terms of images and symbols. Because they are represented as coming directly from a premeditative stage of conscious activity, they carry a convincingness and a fuller impact than they otherwise would. The three symbols that signify everything for Benjy (firelight, the pasture, and Candace) are used so frequently that they come to dominate not only Benjy's consciousness, but the reader's also. Yet, such repetition has a naturalness about it because it comes from a mind as simple as Benjy's is. With Quentin, mental simplicity is not the thing; but obsession tends to give the same effect. Here the significance of the odor-of-honeysuckle image, the wedding announcement symbol, and all of the other symbol or image motifs grows in importance simply by the frequent repetition, which repetition is quite natural to an obsessed mind.

On a more immediate basis, the use of stream-of-consciousness techniques is appropriate in this novel because of the fundamental problem involved in describing an idiot or an obsessed person with any objectivity. Faulkner, among others, has done it out of a stream-of-consciousness context (in *The Hamlet, Wild Palms,* etc.), but never has he been able to get the objective distance necessary to prevent either a bizarre or farcical marring of it except in his stream-of-consciousness novels.

An additional effect Faulkner achieves is a contrast in *not* using stream-of-consciousness techniques in the last two episodes of the novel. It is in these sections that Jason's side of the story is presented. The techniques are soliloquy and conventional omniscient narration, with little attempt to present unspoken thoughts. The meaning this change of technique carries is that Jason's acceptance of the amoral Snopesian world is complete—it pervades his whole mental life; hence on the level of psychic life with which the novel had been dealing, there is no conflict for Jason. His conflicts are entirely in the material world of things and acts, not in the ideal one of thoughts.

So, it would seem on first consideration, are those of the characters in Faulkner's other stream-of-consciousness novel, *As I Lay Dying.* The poverty-stricken, ignorant, hill folk presented there are, however, not Snopeses, despite their Snopes-like qualities of hypocrisy, promiscuity, and avarice. The macabre pilgrimage to bury the dead, which is the central subject of the novel, is motivated by a sense of duty and honor as rigid as any the Sartoris-Compsons might have.

As I Lay Dying is, then, a marginal work in the Faulkner canon. It functions in relation to the whole Snopes-Sartoris drama as a device for repetition on a lighter scale—a minor parallel theme, so to speak. It deals with neither Snopeses nor Sartorises, but it does deal with the question of ethical codes. The method of presentation involves showing the contrast of the Snopes-like external lives of the Bundrens (the selfishness of Anse, the promiscuity of Dewey Dell, etc.) with the Sartoris-like rigidity of their internal sense of form and moral obligation (the fortitude of Addie, the persistence in duty in Cash, the heroism and loyalty of Jewel, etc.). Through the use of soliloquy to present stream of consciousness, this inner aspect of these hill people is eloquently established. Their humanism is primitive and distorted, but it is as rigid and moral as that of the Sartoris clan; and their animalism is as ugly and perverse as is that of the Snopeses—but there is ignorance, not amorality, at the base.

Stream-of-consciousness fiction is essentially a technical feat. Its successful working-out depended on technical resources exceeding those of any other type of fiction. Because this is so, any study of the genre must be essentially an examination of method. A study of devices and form becomes significant if we understand the achievement that justifies all of the virtuosity. Stream of consciousness is not technique for its own sake. It is based on a realization of the force of the drama that takes place in the minds of human beings.

One writer saw it as metaphysically significant, and her own predilections for the reality of visions led her to demonstrate the insight which the ordinary mind is capable of. For Virginia Woolf, the fleeting but vital visions of the human mind had to be expressed within the setting of that mind—and she was right; for she alone has been able to communicate precisely that sense of vision. Another writer saw it as high comedy, and he saw that it was pitiful too. Joyce's insight into man's mind was complemented by an equal insight into man's surface actions. The juxtaposition of the two was material for comedy, because the comparison between man's aspirations and his achievements was for Joyce the stuff of the comic: incongruity so great it could not produce tears, and if one were as faithless as Joyce was, it could not produce visions either. Faulkner saw one aspect of the drama as a tragedy of blood. (In other aspects he saw it as comedy, both high and low.) "The mind, mind has mountains" Faulkner might say; and he would have to add that the human being usually falls from the sheer cliffs to destruction. The tragedy of being conscious of a dying way of life, and the abortive attempts of the mind to lead the individual to isolation from the materials of a decaying reality gave Faulkner his themes. These come to the reader most forcibly in that writer's stream-of-consciousness novels, where the scene can be the one in which the tragedy actually takes place.

What these writers have contributed to fiction is broadly one thing: they have opened up for it a new area of life. They have added mental functioning and psychic existence to the already established domain of motive and action. They have created a fiction centered on the core of human experience, which if it has not been the usual domain of fiction, is not, they have proved, an improper one. Perhaps the most significant thing the stream-of-consciousness writers have demonstrated about the mind has been done obliquely: they have, through their contributions, proved that the human mind, especially the artist's, is too complex and wayward ever to be channeled into conventional patterns. . . .

270   ROBERT HUMPHREY

NOTES

1. In *The Principles of Psychology* (New York, Henry Holt, 1890), I, 239.
2. At least two writers, Frederick Hoffman and Harry Levin, have recognized this loose use of "stream of consciousness." Levin employs in its place the French rhetorical term *monologue intérieur*. Although Levin uses even this term too loosely for any general discussion of that technique, it serves well for his special purposes. I am indebted to him for the basic distinction between the terms in question. See his book, *James Joyce: A Critical Introduction* (Norfolk, Conn., New Directions, 1941), p. 89.
3. James Grier Miller, *Unconsciousness* (New York, J. Wiley and Sons, 1942), p. 18.
4. See the dictionaries of philosophy, particularly *Philosophisches Wörterbuch*, ed. Heinrich Schmidt, 10th ed. (Stuttgart, A. Kröner, 1943), and *The Dictionary of Philosophy*, ed. D. D. Runes (New York, The Philosophical Library, 1942). See also Frederick J. Hoffman's classification of stream-of-consciousness techniques according to four levels of consciousness in *Freudianism and the Literary Mind* (Baton Rouge, La., Louisiana State University Press, 1945), pp. 126–129.
5. For example: Edward Wagenknecht, *Cavalcade of the English Novel from Elizabeth to George VI* (New York, Henry Holt, 1943), p. 505.
6. It is, of course, true that there are several attempts to represent character in fiction in psychoanalytical terms—notably in Conrad Aiken's novels, *Blue Voyage* and *The Great Circle*—but these attempts are for the most part curiosities, and they are finally insignificant.
7. *The Principles of Psychology*, I, 239.
8. "Art of Fiction," *Partial Portraits* (London, Macmillan, 1905), p. 388.
9. *Pilgrimage*, 4 vols. (New York, Alfred A. Knopf, 1938), I, 10.
10. In *Dorothy M. Richardson* (London, Joiner and Steele, 1931), pp. 8 ff.
11. *The Twentieth Century Novel: Studies in Technique* (New York, D. Appleton–Century, 1932), pp. 393 ff.
12. Foreword to *Pilgrimage*, p. 10.
13. I refer particularly to the following: David Daiches, *Virginia Woolf* (Norfolk, Conn., New Directions, 1942); Bernard Blackstone, *Virginia Woolf: A Commentary* (London, Hogarth Press, 1949); and E. M. Forster, *Virginia Woolf* (New York, Harcourt, Brace, 1942).
14. "Modern Fiction," *The Common Reader* (New York, Harcourt, Brace, 1925), p. 212. Other essays in which Virginia Woolf expresses her ideas of reality and the novel are: "How It Strikes a Contemporary," in *The Common Reader; Mr. Bennett and Mrs. Brown* (New York, Harcourt, Brace, 1924); and *A Room of One's Own* (New York, Harcourt, Brace, 1929).
15. *Viking Portable Joyce* (New York, 1947), p. 481.
16. Richard Kain, of the commentators on *Ulysses*, treats the satiric cast of the novel with the most understanding: *Fabulous Voyager* (Chicago, University of Chicago Press, 1947), chaps. i and xv.
17. Ruel E. Foster, "Dream as Symbolic Act in Faulkner," *Perspective*, II (1949).

18. Sumner C. Powell, "William Faulkner Celebrates Easter, 1928," *Perspective,* II (1949).

19. George Marion O'Donnell in a remarkably seminal, if cursory, analysis of Faulkner's work ("Faulkner's Mythology," *Kenyon Review,* I, 1939) establishes this principle of interpretation. It is elaborated by Malcolm Cowley in the introduction to the *Viking Portable Faulkner* (New York, 1946). It is further modified by Robert Penn Warren in two essays that first appeared in *The New Republic* (1946); they are reprinted in *Forms of Modern Fiction,* ed. William Van O'Connor (Minneapolis, University of Minnesota Press, 1948).

PLOT AND STRUCTURE

Strictly speaking, a plot is merely a causal sequence of events arranged in some measure of time that allows a proper growth of motives and sense of duration. But inevitably in reading a story we look forward and backward to happenings and themes widely separated in narration, especially if events are presented not in the sequence they happened but by some principle of order that moves connected episodes closer together. The periodicity of events may remain visible, but the main relationships are established by analogy or typology rather than successive place in time. Also, integral to the actual happenings of a story are things that did not happen but might have, things imagined in a character's mind that stand outside the succession, and various counterplots and concealed strands whose true causal relation does not appear until a late unravelling. Whatever elements keep the main action from proceeding faster (principles of retardation) or give it ironic turns and reversals complicate the surface consequences of plot and hence the concept of plot itself. Without doing it great injustice, in fact, we can think of plot as merely one aspect of technique and method—one of the writer's several tools for probing the psychology, social matter, and cosmos of the work. At a certain point in our discussion, however, such terms as "structure" and "pattern" might prove more useful to describe these total implications of plot: in E. M. Forster's words, pattern *springs from* plot but also includes meaning, image, character, and point of view.

In their comprehensive account of varieties of plot, which reflects the work of Northrop Frye and Erich Auerbach, Kellogg and Scholes include historical, mythic, and mimetic as well as fictional plots. Having previously established a general framework of modes—empirical and mythic primarily—they here define several narrative plots in semi-modal terms, the primitive epic ("an anthology of heroic deeds in chronological order"), picaresque stories, chronological biography and autobiography, and romance and the novel. Such a survey is both historical and formalistic in that, like such essays at Auerbach's, Watt's, and Butor's, it presupposes a vital connection between literary forms and culture. At the same time, it also demonstrates that we can profit from a momentary isolation of formal elements: a narrative-satiric plot by Nathanael West or John Barth will repeat many of the stylistic elements and plot connections of *Candide* despite their cultural and historical separation. Or an epistolary form in whatever culture or time it appears will segment its plot in separate letters and give us the kind of remote dramatic exchange that takes place through the mails. It will have somewhat the same opportunities as its predecessors for confusion and overlapping time sequences when letters cross in the mail. Thus regardless of the specific content of the letters, an epistolary form will demonstrate certain kinds of progression, periodicity, crescendo, and the like.

The tendency of a form to pursue its own ends is good reason, then, to consider form itself as separately as we can in order subsequently to assess its effects on other elements and on our reading of reality *through* it. Plot proves to be especially crucial once we have located all its extensions in the story. Thus while it is natural to assume that character moves action, it can equally well be considered a subordinate element of plot. If a playwright sets out to write a comedy, he will have to assign motives to his hero of the kind that will bring about good fortune. R. S. Crane examines the formal functions of character and incident in *Tom Jones* with this principle in mind and discovers that Tom requires a good deal of luck to arrive at a happy conclusion. The efficient cause of the action in this case is neither character nor the author's eccentricity but something like total form or "decorum." Both fate and Fielding go along with the consistency of the comic work and agree as to what Tom should do before the disentanglement and when the disentanglement should occur. In most cases, we need not establish an order of priority in these elements of pattern: what matters is that the outcome be appropriate to beginning and middle and that no turns of the action violate the work as a whole.

Frank Kermode's essay concerns the structure that a concept of the end gives to the processes that lead to it. He points out that visions of the end were once felt to be applicable to the historical world as well as to fiction and that a like tension exists in the two areas between deterministic patterns of plot and the freedom of people to disturb it. To theologians, mythologers, and philosophers, concepts of the end have traditionally been used to interpret the world of the present: the "end" is normally a "culmination" of history and coincides with revelation, which lays bare the true destiny of the "characters" who have participated in the "story." Without such an ending—a day of judgment or an apocalypse—historical sequences can have no final common ground or necessary relation. It is only by looking forward to an end or backward to a beginning that those in the midst of the "plot" can determine exactly where they stand—even with respect to each other. Hence by giving the world the structure of fiction, myth-creators are able to align temporal sequences and define the relations of all parts to each other by their mutual relationship to their destiny.

Some forms of fiction (such as Christ's parable of the talents) interpret nature according to such divine ends, which are held to exist outside the story and are therefore paradigms or allegorical models of metahistory. But somewhere in the course of Western fiction, perhaps not too long after the writing of *Paradise Lost*, the reading of history as story becomes difficult. "The revealed, authenticated account of the beginning was losing its authority," Kermode writes, and we might say the same of authenticated accounts of the conclusion. From that time onward, literary fiction grows skeptical of all-inclusive paradigms and drops to a plane quite different from the myth-maker's divine plot. Though the idea of an apocalypse continues to haunt modern thought, it either disappears from serious fiction or ceases to be a "second coming" of something historically known and therefore predictive. (By comparison to older views of the end, modern apocalypses are merely destructive cataclysms, images of vengeance invented by bizarre sects for a world that ignores them.) One of Kermode's several points with respect to purpose in fiction is that, though purpose is necessary to any concept of plot as meaningful structure, modern novelists are likely to treat it ironically, aware of the discrepancy between plotted stories and a reality that is plotless and indefinite.

ROBERT SCHOLES and ROBERT KELLOGG

Plot in Narrative

Plot can be defined as the dynamic, sequential element in narrative literature. Insofar as character, or any other element in narrative, becomes dynamic, it is a part of the plot. Spatial art, which presents its materials simultaneously, or in a random order, has no plot; but a succession of similar pictures which can be arranged in a meaningful order (like Hogarth's "Rake's Progress") begins to have a plot because it begins to have a dynamic sequential existence. The images on a strip of motion-picture film are an extreme development of this plot-potential in spatial form. Aristotle, who had the tragic drama mainly in mind, said that plot was the soul of mimetic literary works. In discussing the novel, E. M. Forster quarreled politely with Aristotle and gave character priority over plot. The reasons for this we shall consider when we turn to the characteristic plots of realistic fiction. They are not unlike the reasons which moved Henry James to try to blur the distinction between plot and character. . . . But Aristotle was thinking in absolute terms. He could conceive of a tragedy without much character study (*ethos*) but not of one without action (*praxis*). Though narrative art differs from dramatic in many ways, including some that Aristotle did not know, he was certainly right to insist that in a temporal art form the dynamic and sequential element is the primary one. And this, which he calls *praxis* sometimes and *mythos* sometimes, we refer to as plot. Distinctions have been made from time to time between story, plot, and action. Here we make only the simple one between story as a general term for character and action in narrative form and plot as a more specific term intended to refer to action alone, with the minimum possible reference to character.

Primitive epic narrative is poised between the world of ritual and legend, on the one hand, and the world of history and fiction on the other. As such its plots are in a transitional stage between the artless plotting of folk tradition and the consciously artful or consciously empirical plotting of romance and history. These plots are episodic, and present the deeds (or *gestes*) of a hero in some chronological sequence, possibly beginning with his birth, probably ending with his death. In the *Epic of Gilgamesh,* which is the earliest Western epic preserved in writing and also one of the most primitive, the whole sequence is present. In *Beowulf,* much later but only somewhat less primitive, the episodes are reduced to two major ones, the latter including the hero's death. In the *Iliad,* we are down to a single episode developed at length, with neither the hero's birth nor death included in the time-span of the action. In these three works (which represent three sequential stages of the evolutionary process though they were not composed in chronological sequence) we can trace a major development in narrative plotting. Epic begins as a kind of anthology of heroic deeds in chronological order. Its unity is the simple unity provided by its protagonist, who connects the events chronologically by moving in time from one to the other, and thematically by the continuous elements in his character and the similar situations which they inevitably precipitate. Epic, becoming romanticized, can evolve into an endless proliferation of heroic deeds, as in the Middle Ages the Arthurian and Carolingian cycles did. From the *Chanson de Roland* to *Orlando Furioso* we can trace an evolution of this sort, the simple linear plot of the epic being supplanted by the multifoliate plot of the romance. Or epic can evolve into a tightly constructed narrative centering on a single deed. The Arthurian Cycle leads to the exquisite *Sir Gawain and the Green Knight* and also to such a relatively loose anthology as Malory's *Morte d'Arthur*. Both *Orlando Furioso* and *Sir Gawain and the Green Knight* are manifestations of the romantic impulse to make a beautiful story, but Ariosto's beauty is beauty of adornment and elegant variation, while the *Gawain* poet's beauty is that of balance and restraint.

The linear simplicity of primitive epic—the chronicle of the deeds of the hero—provides the ground plan for the unheroic picaresque narrative. Picaresque presents us with the deeds of an unhero, a rogue, seen through his own eyes and thus located in the actual world; but the picaresque narrative in its plotting is very similar to the epic song of deeds, unified by its single protagonist, but not poised between his birth and death since the picaresque figure normally tells his own life story and is in no position to employ his own birth and death as neat boundaries for his tale. The picaresque episodic plot is the most primitive form of plot employed in the novel, but it has retained its vitality and still flourishes today. The novel, having no form of its own, has borrowed from all its predecessors, and we shall try to keep this in mind as we consider the plot characteristic of the earlier narrative forms, returning now to the epic itself.

The epic plot is to a certain extent bespoken by epic characterization. The plot is inherent in the concept of the protagonist, but that concept is not realized in the narrative until this character is expressed through action. We can see in Homer a movement away from the traditional epic narration of the deeds of the hero. Though Achilles' problem as man-god is a part of his characterization and influences his behavior, Homer is not presenting us with so mythic a narrative as the poets of *Gilgamesh* or *Beowulf*. The notion of starting a story with a plunge *in medias res*, which came to be thought of as a typical "epic" device in Western literature, does not merely mean to Homer—nor to Horace who pointed out the device—starting in the middle and then filling in both ends of the hero's life. Insofar as Achilles' life is the "thing" in question, this narrative—unlike *Gilgamesh*, or *Beowulf*, or the *Chanson de Roland*, or *El Cid*—ends in the middle even as it began there. The deeds of Achilles, or the life of Achilles, or even the death of Achilles are not the subject of this narrative. The plot of the *Iliad* focuses on one episode in the hero's life, just as his characterization focuses on one element of his psyche; and the subject is the same in both—anger. The plot of the *Iliad* is the story of Achilles getting angry —the how and the why of it—and of the appeasement of his anger—the how and why of that. The narrative ends with the funeral of Hector, not with the death of Achilles nor with the fall of Troy; because that funeral represents the triumph of Achilles over his greatest antagonist, himself. It represents the final purgation of his accumulated rage. It glorifies his lesser antagonist Hector, but because it does so through his sufferance alone, it glorifies Achilles more. With the help of the gods he has become himself again; the narrative has reached equilibrium. The voice of the singer of tales ceases its singing.

Great efforts have been made by critics to establish the "unity" of *Beowulf*, by which is meant the artfulness of its narrative. But its unity as a narrative has been forever fixed by its very conception. It has many of the obvious kinds of unity that any heroic narrative about a single protagonist must have. Such unity as we find in the *Iliad,* however, is beyond the *Beowulf* poet's aspirations. His tradition had not progressed to the point where such an essentially fictional conception was available to him. And this is the main point to be made about the plot of the *Iliad.* In it, fiction has played a considerable part, perhaps as strong a part as it could play without projecting the whole narrative into the area of romance. In the great epics as in the great novels, the balance among the various extremes of narrative is a precarious one.

As the traditional epic form breaks down into its empirical and fictional elements, kinds of plotting suitable to these elements tend to be refined and developed. Historical forms emerge quite easily, since they are very close to the forms of primitive heroic narrative. Plot in historical narrative is a chronological affair, covering whatever span of time its subject requires. The simplest forms of historical narrative, appearing in a culture that has writing and a linear concept of time but lacks a developed theory of historiography—as in the European Middle Ages —are chronicles and annals. The chronicle usually begins at whatever point the chronicler believes life to have begun, or his civilization to have been founded, and works its way toward the continuous present, at which point it merges with the annals, which are simply a yearly record of events. This kind of historical writing is to true narrative history as a diary or journal is to true narrative biography or autobiography. In records of this kind we usually feel the lack of two elements essential to narrative art: selectivity and movement. The two are interrelated. In chronicle, annals, and diary the lack of selectivity impedes movement and inhibits the growth of anything like a plot. But the artful diarist who senses a kind of plot in his life will be selecting appropriate materials half unconsciously, as Pepys and Boswell do. And so will the artful annalist or chronicler.

Plot requires (as Aristotle, who was not afraid to utter a necessary banality, observed) a beginning, a middle, and an end. In historical narrative this means that a subject must be discerned in the past and cut off from the irrelevant matters with which it has only a temporal connection: the conflict between Persia and Greece, the Peloponnesian War, the March Up Country of the ten thousand, the Jewish War, or something similar. Such subjects provide ready-made beginnings, middles, and ends for narrative plots. And so does the life of a single man provide a neat formula for plotting. What more perfect beginning than birth or more perfect ending than death? This is simply the old epic formula pushed well into the domain of empirical narrative. This kind of plot can also be idealized and adapted to the uses of fictional narrative as in Xenophon's *Cyropedia*, which is a didactic romance organized along biographical lines, as are most of the Alexander romances and Saints' Lives which descend from Xenophon's seminal combination of biographical form with didactic and romance matter.

The old epic tendency was to present the life of a hero in terms of his most heroic achievements, but the biographer looks for those episodes which are most revealing of the character of his subject. In narratives which are fictional in plotting as well as in spirit the tendency is either to focus on a single episode in the hero's life (the *Iliad*, *Sir Gawain and the Green Knight*) or a single sequence of episodes, such as the interminable interruptions which separate lover from beloved in Greek romance, all of which are interpolated between the moment of falling in love, at which the story proper commences, and the consummation of this love in marriage, where the story inevitably ends. All plots depend on tension and resolution. In narrative the most common plots are the biographical (birth to death) and the romantic (desire to consummation), because these are the most obvious correlatives for the tension and resolution which plot demands. One of the reasons stories have appealed to man for so long a time lies in their neatness. The reader of a narrative can expect to finish his reading having achieved a state of equilibrium—something approaching calm of mind, all passion spent. Insofar as the reader is left with this feeling by any narrative, that narrative can be said to have a plot.

In the ancient world, narrative literature's constant tendency to fragmentation is illustrated thoroughly by the way the empirical narratives concentrate on characterization and the fictional concentrate on adventures. As modern historiography developed in the eighteenth and nineteenth centuries, a further fragmentation became noticeable between the "scientific" and the "artistic" historians. The "artistic" historian insists on retaining plot and character in his work, thus maintaining its place in narrative art. The "scientific" historian subordinates these narrative qualities to impersonal considerations of social and economic forces. Carlyle's *French Revolution* can serve as an example of a consciously artistic history. The rise of scientific history is paralleled by the rise of the novel as a form. The artful historical narrative stands between the hyper-empiricism of scientific history and the romanticized empiricism of the novel, and has had to defend itself from encroachment on both sides. It can be argued that Carlyle's book is at least as fine a work of narrative art as Dickens's novel, A *Tale of Two Cities*, which was admittedly derived from a reading of Carlyle; and that it is in the main a historically accurate work. Yet the serious modern student who must concentrate on the facts has no time for Carlyle, and the less serious or younger student is handed Dickens because the historical pill has a thicker coating of fiction in the novel. A *Tale of Two Cities* is still a staple of the high school curriculum, while the *French Revolution* is hardly read at all. . . .

The main plot forms of empirical narrative which we have considered so far are (a) the historical form, based on an event from the past with its causes and consequences, torn from its irrelevant and casual surroundings and isolated in the form of a narrative, or based on a related sequence of events treated in this manner; and (b) the biographical form, taking its shape from the birth, life, and death of an actual individual. Up to a point the autobiographical form is the same as the biographical form in terms of plot, the most obvious difference between the two being a matter of point of view. But the difference in point of view is inevitably linked with a difference in plot. The resolution of an autobiographical form cannot come from the protagonist's death. This easiest of equilibria to achieve in narrative art is barred to the writer of autobiography. He must find another kind of stasis on which to rest his narrative, or leave it hanging unresolved, "to be continued." This means that some other order of resolution needs to be found for an autobiographical narrative to conclude its plot line with an esthetically satisfying end. In practice this has not often been done. Most autobiographers continue beyond their natural concluding points, aiming toward that unattainable stasis of the narrator's death. But to the extent that the autobiography is a story of the author's inward life, its natural concluding point is not his death but the point at which the author comes to terms with himself, realizes his nature, assumes his vocation. St. Augustine's narrative proper ends with his conversion at the close of Book VIII of the *Confessions*, though the fruits of that conversion in the form of theological discussion and Biblical commentary fill up several more books. Rousseau's narrative also reaches its climax and resolution in its eighth book when he beholds the notice in the *Mercure de France* of the prize offered by the Dijon Academy. He tells us, "The moment I read this I beheld another universe and became another man." And later adds, "All the rest of my life and my misfortunes followed inevitably as a result of that moment's madness." The second part of the *Confessions* continues through a twelfth book, and Rousseau planned a third part which he did not write. Inevitably, once an autobiography continues beyond the moment in which the author comes to terms with his vocation, its interest turns outward and its form becomes open-ended. Cellini's autobiography ends with his departure for Pisa in 1562. Joyce's *A Portrait* (which is autobiographical in plot and content though not in point of view) ends with Stephen's departure for Paris in 1902. Yet how different are these two departures in terms of plot. Cellini is sixty-two years old. His narrative has been open-ended since his vision of God's approval of him and his work, which took place midway in his story. But Joyce's narrative ends after Stephen has accepted his vocation and is accepting the voluntary exile which it entails.

To observe this characteristic of autobiographies is one thing; to wish them all cut short at the most esthetically satisfying place is another. At this point the difference between the reader's attitude toward a work he knows to be fictional and a work he knows to be factual operates so as to bring different esthetic principles into action. When Joyce presents his autobiography in fictional form, calling his central character Dedalus, he serves notice on us that he may take some poetic liberties with the facts of his life. He also contracts to resolve his narrative at an esthetically satisfying and meaningful point. When Wordsworth subtitles his autobiographical narrative "the growth of a poet's mind" he is also contracting to present a shaped and ordered narrative. But a writer of factual autobiography is not under quite the same obligation to shape his story. Sean O'Casey gives us a brilliant portrait of himself growing toward his vocation in the first two volumes of what is now a six-volume work. After that his narrative becomes more memoir than autobiography. His interest turns outward and he fills his pages with brilliant portraits of such figures as Yeats, Lady Gregory, and AE. The first two volumes are an exercise in rather tight, controlled, autobiographical form. After young Sean's vocation is assured and assumed the form loosens and opens up. But it is still narrative and still art. It is art not merely because his portraits of figures like Lady Gregory and AE verge on caricature, but because of his selectivity of detail, because of the way he shapes his chapters toward a crisp conclusion reminiscent of a stage curtain, and because of his prose style, which varies from gutter slang to purple passages but is always artful. And it is narrative because of the chronological ground plan which inevitably provides a loose framework of episodes—crises and resolutions—to stiffen with narrative articulation the loose and journalistic elements of the work. The plotting in that part of O'Casey's narrative which is typical of full-scale autobiography, is the simple chronological plotting of the historical kind of empirical narrative. But the plotting of the early part of this autobiography is based on a traditional pattern which provides it with a much firmer narrative articulation. The Christian story of redemption and atonement, which St. Augustine saw as the pattern reflected in his own history, has been secularized to give shape to the story of the artist or writer. This pattern had been adumbrated in Lucian's brief autobiographical account of how he became a man of letters, but Augustine's demonstration of how pattern and insight could be combined in a full-scale narrative really established the form. A writer like Joyce, aware of the nature of the autobiographical tradition, was in a position to exploit the various facets of this tradition more thoroughly than is usually the case. By making Stephen's true vocation that of "priest of the eternal imagination" he exploits all the tradition of Christian allegory with which Augustine and St. Theresa had invested the form, and all the tradition of the artist's coming of age, which has its equally venerable antecedents in Lucian and Cellini. Thus Joyce can present a narrative that has the appearance of a loosely chronological collection of episodes but is actually as formal and patterned as the Catholic liturgy. In *Ulysses* and *Finnegans Wake* Joyce moved on to new patterns and great narrative experiments. In *A Portrait* he was content to accomplish more in a traditional framework than had ever been accomplished before.

The relationship between patterned and merely chronological narrative we have been considering as an aspect of autobiographical plotting is illustrative of the general situation of historical narrative. Scientific history tends to move away from artistic narrative patterns. So does scientific biography. The impossibility of autobiography becoming scientific combines with the nonavailability of death as a satisfactory form of resolution to keep autobiography within the realm of narrative art. Those histories and biographies which aspire to artistic status tend to move away from merely chronological narrative toward more esthetically satisfying patterns. This means, in effect, that historical narrative will borrow mythical or fictional means of articulation to the extent that it is willing to sacrifice science to art. The artistically minded historian or biographer, even before he writes a word, is looking for esthetically satisfying patterns in the people and events he considers as potential subjects for his work. And every historian or biographer who hopes to reach an audience beyond his fellow professionals is to some extent artistically minded. In the ancient world such a general audience was the only one available, and all historical and biographical narratives were artful. With the rise of professional and academic captive audiences, the need to captivate diminished, allowing the textbook to grow and Carlyle's despised enemy Dryasdust to come into his own. The historian who succeeds in marrying science and art with the fewest sacrifices on either side is no doubt the one with whom Clio, Muse of history, is best pleased. But, like its younger relative the novel, historical narrative is an unstable compound, always threatening to give way too much to one or the other of the opposed fictional and empirical pressures which continually beset it.

Just as historical plotting tends to be less artful than the plotting of traditional epic, fictional plotting tends to be more artful. But the line between fictional and traditional or mythic plotting is not always easy to draw; and, because narrative art never wholly loses its traditional characteristics, fictional plots have a way of establishing themselves as myths just as myths have a way of becoming fictionalized. Though we have touched on the question before, it will probably be well to clarify here what we mean by myth. We can begin to do this by pointing out the ways in which our employment of the term differs from Northrop Frye's influential definition in the *Anatomy of Criticism*. "In terms of narrative," Frye tells us, "myth is the imitation of actions near or at the conceivable limits of human desire." The characters in myth are gods who "enjoy beautiful women, fight one another with prodigious strength, comfort and assist man, or else watch his miseries from the height of their immortal freedom" (p. 136). This definition of myth makes for a certain neatness in discussion, but it does a certain amount of violence to the facts of narrative history. The gods of Ovid's *Metamorphoses* answer to this description, but what of the gods of more primitive mythological narrative? The destruction of Asgard hangs heavy over the gods of Norse mythology. Like men, they must accept their fate. Such myths as those of Attis, Adonis, Osiris, and Tammuz, which figure so prominently in the *Golden Bough*, do not present the gods as involved in actions "at or near the conceivable limits of human desire." These myths are not solely projections of human aspirations. They are projections of human fear as well. The pseudo-myth, like Apuleius' tale of Cupid and Psyche, is closer to Frye's definition than many actually mythic narratives.

Unlike Frye's definition, which emphasizes the supernatural qualities of myth, the definition we have been employing emphasizes its traditional qualities. We have been using the terms "myth" and "traditional narrative" synonymously, because *mythos* in Greek carried this meaning precisely. It is possible, however, to refine our meaning further and to distinguish quite clearly at least three distinct kinds of primitive traditional narrative, which arise in most cultures, out of which what we know as epic poetry sometimes evolves. Bronislaw Malinowski in his study of contemporary primitive society in New Guinea, found that the natives themselves distinguished among three such kinds of tale: the *kukwanebu*, or imaginative folktale, designed to amuse an audience; the *libwogo* or legend, a quasi-historical tale of ordinary or fantastic events, regarded as true history by the audience; and the *liliu* or sacred myth, which is an expression of and justification for primitive theology, manners, and morality. We can see the ways in which epic narrative represents an amalgamation of primitive modes of narration such as these, and we can see how the distinction between the legend, regarded as truth, and the folktale, regarded as amusement, anticipates the tendency of post-epic narrative to separate into fictional and empirical branches. In this primitive culture, however, all three of these kinds of literature are traditional; the stories are passed from one recognized "owner" to his heir. In such a culture newly invented stories must be only somewhat less rare than accurate historical narrative. The most tradition-bound of all forms of narrative in any culture, of course, is the sacred myth; and in such myths we find the most profound revelations of cultural conditions and ancient human attitudes and beliefs.

At first, sacred myth makes its way unchallenged by rational or empirical modes of accounting for natural phenomena. It is preoccupied with the supernatural, and, because of its sacred character, it is especially rigid and traditional. As an embodiment of religious truth it is not to be tampered with or embroidered upon. Confronted with rationalistic criticism, as it was in Greece, myth tends to lose the special character given it by rigidity and preoccupation with the supernatural. Its supernatural elements wither away or present themselves as consciously fictional or allegorical. Its traditional and rigidly preserved stories lend themselves to alteration or adaptation; they become rationalized and humanized or fancifully exaggerated. Once a culture loses its innocence with respect to myth, it can never recapture it. But myth, in yielding up its special characteristics, dies only to be reborn. Because mythic narrative is the expression in story form of deep-seated human concerns, fears, and aspirations, the plots of mythic tales are a store-house of narrative correlatives—keys to the human psyche in story form—guaranteed to reach an audience and move them deeply. Though rationalistic attacks on myth as falsehood tend to invalidate it histori-cally, they are powerless against its psychological potency.

Though the facts are shrouded in the mists of pre-history, we can speculate that sacred myth is the most ancient form of narrative. Before story-telling reached a pitch of sophistication sufficient for it to take amusement or historical recording as its province, it must have been at the service of primitive theology. The sacred myths are rooted in ritual celebration of the most vital concerns of the human race. The function of myth, as Theodore H. Gaster has cogently hypothesized, is to project "the procedures of ritual to the plane of ideal situations, which they are then taken to objectify and reproduce." Sacred myth is a link between magic and religion. It is not an "explanation" of natural phenomena but a gloss on rituals which themselves evolved out of the worship of natural phenomena. These rituals developed as imitative enactments of the cyclical processes of nature, designed to provide magical encouragement to those processes. Though there are many kinds of sacred myth, the most important kind is that associated with rituals celebrating the annual cycle of vegetative life.

So important is this kind of ritual to the concept of plot in narrative that we must pause a moment and consider it. Our knowledge of these matters is a fairly recent development in literary study, and our under-standing of them is far from complete; but Sir James Frazer and the anthropologists and literary scholars who have continued his work have given us a very clear and powerful idea of the nature of such ritual and the kind of role it plays in the articulation of literary materials. Fertility ritual is based on a cyclical concept of time rather than a linear or progressive one. In primitive societies time is seen primarily as a way of dividing the individual year rather than as an accumulation of suc-cessive years. The year is divided by the equinoxes and solstices which mark the sun's annual progress through the heavens and serve as indi-cators of seasonal variations in rainfall, temperature, and other natural phenomena associated with the cycle of vegetative life. In different parts of the world these astronomically designated points in the annual cycle may refer to varying conditions of climate, but they inevitably come to be seen as marking stages in the yearly combat between the forces of fertility and sterility, of life and death, and ultimately of good and evil. The rituals associated with this conflict take a variety of forms. But virtually all the forms of ritual are designed to express one or more of the four major elements in the Seasonal Pattern. The elements are, in Gaster's terminology, rites of "mortification, purgation, invigoration, and jubilation." Such rites frequently find expression in sacred myths which present part or all of this pattern in the form of cosmic narrative, translating the annual magical ritual into a timeless and transcendental shape.

For our consideration of plot in narrative literature two aspects of fertility ritual and the sacred myths associated with it are of crucial importance. Both have to do with developmental processes which affect myth. One concerns the change myth undergoes as the concept of time current in a culture shifts from a primitive, cyclical view to a more sophisticated linear concept. The other concerns the changes myth undergoes when cut off from ritual and subject to merely literary exigencies. Both these changes should be seen against what we may call the primary formal pattern of fertility ritual. In this progression—mortification, purgation, invigoration, and jubilation—we have a cyclical process. Jubilation can be taken as the top of the circle, which is reached when fertility is assured, but inevitably leads to mortification as concern shifts from the accomplished year to the next, in which fertility is not assured. But the cycle is one which can be broken at any point. Ritual tends to be associated with one or two of these four elements in the seasonal pattern, but myth may deal with one, two, or the whole cycle. Both myth in narrative form and mythic drama emerge from such rituals as these. But because of the inherent literary differences between narrative and drama, the sacred materials come to be treated differently in the two forms. Both are subject to a certain amount of what we may call (without pejorative implications) contamination from other literary forms.

Narrative myth, similar to narrative folktale and legend in form, and quite cut off from ritual which is itself dramatic in form, is necessarily more susceptible to this sort of "contamination"; and narrative literature thus achieves its grandest development in ancient literature in the form of epic, which is, as we have insisted, an amalgam of myth, legend, and folktale. But drama is very close in form to ritual and has tended always to emerge as a form under theological auspices, whether in ancient Greece or medieval Europe. Thus drama has inevitably retained more of the ritualistic pattern than has narrative. The rituals which seem to have had the most profound influence on Greek drama, and hence on Western culture, are four types singled out by F. M.

Cornford in *The Origins of Attic Comedy:* 1) The Carrying Out of Death, 2) The Battle of Summer and Winter, 3) The Young and the Old King, 4) Death and Resurrection. Gilbert Murray and Cornford have traced both the tragic and comic drama in Greece to these same ritual types. The difference between tragic and comic drama begins as a difference in attitude toward the sacred materials, associated with a difference in emphasis. As the evolution from ritual brings drama further and further into the realm of esthetic considerations, the esthetic impulse toward neatness of form (which in drama dominates the impulse to adorn and elaborate) reinforces the original tendency of tragic and comic drama to concentrate on the opposite aspects of the cycle inherited from ritual. Tragedy tends to specialize in mortification and purgation, while comedy tends to specialize in invigoration and jubilation. Aeschylean tragedy often took the form of cyclical trilogies which comprehended much of the full seasonal pattern, but the later dramatists tended to move away from tragic cycles to individual dramas which concentrated on the fearful side of the seasonal pattern, developing a typical plot design based on a sequence of events leading to death or expulsion from society. In comedy the joyful side of the seasonal pattern is emphasized, its typical plots leading to marriage, celebration, and reunion or reconciliation with society. These formulations, originally dramatic, inevitably influenced narrative literature in a variety of ways: tragedy directly affecting plotting in narrative history; comedy directly affecting plotting in romance; and the novel ultimately drawing upon both tragic and comic formulations, often simultaneously.

This evolution and separation of comic and tragic plots is the most significant change undergone by mythic materials when cut off from ritual theology. The other change in mythic materials which is of great importance for narrative literature has to do with the shift from myth seen in the context of a cyclical concept of time, to myth seen against a linear or progressive concept. This change in the human conception of time is an aspect of that universal movement toward a rational understanding of the cosmos which tends to make itself felt in most cultures but is virtually the identifying characteristic of our Western culture. The crucial point which must be made in discussing the relationship of this temporal concept to myth and literature is made by Gaster in discussing the significance of the struggle between Baal and Yam in the Canaanite seasonal myth. In this struggle Baal represents the forces which must triumph if the annual cycle is to be renewed and the fertility of nature assured for another year. The relation of this conflict to developing concepts of time is made so clearly by Gaster that we can do no better than quote it here directly.

> The fight of god [Baal] and dragon [Yam]—a counterpart of that enacted in ritual in order to bring in the new lease of life— is a constant theme of seasonal myths throughout the world. Moreover as the concept of time develops from the cyclic to the progressive, this fight comes to be projected both *back- ward* into cosmogony and *forward* into eschatology; for that which was regarded in more primitive thought as the neces- sary preliminary to each successive lease of life comes now to be regarded as the necessary preliminary to the entire series and likewise to the establishment of the new dispensation at the end of the present order. In the familiar language of Judeo-Christian cosmogony and apocalypse, the God who en- gaged and vanquished Leviathan at the beginning of days will perforce do so again at the end of them in order to usher in the New Age.

The whole journey of man in Judeo-Christian sacred myth falls be- tween Genesis and Apocalypse, the first and last books of the Bible: between birth and that death which constitutes rebirth; between the deathless life of perfection in the Garden of Eden followed by expul- sion and subjection to death, and the deliverance from death in the City of God, the New Jerusalem. The annual cycle of fertility ritual becomes, with the progressive concept of time which informs Jewish and Christian sacred myth, a linear spiral with a beginning and an end: the death-which-is-birth at the end of the spiral being the counterpart of the birth-which-is-death that begins it.

The full narrative pattern of sacred myth we have been considering involves both the descent from perfection, which corresponds to morti- fication and purgation in ritual, and the ascent to the new ideal state, which corresponds to the invigoration and jubilation of ritual. The pattern of descent, or fall, corresponds to the tragic pattern in drama; the pattern of ascent, or rise, corresponds to the comic pattern in drama. But we can distinguish to some extent between the forms of tragedy and comedy as they evolved in Greek drama and the broad falling-rising pattern of narrative myth. Both comedy and tragedy in Greece evolved away from sacred mythology toward a kind of literary perfection of their forms. This evolution involved a displacement of the ritualistic pattern by other kinds of pattern, as the frame of reference became less cosmic and more human. As tragedy and comedy moved toward their esthetic fulfillment, tragedy found its area of concern located in past time, an earlier and more heroic age, and it found its specific story materials crystalized in narrative literature such as Homeric epic, which itself included in the epic amalgam elements of displaced sacred myth. That the tragic dramatist should single out the most mythic material in his narrative sources is not a coincidence but an inevitability. Tragedy came to be dominated in Greece by a fairly narrow range of plot possibilities. As Cornford has pointed out, "the tragedian had to take some traditional story ('myth') with its quasi-historic characters, and, although he might modify details and even invent new characters, he could not alter the most important incidents." As comedy evolved in Greek drama it came to concentrate on contemporary rather than past materials, ordering these thematically on the loose structure inherited from ritual. Where tragedy has a *mythos*, comedy has a *logos* or informing idea. The domination of inherited plot in tragedy forced the tragic dramatists to exceptional exercises in creative characterization. Since plot remained much the same and was the dominating "soul" of tragic drama, the tragic dramatists were forced to create individual characters of extraordinary intensity to provide the motivation which the plot demanded but did not necessarily furnish. Comic dramatists, on the other hand, turned to quasi-realistic characterization based on figures copied from contemporary life. Cornford discerns in the progress of comedy "a steady drift from Mystery to Mime," in which characterization tends to shift from professional types (the Swaggering Soldier and the Learned Doctor) to character types based on an elaborate classification according to age, sex, and disposition. The "perfection" of comic form consists in the combination of generalized characters typical of contemporary life with a flexible plot formula based on intrigue and leading to marriage. This is the shape assumed by New Comedy in Greece and all its descendants. The "perfection" of tragic form consists in the discovery or adaptation of specific characters and plots to the quite rigid pattern of pride, flaw, downfall, and recognition which Aristotle discerned and established as the ideal tragic pattern.

Romance, with its desire to please an audience, takes over the joyful pattern of comic drama, gives it the expanded, cinemascope production so easily achieved in narrative, and substitutes rich rhetoric and lush description for the tomfoolery of comic drama. The romantic desire to adorn, to beautify, and to induce pleasurable suspense, results in the suppression of the purely funny elements in comedy, which are not really in the plotting but in the treatment of the plotting. In *Tom Jones* we can see Fielding putting the funny elements back into the romance plot, where they naturally fit very well. And we can discern in Fielding's literary ancestor Longus, a similar disposition, though not carried nearly so far, to bring romance back to the comic earth from which it originally sprang.

If in pure romance we can see a refined and displaced aspect of fertility ritual, we can find in didactic fiction or fable a reaching back toward the materials of sacred myth. The Biblical pattern of fall and rise, expulsion from Eden and ascent to the New Jerusalem, death and resurrection, is in itself, as we have suggested, a projection into a progressive time scheme of the old seasonal cycle. Didactic narrative in the West has been primarily a Christian preserve, reaching its greatest development in the late Middle Ages and the Renaissance. Such allegorists as Dante and Spenser deliberately construct their narratives on the Biblical plan, and even St. Augustine presents the story of his own life in the form of the great Christian archetype. The Bible, as the great and inviolable compendium of Christian sacred myth, is a storehouse for narrative artists who wish to reinforce their stories with traditionally meaningful materials, or who wish to borrow patttterns for the articulation of their narratives.

The concepts of the Garden of Eden and the New Jerusalem influence Western literature in ways more subtle than patterns of plotting. The concept of the Fall, the view of man as inferior to his ancestors who lived in a Golden Age, has influenced the tone of narratives from Ovid's *Metamorphoses* to Willa Cather's *O Pioneeers!* And similarly, the concept of the New Jerusalem, the view of man as progressing toward the City of God, has had an enormous influence, especially in the secularized form of the Utopian narrative. The possibility of mankind achieving the ideal society on earth is pre-Christian, reaching an elaborate embodiment in Plato's *Republic;* but in the Christian world it inevitably either conflicts with or merges with the Christian City of God. To conceive of the ideal city as possibly realizable on earth, of the New Jerusalem built, as Blake put it, "in England's green and pleasant land," smacks of heresy, but it is nonetheless fundamental to all liberal and progressive thinking. A different view on this crucial question is one of the great causes of the hostility between the Church and Marxism. In didactic narrative those fictions we now call Utopian accept this progressive possibility (B. F. Skinner's *Walden Two* for instance) while those fictions we now call anti-Utopian (Orwell's *1984*) reject it. The whole idea of projecting a narrative into the future is a terribly daring one, and is one of the latest narrative possibilities to be discovered and exploited in Western literature. The journey in space, however fantastic, has a pedigree going back to Lucian at least; but the journey forward in time is really a development of the nineteenth century. The possibility has been there ever since the progressive concept of time evolved and the New Jerusalem was established as the future boundary of human existence, to go with the past boundary of the creation. But not until very recently has narrative literature been able to do much with this future. The great proliferation of science fiction narrative in our time is due to the opening of this virgin territory; and the scramble for its occupation has involved writers mainly concerned with fictional romance as well as those concerned with didactic fiction. At last these forms have found their true and natural territory. Just as myth and history belong to the past and mimesis to the present, pure romance really belongs to the future, which is absolutely cut off from any possible reference to truth of fact or truth of sensation. This fragment of narrative evolution, so recently achieved, should give us some sense of the great, continuing, and inexorable process in which narrative art is involved. The schools and the professional men of letters have been slow to come to terms with the concept of futuristic fiction, but, inevitably, they will adjust. The romance of the future is very much our own literature and we must begin to understand it. Its plots can be derived from the old Greek romance plots of separation, danger, and reunion; or from the simple and ancient plan of travel— the road or journey narrative; or from the various Utopian and anti-Utopian formulas already devised. But its possibilities for variation of adventures and expression of ideas are limited only by the limitations of the human mind to conceive them. To criticism, however, the future is closed, and we must return here to consider one of the plot patterns most frequently employed in romance.

The journey to a distant goal (as in the *Aeneid*), and the return home (as in the *Odyssey*), and the quest, which involves voyage out, achievement, and return (as in the *Argonautica*) are typical plots of that heroic romance which lies between primitive epic and erotic romance. The traditional romantic narratives of the Renaissance, from

Orlando Furioso at the beginning to the *Grand Cyrus* at the end, tend to combine the heroic and erotic materials in a more equal balance than either Greek romance, which emphasizes the erotic, or ancient literary epic, which emphasizes the heroic. But from Apollonius Rhodius on, the combination of quest and love in narrative had been established and was available. The chivalric ideal and the ideal of courtly love, both so important to the later Middle Ages, offered the perfect intellectual foundation for the combination of heroic and erotic romance. Combined with Christian sacred myth, with its spiritualizing tendencies, this sort of intellectual milieu produced such humanistic romances as Tasso's *Gerusalemme Liberata* and Spenser's *Faerie Queene*.

We have discussed historical, mythic, and fictional plot forms. It remains now to consider the plot forms usually adopted by mimetic narrative. With respect to plot the mimetic is the antithesis of the mythic. We can see this clearly in the ancient drama, which developed the Mime, a form of dramatic representation quite different from both tragedy and New Comedy in its plotting. Cornford describes it this way: "As practised by the Alexandrian writers, the Mime has no action at all; it represents characters in a situation which does not change. The interest is entirely focussed on the study of character, and no preoccupation with larger issues stands in the way of extreme realism." The ancient Mime, of course, like the Theophrastian Character, was interested in general character types, not in unique individuals. The main lesson of Auerbach's *Mimesis*—the most unshakable and valuable part of that excellent work—is that the great realistic narratives combine the tragic concern for the individual with the comic concern for society to produce a representation of reality which is a just reflection of actual conditions and at the same time displays a tragic and problematic concern for the individual, regardless of his place in the social hierarchy. The typical figure of the Theophrastian Character is not an individual but a representative of a social deformity, and thus is properly presented comically and held up to a ridicule based upon social norms. The problematic quality which marks the great serious novels is to a considerable extent the result of the novelists' insistence on inserting individualized characters into typical situations, or—stated another way—tragic characters in comic situations. We can see this happening in the drama before it happens in the novel. One of Shakespeare's great gifts as a creator of character is his ability to fill the mold of type with individuality. Like the great novelists, who learned so much from him, Shakespeare is one of those writers who projects himself into his characters, seeing things from their point of view. Rhymer's criticism of him is based on his failure to construct in the old rhetorical way, from the outside, according to type. We all know that Rhymer was wrong in his judgment of Shakespearean characterization, but we are less aware that the observation on which he based this judgment was a shrewd one. Shakespeare does not create his characters according to type, in the old rhetorical way. The character Shylock in the *Merchant of Venice* is an instance of a social type (the grasping, Jewish usurer) individualized beyond the point appropriate for comic treatment. The poetry of some of Shylock's lines ("Hath not a Jew eyes?") tends to thrust this character out of the comic realm into the problematic, if not the tragic. Similarly, in the *Misanthrope* Molière presented a social type with more individuality than a stock figure, the "misanthropic man" of a Mime or Character, should properly possess. Rousseau could take Alceste in Molière's play seriously—too seriously no doubt; and Shylock, in the nineteenth century could be played as a tragic figure—another excess; but these excesses were possible only because of the problematic quality derived from the presence of individual or tragic "toads" in social or comic "gardens." What are Julien Sorel, Raskolnikov, Emma Bovary, and Anna Karenina but individuals in a mimetic world acting out the pattern of their mythic destinies?

The novelists who created these characters were not only borrowing the old tragic pattern for the articulation of their plots; they often achieved rich and complex ironic effects because of the incongruity of the mythic pattern in the world of the nineteenth century. George Eliot's complaint that no life so heroic as St. Theresa's existed for Dorothea Brooke is a milder echo of Stendhal's complaint about the banality of the nineteenth century and Flaubert's hatred of the bourgeoisie who seemed to typify his age. The decorum of separate tragic and comic formulations had given way by the nineteenth century to a powerful new impulse to find a common vehicle which would unite the neoclassical realism of social type and the romantic realism of unique individuality. The novel's great virtue lay in finding a way to combine the tragic concern for the individual with the comic concern for society. That the novelists called this impulse "realism" and felt that they had arrived at the ultimate way of representing "reality" must not deceive us. Theirs was simply a new decorum, more easily achieved in narrative than drama, and itself subject to alteration as new ways of conceiving of the individual and society became available. The new sciences of psychology and sociology had their inevitable effect on the artistic representation of the individual and society, providing new schemes of meaning and new kinds of plotting for the use of narrative artists; but they also disputed with art for the control of the representation of actuality, driving both narrative and dramatic art ultimately away from essentially mimetic or realistic formulations. Before the rise of these latest branches of science, literature controlled the present; just as before the rise of scientific historiography it controlled the past. History was so clearly an art in the ancient world because historiography had not become quite scientific enough for scientific history to dispute with artistic history. Just so in the nineteenth century did the novel control the field of present social and psychological reality, while the sciences of society and the psyche were slowly and painfully being born. Now, however, these sciences are strong and active, forcing narrative artists either to embrace them and write fiction which accommodates the scientific truth of psychology and sociology in order to be "realists," or give over "realism" entirely, as Proust and Joyce discerned, in order to find a new dispensation under which narrative art may prosper. But we anticipate. The rise of realistic fiction begins with the recognition of social, intellectual, and emotional types, and their presentation for comic and satiric purposes.

The revival of Theophrastian Characters in the seventeenth century is a prelude, perhaps an indispensable one, to the rise of novelists like Fielding who are primarily concerned with the representation of general character types. Fielding could employ such generalized characters in his plot-dominated kind of fiction with enormous success, but the ultimate in mimetic characterization requires a greater freedom from plot than Fielding allowed himself in *Tom Jones*. The ultimate form of mimetic plot is the "slice of life," virtually an "unplot." The naturalistic novelists often aimed at this kind of form, but its achievement really carries narrative into the domain of the sociologist, who, with his tape recorder can produce a book like *The Children of Sanchez*— powerful, vivid, and truer to the facts of life than any made-up narrative can hope to be. All the narrative forms, if pushed to their ultimate capabilities and purged of "impurities," disappear into the outer fringes of the world of art or of the actual world. Historical narrative becomes scientific and bloodless. Mimetic narrative becomes sociological or psychological, turning into the case history. Didactic narrative becomes hortatory or metaphysical. Romance, the only narrative form which is ineluctably artistic, since it is the product of the story-telling impulse at its purest, diminishes in interest as its perfection carries it too far from the world of ideas or from the actual world. A pure story, without ideas or imitation of actuality to tie it to human concerns and experiences, would be, if such a possibility were realizable, totally uninteresting to adult readers. In some children's stories this infinitude of inanity is approached. But, in general, narrative artists have sensed the dangers of purity in their art and shied away from it, consciously or not. The narratives which men have admired most are those which have combined most powerfully and copiously the various strands of narrative: the epic and the novel. The epic, dominated by its mythic and traditional heritage, nevertheless included fictional, historical, and mimetic materials in its powerful amalgam. The novel, dominated by its growing realistic conception of the individual in an actual society, nevertheless has drawn upon mythic, historical, and romantic patterns for its narrative articulation. The great historical narratives and the great allegorical romances also have combined many of the strands of narrative in their rich fabrics. Romance turns to didactic allegory or mimetic characterization in order to enrich itself. History turns to mythic plotting or romantic adventure in order to captivate and move its audience. Myth, mimesis, history, romance, and fable all function so as to enhance one another and reward the narrative artist whose mind and art are so powerful that he can contain and control the richest combination of narrative possibilities.

The possibilities for the future of narrative literature lie in the new combinations which may be worked out between the novel, now clearly emerged as a form, and such older forms as romance and history. As Henri Focillon pointed out in *The Life of Forms in Art*, artistic forms all tend to follow a cyclical pattern which can be described in four stages: primitive, classical, mannered, and baroque. The novel reached its classical form in the period from Stendhal to Tolstoy; it moved toward mannerism in the Edwardians, as writers like Galsworthy, Bennett, and Proust stretched the form in the direction of sequence novels like those now being written by Snow and Powell or the endless narratives of comic strip and soap opera; it moved toward the baroque in Joyce, Faulkner, and Beckett, who twisted and strained the realistic norm to the breaking point. After the baroque, according to Focillon, comes a return to primitivism, which we might find in the contemporary return to picaresque narration. But literary forms are not precisely the same as forms in the plastic arts such as Focillon had in mind, and the novel's turn toward the baroque means a re-turn toward narrative romance as well as a renewed interest in primitive myth.

The novel, a form dominated by the mimetic impulse, has always borrowed its plot materials from other forms. We can see a gradual shift in the sources for novel plots from the beginnings of the form in the seventeenth century to the present time. *Don Quixote*, the great progenitor of the form, is, in its plot, a compromise between the romantic quest pattern and the life-to-death pattern of historical biography. *Lazarillo de Tormes*, the lesser, earlier, but no less influential progenitor of the novel, exhibits in its picaresque form the elements of simple road or journey narrative and the chronological pattern of historical autobiography. These two combinations (biography-quest and autobiography-journey) dominate the rise of the novel. *Gil Blas* and its imitators represent the autobiography-journey pattern; *Tom Jones* and its successors, the biography-quest pattern. Of course, the two flow together. Smollett in *Roderick Random*, for example, casually grafts a romantic love-quest plot onto his essentially picaresque pattern. But, in general, eighteenth-century novels stick to picaresque, historico-biographical, and erotic plot formulations. What they avoid, and what the realistic novelists of the nineteenth century frequently turn to in their greatest works, is the tragic plot formula leading to violent death and/or expulsion from society. Approaches toward this in the eighteenth century, such as Richardson's *Clarissa* and the Abbé Prévost's *Manon Lescaut* stand out by virtue of their singularity. But the novels we think of as representative of the great period of realistic fiction on the European continent—*The Red and the Black, Madame Bovary, Crime and Punishment, Anna Karenina, Fathers and Sons*—generally reflect a careful adherence (deliberate or not) to the ancient tragic formula. These great realistic novels generate their power by the tension they exploit between their mimetic and mythic characteristics. The characters are highly individualized versions of recognizable social types, and the patterns through which they move are woven out of the *mythos* of the tragic drama. The actions are heroic, but the characters themselves are more intimately revealed to us than the monolithic creatures we associate with heroic narratives; they are more penetrable than even the carefully sculptured characters of Euripidean drama.

As, in the novel, mimetic narrative tends to expand and develop its treatment of characters' inner lives, the most tragic character becomes the one capable of the most intense feelings. Modern tragedy is always tragedy of intensity. As tragedy of intensity came to be understood as the mimetic alternative to the old mythic pattern which required violence of catastrophe, the realistic novelists began to make a theoretical case for what they felt to be a new and more realistic kind of tragedy. The old formulations seemed too mythic, too much of the theater perhaps, and the novelists worked toward a kind of plotting appropriate to the new, realistic concept of tragedy. In the passage from *Middlemarch* quoted on page 197, George Eliot is redefining tragedy in a more mimetic way. Arnold Bennett in *The Old Wives' Tale* followed her lead in an attempt to define tragedy so as to make it the province of mimetic narrative. The naturalists found in Darwin's natural selection the deterministic qualities they needed for a new fatalistic element in literature to take the place of the Erinyes which ruled men's lives under the old mythic dispensation. We can see in such a typically Edwardian novelist as Arnold Bennett an attempt to present the new kind of ordinary tragedy in a plot structure which was itself more ordinary. In getting away from the tragic formula leading to violent catastrophe, Bennett turned back to a historical pattern based on chronology, as the old affinities between myth and history reasserted themselves. Bennett's actuarial view of humanity reintroduces through sheer chronological perspective a deterministic aspect into narrative art, with time, rather than fate, managing the catastrophe. Bennett attempts to generate tragic and comic responses to the lives of Sophia and Constance based not on the mythic patterns of tragedy and comedy but on a chronological plan which leads the reader through pale replicas of invigoration and mortification.

With the coming of the twentieth century, plotting in narrative became dominated by time as it never had been before. First the old chronological formulas of the various kinds of historical narrative were given their most thorough employment yet in non-historical narrative; then plots began to be developed which were based on rearranging time so that the resolution became not so much a stasis of concluded action as a stasis of illumination, when the missing pieces of the temporal jigsaw puzzle were all finally in place and the picture therefore complete. In the *Forsyte Saga* Galsworthy revived the old chronological plan of the Icelandic family saga, continuing the story of the Forsytes for several generations. This kind of narrative tends toward open-endedness. It need not ever be resolved but may be continued indefinitely like the lives of characters in comic strips or soap operas. D. H. Lawrence used something like this plan in *The Rainbow* and *Women in Love,* and its elements still appear in sequence novels like C. P. Snow's *Strangers and Brothers* and Anthony Powell's *Music of Time.* The movement toward the chronological plot in modern narrative is part of the general movement to emphasize character in narrative. The loose chronological plot frees characterization from dramatic exigencies and allows it to be developed without being cramped by the necessary preparations for a mythic end. Such a simple and relatively primitive form of the novel as the picaresque has retained its vitality precisely because its episodic pattern allows for free and full character development without interference from the requirements of a tightly-knit plot. E. M. Forster's assertion that despite Aristotle character must take precedence over plot is very much the assertion of a modern, mimetically oriented novelist.

The rise of modern psychology, itself a phenomenon of the later nineteenth century, marks the zenith of mimetic narrative. It also provides some new variations for the old, autobiographical plot pattern of discovery of true vocation. Joyce's *A Portrait* is in the old pattern of Lucian and St. Augustine, but Lawrence's autobiographical novel, *Sons and Lovers,* is not. There is a bit of family saga in the plotting of *Sons and Lovers,* but the novel's real plot is the story of Paul Morel's attempt to solve the problems generated by his special relationship with his mother. A plot summary of this novel could be couched in the standard terms of clinical psychology without doing much violence to the story. After Freud's theories became widely available, the new psychological plot became almost as much a formula as the old Greek romance plot. The discovery of the self, the recovery from the trauma or wound in the psyche, offered narrative artists a new kind of comic formulation referable to psychology rather than to myth. Destruction of the individual due to trauma rather than *hamartia* offered a new scheme for tragedy. The ritualistic-romantic quest for the Grail is metamorphosed in modern fiction into the psychological search for identity. Some of the problems posed by the new interest in psychological characterization have been considered in Chapter 5 above. But its general effect has been to drive the old romantic formulations out of serious fiction and into the realm Graham Greene has called "entertainment." Such a division between novels and entertainments is characteristic of the current tendency of the novel to fragment.

Character and plot, once again, are tending to separate. Serious works, in which the empirical is emphasized get the characters; adventure stories get the plots. Novelists from Fielding to Tolstoy have resisted this tendency, but modern novelists are finding it increasingly hard to resist. In *Ulysses* Joyce's narrative hangs loosely on its borrowed Homeric framework, but its concern is really with character, not plot. It is more of a portrait than *A Portrait of the Artist*—more static, less dynamic; more mimetic, less mythic. Proust's great narrative also nods at the conventional with its autobiographical plot of self-discovery and assumption of vocation, but it too is more interested in character than plot. To provide some kind of tension and resolution for narratives which compromise so little with traditional plot forms, the modern novelist has sought to borrow techniques of organization from painting and music. To call a narrative work "a portrait" is to warn the reader at once not to expect much action, to look for resolution in the completion of an artistic pattern rather than in a stasis achieved in the lives of the characters. In his precocious first draft of *A Portrait* Joyce defined a literary portrait as an attempt to present the past not in "its iron memorial aspect" but as a "fluid succession of presents." Thus a portrait should be "not an identificative paper but rather the curve of an emotion."

The older novelists used to like to wind up a narrative by telling us what happened to everybody "afterwards." We can find this in Balzac and George Eliot as well as in Dickens. A modern writer like Lawrence Durrell, however, can end his *Alexandria Quartet* with "workpoints" which indicate ways in which the narrative could be extended backward and forward in time, indicating just how artificial is the equilibrium we seem to have reached at the end of the fourth volume. Music, like painting, has been pressed into service by narrative artists seeking new varieties of tension and resolution to supplant the traditional culminations of stories. E. M. Forster has singled out the recurring musical phrase in Proust as an example of "rhythm" in fiction, just as he cited the hourglass shape of James's *The Ambassadors* as an example of "pattern." But in a larger sense Proust's novel is rhythmic and musical in the way situations are repeated as variations on a theme, in the way characters group, separate, and regroup themselves as in a dance to what Anthony Powell has called *The Music of Time*. Proust's, Powell's, and Durrell's major works all nod at traditional plotting of the autobiographical and chronological kind, but they combine this with more serious attention to themes and variations. Where Galsworthy and Bennett gave most of their allegiance to time, these writers give theirs to music, having found in that art an esthetic principle which enables them to deal with time more creatively, as time is dealt with in music, and achieve beauty of form without sacrificing characterization to the resolution of a traditional plot.

On the whole, however, of all the aspects of narrative, plot seems to be not only the most essential but also the least variable, insofar as its general outlines are concerned. We demand variety of incident more than we demand variety of plot in our fiction. When we pick up a modern picaresque tale, whether it is narrated by Felix Krull or Augie March, we know in a general way what to expect. We know our destination though we do not know specifically what scenes we shall pass by the way. The specifics of incident admit of as much variation as the specifics of characterization, and it is in this area that we expect an author to exercise his originality in plotting. Plot, in the large sense, will always be *mythos* and always be traditional. For an author like Jane Austen one plot, in this large sense, can suffice for all her novels. But there are some smaller senses of the word "plot" which we have not yet considered, that must at least be mentioned before we can conclude.

Every separable element in a narrative can be said to have its own plot, its own little system of tension and resolution which contributes its bit to the general system. Not only every episode or incident but every paragraph and every sentence has its beginning, middle, and end. It is in these small areas rather than in the large ones we have been considering that individual achievement may be properly assesssed. Here, we may distinguish the master from the hack or journeyman. Here every work becomes a thing in itself rather than a part of some complex generic tradition. In a plot-summary we often cannot tell a great work from a feeble one. What we respond to in the greatest narratives is the quality of mind transmitted to us through the language of characterization, motivation, description, and commentary —the intelligence and sensitivity with which the fictional events are related to the perceivable world or the world of ideas: the accuracy and insight of the artist's picture of the brazen world in which we live, or the beauty and idealism of the golden world created in the fiction. Quality of mind (as expressed in the language of characterization, motivation, description, and commentary) not plot, is the soul of narrative. Plot is only the indispensable skeleton which, fleshed out with character and incident, provides the necessary clay into which life may be breathed.

R. S. CRANE

The Concept of Plot and the Plot of *Tom Jones*

Of all the plots constructed by English novelists that of *Tom Jones* has probably elicited the most unqualified praise. There is "no fable whatever," wrote Fielding's first biographer, that "affords, in its solution, such artful states of suspence, such beautiful turns of surprise, such unexpected incidents, and such sudden discoveries, sometimes apparently embarrassing, but always promising the catastrophe, and eventually promoting the completion of the whole." [1] Not since the days of Homer, it seemed to James Beattie, had the world seen "a more artful epick fable." "The characters and adventures are wonderfully diversified: yet the circumstances are all so natural, and rise so easily from one another, and co-operate with so much regularity in bringing on, even while they seem to retard, the catastrophe, that the curiosity of the reader . . . grows more and more impatient as the story advances, till at last it becomes downright anxiety. And when we get to the end . . . we are amazed to find, that of so many incidents there should be so few superfluous; that in such variety of fiction there should be so great probability; and that so complex a tale should be perspicuously conducted, and with perfect unity of design." [2] These are typical of the eulogies that preceded and were summed up in Coleridge's famous verdict in 1834: "What a master of composition Fielding was! Upon my word, I think the Oedipus Tyrannus, The Alchemist, and Tom Jones, the three most perfect plots ever planned." [3] More recent writers have tended to speak less hyperbolically and, like Scott, to insist that "even the high praise due to the construction and arrangement of the story is inferior to that claimed by the truth, force, and spirit of the characters," [4] but it is hard to think of any important modern discussion

From *Critics and Criticism: Ancient and Modern.* Copyright 1952 by The University of Chicago Press. Reprinted by permission of the author.

of the novel that does not contain at least a few sentences on Fielding's "ever-to-be-praised skill as an architect of plot." [5]

I

The question I wish to raise concerns not the justice of any of these estimates but rather the nature and critical adequacy of the conception of plot in general and of the plot of *Tom Jones* in particular that underlies most if not all of them. Now it is a striking fact that in all the more extended discussions of Fielding's masterpiece since 1749 the consideration of the plot has constituted merely one topic among several others, and a topic, moreover, so detached from the rest that once it is disposed of the consideration of the remaining elements of character, thought, diction, and narrative technique invariably proceeds without further reference to it. The characters are indeed agents of the story, but their values are assessed apart from this, in terms sometimes of their degrees of conformity to standards of characterization in literature generally, sometimes of the conceptions of morality they embody, sometimes of their relation to Fielding's experiences or prejudices, sometimes of their reflection, taken collectively, of the England of their time. The other elements are isolated similarly, both from the plot and from one another: what is found important in the thought, whether of the characters or of the narrator, is normally not its function as an artistic device but its doctrinal content as a sign of the "philosophy" of Fielding; the style and the ironical tone of the narrative are frequently praised, but solely as means to the general literary satisfaction of the reader; and, what is perhaps more significant, the wonderful comic force of the novel, which all have delighted to commend, is assumed to be independent of the plot and a matter exclusively of particular incidents, of the characters of some, but not all, of the persons, and of occasional passages of burlesque or witty writing.[6]

All this points to a strictly limited definition of plot as something that can be abstracted, for critical purposes, from the moral qualities of the characters and the operations of their thought. This something is merely the material continuity of the story considered in relation to the general pleasure we take in any fiction when our curiosity about the impending events is aroused, sustained, and then satisfied to a degree or in a manner we could not anticipate. A plot in this sense—the sense in which modern novelists pride themselves on having got rid of plot—can be pronounced good in terms simply of the variety of incidents it contains, the amount of suspense and surprise it evokes, and the ingenuity with which all the happenings in the beginning and middle are made to contribute to the resolution at the end. Given the definition, indeed, no other criteria are possible, and no others have been used by any of the critics of *Tom Jones* since the eighteenth century who have declared its plot to be one of the most perfect ever planned. They have uniformly judged it as interesting story merely— and this whether, as by most of the earlier writers, "the felicitous contrivance and happy extrication of the story" is taken to be the chief "beauty" of the novel or whether, as generally nowadays, preference is given to its qualities of character and thought. It is clearly of plot in no completer sense than this that Oliver Elton is thinking when he remarks that, although some "have cared little for this particular excellence, and think only of Partridge, timorous, credulous, garrulous, faithful, and an injured man; of Squire Western, and of the night at Upton, and of wit and humour everywhere," still "the common reader, for whom Fielding wrote, cares a great deal, and cares rightly, for plot; and so did Sophocles." [7]

When plot is conceived thus narrowly, in abstraction from the peculiar characters and mental processes of the agents, it must necessarily have, for the critic, only a relatively external relation to the other aspects of the work. That is why, in most discussions of *Tom Jones*, the critical treatment of the plot (as distinguished from mere summary of the happenings) is restricted to the kind of enthusiastic general appreciation of which I have given some examples, supplemented by more particular remarks on various episodes, notably those of the Man of the Hill and of Mrs. Fitzpatrick, which appear to do little to advance the action. The plot, in these discussions, is simply one of several sources of interest and pleasure afforded by a novel peculiarly rich in pleasurable and interesting things, and the problem of its relation to the other ingredients is evaded altogether. Occasionally, it is true, the question has been faced; but even in those critics, like W. L. Cross and Oliver Elton, who have made it most explicit, the formulas suggested never give to the plot of *Tom Jones* the status of more than an external and enveloping form in relation to which the rest of the novel is content. It is not, as they see it, an end but a means, and they describe it variously, having no language but metaphor for the purpose, as a "framework" in which character (which is Fielding's "real 'bill of fare' ") is "set"; as a device, essentially "artificial," for bringing on the stage "real men and women"; as a "mere mechanism," which, except now and then in the last two books, "does not obtrude," for keeping readers alert through six volumes.[8]

I do not believe, however, that it is necessary to remain content with this very limited and abstract definition of plot or with the miscellaneous and fragmentized criticism of works like *Tom Jones* that has always followed from it. I shall assume that any novel or drama not constructed on didactic principles [9] is a composite of three elements, which unite to determine its quality and effect—the things that are imitated (or "rendered") in it, the linguistic medium in which they are imitated, and the manner or technique of imitation; and I shall assume further that the things imitated necessarily involve human beings interacting with one another in ways determined by, and in turn affecting, their moral characters and their states of mind (i.e., their reasonings, emotions, and attitudes). If this is granted, we may say that the plot of any novel or drama is the particular temporal synthesis effected by the writer of the elements of action, character, and thought that constitute the matter of his invention. It is impossible, therefore, to state adequately what any plot is unless we include in our formula all three of the elements or causes of which the plot is the synthesis; and it follows also that plots will differ in structure according as one or another of the three causal ingredients is employed as the synthesizing principle. There are, thus, plots of action, plots of character, and plots of thought. In the first, the synthesizing principle is a completed change, gradual or sudden, in the situation of the protagonist, determined and effected by character and thought (as in *Oedipus* and *The Brothers Karamazov*); in the second, the principle is a completed process of change in the moral character of the protagonist, precipitated or molded by action, and made manifest both in it and in thought and feeling (as in James's *The Portrait of a Lady*); in the third, the principle is a completed process of change in the thought of the protagonist and consequently in his feelings, conditioned and directed by character and action (as in Pater's *Marius the Epicurean*). All these types of construction, and not merely the first, are plots in the meaning of our definition; and it is mainly, perhaps, because most of the familiar classic plots, including that of *Tom Jones*, have been of the first kind that so many critics have tended to reduce plot to action alone.[10]

If this is granted, we may go farther. For a plot, in the enlarged sense here given to the term, is not merely a particular synthesis of particular materials of character, thought, and action, but such a synthesis endowed necessarily, because it imitates in words a sequence of human activities, with a power to affect our opinions and emotions in a certain way. We are bound, as we read or listen, to form expectations about what is coming and to feel more or less determinate desires relatively to our expectations. At the very least, if we are interested at all, we desire to know what is going to happen or how the problems faced by the characters are going to be solved. This is a necessary condition of our pleasure in all plots, and there are many good ones—in the classics of pure detective fiction, for example, or in some modern psychiatric novels—the power of which depends almost exclusively on the pleasure we take in inferring progressively, from complex or ambiguous signs, the true state of affairs. For some readers and even some critics this would seem to be the chief source of delight in many plots that have obviously been constructed on more specific principles: not only *Tom Jones*, as we have seen, but *Oedipus* has been praised as a mystery story, and it is likely that much of Henry James's popularity is due to his remarkable capacity for provoking a superior kind of inferential activity. What distinguishes all the more developed forms of imitative literature, however, is that, though they presuppose this instinctive pleasure in learning, they go beyond it and give us plots of which the effects derive in a much more immediate way from the particular ethical qualities manifested in their agents' actions and thoughts vis-à-vis the human situations in which they are engaged. When this is the case, we cannot help becoming, in a greater or less degree, emotionally involved; for some of the characters we wish good, for others ill, and, depending on our inferences as to the events, we feel hope or fear, pity or satisfaction, or some modification of these or similar emotions. The peculiar power of any plot of this kind, as it unfolds, is a result of our state of knowledge at any point in complex interaction with our desires for the characters as morally differentiated beings; and we may be said to have grasped the plot in the full artistic sense only when we have analyzed this interplay of desires and expectations sequentially in relation to the incidents by which it is produced.

It is, of course, an essential condition of such an effect that the writer should so have combined his elements of action, character, and thought as to have achieved a complete and ordered whole, with all the parts needed to carry the protagonist, by probable or necessary stages, from the beginning to the end of his change: we should not have, otherwise, any connected series of expectations wherewith to guide our desires. In itself, however, this structure is only the matter or content of the plot and not its form; the form of the plot—in the sense of that which makes its matter into a definite artistic thing—is rather its distinctive "working or power," as the form of the plot in tragedy, for example, is the capacity of its unified sequence of actions to effect through pity and fear a catharsis of such emotions.

But if this is granted, then certain consequences follow for the criticism of dramas and novels. It is evident, in the first place, that no plot of this order can be judged excellent *merely* in terms of the unity of its action, the number and variety of its incidents, or the extent to which it produces suspense and surprise. These are but properties of its matter, and their achievement, even to a high degree, in any particular plot does not inevitably mean that the emotional effect of the whole will not still be diffused or weak. They are, therefore, necessary, but not sufficient, conditions of a good plot, the positive excellence of which depends upon the power of its peculiar synthesis of character, action, and thought, as inferable from the sequence of words, to move our feelings powerfully and pleasurably in a certain definite way.

But this power, which constitutes the form of the plot, is obviously, from an artistic point of view, the most important virtue any drama or novel can have; it is that, indeed, which most sharply distinguishes works of imitation from all other kinds of literary productions. It follows, consequently, that the plot, considered formally, of any imitative work is, in relation to the work as a whole, not simply a means— a "framework" or "mere mechanism"—but rather the final end which everything in the work, if that is to be felt as a whole, must be made, directly or indirectly, to serve. For the critic, therefore, the form of the plot is a first principle, which he must grasp as clearly as possible for any work he proposes to examine before he can deal adequately with the questions raised by its parts. This does not mean that we cannot derive other relevant principles of judgment from the general causes of pleasure operative in all artistic imitations, irrespective of the particular effect, serious or comic, that is aimed at in a given work. One of these is the imitative principle itself, the principle that we are in general more convinced and moved when things are "rendered" for us through probable signs than when they are given merely in "statement," without illusion, after the fashion of a scenario.[11] Critical judgments, valid enough if they are not taken absolutely, may also be drawn from considerations of the general powers of language as a literary medium, of the known potentialities or requirements of a given manner of representation (e.g., dramatic or narrative), and of the various conditions of suspense and surprise. We are not likely to feel strongly the emotional effect of a work in which the worse rather than the better alternatives among these different expedients are consistently chosen or chosen in crucial scenes. The same thing, too, can be said of works in which the thought, however clearly serving an artistic use, is generally uninteresting or stale, or in which the characters of the agents, though right enough in conception for the intended effect, are less than adequately "done" or fail to impress themselves upon our memory and imagination, or in which we perceive that the most has not been made of the possibilities implicit in the incidents. And there is also a kind of judgment, distinct from any of these, the object of which is not so much the traits of a work that follow from its general character as an imitative drama or novel as the qualities of intelligence and moral sensibility in its author which are reflected in his conception and handling of its subject and which warrant us in ascribing "greatness," "seriousness," or "maturity" to some products of art and in denying these values to others no matter how excellent, in a formal sense, the latter may be.

Such criticism of parts in the light of general principles is indispensable, but it is no substitute for—and its conclusions, affirmative as well as negative, have constantly to be checked by—the more specific kind of criticism of a work that takes the form of the plot as its starting point and then inquires how far and in what way its peculiar power is maximized by the writer's invention and development of episodes, his step-by-step rendering of the characters of his people, his use and elaboration of thought, his handling of diction and imagery, and his decisions as to the order, method, scale, and point of view of his representation. . . .

[Concerning *Tom Jones*], there are not many novels of comparable length in which the various parts are conceived and developed with a shrewder eye to what is required for a maximum realization of the form.[12] A few examples of this will have to serve, and it is natural to start with the manner in which Fielding handles the incidents that follow directly from Tom's mistakes. The pattern of all of these is much the same. Tom first commits an indiscretion, which is then discovered, and the discovery results in his immediate or eventual embarrassment. Now it is clear that the comic pleasure will be enhanced in proportion as, in each incident, the discovery is made unexpectedly and by precisely those persons whose knowledge of what Tom has done will be most damaging to him, and by as many of these as possible so that the consequences for him are not simple but compounded. Fielding understood this well, and the effects of his understanding are repeatedly evident in *Tom Jones*, from Book IV to the end of the complication. Consider, for example, how he manages the discovery of Tom's original entanglement with Molly. It is necessary, of course, when Molly is arrested after the fight in the churchyard, that Tom should at once rush to Allworthy with his mistaken confession; but it is not necessary—only highly desirable—that he should intervene in the fight himself as Molly's champion, that Blifil and Square should be with him at the time, that the news of the arrest should reach him while he is dining with Western and Sophia, whose charm he is just beginning to perceive, and that, when he leaves in a hurry, the Squire should joke with his daughter about what he suspects. Or, again, there is the even more complicated and comically disastrous sequence that begins with Tom's drunkenness after Allworthy's recovery. This in itself is ridiculous, since we know the illness has never been serious; but observe how the succeeding embarrassments are made to pile up: Tom's hilarious joy leading to his fight with Blifil; this to his retirement to the grove, his romantic meditation on Sophia, and his surrender to Molly; this to the discovery of his new folly by Blifil and Thwackum; this to the second fight, much bloodier than the first; and this in turn, when the Westerns unexpectedly appear on the scene, to Sophia's fresh discovery of Tom's wildness and, what is much more serious, to the misconstruction of her fainting fit by her aunt, with results that lead presently to the proposal of a match with Blifil, the foolish intervention of Tom, the discovery by Western of the true state of affairs, his angry appeal to Allworthy, Blifil's distorted version of what has happened, Tom's expulsion from home, and Sophia's imprisonment. All this is probable enough, but there is something of the comically wonderful in the educing of so many appropriately extreme consequences from a cause in itself so apparently innocent and trivial. And the same art of making the most out of incidents for the sake of the comic suspense of the plot can be seen at work through the rest of the novel: in the great episode at Upton, for example, where all the happenings are contrived to produce, immediately or remotely, a maximum of pseudo-serious suffering for Tom, and also in the various later scenes in which the discovery to Sophia of Tom's intrigue with her cousin is first narrowly averted, with much embarrassment to him, and then finally made under circumstances that could hardly be worse for the young man. A less accomplished artist seeking to achieve the same general effect through his plot would certainly have missed many of these opportunities.

A less accomplished artist, again, would never have been able to invent or sustain characters so good for the form, as well as so interesting in themselves, as the two Westerns and Partridge. We need not dwell on the multiple uses to which these great humorists are put; it is more important, since the point has been less often discussed, or discussed in part to Fielding's disadvantage, to consider what merits can be found in his handling of the other characters, such as Tom himself, Allworthy, Sophia, and Blifil, who are intended to seem morally sympathetic or antipathetic to us and comically inferior only by virtue of their erroneous acts. With the exception of Sophia, who is made charming and lively enough to constitute in herself good fortune for Tom, they are not endowed with any notably particularized traits, and the question for criticism is whether, given the comic form of the novel as a whole, any more lifelike "doing" would not have entailed a departure from the mean which this imposed. I think the answer is clear for Blifil: he must be made to seem sufficiently formidable in the short run to arouse comic apprehension for Tom but not so formidable as to excite in us active or prolonged feelings of indignation; and any further individualizing of him than we get would almost certainly have upset this balance to the detriment of the whole. The answer is clear also, I think, for Tom. We must consistently favor him against his enemies and think it probable that he should suffer acute embarrassment and remorse when he discovers the consequences of his mistakes; but, on the other hand, any appreciably greater particularizing of his sympathetic traits than is attempted would inevitably have made it difficult for us not to feel his predicaments as seriously as he does himself, and that would have been an error; it is not the least happy of Fielding's inventions, for example, that he repeatedly depicts Tom, especially when he is talking to Sophia or thinking about her, in terms of the clichés of heroic romance. There remains Allworthy, and concerning him the chief doubt arises from a consideration of the important part he is given, along with Sophia, in the definition of Tom's final good fortune. For the purposes of the comic complication it is sufficient that we should see him acting in the character of a severely just magistrate who constantly administers injustice through too great trust in his knowledge of men; it is not for this, however, but for his "amiability" that Tom loves him and cherishes his company in the end; yet of Allworthy's actual possession of that quality we are given few clear signs.

A whole essay, finally, could be written on the masterly way in which Fielding exploited the various devices implicit in his third-person "historical" mode of narration in the service of his comic form.

Broadly speaking, his problem was twofold: first, to establish and maintain in the reader a general frame of mind appropriate to the emotional quality of the story as a whole and, second, to make sure that the feelings aroused by his characters at particular moments or stages of the action were kept in proper alignment with the intended over-all effect.

That the first problem is adequately solved there can be little doubt; long before we come to the incidents in which Tom's happiness is put in jeopardy by his own blunders and the malice of Blifil, we have been prepared to expect much unmerited calamity and distress for him, and at the same time to view the prospect without alarm. Our security would doubtless have been less had not Fielding chosen to represent at length the events contained in Books I and II, with the vivid impressions they give of the fallibility of Allworthy on the one hand and of the impotence for permanent harm of the elder Blifil on the other: we cannot but look forward to a repetition of this pattern in the later parts of the novel. This is less important, however, as a determinant of our frame of mind than the guidance given us by the clearly evident attitude of Fielding's narrator. He is, we perceive, a man we can trust, who knows the whole story and still is not deeply concerned; one who understands the difference between good men and bad and who can yet speak with amused indulgence of the first, knowing how prone they are to weakness of intellect, and with urbane scorn, rather than indignation, of the second, knowing that most of them, too, are fools. This combination of sympathetic moral feeling with ironical detachment is bound to influence our expectations from the first, and to the extent that it does so, we tend to anticipate the coming troubles with no more than comic fear.

It is when the troubles come, in Book V and later, that Fielding's second problem emerges; for, given the kinds of things that then happen to Tom and especially the seriousness with which, as a good man, he necessarily takes them, there is always a danger that our original comic detachment may give way, temporarily, to tragicomic feelings of fear, pity, and indignation. That this seldom happens is another sign of how successfully, in *Tom Jones*, the handling of the parts is kept consonant with the formal demands of the whole. It is a question primarily of maximizing the general comic expectations of the reader by minimizing the possible noncomic elements in his inferences about particular situations; and the devices which Fielding uses for the purpose are of several kinds. Sometimes the result is achieved by preventing our attention from concentrating long or closely on potential causes of distress for Tom; it is notable, for example, that we are given no representation of Blifil scheming Tom's ruin before his speech to Allworthy in Book VI, chapter xi, and that from this point until Book XVI Blifil and his intentions are not again brought to the fore. Sometimes the device consists in slurring over a painful scene by generalized narration and then quickly diverting us to an obviously comic sequence in another line of action: this is what Fielding does, to excellent effect, with the incident of Tom's condemnation and banishment; we should feel much more keenly for him if, in the first place, we were allowed to hear more of his talk with Allworthy and, in the second place, were not plunged so soon after into the ridiculous quarrels of the Westerns. Or, again, the expedient may take the simple form of a refusal by the narrator to describe feelings of Tom which, if they were represented directly and at length, might easily excite a noncomic response; as in the accounts of his "madness" at Upton after he finds Sophia's muff and of the torments he endures ("such that even Thwackum would almost have pitied him") when her message of dismissal comes to him in prison. And the same general minimizing function is also served by the two episodes in the middle part of the novel which have occasioned so much discussion among critics. Both the story told to Tom by the Man of the Hill and that recounted to Sophia by Mrs. Fitzpatrick, however much they owe to the convention of interpolated narratives which Fielding had inherited, along with other devices, from the earlier writers of "comic romance," are clearly designed as negative analogies to the moral state of the listeners, from which the reader is led to infer, on the eve of the most distressing part of the complication for the hero and heroine, that nothing that may happen to them will be, in comparison, very bad.

The controlling influence of the form can be seen in all these expedients, and it is no less apparent in Fielding's handling of the intrigue upon which the action of the novel ultimately depends—Bridget's affair with Summer, her scheme of temporary concealment and eventual disclosure of Tom's parentage, and the frustration of the second of these intentions, until the denouement, by Blifil. Without this series of events and the consequences they entail in the opinions and acts of the characters, the plot as we have it could not have existed; but there was nothing in the nature of the events themselves to prescribe the particular manner in which they must be brought before the reader. At least two alternative modes of procedure were open to Fielding besides the one he actually chose. He could, on the one hand, have let the reader into the secret, either from the beginning or at the point in Book V where Bridget's dying message is brought by Dowling: in the former case a brief statement by the narrator would have been suffi- cient (since he plainly knows the facts); in the latter case, a brief report, for which there are precedents elsewhere in the novel, of Bli- fil's thoughts. Or, on the other hand, he could have contrived to keep our curiosity regarding the mystery more continuously and actively awake, especially in the long stretches of the story between Book III and the final scenes in London: this need not again have required any invention of new incidents, but only manipulations of the narrative dis- course, such as an explicit direction of the reader's mind to the circum- stance that Dowling brought a letter from Bridget as well as the news of her death, a hint that Blifil now had some new and surprising infor- mation about Tom, and an occasional reminder thereafter that the full truth concerning Tom's birth was still to be learned and that it might, when known, have important bearings, for good or possibly for ill, upon his fortunes.

Given, however, the form which Fielding, according to our hypothe- sis, was attempting to impose on the materials of his plot, with its dis- tinctive line of seriocomic expectations and desires, either of these two courses would clearly have been incorrect. The second would have in- jected into the middle sections of the narrative a competing principle of suspense, diverting our attention unduly from the question of what is likely to befall Tom as a result of his mistakes to the question of who he is; the novel would then have become in fact the mystery story which, on a partial and erroneous view, it has sometimes been taken to be. And the consequences of the other course would have been equally, perhaps more, disruptive. For the complication in that case would have become, in large part, the story of a completely foreseen and wished- for discovery repeatedly deferred, with the result, on the one hand, that our complacency about the eventual outcome would have been increased to such a degree as sensibly to lessen our comic fear and hence our comic mirth in the successive anticlimactic reversals and, on the other hand, that our preoccupation with the comic aspects of Tom's well-intentioned blunderings would have tended to give way exces- sively to a concern with the original injustice done him by Bridget and with the villainy of Blifil. A mean between emphasis on the existence of a mystery and full revelation of the secret to the reader was therefore indicated as the right technique, and it was his perception of this that guided Fielding's procedure both in Books I and II, where the question of Tom's parentage is formally inquired into by Allworthy and settled to his own satisfaction, and in Books V–XVII, where the question is reopened, in intent but not in result, first by the confession of Bridget and then by the advances of Dowling to Tom. Something close to the proper mean is achieved by concentrating the narrative in the opening books on the objective acts and declarations of Bridget, Jenny, and Partridge subsequent to the finding of Tom in Allworthy's bed and representing these by signs sufficiently ambiguous so that, although we discount the inferences drawn by Allworthy from the behavior of the two supposed parents, we are yet given no adequate premises from which to reason to any particular alternative explanation. We surmise that one will ultimately be forthcoming, but in the meantime we are easily persuaded by the narrator to suspend our curiosity, especially since we perceive that neither of Allworthy's discoveries will make any difference in his treatment of Tom. We are predisposed therefore to yield our attention to the events recounted in the middle books of the novel without active speculation concerning their remoter causes or growing impatience for further disclosures. Ambiguous disclosures do indeed continue to be made. There is the pervasive irony (in the world of this novel) of a young man assumed by nearly everyone in his circle, including himself, to be base-born who yet manifests all the signs, in appearance and sensibility, of being a gentleman and is regularly taken as one by strangers until they learn his story; and there are also the more specific clues to the real state of affairs afforded by Bridget's increasing preference for Tom as he grows up, the suddenly intensified animosity of Blifil toward the foundling after he learns the content of Bridget's message, Partridge's disavowal of the role in which he has been cast as Tom's father, and, most pointed of all, Dowling's sly reference to "your uncle" in the interview which he forces on Tom in Book XII. But though hints of the truth are thus given in the events themselves, it is only in retrospect, at the moment of the discovery scene in Book XVIII, that we grasp their cumulative import; so effectively, in the narrator's discourse up to the very eve of this scene, has the question of who Tom is been kept subordinate to the question, upon which the main comic effect depends, of what will immediately follow from his imprudent acts. . . .

316   R. S. CRANE

NOTES

1. Arthur Murphy (1762), quoted in Frederic T. Blanchard, *Fielding the Novelist: A Study in Historical Criticism* (New Haven, 1927), p. 161.
2. *Dissertations Moral and Critical* (1783), quoted in Blanchard, pp. 222–23.
3. *Ibid.*, pp. 320–21.
4. *Ibid.*, p. 327.
5. The phrase is Oliver Elton's in *A Survey of English Literature, 1730–1780* (New York, 1928), I, 195. See also Wilbur L. Cross, *The History of Henry Fielding* (New Haven, 1918), II, 160–61; Aurélien Digeon, *Les Romans de Fielding* (Paris, 1923), pp. 210–16; Elizabeth Jenkins, *Henry Fielding* (London, 1947), pp. 57–58; and George Sherburn, in *A Literary History of England*, ed. Albert C. Baugh (New York and London, 1948), pp. 957–58; cf. his interesting Introduction to the "Modern Library College Editions" reprint of *Tom Jones* (New York, 1950), pp. ix–x.
6. The explanation of this procedure lies, partly at least, in a still unwritten chapter in the history of criticism. When works of prose fiction became objects of increasingly frequent critical attention in the eighteenth century, it was natural that the new form should be discussed in terms of its obvious analogies, both positive and negative, to drama and epic and that critics of novels should consequently, avail themselves, of the familiar categories of "fable," "characters," "sentiments," and "language" which had been long established, in the neoclassical tradition, as standard devices for the analysis of tragedies, comedies, and heroic poems. In remote origin these distinctions derived from the four qualitative "parts" which Aristotle had shown to be common to tragedy and epic (cf. *Poetics* 5. 1449^{b}15 ff.; 24. 1459^{b}8–11). In the course of their transmission to the eighteenth century, however—as a result partly of the influence of Horace and partly of a complex of more general causes operative from the beginnings of Aristotelian commentary in the Renaissance . . . the analytical significance of the scheme had undergone a radical change. For Aristotle, concerned with the construction of poetic wholes that afford "peculiar pleasures" through their imitations of different species of human actions, the four terms had designated the essential elements upon the proper handling and combination of which, relatively to the intended over-all effect, the quality of a tragedy or epic necessarily depends. They are distinct parts in the sense of being variable factors in the complex problem of composing works which, when completed, will produce their effects, synthetically, as organic wholes. Hence it is that in the *Poetics* they are treated, not discretely as co-ordinate topics, but hierarchically in a causal sequence of form-matter or end-means relationships in which plot is the most inclusive or architectonic of the four, subsuming all the others as its poetic matter; in which character, while subordinated materially to plot and effect, is similarly a formal or organizing principle with respect to thought and diction; in which thought, while functioning as matter relatively to character, incident, and effect, is the form which immediately controls the choice and arrangement of language in so

far as this is employed as a means to imitative rather than ornamental ends; and in which diction, though necessarily having a form of its own by virtue of its rhythmical, syntactical, and "stylistic" figuration, is the underlying matter which, as significant speech, at once makes possible all the other "parts" and is in turn, mediately or immediately, controlled by them. The nature of the four elements is such, in short, that, although a critic in his analysis of a given tragedy or epic may take any one of them as his primary object of attention, he can make no adequate judgment of the poet's success or failure with respect to it without bringing into his discussion all the others to which it is related, directly or indirectly, either as matter or as form.

Of this causal scheme only the general outlines survived in the doctrines of subsequent critics in the "Aristotelian" line. The distinction of the four parts was retained and, along with it, the substance of the rules which Aristotle had formulated for their handling; what disappeared was precisely the rationale which in the *Poetics* had justified not only the rules but the discrimination, definition, and ordering of the parts themselves. In its place various new principles and schemes of analysis were substituted by different theorists and critics, the general tendency of which was to make of poetics a practical rather than a productive art and hence to reduce tragedy and epic to modes of ethical or rhetorical discourse designed to serve, each in its specialized way, the common purposes of all such discourse, namely, the delight and instruction of mankind. The consequence was that, although critics continued to distinguish aspects of tragedies and epics that corresponded roughly with the Aristotelian "parts" and although these served to determine the framework of the discussion at least in the most systematic treatises and essays, the discussion itself no longer turned on the nature and functional interrelations of the four parts as elements in an artistic synthesis of a particular kind but on the general qualities which the poet ought to aim at in each, in order to enhance its independent power of pleasing, moving, and edifying spectators or readers. And when this apparatus was carried over from the statement of tragic or epic theory to the practical criticism of tragedies or epics (as in Addison's papers on *Paradise Lost* or Pope's Preface to the *Iliad*), the disjunction of the four elements tended to become still more marked. They were no longer functional parts in an organic whole but so many relatively discrete *loci* of critical praise and blame; and critics could write *seriatim* of the beauties or defects in the fable, characters, sentiments, and language of a given tragedy or heroic poem without assuming any synthesizing principles more specific than the decorum of the genre or the necessity (e.g.) that the sentiments expressed should be consonant with the characters of the persons who uttered them (many illustrations of the procedure may be found in H. T. Swedenberg, Jr., *The Theory of the Epic in England, 1650–1800* [Berkeley and Los Angeles, 1944]; cf. the Index under "Fable or action," "Characters," "Sentiments in the epic," and "Language of the epic").

It was at this stage in the history of the Aristotelian "parts" that they entered into the criticism, both general and applied, of modern prose fiction. See, for example, besides many notices of novels in the *Monthly Review* and the *Critical Review*, the anonymous *Critical Remarks on Sir Charles Grandison, Clarissa, and Pamela* (1754); Arthur Murphy's "Essay on the Life and

Genius of Henry Fielding," in *The Works of Henry Fielding* (1762); James Beattie's "On Fable and Romance," in his *Dissertations* (1783); and John More's "View of the Commencement and Progress of Romance," in *The Works of Tobias Smollett* (1797). In spite of the general indifference of criticism since about 1750 to questions specific to the various poetic kinds (see above, pp. 14, 459), the tradition of method thus established has persisted, especially in academic circles, to the present day; its influence still lingers in the topical divisions of treatises or textbooks dealing with the technique of fiction; and it still provides the commonplaces of a good many "studies" of novelists and novels (e.g., the pages on *Tom Jones*, already referred to, in Elton's *Survey*). The undoubted deficiencies of the scheme (in its neoclassical degradation) as an instrument of critical analysis and judgment have not passed unnoticed in recent years, particularly among critics of the *Scrutiny* group, who point out, justly enough, that "plot" and "character" are treated in a fashion that abstracts them unduly from the continuum of the novelist's language through which alone they affect us. These critics, however, are usually content to offer, as a positive substitute for the traditional scheme, only a still more extreme reduction of Aristotle's principles, in which everything in the discussion of a novel is made to turn on the relations between diction, in the sense of the author's "verbal arrangements," and thought, in the sense of the "experience" which he communicates by imposing "the pattern of his own sensibility" on the reader through the medium of language. See, for example, Martin Turnell, "The Language of Fiction," *Times Literary Supplement*, August 19, 1949, pp. 529–31; reprinted in his *Novel in France* (New York, 1951).

7. *Op. cit.*, I, 195.

8. Cross, *op. cit.*, II, 159–61; Elton, *op. cit.*, I, 195–96.

9. See *Critics and Criticism* (original ed.), pp. 588–92.

10. This accounts in large part, I think, for the depreciation of "plot" in E. M. Forster's *Aspects of the Novel*, and for his notion of a rivalry between "plot" and "character," in which one or the other may "triumph." For a view much closer to that argued in this essay see Elizabeth Bowen, "Notes on Writing a Novel," *Orion*, II (1945), 18 ff.

11. The meaning and force of this will be clear to anyone who has compared in detail the text of *The Ambassadors* with James's preliminary synopsis of the novel (*The Notebooks of Henry James* [New York, 1947], pp. 372–415). See also the excellent remarks of Allen Tate, apropos of *Madame Bovary*, in his "Techniques of Fiction" (*Forms of Modern Fiction*, ed. William Van O'Connor [Minneapolis, 1948], esp. pp. 37–45).

12. I am indebted for several points in what follows to an unpublished essay by one of my students, Mr. Melvin Seiden.

E. M. FORSTER

Pattern and Rhythm

Our interludes, gay and grave, are over, and we return to the general scheme of the course. We began with the story, and having considered human beings, we proceeded to the plot which springs out of the story. Now we must consider something which springs mainly out of the plot, and to which the characters and any other element present also contribute. For this new aspect there appears to be no literary word— indeed the more the arts develop the more they depend on each other for definition. We will borrow from painting first and call it the pattern. Later we will borrow from music and call it rhythm. Unfortunately both these words are vague—when people apply rhythm or pattern to literature they are apt not to say what they mean and not to finish their sentences: it is, "Oh, but surely the rhythm . . ." or "Oh, but if you call that pattern . . ."

Before I discuss what pattern entails, and what qualities a reader must bring to its appreciation, I will give two examples of books with patterns so definite that a pictorial image sums them up: a book the shape of an hour-glass and a book the shape of a grand chain in that old-time dance, the Lancers.

Thais by Anatole France is the shape of an hour-glass.

There are two chief characters, Paphnuce the ascetic, Thais the courtesan. Paphnuce lives in the desert, he is saved and happy when the book starts. Thais leads a life of sin in Alexandria, and it is his duty to save her. In the central scene of the book they approach, he succeeds; she goes into a monastery and gains salvation, because she has met him, but he, because he has met her, is damned. The two characters converge, cross, and recede with mathematical precision, and part of the pleasure we get from the book is due to this. Such is

319

the pattern of *Thais*—so simple that it makes a good starting point for a difficult survey. It is the same as the story of *Thais*, when events unroll in their time-sequence, and the same as the plot of *Thais*, when we see the two characters bound by their previous actions and taking fatal steps whose consequence they do not see. But whereas the story appeals to our curiosity and the plot to our intelligence, the pattern appeals to our aesthetic sense, it causes us to see the book as a whole. We do not see it as an hour-glass—that is the hard jargon of the lecture room which must never be taken literally at this advanced stage of our inquiry. We just have a pleasure without knowing why, and when the pleasure is past, as it is now, and our minds are left free to explain it, a geometrical simile such as an hour-glass will be found helpful. If it was not for this hour-glass the story, the plot, and the characters of Thais and Paphnuce would none of them exert their full force, they would none of them breathe as they do. "Pattern," which seems so rigid; is connected with atmosphere, which seems so fluid.

Now for the book that is shaped like the grand chain: *Roman Pictures* by Percy Lubbock.

Roman Pictures is a social comedy. The narrator is a tourist in Rome; he there meets a kindly and shoddy friend of his, Deering, who rebukes him superciliously for staring at churches and sets him out to explore society. This he does, demurely obedient; one person hands him on to another; café, studio, Vatican and Quirinal purlieus are all reached, until finally, at the extreme end of his career he thinks, in a most aristocratic and dilapidated palazzo, whom should he meet but the second-rate Deering; Deering is his hostess's nephew, but had concealed it owing to some backfire of snobbery. The circle is complete, the original partners have rejoined, and greet one another with mutual confusion which turns to mild laughter.

What is so good in *Roman Pictures* is not the presence of the "grand chain" pattern—anyone can organize a grand chain—but the suitability of the pattern to the author's mood. Lubbock works all through by administering a series of little shocks, and by extending to his characters an elaborate charity which causes them to appear in a rather worse light than if no charity was wasted on them at all. It is the comic atmosphere, but sub-acid, meticulously benign. And at the end we discover to our delight that the atmosphere has been externalized, and that the partners, as they click together in the marchesa's drawing-room, have done the exact thing which the book requires, which it required from the start, and have bound the scattered incidents together with a thread woven out of their own substance.

Thais and *Roman Pictures* provide easy examples of pattern; it is not often that one can compare a book to a pictorial object with any accuracy, though curves, etc., are freely spoken of by critics who do not quite know what they want to say. We can only say (so far) that pattern is an aesthetic aspect of the novel, and that though it may be nourished by anything in the novel—any character, scene, word—it draws most of its nourishment from the plot. We noted, when discussing the plot, that it added to itself the quality of beauty; beauty a little surprised at her own arrival: that upon its neat carpentry there could be seen, by those who cared to see, the figure of the Muse; that Logic, at the moment of finishing its own house, laid the foundation of a new one. Here, here is the point where the aspect called pattern is most closely in touch with its material; here is our starting point. It springs mainly from the plot, accompanies it like a light in the clouds, and remains visible after it has departed. Beauty is sometimes the shape of the book, the book as a whole, the unity, and our examination would be easier if it was always this. But sometimes it is not. When it is not I shall call it rhythm. For the moment we are concerned with pattern only.

Let us examine at some length another book of the rigid type, a book with a unity, and in this sense an easy book, although it is by Henry James. We shall see in it pattern triumphant, and we shall also be able to see the sacrifices an author must make if he wants his pattern and nothing else to triumph.

The Ambassadors, like *Thais*, is the shape of an hour-glass. Strether and Chad, like Paphnuce and Thais, change places, and it is the realization of this that makes the book so satisfying at the close. The plot is elaborate and subtle, and proceeds by action or conversation or meditation through every paragraph. Everything is planned, everything fits; none of the minor characters are just decorative like the talkative Alexandrians at Nicias' banquet; they elaborate on the main theme, they work. The final effect is pre-arranged, dawns gradually on the reader, and is completely successful when it comes. Details of intrigue, of the various missions from America, may be forgotten, but the symmetry they have created is enduring.

Let us trace the growth of this symmetry.[1]

Strether, a sensitive middle-aged American, is commissioned by his old friend, Mrs. Newsome, whom he hopes to marry, to go to Paris and rescue her son Chad, who has gone to the bad in that appropriate city. The Newsomes are sound commercial people, who have made money over manufacturing a small article of domestic utility. Henry James never tells us what the small article is, and in a moment we shall understand why. Wells spits it out in *Tono Bungay,* Meredith reels it out in *Evan Harrington,* Trollope prescribes it freely for Miss Dunstable, but for James to indicate how his characters made their pile—it would not do. The article is somewhat ignoble and ludicrous—that is enough. If you choose to be coarse and daring and visualize it for yourself as, say, a button-hook, you can, but you do so at your own risk: the author remains uninvolved.

Well, whatever it is, Chad Newsome ought to come back and help make it, and Strether undertakes to fetch him. He has to be rescued from a life which is both immoral and unremunerative.

Strether is a typical James character—he recurs in nearly all the books and is an essential part of their construction. He is the observer who tries to influence the action, and who through his failure to do so gains extra opportunities for observation. And the other characters are such as an observer like Strether is capable of observing—through lenses procured from a rather too first-class oculist. Everything is adjusted to his vision, yet he is not a quietist—no, that is the strength of the device; he takes us along with him, we move as well as look on.

When he lands in England (and a landing is an exalted and enduring experience for James, it is as vital as Newgate for Defoe; poetry and life crowd round a landing): when Strether lands, though it is only old England, he begins to have doubts of his mission, which increase when he gets to Paris. For Chad Newsome, far from going to the bad, has improved; he is distinguished, he is so sure of himself that he can be kind and cordial to the man who has orders to fetch him away; his friends are exquisite, and as for "women in the case" whom his mother anticipated, there is no sign of them whatever. It is Paris that has enlarged and redeemed him—and how well Strether himself understands this!

> His greatest uneasiness seemed to peep at him out of the possible impression that almost any acceptance of Paris might give one's authority away. It hung before him this morning, the vast bright Babylon, like some huge iridescent object, a jewel brilliant and hard, in which parts were not to be dis-

criminated nor differences comfortably marked. It twinkled and trembled and melted together; and what seemed all surface one moment seemed all depth the next. It was a place of which, unmistakably, Chad was fond; wherefore, if he, Strether, should like it too much, what on earth, with such a bond, would become of either of them?

Thus, exquisitely and firmly, James sets his atmosphere—Paris irradiates the book from end to end, it is an actor though always unembodied, it is a scale by which human sensibility can be measured, and when we have finished the novel and allow its incidents to blur that we may see the pattern plainer, it is Paris that gleams at the centre of the hour-glass shape—Paris—nothing so crude as good or evil. Strether sees this soon, and sees that Chad realizes it better than he himself can; and when he has reached this stage of initiation the novel takes a turn: there is, after all, a woman in the case; behind Paris, interpreting it for Chad, is the adorable and exalted figure of Mme. de Vionnet. It is now impossible for Strether to proceed. All that is noble and refined in life concentrates in Mme. de Vionnet and is reinforced by her pathos. She asks him not to take Chad away. He promises—without reluctance, for his own heart has already shown him as much—and he remains in Paris not to fight it but to fight for it.

For the second batch of ambassadors now arrives from the New World. Mrs. Newsome, incensed and puzzled by the unseemly delay, has dispatched Chad's sister, his brother-in-law, and Mamie, the girl whom he is supposed to marry. The novel now becomes, within its ordained limits, most amusing. There is a superb set-to between Chad's sister and Mme. de Vionnet, while as for Mamie—here is disastrous Mamie, seen as we see all things, through Strether's eyes.

As a child, as a "bud," and then again as a flower of expansion, Mamie had bloomed for him, freely, in the almost incessantly open doorways of home; where he remembered her at first very forward, as then very backward—for he had carried on at one period, in Mrs. Newsome's parlours, a course of English literature reinforced by exams and teas—and once more, finally, as very much in advance. But he had kept no great sense of points of contact; it not being in the nature of things at Woollett that the freshest of the buds should find herself in the same basket with the most withered of the winter apples. . . . He none the less felt now, as he sat with the charming girl, the signal growth of a confidence. For she *was* charming, when all was said, and none the less so for the visible habit and practice of freedom and fluency. She was charming, he was aware, in spite of the fact that if he hadn't found her so he would have found her something he should have been in peril of expressing as "funny." Yes, she was funny, wonderful Mamie, and without dreaming it; she was bland, she was bridal—with never, that he could make out as yet, a bridegroom to support it; she was handsome and portly, and easy and chatty, soft and sweet and almost disconcertingly reassuring. She was dressed, if we might so far discriminate, less as a young lady than as an old one—had an old one been supposable to Strether as so committed to vanity; the complexities of her hair missed moreover also the looseness of youth; and she had a mature manner of bending a little, as to encourage and reward, while she held neatly in front of her a pair of strikingly polished hands: the combination of all of which kept up about her the glamour of her "receiving," placed her again perpetually between the windows and within sound of the ice cream plates, suggested the enumeration of all the names, gregarious specimens of a single type, she was happy to "meet."

Mamie! She is another Henry James type; nearly every novel contains a Mamie—Mrs. Gereth in *The Spoils of Poynton* for instance, or Henrietta Stackpole in *The Portrait of a Lady*. He is so good at indicating instantaneously and constantly that a character is second-rate, deficient in sensitiveness, abounding in the wrong sort of worldliness; he gives such a character so much vitality that its absurdity is delightful.

So Strether changes sides and loses all hopes of marrying Mrs. Newsome. Paris is winning—and then he catches sight of something new. Is not Chad, as regards any fineness in him, played out? Is not Chad's Paris after all just a place for a spree? This fear is confirmed. He goes for a solitary country walk, and at the end of the day he comes across Chad and Mme. de Vionnet. They are in a boat, they pretend not to see him, because their relation is at bottom an ordinary liaison, and they are ashamed. They were hoping for a secret week-end at an inn while their passion survived; for it will not survive, Chad will tire of the exquisite Frenchwoman, she is part of his fling; he will go back to his mother and make the little domestic article and marry Mamie. They know all this, and it is revealed to Strether though they try to hide it; they lie, they are vulgar—even Mme. de Vionnet, even her pathos, once so exquisite, is stained with commonness.

> It was like a chill in the air to him, it was almost appalling, that a creature so fine could be, by mysterious forces, a creature so exploited. For, at the end of all things, they *were* mysterious; she had but made Chad what he was—so why could she think she had made him infinite? She had made him better, she had made him best, she had made him anything one would; but it came to our friend with supreme queerness that he was none the less only Chad. The work, however admirable, was nevertheless of the strict human order, and in short it was marvellous that the companion of mere earthly joys, of comforts, aberrations—however one classed them— within the common experience, should be so transcendently prized.
>
> She was older for him tonight, visibly less exempt from the touch of time; but she was as much as ever the finest and subtlest creature, the happiest apparition, it had been given him, in all his years, to meet; and yet he could see her there as vulgarly troubled, in very truth, as a maidservant crying for a young man. The only thing was that she judged herself as the maidservant wouldn't; the weakness of which wisdom too, the dishonour of which judgment, seemed but to sink her lower.

So Strether loses them too. As he says: "I have lost everything—it is my only logic." It is not that they have gone back. It is that he has gone on. The Paris they revealed to him—he could reveal it to them now, if they had eyes to see, for it is something finer than they could ever notice for themselves, and his imagination has more spiritual value than their youth. The pattern of the hour-glass is complete; he and Chad have changed places, with more subtle steps than Thais and Paphnuce, and the light in the clouds proceeds not from the well-lit Alexandria, but from the jewel which "twinkled and trembled and melted together, and what seemed all surface one moment seemed all depth the next."

The beauty that suffuses *The Ambassadors* is the reward due to a fine artist for hard work. James knew exactly what he wanted, he pursued the narrow path of aesthetic duty, and success to the full extent of his possibilities has crowned him. The pattern has woven itself with modulation and reservations Anatole France will never attain. Woven itself wonderfully. But at what sacrifice!

So enormous is the sacrifice that many readers cannot get interested in James, although they can follow what he says (his difficulty has been much exaggerated), and can appreciate his effects. They cannot grant his premise, which is that most of human life has to disappear before he can do us a novel.

He has, in the first place, a very short list of characters. I have already mentioned two—the observer who tries to influence the action, and the second-rate outsider (to whom, for example, all the brilliant opening of *What Maisie Knew* is entrusted). Then there is the sympathetic foil—very lively and frequently female—in *The Ambassadors.* Maria Gostrey plays this part; there is the wonderful rare heroine, whom Mme. de Vionnet approached and who is consummated by Milly in *The Wings of the Dove;* there is sometimes a villain, sometimes a young artist with generous impulses; and that is about all. For so fine a novelist it is a poor show.

In the second place, the characters, beside being few in number, are constructed on very stingy lines. They are incapable of fun, of rapid motion, of carnality, and of nine-tenths of heroism. Their clothes will not take off, the diseases that ravage them are anonymous, like the sources of their income, their servants are noiseless or resemble themselves, no social explanation of the world we know is possible for them, for there are no stupid people in their world, no barriers of language, and no poor. Even their sensations are limited. They can land in Europe and look at works of art and at each other, but that is all. Maimed creatures can alone breathe in Henry James's pages—maimed yet specialized. They remind one of the exquisite deformities who haunted Egyptian art in the reign of Akhenaton—huge heads and tiny legs, but nevertheless charming. In the following reign they disappear.

Now this drastic curtailment, both of the numbers of human beings and of their attributes, is in the interests of the pattern. The longer James worked, the more convinced he grew that a novel should be a whole—not necessarily geometric like *The Ambassadors,* but it should accrete round a single topic, situation, gesture, which should occupy the characters and provide a plot, and should also fasten up the novel on the outside—catch its scattered statements in a net, make them cohere like a planet, and swing through the skies of memory. A pattern must emerge, and anything that emerged from the pattern must be pruned off as wanton distraction. Who so wanton as human beings? Put Tom Jones or Emma or even Mr. Casaubon into a Henry James book, and the book will burn to ashes, whereas we could put them into one another's books and only cause local inflammation. Only a Henry James character will suit, and though they are not dead—certain selected recesses of experience he explores very well—they are gutted of the common stuff that fills characters in other books, and ourselves. And this castrating is not in the interests of the Kingdom of Heaven, there is no philosophy in the novels, no religion (except an occasional touch of superstition), no prophecy, no benefit for the superhuman at all. It is for the sake of a particular aesthetic effect which is certainly gained, but at this heavy price.

H. G. Wells has been amusing on this point, and perhaps profound. In *Boon*—one of his liveliest works—he had Henry James much upon his mind, and wrote a superb parody of him.

> James begins by taking it for granted that a novel is a work of art that must be judged by its oneness. Some one gave him that idea in the beginning of things and he has never found it out. He doesn't find things out. He doesn't even seem to want to find things out. He accepts very readily and then—elaborates. . . . The only living human motives left in his novels are a certain avidity and an entirely superficial curiosity. . . . . His people nose out suspicions, hint by hint, link by link. Have you ever known living human beings do that? The thing his novel is *about* is always there. It is like a church lit but with no congregation to distract you, with every light and line focussed on the high altar. And on the altar, very reverently placed, intensely there, is a dead kitten, an egg shell, a piece of string. . . . Like his *Altar of the Dead* with nothing to the dead at all. . . . For if there was, they couldn't all be candles, and the effect would vanish.

Wells sent *Boon* as a present to James, apparently thinking the master would be as much pleased by such heartiness and honesty as was he himself. The master was far from pleased, and a most interesting correspondence ensued.[2] Each of the eminent men becomes more and more himself as it proceeds. James is polite, reminiscent, bewildered, and exceedingly formidable: he admits that the parody has not "filled him with a fond elation," and regrets in conclusion that he can sign himself "only yours faithfully, Henry James." Wells is bewildered too, but in a different way; he cannot understand why the man should be upset. And, beyond the personal comedy, there is the great literary importance of the issue. It is this question of the rigid pattern: hourglass or grand chain or converging lines of the cathedral or diverging lines of the Catherine wheel, or bed of Procrustes—whatever image you like as long as it implies unity. Can it be combined with the immense richness of material which life provides? Wells and James would agree it cannot, Wells would go on to say that life should be given the preference, and must not be whittled or distended for a pattern's sake. My own prejudices are with Wells. The James novels are a unique possession and the reader who cannot accept his premises misses some valuable and exquisite sensations. But I do not want more of his novels, especially when they are written by someone else, just as I do not want the art of Akhenaton to extend into the reign of Tutankhamen.

That then is the disadvantage of a rigid pattern. It may externalize the atmosphere, spring naturally from the plot, but it shuts the doors on life and leaves the novelist doing exercises, generally in the drawing-room. Beauty has arrived, but in too tyrannous a guise. In plays— the plays of Racine, for instance—she may be justified because beauty can be a great empress on the stage, and reconcile us to the loss of the men we knew. But in the novel, her tyranny as it grows powerful grows petty, and generates regrets which sometimes take the form of books like *Boon*. To put it in other words, the novel is not capable of as much artistic development as the drama: its humanity or the grossness of its material hinder it (use whichever phrase you like). To most readers of fiction the sensation from a pattern is not intense enough to justify the sacrifices that made it, and their verdict is "Beautifully done, but not worth doing."

Still this is not the end of our quest. We will not give up the hope of beauty yet. Cannot it be introduced into fiction by some other method than the pattern? Let us edge rather nervously towards the idea of "rhythm."

Rhythm is sometimes quite easy. Beethoven's Fifth Symphony, for instance, starts with the rhythm "diddidy dum," which we can all hear and tap to. But the symphony as a whole has also a rhythm—due mainly to the relation between its movements—which some people can hear but no one can tap to. This second sort of rhythm is difficult, and whether it is substantially the same as the first sort only a musician could tell us. What a literary man wants to say though is that the first kind of rhythm, the diddidy dum, can be found in certain novels and may give them beauty. And the other rhythm, the difficult one—the rhythm of the Fifth Symphony as a whole—I cannot quote you any parallels for that in fiction, yet it may be present.

Rhythm in the easy sense, is illustrated by the work of Marcel Proust.[3]

Proust's conclusion has not been published yet, and his admirers say that when it comes everything will fall into its place, times past will be recaptured and fixed, we shall have a perfect whole. I do not believe this. The work seems to me a progressive rather than an aesthetic confession, and with the elaboration of Albertine the author was getting tired. Bits of news may await us, but it will be surprising if we have to revise our opinion of the whole book. The book is chaotic, ill-constructed, it has and will have no external shape; and yet it hangs together because it is stitched internally, because it contains rhythms.

There are several examples (the photographing of the grandmother is one of them) but the most important from the binding point of view is his use of the "little phrase" in the music of Vinteuil. It does more than anything else—more even than the jealousy which successively destroys Swann, the hero, and Charlus—to make us feel that we are in a homogeneous world. We first hear Vinteuil's name in hideous circumstances. The musician is dead—an obscure little country organist, unknown to fame—and his daughter is defiling his memory. The horrible scene is to radiate in several directions, but it passes, we forget about it.

Then we are at a Paris salon. A violin sonata is performed and a little phrase from its andante catches the ear of Swann and steals into his life. It is always a living being, but takes various forms. For a time it attends his love for Odette. The love affair goes wrong, the phrase is forgotten, we forget it. Then it breaks out again when he is ravaged by jealousy, and now it attends his misery and past happiness at once, without losing its own divine character. Who wrote the sonata? On hearing it is by Vinteuil, Swann says, "I once knew a wretched little organist of that name—it couldn't be by him." But it is, and Vinteuil's daughter and her friend transcribed and published it.

That seems all. The little phrase crosses the book again and again, but as an echo, a memory; we like to encounter it, but it has no binding power. Then, hundreds and hundreds of pages on, when Vinteuil has become a national possession, and there is talk of raising a statue to him in the town where he has been so wretched and so obscure, another work of his is performed—a posthumous sextet. The hero listens —he is in an unknown rather terrible universe while a sinister dawn reddens the sea. Suddenly for him and for the reader too, the little phrase of the sonata recurs—half heard, changed, but giving complete orientation, so that he is back in the country of his childhood with the knowledge that it belongs to the unknown.

We are not obliged to agree with Proust's actual musical descriptions (they are too pictorial for my own taste): but what we must admire is his use of rhythm in literature, and his use of something which is akin by nature to the effect it has to produce—namely a musical phrase. Heard by various people—first by Swann, then by the hero—the phrase of Vinteuil is not tethered; it is not a banner such as we find George Meredith using—a double-blossomed cherry tree to accompany Clara Middleton, a yacht in smooth waters for Cecilia Halkett. A banner can only reappear, rhythm can develop, and the little phrase has a life of its own, unconnected with the lives of its auditors, as with the life of the man who composed it. It is almost an actor, but not quite, and that "not quite" means that its power has gone towards stitching Proust's book together from the inside, and towards the establishment of beauty and the ravishing of the reader's memory. There are times when the little phrase—from its gloomy inception, through the sonata into the sextet—means everything to the reader. There are times when it means nothing and is forgotten, and this seems to me the function of rhythm in fiction; not to be there all the time like a pattern, but by its lovely waxing and waning to fill us with surprise and freshness and hope.

Done badly, rhythm is most boring, it hardens into a symbol and instead of carrying us on it trips us up. With exasperation we find that Galsworthy's spaniel John, or whatever it is, lies under the feet again; and even Meredith's cherry trees and yachts, graceful as they are, only open the windows into poetry. I doubt that it can be achieved by the writers who plan their books beforehand, it has to depend on a local impulse when the right interval is reached. But the effect can be exquisite, it can be obtained without mutilating the characters, and it lessens our need of an external form.

That must suffice on the subject of easy rhythm in fiction: which may be defined as repetition plus variation, and which can be illustrated by examples. Now for the more difficult question. Is there any effect in novels comparable to the effect of the Fifth Symphony as a whole, where, when the orchestra stops, we hear something that has never actually been played? The opening movement, the andante, and the trio-scherzo-trio-finale-trio-finale that composes the third block, all enter the mind at once, and extend one another into a common entity. This common entity, this new thing, is the symphony as a whole, and it has been achieved mainly (though not entirely) by the relation between the three big blocks of sound which the orchestra has been playing. I am calling this relation "rhythmic." If the correct musical term is something else, that does not matter; what we have now to ask ourselves is whether there is any analogy to it in fiction.

I cannot find any analogy. Yet there may be one; in music fiction is likely to find its nearest parallel.

The position of the drama is different. The drama may look towards the pictorial arts, it may allow Aristotle to discipline it, for it is not so deeply committed to the claims of human beings. Human beings have their great chance in the novel. They say to the novelist: "Recreate us if you like, but we must come in," and the novelist's problem, as we have seen all along, is to give them a good run and to achieve something else at the same time. Whither shall he turn? not indeed for help but for analogy. Music, though it does not employ human beings, though it is governed by intricate laws, nevertheless does offer in its final expression a type of beauty which fiction might achieve in its own way. Expansion. That is the idea the novelist must cling to. Not completion. Not rounding off but opening out. When the symphony is over we feel that the notes and tunes composing it have been liberated, they have found in the rhythm of the whole their individual freedom. Cannot the novel be like that? Is not there something of it in *War and Peace?*—the book with which we began and in which we must end. Such an untidy book. Yet, as we read it, do not great chords begin to sound behind us, and when we have finished does not every item—even the catalogue of strategies—lead a larger existence than was possible at the time?

NOTES

1. There is a masterly analysis of *The Ambassadors* from another standpoint in *The Craft of Fiction.*
2. See the *Letters of H. James,* Vol. II.
3. The first three books of *A la recherche du temps perdu* have been excellently translated by C. K. Scott Moncrieff under the title of *Remembrance of Things Past,* A. & C. Boni.

FRANK KERMODE

The End

. . . I begin by discussing fictions of the End—about ways in which, under varying existential pressures, we have imagined the ends of the world. This, I take it, will provide clues to the ways in which fictions, whose ends are consonant with origins, and in concord, however unexpected, with their precedents, satisfy our needs. So we begin with Apocalypse, which ends, transforms, and is concordant.

Broadly speaking, apocalyptic thought belongs to rectilinear rather than cyclical views of the world, though this is not a sharp distinction; and even in Jewish thought there was no true apocalyptic until prophecy failed, for Jewish apocalyptic belongs to what scholars call the Intertestamentary Period. But basically one has to think of an ordered series of events which ends, not in a great New Year, but in a final Sabbath. The events derive their significance from a unitary system, not from their correspondence with events in other cycles.

This changes the events themselves, and the temporal relations between them. In Homer, we are told, the Odyssean episodes are related by their correspondence with a cyclic ritual; the time between them is insignificant or null.[1] Virgil, describing the progress of Aeneas from the broken city of Troy to a Rome standing for empire without end, is closer to our traditional apocalyptic, and that is why his *imperium* has been incorporated into Western apocalyptic as a type of the City of God. And in the journey of Aeneas the episodes are related internally; they all exist under the shadow of the end. Erich Auerbach makes a similar point in the opening chapter of *Mimesis,* where he contrasts the story of the scar of Odysseus with the story of the sacrifice of

Isaac—the second story has continually to be modified by reference to what is known of the divine plan from the Creation to the Last Days: it is perpetually open to history, to reinterpretation—one remembers how central the story was to Kierkegaard—in terms of changed human ways of speaking about the single form of the world. *The Odyssey* is not, in this way, open. Virgil and Genesis belong to our end-determined fictions; their stories are placed at what Dante calls the point where all times are present, *il punto a cui tutti li tempi son presenti;* or within the shadow of it. It gives each moment its fullness. And although for us the End has perhaps lost its naïve *imminence,* its shadow still lies on the crises of our fictions; we may speak of it as *immanent.*

This is a position I shall try to justify in my second talk. Meanwhile let me assume it. In their general character our fictions have certainly moved away from the simplicity of the paradigm; they have become more "open." But they still have, and so far as one is capable of prediction must continue to have, a real relation to simpler fictions about the world. Apocalypse is a radical instance of such fictions and a source of others. I shall be speaking of it both as type and source. In view of my own limitations and because the end of one's lecture is always immanent, I shall go in for drastic foreshortenings; but if I concentrate on aspects of the topic important to my argument, I do so, I hope, without falsifying the others.

The Bible is a familiar model of history. It begins at the beginning ("In the beginning . . .") and ends with a vision of the end ("Even so, come, Lord Jesus"); the first book is Genesis, the last Apocalypse. Ideally, it is a wholly concordant structure, the end is in harmony with the beginning, the middle with beginning and end. The end, Apocalypse, is traditionally held to resume the whole structure, which it can only do by figures predictive of that part of it which has not been historically revealed. The Book of Revelation made its way only into the canon—it is still unacceptable to Greek Orthodoxy—perhaps because of learned mistrust of over-literal interpretation of the figures. But once established it showed, and continues to show, a vitality and resource that suggest its consonance with our more naïve requirements of fiction.

Men, like poets, rush "into the middest," [2] *in medias res,* when they are born; they also die *in mediis rebus,* and to make sense of their span they need fictive concords with origins and ends, such as give meaning to lives and to poems. The End they imagine will reflect their irreducibly intermediary preoccupations. They fear it, and as far as we can see have always done so; the End is a figure for their own deaths. (So, perhaps, are all ends in fiction, even if represented, as they are for example by Kenneth Burke, as cathartic discharges.)

It is sometimes argued—as by those very different critics, D. H. Lawrence and Dr. Austin Farrar [3]—that behind Revelation there lies a strictly inexplicable set of myths that have been overlaid by later topical applications; but what human need can be more profound than to humanize the common death? When we survive, we make little images of moments which have seemed like ends; we thrive on epochs. Fowler observes austerely that if we were always quite serious in speaking of "the end of an epoch" we should live in ceaseless transition; recently Mr. Harold Rosenberg has been quite seriously saying that we do.[4] Scholars are devoted to the epoch, and philosophers—notably Ortega y Gasset and Jaspers—have tried to give the concept definition.[5] The matter is entirely in our own hands, of course; but our interest in it reflects our deep need for intelligible Ends. We project ourselves— a small, humble elect, perhaps—past the End, so as to see the structure whole, a thing we cannot do from our spot of time in the middle.

Apocalypse depends on a concord of imaginatively recorded past and imaginatively predicted future, achieved on behalf of us, who remain "in the middest." Its predictions, though figurative, *can* be taken literally, and as the future moves in on us we may expect it to conform with the figures. Many difficulties arise from this expectation. We ask such questions as, who is the Beast from the Land? the Woman Clothed with the Sun? What is meant by this number, and to what events do the Seven Seals refer? Where, on the body of history, shall we look for the scars of that three-and-a-half years' reign? What is Babylon, who is the Knight Faithful and True? We may be sure that we can from our special point of vantage work out the divisions of history in accordance with these figures, and that we must be right, if only because the state of the world shows so clearly that the second coming is at hand, *donec finiatur mundus corruptionis*. The great majority of interpretations of Apocalypse assume that the End is pretty near. Consequently the historical allegory is always having to be revised; time discredits it. And this is important. Apocalypse can be disconfirmed without being discredited. This is part of its extraordinary resilience. It can also absorb changing interests, rival apocalypses, such as the Sibylline writings. It is patient of change and of historiographical sophistications. It allows itself to be diffused, blended with other varieties of fiction—tragedy, for example, myths of Empire and of Decadence—and yet it can survive in very naïve forms. Probably the most sophisticated of us is capable at times of naïve reactions to the End.

Let us look for a moment at some features of naïve apocalyptism. The early Christians were the first to experience the disconfirmation of literal predictions; it has been said that the apostasies of the second century were the consequence of this "eschatological despair," as Bultmann calls it.[6] But literal disconfirmation is thwarted by typology, arithmology, and perhaps by the buoyancy of chiliasts in general. Thus a mistaken prediction can be attributed to an error of calculation, either in arithmetic or allegory. And if you insist that Nero is Antichrist, or Frederick II the Emperor of the Last Days, you need not be too depressed if your choice should die too early, since at this level of historical abstraction you can always believe he will return at a convenient season; and you will even find Sibylline texts to support you.

Given this freedom, this power to manipulate data in order to achieve the desired consonance, you can of course arrange for the End to occur at pretty well any desired date, but the most famous of all predicted Ends is A.D. 1000. It is now thought that earlier historians exaggerated the "Terrors" of that year, but it need not be doubted that it produced a characteristic apocalypse-crisis. The opinion of St. Augustine, that the millennium was the first thousand years of the Christian era, supported the feeling that the world was reaching its term, and that the events of Apocalypse, already given memorable iconographic form, were to ensue. The Terrors and Decadence are two of the recurring elements in the apocalyptic pattern; Decadence is usually associated with the hope of renovation. Another permanent feature of the pattern was also illustrated in the crisis of the year 1000, and this I shall call clerkly scepticism. The Church frowned on precise predictions of the End. One such protest was the *Libellus de Antechristo* of Adso. He was a monk who in 954 argued that the end of the world cannot be predicted, and in any case cannot come until the full restoration of the Empire (ultimately a Sibylline doctrine). It can only happen after a Frankish emperor, following a peaceful universal reign, has deposited his sceptre on the Mount of Olives. The Church persistently tried to de-mythologize Apocalypse, though obviously Adso was discrediting arithmological fictions by substituting what seem to us equally fantastic imperial fictions. In fact the mythology of Empire and of Apocalypse are very closely related. Anyway, there was something that might be called scepticism among the learned—a recognition

that arithmetical predictions of the End are bound to be disconfirmed. . . .

This has relevance to literary plots, images of the grand temporal
consonance; and we may notice that there is the same co-existence of
naïve acceptance and scepticism here as there is in apocalyptic. Broadly
speaking, it is the popular story that sticks most closely to established
conventions; novels the clerisy calls "major" tend to vary them, and
to vary them more and more as time goes by. I shall be talking about
this in some detail later, but a few brief illustrations might be useful
now. I shall refer chiefly to one aspect of the matter, the falsification
of one's expectation of the end.

The story that proceeded very simply to its obviously predestined
end would be nearer myth than novel or drama. Peripeteia, which has
been called the equivalent, in narrative, of irony in rhetoric, is present
in every story of the least structural sophistication. Now peripeteia
depends on our confidence of the end; it is a disconfirmation followed
by a consonance; the interest of having our expectations falsified is
obviously related to our wish to reach the discovery of recognition by
an unexpected and instructive route. It has nothing whatever to do
with any reluctance on our part to get there at all. So that in assimi-
lating the peripeteia we are enacting that readjustment of expectations
in regard to an end which is so notable a feature of naïve apocalyptic.

And we are doing rather more than that; we are, to look at the matter
in another way, re-enacting the familiar dialogue between credulity
and scepticism. The more daring the peripeteia, the more we may feel
that the work respects our sense of reality; and the more certainly we
shall feel that the fiction under consideration is one of those which,
by upsetting the ordinary balance of our naïve expectations, is finding
something out for us, something *real*. The falsification of an expectation
can be terrible, as in the death of Cordelia; it is a way of finding
something out that we should, on our more conventional way to the
end, have closed our eyes to. Obviously it could not work if there were
not a certain rigidity in the set of our expectations.

The degree of rigidity is a matter of profound interest in the study
of literary fictions. As an extreme case you will find some novel, probably contemporary with yourself, in which the departure from a basic
paradigm, the peripeteia in the sense I am now giving it, seems to
begin with the first sentence. The schematic expectations of the reader
are discouraged immediately. Since by definition one seeks the maxi-

mum peripeteia (in this extended sense) in the fiction of one's own time, the best instance I can give is from Alain Robbe-Grillet.[7] He refuses to speak of his "theory" of the novel; it is the old ones who talk about the need for plot, character, and so forth, who have the theories. And without them one can achieve a new realism, and a narrative in which "le temps se trouve coupé de la temporalité. Il ne coule plus." And so we have a novel in which the reader will find none of the gratification to be had from sham temporality, sham causality, falsely certain description, clear story. The new novel "repeats itself, bisects itself, modifies itself, contradicts itself, without even accumulating enough bulk to constitute a past—and thus a 'story,' in the traditional sense of the word." The reader is not offered easy satisfactions, but a challenge to creative co-operation.

When Robbe-Grillet wrote *Les Gommes* he was undoubtedly refining upon certain sophisticated conventions developed by Simenon in the Maigret novels; but in those the dark side of the plot is eventually given a reasonable explanation, whereas in Robbe-Grillet the need for this has gone. Rival versions of the same set of facts can co-exist without final reconciliation. The events of the day are the events of the novel, and on the first page we are told that they will "encroach upon the ideal order, cunningly introducing an occasional inversion, a discrepancy, a warp, in order to accomplish their work." The time of the novel is not related to any exterior norm of time. So, in *La Jalousie,* the narrator is explicitly "unconcerned with chronology," perceiving only that here and now in which memory, fantasy, anticipation of the future may intrude, though without sharp differentiation. The story does move forward, but without reference to "real" time, or to the paradigms of real time familiar from conventional novels.

It is a question how far these books could make their effect if we were genuinely, as Robbe-Grillet thinks we should be, indifferent to all conventional expectations. In some sense they must be there to be defeated. Thus, in another novel, *In the Labyrinth,* the soldier who is the central figure only slowly emerges (in so far as he does emerge) from other things, the objects described with equal objectivity, such as the mysterious packet he carries (why is it mysterious? that is a conventional expectation, to be defeated later) or a street, or wallpaper. The soldier has a mission; as you expect to hear about it you are given minute descriptions—of snow on windowsills, of polish on a boot, of the blurred rings left by glasses on a wooden tabletop. There is an unhelpful child, who comes in again and again, confusing one about one's way, asking questions. There is a woman who gives the soldier food, and a photograph mysteriously (why?) related to the soldier himself and what he is doing. It seems he has arrived at the unknown place he seeks; but no, he has not, for he is back at an earlier point in the story, though he does not seem to have been dreaming. He even sees himself in the street. The book makes its own unexpected, unexpectable designs; this is *écriture labyrinthine*, as *Les Gommes* is writing with an eraser. The story ends where it began, within the immediate perceptual field of a narrator. It is always *not* doing things which we unreasonably assume novels ought to do: connect, diversify, explain, make concords, facilitate extrapolations. Certainly there is no temporality, no successiveness. In Robbe-Grillet's latest novel the same character is murdered four times over (an extension of the device already used in *Les Gommes*). This is certainly a shrewd blow at paradigmatic expectations.

Still, this is very modern and therefore very extreme. As a method Robbe-Grillet's owes a good deal to those of Sartre and Camus, and it is obvious that both *La Nausée* and *L'Etranger* are strikingly original and unconventional fictions; yet in the view of the younger man, Camus was incapable of breaking completely with the old myths of narrative, the old anthropomorphism, and Robbe-Grillet calls him a tragic humanist. Sartre in his own way is just as old-fashioned, his world "entièrement tragifié." And it is true that even in these novels, and much more in *Les Chemins de la liberté* and in *La Peste*, Sartre and Camus are less contemptuous than Robbe-Grillet of paradigm and expectation.

For example, the first chapter of *La Peste* is not so different from one of Scott's leisurely overtures; it talks about the "setting," Oran, and although it contains what might be called typological ironies— indications of the ways in which Oran, in the book, might stand for any community, or for some particular communities (France, for example, on the eve of the Occupation)—these are not obtrusive. The "real" opening follows, and striking though it may be—"When leaving his surgery on the morning of 16 April, Dr. Bernard Rieux felt something soft under his foot"—it is no great departure from the famous norm of an opening sentence, "The Marquise went out at five o'clock." So at the end: the end of the plague might seem a natural close, but it goes on, and Rieux, now known to be the narrator, adds a few words to moralize the situation: in happy cities which do not like death it is easy to ignore the existence of the plague bacillus, and so on. This is, however, not the old ending that panders to temporal expectations, the sort described (in its comic mode) by Henry James as "a distribution at the last of prizes, pensions, husbands, wives, babies, millions, appended paragraphs, and cheerful remarks." [8] In fact Camus has put the conventional opening and close to original use; for without the opening and the close it would certainly be less easy to argue, as is commonplace, that the book is "really about" the Occupation, or "really about" more abstract issues. The peripeteia is there all right, but it bears more directly upon the conventions which make it possible. *La Peste* is what the analysts call "over-determined," is susceptible to multiple readings, because of the slightly extra-paradigmatic way of proceeding I have tried to sketch in. There is other evidence; it even contains the opening of a rival novel, intensely conventional, and the sermons are also peripeteias. *La Peste* is much more like a "novel" than *Dans le labyrinthe*, but it has anti-novelistic devices; as all good novels, on the French definition of the anti-novel, must have.

Let me, to get the situation clearer, choose at random one more novel, an older one again, which has the advantage of being universally regarded as a remarkable masterpiece: Dostoevsky's *The Idiot*. To put it at its lowest, this novel abounds in surprising things. But it starts off with the Warsaw train rapidly approaching St. Petersburg "at about nine o'clock in the morning at the end of November," and tells us that the train contains Prince Myshkin and Rogozhin. They are elaborately described, and the other principal, Nastasya Filippovna, is discussed in some detail before the train gets in. Even Lebedev is there. The prince is called a "holy fool." It seems that nothing in the story is being held back. And indeed the book ends, thirteen or fourteen reading hours later, with Rogozhin and Myshkin together beside the dead Nastasya, the corpse with its one hovering fly, the murderer, and the idiot consoling him. Or so it would end, were it not that Dostoevsky found the paradigms convenient in their place; he writes a "conclusion," completely perfunctory and traditional, in which he tells you what became of the surviving characters, one of those ends so despised by Henry James.

It would be of little use at this point to introduce more examples. In the *nouveau roman* of Robbe-Grillet there is an attempt at a more or less Copernican change in the relation between the paradigm and the text. In Camus the counter-pointing is less doctrinaire; in Dostoevsky there is no evidence of any theoretical stand at all, simply rich originality within or without, as it chances, normal expectations.

All these are novels which most of us would agree (and it is by a consensus of this kind only that these matters, quite rightly, are determined) to be at least very good. They represent in varying degrees that falsification of simple expectations as to the structure of a future which constitutes peripeteia. We cannot, of course, be denied an end; it is one of the great charms of books that they have to end. But unless we are extremely naïve, as some apocalyptic sects still are, we do not ask that they progress towards that end precisely as we have been given to believe. In fact we should expect only the most trivial work to conform to pre-existent types.

It is essential to the drift of all these talks that what I call the scepticism of the clerisy operates in the person of the reader as a demand for constantly changing, constantly more subtle, relationships between a fiction and the paradigms, and that this expectation enables a writer much inventive scope as he works to meet and transcend it. The presence of such paradigms in fictions may be necessary—that is a point I shall be discussing later—but if the fictions satisfy the clerisy, the paradigms will be to a varying but always great extent attenuated or obscured. The pressure of reality on us is always varying, as Stevens might have said: the fictions must change, or if they are fixed, the interpretations must change. Since we continue to "prescribe laws to nature"—Kant's phrase, and we do—we shall continue to have a relation with the paradigms, but we shall change them to make them go on working. If we cannot break free of them, we must make sense of them. . . .

It may be useful to have some kind of summary account of what I've been saying. The main object is the critical business of making sense of some of the radical ways of making sense of the world. Apocalypse and the related themes are strikingly long-lived; and that is the first thing to say about them, although the second is that they change. The Johannine acquires the characteristics of the Sibylline Apocalypse, and develops other subsidiary fictions which, in the course of time, change the laws we prescribe to nature, and specifically to time. Men of all kinds act, as well as reflect, as if this apparently random collocation of opinion and predictions were true. When it appears that it cannot be so, they act as if it were true in a different sense. Had it been otherwise, Virgil could not have been *altissimo poeta* in a Christian tradition; the Knight Faithful and True could not have appeared in the opening stanzas of *The Faerie Queene*. And what is far more puzzling, the City of Apocalypse could not have appeared as a modern Babylon, together with the "shipmen and merchants who were made rich by her" and by the "inexplicable splendour" of her "fine linen, and purple and scarlet," in *The Waste Land,* where we see all these things, as in Revelation, "come to nought." Nor is this a matter of literary allusion merely. The Emperor of the Last Days turns up as a Flemish or an Italian peasant, as Queen Elizabeth or as Hitler; the Joachite transition as a Brazilian revolution, or as the Tudor settlement, or as the Third Reich. The apocalyptic types—empire, decadence and renovation, progress and catastrophe—are fed by history and underlie our ways of making sense of the world from where we stand, in the middest.

But the more learned the cleric, whether theologian, poet, or novelist, the "higher" the kind he practises, the more subtly are these types overlaid. That which seemed a straightforward prediction becomes an obscure figure. As the predictions go wrong, it emerges that it is not merely upon the people of a certain moment but upon all men that the ends of the world have come. Apocalypse, which succeeded prophecy, merges with tragedy; the humble elect survive not all the kings of the earth as in Revelation, but the one king whose typical story is enacted before them. When tragedy established itself in England it did so in terms of plots and spectacle that had much more to do with medieval apocalypse than with the *mythos* and *opsis* of Aristotle. Later, tragedy itself succumbs to the pressure of "demythologizing"; the End itself, in modern literary plotting loses its downbeat, tonic-and-dominant finality, and we think of it, as the theologians think of Apocalypse, as immanent rather than imminent. Thus, as we shall see, we think in terms of crisis rather than temporal ends; and make much of subtle disconfirmation and elaborate peripeteia. And we concern ourselves with the conflict between the deterministic pattern any plot suggests, and the freedom of persons within that plot to choose and so to alter the structure, the relations of beginning, middle, and end.

Naïvely predictive apocalypses implied a strict concordance between beginning, middle, and end. Thus the opening of the seals had to correspond to recorded historical events. Such a concordance remains a deeply desired object, but it is hard to achieve when the beginning is lost in the dark backward and abysm of time, and the end is known to be unpredictable. This changes our views of the patterns of time, and in so far as our plots honour the increased complexity of these ways of making sense, it complicates them also. If we ask for comfort from our plots it will be a more difficult comfort than that which the archangel offered Adam:

> How soon hath thy prediction, Seer blest,
> Measur'd this transient World, the race of Time,
> Till time stands fix'd.

But it will be a related comfort. In our world the material for an es-chatology is more elusive, harder to handle. It may not be true, as the modern poet argues, that we must build it out of "our loneliness and regret"; the past has left us stronger materials than these for our arti-fice of eternity. But the artifice of eternity exists only for the dying generations; and since they choose, alter the shape of time, and die, the eternal artifice must change. The golden bird will not always sing the same song, though a primeval pattern underlies its notes.

In my next talk I shall be trying to explain some of the ways in which that song changes, and talking about the relationship between apocalypse and the changing fictions of men born and dead in the middest. It is a large subject, because the instrument of change is the human imagination. It changes not only the consoling plot, but the structure of time and the world. One of the most striking things about it was said by Stevens in one of his adages; and it is with this suggestive saying that I shall mark the transition from the first to the second part of my own pattern. "The imagination," said this student of changing fictions, "the imagination is always at the end of an era." Next time we shall try to see what this means in relation to our problem of making sense of the ways we make sense of the world.

NOTES

1. See Georg Róppen and Richard Sommer, *Strangers and Pilgrims*, Oslo, 1964, pp. 19 and 355; Rhys Carpenter, *Folk Tale, Fiction and Saga in the Homeric Epics*, Berkeley, 1958; and Erich Auerbach, *Mimesis*, translated by Willard Trask, Princeton, 1953.
2. ". . . a Poet thrusteth into the middest, euen where it most concerneth him, and there recoursing to the thinges forepaste, and diuining of thinges to come, maketh a pleasing analysis of all." Sir Philip Sidney, *Apology for Poetry.*
3. See *Apocalypse*, London, 1932, and *The Rebirth of Images*, London, 1949.
4. See *The Tradition of the New*, New York, 1962.
5. See Ortega y Gasset, *Man and Crisis*, New York, 1958, and K. Jaspers, *Man in the Modern Age*, London, 1951, Introduction.
6. See R. Bultmann, *The Presence of Eternity*, New York, 1957.
7. See Alain Robbe-Grillet, *Pour un nouveau roman*, Paris, 1963, p. 168. Other quotations from the recent translation by Barbara Wright in *Snapshots and Towards a New Novel*, London, 1965 (published 1966).
8. In the Preface to *Roderick Hudson.*

CHARACTER

If considering fiction in terms of "plot and structure," as in the previous section, seems to detach it from life and set it entirely within the frame of art, discussing "character" would seem to vitalize fiction by returning it to the familiar world of human personality. But perhaps we need to remind ourselves that fictional characters look in two directions, out toward life and in toward art. Both directions are suggested by the word "character" itself, which can distinguish literary personages ("characters") from real persons and can associate the two through their common possession of the moral and psychological traits called "character." Thus we may find ourselves admiring at one moment the in-depth realism and vividness of a Huck Finn or an Augie March and, at the next, the way such characters, through contrasts, parallels, and analogies to other characters and themselves, contribute as structural elements to the design of the work.

This dual aspect of "character" as both lifelike and artlike is reflected in David Daiches's essay. Examining the art by which characters are revealed to us in all their apparent naturalness of personality, he points out how three traditional methods of characterization, each dependent on a sequential development in time, have given way in some

343

quarters to the stream of consciousness method, which by tuning in on the unconscious and preconscious levels of mind where past and present interpenetrate is able to create a fuller sense of character than was formerly possible.

W. H. Harvey is not concerned with methods of characterization but with the knowledge of character we obtain from observing the relation of characters to environmental contexts, specifically (in the chapter printed here) the context of "things." Various "mind-thing" relationships are possible, ranging from those in which things have a rather primitive, anthropomorphic life of their own to those in which they are merely so much ephemeral grist for the all-consuming mills of consciousness. The modern sense of alienation from things (and the fear of being reduced to thing-ness) may result in works that equate the ethical autonomy of the individual to the aesthetic autonomy of the work of art, moral control and artistic control becoming metaphors for one another.

This association of aesthetics and ethics is also reflected in Alan Friedman's essay, which urges the indivisibility of narrative and moral form. In their responses to events, characters define both their experiences and themselves as well. Thus Friedman finds a fictional event to be not merely an element of plot but a moment in the creation of self; and thus the moral movement of characters from innocence to experience within the work is built into the narrative structure of fiction.

DAVID DAICHES

Character

Should the personalities of characters in fiction emerge from a chronological account of a group of events and the characters' reactions to
those events, or is it the duty of the novelist to take time off, as it were,
in order to give a rounded description of the characters at the point
when they are introduced into the story? Novelists have employed
either of these two methods, and some have employed both at once.
Sometimes the character as we see him first is a shadowy and indeterminate creature, but after his reactions to a chronological series of
events have been presented we feel that he is now a living personality.
In other novels we are given a descriptive portrait of the character first,
so that we know what to expect, and the resulting actions and reactions
of the character provide a filling-in and elaboration whose justness we
can appreciate by comparison with the original portrait.

In Thomas Hardy's *Mayor of Casterbridge* there is no set description of Michael Henchard's character at the beginning of the book or,
indeed, anywhere else. In the first chapter he is simply a young man,
and Hardy continues to call him "the man" until the first episode is
concluded. True, we have an account of Michael's physical appearance
("The man was of fine figure, swarthy, and stern in aspect," etc.) but
that is all. There is no hint of his real nature—his personality. That
emerges as the story proceeds—emerges from the story itself, from the
account of what Michael does, and the way in which he reacts to the
doings of others. It might be argued that his character is not fully presented until the story is concluded, and the only way Hardy has by
then managed to give us a full view of his character has been by taking
him through a long and varied sequence of events. Any criterion of
consistency we may apply can concern only the relation of one action

From *The Novel and the Modern World.* Copyright © 1960 by The University of Chicago Press. Reprinted by permission of the publisher.

or reaction of Michael to another; there can be no referring back to an original prose portrait, because the author has not given us one.

That is one way of presenting character. The other, and perhaps the commoner, way is illustrated as well as anywhere in the third chapter of Trollope's *Barchester Towers*. The chapter is entitled "Dr. and Mrs. Proudie" and is a complete formal account of the characters of Dr. Proudie and his wife. First a general sketch of Dr. Proudie's personality and habits of mind, then an account of his career, then further expansion of his present nature and attitude. Then Mrs. Proudie is taken up and similarly treated. By the end of the chapter we know exactly who and what these two characters are: we know no more about their characters at the end of the book—we have only seen the application to particular events of the general principles already enunciated. The interest of the book lies in these events and in our noting and approving how the characters run true to form throughout.

Most effective of all from the point of view of those whose chief interest in fiction lies in its psychological aspects is the technique which combines the foregoing two methods. Any one of Jane Austen's novels would provide a good example of this. *Emma,* for example, begins as follows:

> Emma Woodhouse, handsome, clever, and rich, with a comfortable home and happy disposition, seemed to unite some of the best blessings of existence; and had lived nearly twenty-one years in the world with very little to distress or vex her. . . .
>
> The real evils . . . of Emma's situation were the power of having rather too much her own way, and a disposition to think a little too well of herself; these were the disadvantages which threatened alloy to her many enjoyments. The danger, however, was at present so unperceived, that they did not by any means rank as misfortunes with her. . . .

And so on. In the first chapter we are given a fairly adequate sketch of Emma's character and circumstances. Yet we do not know Emma completely. A full understanding of her nature comes only after we have watched her reactions to the events which constitute the story and have studied her own part in the shaping of those events. Jane Austen has availed herself of both of our two methods: she starts with the inset character sketch, yet it is not complete, even as a character sketch, until we have seen Emma in her relations with Harriet Smith,

Jane Fairfax, Mr. Elton, Mr. Knightley, and others. Whether or not there comes a point in the course of the novel, before the actual conclusion, where we feel that we know the real Emma, is a matter that individual readers may wrangle over; what concerns us here is to notice Jane Austen's method of showing us the kind of person that Emma is. Trollope shows us a known constant in varied circumstances, and our pleasure lies in recognizing the truth of the resulting description of behavior. Jane Austen shows us a partially known variant (variant for the reader just because partially known) in varied circumstances, and our pleasure lies in the progressively enhanced knowledge of that variant which the resulting description of behavior brings us—until there comes a point at which the variant becomes a constant, as we know the limiting bounds within which it moves. Hardy shows us an unknown defining itself by its reactions to the circumstances with which it is brought into contact. In all three cases a consistent character portrait emerges, but in each case the method of portraying—and the point at which the portrait is complete—is different. It might be noted that in Jane Austen's case minor characters are often portrayed by the first method: Mr. Woodhouse, for example, is presented complete at his first appearance and is made to act consistently throughout.

These two methods, separately or in combination, have been the stock methods of presenting character in fiction from the beginnings of the novel until modern times. Their prototypes are, respectively, the "Character" as practiced originally by Theophrastus and widely imitated in France and England in the seventeenth century, and the simple adventure story. You put a character into a story, or you arrange a story so that a character emerges—to make a very blunt distinction. In recent times, partly as a result of increased speculation into the nature of states of consciousness, writers have become dissatisfied with these traditional methods. They have realized that a psychologically accurate account of what a man is at any given moment can be given neither in terms of a static description of his character nor in terms of a group of chronologically arranged reactions to a series of circumstances. They have become interested in those aspects of consciousness which cannot be viewed as a progression of individual and self-existing moments, but which are essentially dynamic rather than static in nature and are independent of the given moment. The present moment is specious; it denotes the ever fluid passing of the "already" into the "not yet," and therefore retrospect and anticipation constitute the very essence of consciousness at any specified time. In other words, the relation of consciousness to time is not the simple one of events to time, but is independent of chronological sequence in a way that events are not. Further, the quality of my experience of any new phenomenon (and hence my reaction to any new circumstance) is conditioned by a group of similar experiences scattered up and down through past time, the association of which with the present experience is what makes the present experience what it is. A novelist might try to indicate this by such digression as, "That reminded him of . . . ," or "There flashed through his brain a memory of . . . ," or similar formulas, but modern writers have come to feel that this is too clumsy and artificial a way of expressing the mind's independence of chronological sequence. Some more fluid technique must be devised which will enable the author to utilize constantly those ever present contacts with the past which constitute the very stuff of consciousness. The static character sketch is, in the view of these writers, an arbitrary formalization of the real facts, while, on the other hand, to make the presentation of states of mind dependent on the step-by-step relation of a sequence of events in time is to impose on the mental activity of men a servile dependence on chronology which is not in accordance with psychological fact. It was as a way out of this difficulty (arising from a new realization of the complex and fluid nature of consciousness and the desire to utilize this realization in the portrayal of character) that the "stream of consciousness" technique was introduced into fiction.

Looked at from one point of view, the "stream of consciousness" technique is a means of escape from the tyranny of the time dimension. It is not only in distinct memories that the past impinges on the present, but also in much vaguer and more subtle ways, our mind floating off down some channel superficially irrelevant but really having a definite starting-off place from the initial situation; so that in presenting the characters' reactions to events, the author will show us states of mind being modified by associations and recollections deriving from the present situation (in a sense *creating* the present situation) but referring to a constantly shifting series of events in the past. Now, if this presentation of a state of mind is done with care and skill, the author will be able to kill two birds with one stone: he will be able to indicate the precise nature of the present experience of his character and at the same time he will be giving, incidentally, facts about the character's life previous to this moment—previous, in all probability, to the moment at which the book opens; and thus though the chronological scheme of the novel may comprise only a very limited time, one day, for example, the characters will emerge complete, both historically and psychologically.

This technique is, as has been mentioned, an extension of the more traditional memory digression. But a story which claims to unite in mutual progress the event and the character's reaction to the event, so that the mental picture is always dependent on the physical situation, can exploit the points in consciousness where the past impinges on, and indeed conditions, the present only as a digression, as an exception to the rule, which will become wearisome and disintegrating to the story if indulged in to any extent. What the "stream of consciousness" technique enables the writer to do is to claim a validity for these references and impingements, a validity in their own right as it were, because it is through their means that the story is presented completely and welded into a unity. The new method of describing states of mind becomes a new technique of story-telling.

Consider the actual story in Virginia Woolf's *Mrs. Dalloway*. If we were to judge it by the chronological time scheme, we should say that it was the story of one day in the life of a middle-aged woman. But it is not that: the story embraces much of Mrs. Dalloway's past life and her relations with other characters in the past as well as in the present, so that, even judging the story on the simple narrative level, we can see that it is more than the story of one day's activity. This inclusion of so much of Mrs. Dalloway's past life is made possible by the way in which her ever-changing state of mind is described. True, the time sequence is marked off almost rigidly by such an obvious device as the striking of clocks (we shall discuss this point in more detail in a later chapter); but the very reason why the chronological framework has to be kept so constantly before the reader's attention is just because it is a framework, and nothing more. It is not the substance of the story, as it would be in any traditional novel; it is the mere skeleton which supports the living flesh and blood of the novel. Fixing her character physically at a given point in time and space, Mrs. Woolf is free to follow the character's "stream of consciousness" up and down in these two dimensions. It is as though we are led away up a winding tributary, but, having previously marked with some easily distinguished object the point where the tributary joins the main stream, we are able to find our way back at any moment. The significance of a novel like *Mrs. Dalloway* lies—to continue the metaphor—in the tributaries explored rather than in the main stream. The main stream is important only because it is from it that we take our bearings and with reference to it that we chart our position at any given moment. The line along which we move in the traditional chronological novel becomes, in a novel of this kind, one of the axes of a graph on which the curve of our journey is plotted, and we refer to the axis only when we want to check up on our position.

Thus the "stream of consciousness" technique is not simply a method of describing states of mind, because the method has implications for the whole technique of narrative and character drawing. If we ask ourselves why Joyce in *Ulysses* is able, while confining his chronological framework to the events of a single day, to relate so much more than merely the events of that single day and to make his hero perhaps the most complete and rounded character in all fiction, the answer lies in the potentialities—potentialities for narrative as well as for psychological analysis—of this new method of describing mental attitudes.

But the advantages for psychological analysis need not be minimized. The realization, which this technique implies, of the fact that personality is in a constant state of unstable equilibrium, that a mood is never anything static but a fluid pattern "mixing memory with desire," marks an important new development in the tradition of psychological fiction that has come down to us from Richardson. Richardson tried to present immediately the mood and thought of his characters by weaving his novels out of their letters. The defect here, from the modern standpoint, is that letters written to a given correspondent are bound to be subject to rigid formal limitations which prohibit the direct and adequate expression of states of mind. Only formalized aspects of an attitude can be expressed to any given audience (as every audience, even if the letter is a letter to the press, is a strictly defined and limited audience) however indefatigable a correspondent the character may be. The inhibiting effect of the audience would make the epistolary technique unacceptable to the modern psychological novelist. The diary would seem a more helpful device here than the letter; but the author will always be at a loss to render convincing the desire of the character to express completely and effectively his states of mind with reference to the given circumstances. No, if the characters are not to be either incredibly frank and self-conscious letter-writers or continuously introverted egoists, the responsibility for putting the "stream of consciousness" onto paper must not be laid on the characters but assumed in full by the author. The technique of Dorothy Richardson or Virginia Woolf or James Joyce is in this respect no more "real" than any other: it is a convention like other conventions, and it depends on our acceptance of the author's omniscience with no limitation whatsoever; but, once the convention is accepted, it makes possible the presentation of aspects of personality and of states of mind which were not possible in fiction utilizing other techniques and other conventions.

That we are what we are in virtue of what we have been is an obvious platitude; but the full utilization of the psychological aspects of this fact to build up a new technique in fiction is a comparatively recent development in the history of literature. The wheel has come full circle since the days when seventeenth-century wits wrote "characters" of types or eccentrics. Novelists who employ the "stream of consciousness" technique would deny that character *portrayal* is possible for the fiction writer at all: character is a process not a state, and the truth about men's reactions to their environment—and what is a man's character but his reactions to environment, actual and potential?—can be presented only through some attempt to show this process at work. An understanding of this view can help us to understand one of the main directive forces at work in contemporary fiction.

If we may return for a moment to the two traditional methods of presenting character discussed at the beginning of this chapter—the complete initial portrait followed by events which confirm the portrait and the emergence of the complete character from the action—we may note that a third method is frequently distinguished by students of fiction. This is the method which shows the character changing or developing, so that while the initial portrait is valid with reference to the situation presented at the beginning of the novel, it ceases to be valid by the time the novel is concluded. As a result of the circumstances in which the character finds himself throughout the course of the story, his nature is modified and we are finally confronted with a different person from the one we met at the beginning. Now, to distinguish this method as essentially a different technique seems to be the result of a certain confusion. It is of course possible to make a character really change in the course of the action: we know how in many popular novels the villain reforms at the end and becomes a good man. But such sudden and radical change as this—we recall Mr. Alfred Jingle's distressing conversion at the end of the *Pickwick Papers*—is never convincing in terms of psychological probability. Development, however, as distinct from such crude change, is more regular in good fiction. This is in essence but one aspect of our second method, when the character, incompletely presented at the beginning, does not emerge completely until the action has taken place. The final character is different, in the sense that events have made actual elements in his nature which before were only potential. The completeness of a character is judged by the degree to which its potentialities are realized. Thus, one reason why there is no complete portrayal at the beginning, why the portrayal is not complete until after we have seen the character in action, may be because the character was not meant to be a complete character until after these events had brought to light what was hitherto dormant. There is such a thing as an incomplete character in life. It may be such a character that the author introduces to us at the beginning of his story, while eventually we see the character made complete by experience. It will be seen that this is a modification of what we have called the second method rather than a quite separate method.

This point may be made clearer if we take an example from drama, where this development is more regular. Take the stock example of *King Lear*. King Lear is a different man at the end of the play from the man he was in Act I. Experience has altered his attitude, and we can actually see that process of modification at work throughout the play. Yet the circumstances presented in the play do not so much *change* Lear's character as bring out aspects of it which hitherto events had not conspired to release. This is a very different thing from the formal conversion of a villain to a reformed character. A character is not fully revealed until brought into the necessary testing circumstances, and an author can introduce us to a character either before or after he has met with such circumstances. There is a difference between change as the fulfilment of latent potentialities and change as the entire alteration of what previously existed. Consider Jane Austen's *Emma* again. True, Emma's character develops: she is more sensible in her attitude to specific things when we leave her than she was when we found her. But this is simply because her inherent common sense, a characteristic of hers all along, has had an opportunity of confronting experiences with which she was hitherto unfamiliar. Her rationality has applied itself to new premises and made the necessary deductions; and in the future she will always be in possession of those deductions. The change in Emma is of course very trivial when compared with that in Lear; but the difference is one of degree and not of kind. (Changes which are a result of physical or biological development are naturally in quite a different category. An adult is a different character from the child he once was. It might even be argued that for the purposes of plot in fiction they represent two separate characters. Novels whose central figure is shown progressing from infancy to manhood are liable to be episodic; no single presentation of character emerges from the work as a whole.)

What has the "stream of consciousness" technique to offer in presenting development in character? The situation here is very different from that present with either of the traditional methods; because by the adequate exploitation of states of mind and by following up all the paths suggested by the impinging of the past, in its multifarious variety, on the present, the nature of potentiality in character can be indicated even without our being shown the occurrence of events that would make those potentialities actual. The most interesting case in point here is the character of Stephen Dedalus in *Ulysses*. We see Stephen still a young man, immature, foolish, in many respects undeveloped. We are not shown him at all in his maturity—nothing in the book anticipates that day in June, 1904. Yet the fulness of implication provided by Joyce's method of presenting the consciousness of his characters is such that by the time the book closes we know the whole of Stephen, even though the whole of him is not yet, as it were, made actual. We can see the germ of the future in the present and without looking beyond the present. In Mrs. Dalloway, too, though the method is applied to her very much less intensely (and she is already a woman near the end of her life), we have a feeling by the end of the book that we know not only what she is and has been but what she might have been—we know all the unfulfilled possibilities in her character. In a character whose life is almost complete, unfulfilled possibilities are mere "might have beens"; in a character who has not yet reached complete maturity, such potentialities reveal also what may be.

If Joyce's method had been applied to the character of Lear it would have been possible, within a chronological framework comprising one day in Lear's life before the tragedy occurred, to make the reader aware of those potentialities in his character that in the play we do not see until they are made actual by events. The "stream of consciousness" method, at its most subtle and most intense, is able to achieve by depth what the traditional method achieves by extension. It provides a method of presenting character outside time and place, in the double sense that, first, it separates the presentation of consciousness from the chronological sequence of events, and, second, it enables the quality of a given state of mind to be investigated so completely, by means of pursuing to their end the remote mental associations and suggestions, that we do not need to wait for time to make the potential actual before we can see the whole.

W. H. HARVEY

Character and the Context of Things

In the next three chapters I shall deal with elements of character rather
than with techniques of characterization. Of course, the two can never
really be separated. In real life our sense of character naturally varies
with our powers of perception and understanding. We see in others
only what we are able to see and this ability then forms for others part
of our own character. We value qualities of sensitivity, tact, sympathy,
the unafraid acceptance of intensity or contradiction—qualities, we say,
which make us more fully human in that through them we respond
more fully to others. There is no *necessary* connection between many
of these qualities and the power to express them. We probably all know
the man whose profound knowledge of human nature expresses itself
only in silence or in platitude. We certainly know the man whose brilliant epigrams only disguise his ignorance or fear or hatred of anything beneath the surface.

As in life, so in art. We do not mean enough by technique if we
mean only those particular skills or methods of articulation—control of
dialogue, point of view, stream of consciousness and so on. Behind
these particular skills may or may not lie the really valuable qualities
of human vision, understanding and response. On the one hand, a
novelist may conscientiously include in his work every aspect of character and yet remain finally unperceptive because he lacks the technique whereby these elements are composed into a living whole.
Technical inadequacy here points to a more radical failure of the
imagination. If we are to choose only from the first order of art, then
Romola strikes me as a failure of this kind; of course, such failures
become more common as we descend the ladder of talent. On the other
hand, we know that an elegant technician may corruscate in a human

From *Character and the Novel*. Copyright © 1965 by W. J. Harvey. Reprinted by permission of the author's literary estate, Chatto and Windus,
Ltd., and Cornell University Press.

void while someone like Dreiser—clumsy, technically outrageous—still has the power of deeply moving the reader because the life he has imagined is indeed alive. Imagination here stands for the incalculable and indescribable factor in the creative process. As I have said, I shall try to describe what might be called the raw material of character rather than techniques of characterization. But even here language may betray us if it suggests a process of manufacture; a more appropriate metaphor is that of conception, gestation, birth and growth—more appropriate because more mysterious. As critics we can never do more than guess or hint at what happens with the conjunction of vision and technique.

II

When, in real life, we try to describe a person's character we generally speak in terms of a discrete identity. We think of it as something unique and separable from all other identities. We do this, of course, because the most intimate sense of character we can possibly have—our knowledge of self—is of this kind. No matter what image we have of our own identity—as the secret, central ego lurking behind a gallery of social personae, as the ghost in the machine, as a pattern, as a flux, as a hard, stable core within the flux—we still think of it as unique, isolate, discrete. From this we extrapolate a similar sense of the characters of others; they may be private and unknowable but they are like us at least in this respect. There can, of course, be no evidence for this assumption since when we experience another person we do so within a context which is inseparable from the experience itself. We can never know another in himself since in the very act of knowing our presence creates the context on which knowledge depends. The data by which we describe character are the aggregate of our experience in a number of situations, relationships, contexts. Without these contexts the characters of others do not make sense for us. We can have what may be called intrinsic knowledge of ourselves; we can only have contextual knowledge of others.

It is tempting to draw parallels between our experience of life and of fictional characters. Thus it is ridiculous to isolate characters from a novel and discuss them as totally autonomous entities; the novel itself is nothing but a complicated structure of artificially formed contexts parallel to those within which we experience real people. But can we go further than this? Can we say that the author, however he may disguise himself, is to his characters what we are to other people—the one context that must exist if we are to experience anything at all? The answer here must be no; in this case the analogy is false. For the author is not to his characters as we are to other people; his relationship to them is not human but god-like. However invisible he may make himself, whatever narrative techniques he may use to conceal his exit from his fiction, the novelist is and must be both omnipotent and omniscient. The last word is, both literally and metaphorically, his alone.

This being so, the novelist may confer on us his god-like power and privilege; we, too, can see the fictional character in his private self, secret, entirely solitary. Life allows only intrinsic knowledge of self, contextual knowledge of others; fiction allows both intrinsic and contextual knowledge of others. Many modern critics, of course, have regarded this god-like vision as illegitimate, as something inimical to the truth of fiction. These theoretical objections have their correlative in creative practice; the novelist's abdication of his god-like prerogatives is a central fact of modern fiction. While it may result from adherence to a philosophical theory or simply from a loss of nerve, this refusal to allow intrinsic knowledge of other characters merely creates a new kind of novel; it does not prove that this new kind is the *only* truthful sort of fiction. It is surely fair to say that the omniscient author of the classical novel destroys no necessary fictional illusion. On the contrary, he often creates a world which seems more real than many of those created by his more timid or more scrupulous successors. To say that because in real life we can only have contextual knowledge of others, therefore we can only be allowed a similar knowledge in fiction seems to me a naïve mistake. It is akin to the confusion of those neo-classical critics who demanded a strict adherence to the unities, lest the dramatic illusion be destroyed. The "suspension of disbelief" involved in reading what we *know* to be fiction seems to me to pose no special psychological difficulty; every day we make more daring and radical assumptions about other people in real life. Surely the fact that we are allowed intrinsic knowledge of other characters is a prime reason for our enjoyment of fiction; the imaginative release from our actual imprisonment within our own single point of view is one of the great consolations of art.

It is, however, on contextual knowledge of character that I wish to concentrate. Remarkably few great novelists have attempted a really prolonged revelation of a single centre of consciousness treated entirely as though from within. In most cases the mimetic richness of a novel derives from the writer showing us his characters functioning within a wide variety of contexts, situations, relationships. Early in *A Portrait of the Artist as a Young Man,* Stephen Dedalus turns to his geography book, on the flyleaf of which he has written:

> Stephen Dedalus
> Class of Elements
> Clongowes Wood College
> Sallins
> County Kildare
> Ireland
> Europe
> The World
> The Universe

This is an apt paradigm of the sense of plurality, of interlocking circles and multiple relationships, through which we move in our everyday lives. Reality in this sense is nothing but an incredibly complicated pattern of contexts, a pattern which moves in time and which ripples continuously outwards, as though from Stephen Dedalus to the Universe, until we can discern no pattern at all. Hence *any* formal limitation must be artificial and where to draw the line becomes a prime problem for the novelist. As Henry James puts it:

> Really, universally, relations stop nowhere, and the exquisite problem of the artist is eternally but to draw, by a geometry of his own, the circle within which they shall happily *appear* to do so. He is in the perpetual predicament that the continuity of things is the whole matter, for him, of comedy and tragedy; that this continuity is never, by the space of an instant or an inch, broken, and that, to do anything at all, he has at once intensely to consult and intensely to ignore it.[1]

Granted this, then one part of the truth of any novel will depend on the novelist's power of persuading us to accept these formal limitations. This he may do by working within some convention which, once accepted by the reader, permits him to concentrate intensely on the area of life thus circumscribed. The convention is, so to speak, a signal to the reader—"*This* is what you may accept. Pay *this* kind of attention." A simple example would, I suppose, be the "once upon a time" formula of the fairly-tale; a more sophisticated kind is the device of descriptive interchapters in Virginia Woolf's *The Waves*. Alternatively, the novelist may so disguise the frontiers of his fiction that we sense beyond the story the continuum of life itself. In this way the reader's experience of fiction merges imperceptibly into other, "real-life" experiences just as, in actuality, one context of our lives overlaps with another. This disguise, this effect of blurring the frontiers of fiction and life, is again the product of art, whether naïve or crafty. A crude example, I think, is the technique of montage used by Dos Passos in *U.S.A.*; we may contrast with this the author's addresses to the reader in *Tom Jones*. These may look simple minded when compared with modern technical experiments but are, I believe, sophisticated and designed to produce quite complicated effects upon the reader. At first sight they might seem to be conventional devices artificially delimiting the area of the novel. But they have the opposite effect, raising the novel to the magnitude of life itself and giving the fictional world a wonderful openness which is then played off against the formal intricacy of the plot.

III

To catalogue the various contexts which produce the density of relationships characterizing our everyday experience would be tedious and, since they constantly interact, misleading. We must risk both tedium and distortion, however, if we are to realize the extreme complexity of the problem. For what we are attempting is a descriptive analysis of the quality of experience and in such a task method and subject stand in much the same relationship as a chemical formula to the distinctive tang of a fruit on the palate. So much is fugitive, evanescent, dies under scrutiny; nevertheless we must labour, however clumsily, to follow the imaginative artist in his pursuit of experience. Let us start, at least, from relative simplicity by considering the least complex of human contexts—our relation, that is, to *things,* to the world of inanimate objects.

> "When you've lived as long as I you'll see that every human being has his shell and that you must take the shell into account. By the shell I mean the whole envelope of circumstances. There's no such thing as an isolated man or woman;

we're each of us made up of some cluster of appurtenances. What shall we call our 'self'? Where does it begin? Where does it end? It overflows into everything that belongs to us— and then it flows back again. I know a large part of myself is in the clothes I choose to wear. I've a great respect for *things!* One's self—for other people—is one's expression of one's self; and one's house, one's furniture, one's garments, the books one reads, the company one keeps—these things are all expressive."

(*The Portrait of a Lady*, Chapter 19)

Madame Merle's excursion into metaphysics raises a great many questions about the nature of character—indeed, more than character, for without her viewpoint what would become of our old thematic friend, Appearance and Reality? But she also states with finality the most obvious *function* in fiction of the various relationships assumed to exist between people and objects. This function is to create settings which, as Wellek and Warren observe, "may be viewed as metonymic, or metaphoric, expressions of character." This function has so often been the object of critical attention that I shall not discuss it further here. My concern is with some less obvious and more problematical aspects of the relations established between mind and things.

We may begin with a passage from the superb eleventh chapter of *Our Mutual Friend*, which describes a dinner party at the Podsnaps:

Mr. and Mrs. Veneering, and Mr. and Mrs. Veneering's brand-new bride and bridegroom, were of the dinner company; but the Podsnap establishment had nothing else in common with the Veneerings. Mr. Podsnap could tolerate taste in a mushroom man who stood in need of that sort of thing, but was far above it himself. Hideous solidity was the characteristic of the Podsnap plate. Everything was made to look as heavy as it could, and to take up as much room as possible. Everything said boastfully, "Here you have as much of me in my ugliness as if I were only lead; but I am so many ounces of precious metal worth so much an ounce;—wouldn't you like to melt me down?" A corpulent straddling epergne, blotched all over as if it had broken out in an eruption rather than been ornamented, delivered this address from an unsightly silver platform in the centre of the table. Four silver wine-coolers, each furnished with four staring heads, each head obtrusively carrying a big silver ring in each of its ears, conveyed the sentiment up and down the table, and handed it on to the pot-bellied silver salt-cellars. All the big silver spoons and forks widened the mouths of the company expressly for the purpose of thrusting the sentiment down their throats with every morsel they ate.

It is not enough to say that the dinner table is merely metonymic, that it simply reflects or symbolizes the qualities of Podsnappery. The passage may begin in that way but any sense of equivalence is soon overtaken by a livelier fantastication of the prose. The objects in a sense *become* Podsnap and his guests; in the sustained exuberance of the conceit salt-cellar and spoon live a life of their own far more intense than that of the assembled company, who suffer for a moment the unnatural reverse of becoming merely objects. All critics have remarked on Dickens's power of animating the inanimate world; none better than R. H. Horne who in an early essay compares him with Hogarth:

> There is a profusion and prodigality of character in the works of these two artists. A man, woman, or child, cannot buy a morsel of pickled salmon, look at his shoe, or bring in a mug of ale; a solitary object cannot pass on the other side of the way; a boy cannot take a bite at a turnip or hold a horse; a by-stander cannot answer the simplest question; a dog cannot fall into a doze; a bird cannot whet his bill; a pony cannot have a peculiar nose, nor a pig one ear, but out peeps the first germ of "a character." Nor does the ruling tendency and seed-filled hand stop with such as these; for inanimate objects become endowed with consciousness and purpose, and mingle appropriately in the background of the scene. Sometimes they even act as principals, and efficient ones too. . . .[2]

The good thing about Horne's comment is the way in which he connects two main characteristics of Dickens's fictional world. The Dickensian qualities of abundance and prodigality are such that, moving with him through his imaginatively crowded world, we seem continually to be bumping into things. This is a world of perpetual small collisions. At a pinch, we might say that this was an objective quality of his age, that a Victorian drawing room, for example, literally was crowded with objects. But it was also a quality of his imagination since this dense world of things is also alive; it has a comic or malign energy of its own. Dickens's imagination is primitive, animistic. I think we misread him slightly if we take his quickening power as merely conceit or metaphor or symbol; I believe this inanimate world was, for him, literally alive. There is nothing very odd in this; when a pencil breaks or we stub our toe in the dark we often have, in a transient way, this primitive sense of objects stubbornly leading a mysterious life of their own, a life which sometimes thwarts or obtrudes into ours. Most of us have vestigial terrors which are the feeble descendants of a magical view of the world. This primitive, animistic sense of things not just as "out-there," opaque, other-than-us, but also as alive, hostile or benevolent, is only one end of a whole scale of relationships between mind and the world of objects. Up and down this scale the novelist may range at will. Its centre—that which we take to be both norm and normal—is surely represented in fiction by Tolstoy, in whose work, as F. G. Steiner says, "Physical objects derive their *raison d'être* and solidity from the human context." Mr. Steiner at this point in his argument is contrasting Tolstoy's humanistic attitude to the world of things with that of Flaubert; he quotes from *Madame Bovary* the famous description of Charles's schoolboy cap:

> It was a headgear of composite order, containing elements of an ordinary hat, a hussar's busby, a lancer's cap, a sealskin cap and a nightcap; one of those wretched things whose mute hideousness suggests unplumbed depths, like an idiot's face. Ovoid and stiffened with whalebone, it began with three convex strips, then followed alternating lozenges of velvet and rabbit's fur, separated by a red band; then came a kind of bag, terminating in a cardboard-lined polygon intricately decorated with braid. From this hung a long, excessively thin cord, ending in a kind of tassel of gold netting. The cap was new; its peak was shiny.[3]

The object here is more truly metonymic, but Mr. Steiner is surely right to dismiss those critics who load this passage with tremendous symbolic import. While it may throw *some* light on Charles's character it also communicates a kind of linguistic desperation in the face of a contingent and multitudinous world of objects—as though the author has said to himself, "At least I will pin *this* down in a definitive manner." By contrast, Tolstoy moves freely and confidently through his imagined world which seems denser, of greater plenitude, precisely because he does not lavish his attention on detail in the way that Flaubert does. Tolstoy is lord of creation—at least of his creation—and things retreat before him to their humble place in a centrally human world.

If we travel further down the scale of mind—thing relationships, from the primitive imagination of Dickens, through the human centrality of Tolstoy, past the desperation of Flaubert, then we arrive at something like this:

> "We went back to look for Minta's brooch," he said, sitting down by her. "We"—that was enough. She knew from the effort, the rise in his voice to surmount a difficult word that it was the first time he had said "we." "We" did this, "we" did that. They'll say that all their lives, she thought, and an exquisite scent of olives and oil and juice rose from the great brown dish as Martha, with a little flourish, took the cover off. The cook had spent three days over that dish. And she must take great care, Mrs. Ramsay thought, diving into the soft mass, to choose a specially tender piece for William Bankes. And she peered into the dish, with its shiny walls and its confusion of savoury brown and yellow meats, and its bay leaves and its wine, and thought: This will celebrate the occasion—a curious sense rising in her, at once freakish and tender, of celebrating a festival, as if two emotions were called up in her, one profound—for what could be more serious than the love of man for woman, what more commanding, more impressive, bearing in its bosom the seeds of death; at the same time these lovers, these people entering into illusion glittering eyed, must be danced round with mockery, decorated with garlands.
>
> "It is a triumph," said Mr. Bankes, laying his knife down for a moment. He had eaten attentively. It was rich; it was tender. It was perfectly cooked.[4]

There is here, as in Flaubert, a desperation in face of the world of objects. But whereas Flaubert reacts by attempting to capture the thing in itself, objective, in all its bizarre detail, Virginia Woolf tries to pin the thing down at the moment when it deliquesces into the consciousness of her characters. The sensuous richness of so much of her prose is not, as it might at first seem, her tribute to a crowded world of autonomous objects since for her all things ultimately become mind-stuff, entering the glow of that "luminous halo" which is her metaphor for life itself. Virginia Woolf is perhaps too often a naïve Berkeleyan since *esse percipi est* is only one side of the equipoise between mind and the world of objects. The other side is our sense that objects *resist* our attention, that they remain opaque, stubbornly themselves. This sense is abundant in Dickens—it is a source of his metaphoric rich-ness—but is deficient in Virginia Woolf. To dine with the Podsnaps is to surrender to a world of things sensed as living a life of its own; to dine with the Ramsays is to celebrate a triumph of mind over matter. For in the passage I have quoted from *To the Lighthouse*, the book as well as the dinner has been beautifully cooked. Behind the perfection of the Bœuf-en-Daube, with its subtle blend of ingredients, is Mrs. Ramsay's triumph in blending and reconciling the human ingredients of her dinner party; Mr. Bankes pays tribute to both successes. And behind Mrs. Ramsay, of course, stands Virginia Woolf triumphantly blending the elements of life into her art. The extreme self-conscious-ness of this process is evident—"this will celebrate the occasion," Mrs. Ramsay thinks. This is one reason why Virginia Woolf's novels, though containing many striking and beautiful effects, are in the last analysis irritating. The metaphoric vivacity of Dickens's prose only enhances the independence of the objects described; Virginia Woolf, by con-trast, allows the external world too little freedom. The sensibility of her characters too easily digests whatever it encounters. We are left with facts of mind where sometimes we hunger for simple, brute facts. Moreover—this is a different but related complaint—the mind which thus transmutes is far too limited, allowing little dramatic variety; most of her characters metamorphose the world in strikingly similar ways. The results achieved are rich but narrow; intensity is purchased at too great a cost. After so much Bœuf-en-Daube one hungers for plain bread-and-cheese.

If we go still further in our scale of mind–thing relationships, be-yond Virginia Woolf, then we encounter something like Roquentin's famous confrontation with the chestnut tree:

> Absurdity; another word; I struggle against words; down there I touched the thing. But I wanted to fix the absolute character of this absurdity here. A movement, an event in the tiny coloured world of men is only relatively absurd: by rela-

tion to the accompanying circumstances. A madman's ravings, for example, are absurd in relation to the situation in which he finds himself, but not in relation to his delirium. But a little while ago I made an experiment with the absolute or the absurd. This root—there was nothing in relation to which it was absurd. Oh, how can I put it in words? Absurd: in relation to the stones, the tufts of yellow grass, the dry mud, the tree, the sky, the green benches. Absurd, irreducible; nothing—not even a profound, secret upheaval of nature—could explain it. Evidently I did not know everything, I had not seen the seeds sprout, or the tree grow. But faced with this great wrinkled paw, neither ignorance nor knowledge was important; the world of explanations and reasons is not the world of existence. A circle is not absurd, it is clearly explained by the rotation of a straight segment around one of its extremities. But neither does a circle exist. This root, on the other hand, existed in such a way that I could not explain it. Knotty, inert, nameless, it fascinated me, filled my eyes, brought me back unceasingly to its own existence. In vain to repeat: "This is a root"—it didn't work any more. I saw clearly that you could not pass from its function as a root, as a breathing pump, *to that,* to this hard and compact skin of a sea lion, to this oily, callous, headstrong look. The function explained nothing: it allowed you to understand generally that it was a root, but not *that one* at all. This root, with its colour, shape, its congealed movement, was . . . below all explanation. Each of its qualities escaped it a little, flowed out of it, half solidified, almost became a thing; each one was *in the way* in the root and the whole stump now gave me the impression of unwinding itself a little, denying its existence to lose itself in a frenzied excess. I scraped my heel against this black claw: I wanted to peel off some of the bark. For no reason at all, out of defiance, to make the bare pink appear absurd on the tanned leather; to *play* with the absurdity of the world. But, when I drew my heel back, I saw that the bark was still black.[5]

This passage, which perhaps suffers more than the others in being wrenched from its context, is really the extension of an insight which has come to Roquentin a few pages earlier, when he ponders the seat of a tramcar in which he is travelling:

Things are divorced from their names. They are there, grotesque, headstrong, gigantic and it seems ridiculous to call
them seats or say anything at all about them: I am in the
midst of things, nameless things. Alone, without words, de-
fenceless, they surround me, are beneath me, behind me,
above me. They demand nothing, they don't impose themselves; they are there.[6]

It is clear, even from these short extracts, that part of *La Nausée*
is concerned with dramatizing the struggle of a mind to leap through
the void that separates it from the world of things and to make sense
of a totally senseless universe. The desperation of both the effort and
the inevitable defeat is to be sensed in the language, particularly in
its quality of powerful but slightly sinister metaphor. The thing, the
tree-root, can be named, but the name is divorced from the thing;
that its "absolute character" can never be fixed is shown by the drastic
metamorphoses it undergoes—a breathing pump, a sea-lion, a black
claw. The prose oscillates between that and a kind of abstraction—
"a circle is not absurd"—which enacts, I suppose, the effort of the mind
to come to terms with the vigour and plenitude of an external world
totally subversive of all logic. Even to speak in these terms is to do the
passage an injustice, since what appears as metaphorical is also, in a
sense, literal. In a world where, as Roquentin says, "the essential thing
is contingency," where no necessary or stable relationships are to be
discerned, which is sensed primarily as a viscous flux, such metamorphoses are not impossible. Why, in this totally random world,
should a root *not* become a black claw or the seat of a tramcar change
into the upturned belly of a dead donkey? The prose does more than
play with such questions; behind it is a serious and sophisticated
philosophy. Yet, oddly enough, our scale of mind—thing relationships
seems almost to be circular, with its extremes meeting; the philosophic imagination of Sartre seems much more akin to the primitive
imagination of Dickens than to anything else we have encountered.

IV

Alienation has unfortunately become something of a cant word in
many kinds of intellectual discourse, including literary criticism. But
it is the right and inevitable word if we are to see the passages I have
quoted as representative rather than arbitrary. Its primary connota-

tions are, of course, social; it directs us to such topics as the replacement of community by mass or the breakdown in communication between the artist and any coherent audience. If its effects have been primarily social so, we may agree, was its cause; I see little to quarrel with in the Marxist thesis that alienation is a product of complex industrial and capitalist societies. But a contributory cause was certainly the decline of a theology in which man's relation to his world was given stability by being part of a divinely-ordered cosmos. We need not discuss how the breakdown of this world-view was related to social and economic changes. But we should notice that one of the series of correspondences supposed to exist between microcosm and macrocosm presupposed a stable relation between the world of things and man's mind,

> that ocean where each kind
> Does streight its own resemblance find.

At first the grandeur and order of the Newtonian universe buttressed the coherence and stability of this world view. But as the idea of rational man living in a rational universe crumbles, as scientific laws turn into mere high-order probabilities, as the possibility of certain knowledge dwindles and as the necessary turns into the contingent, so the novelist comes to inhabit an exciting but unstable world. I am not, of course, suggesting a simple relationship between intellectual cause and imaginative response; no doubt there is a cultural time-lag and no doubt diffusion means distortion. But gradually man's view of his world changes and gradually this affects the novelist's response; we move from confidence to uncertainty, from stability to flux, from the assurance that we know what is normal to Roquentin's sense of the absurd. The effects of this breakdown—of alienation—are discernible in every aspect of life, including man's relation to the world of things.

The breakdown usually takes one of two forms. There is the common Romantic nightmare—particularly acute in Coleridge—of the material world when the creative mind fails in its seminal function; a universe of little things, dry, disconnected, dead. But it is the second kind of alienation that I wish to stress, one denounced by Carlyle and Ruskin, not to speak of Marx himself. This is the view of man as victim of the cash-nexus and the industrial jungle; man as reduced to the status of a mere thing, an extension of the lever or the loom; man as an object to be manipulated and exploited.

Most novelists view with abhorrence this reduction of man to thing. This is partly because most of them write from within a liberal world view with its respect for people as autonomous beings, as ends-in-themselves. But this respect is also inherent in the nature of their craft; acutely aware of the dangers of creating puppets, they must strive to give at least the illusion of autonomy to their characters. Hence most of them react sharply to this aspect of alienation; manipulation of other people, the reduction of man to object, quickly become objects of attack in their fiction. This is certainly what happens in the extract quoted from *Our Mutual Friend,* constituting the important difference between Dickens and Sartre. For Dickens's primitive imagination of the world is given moral point and direction by a mind that is, in the last analysis, in confident control, whereas Sartre's protagonist is helpless in face of a totally contingent world of objects.

It is rare for the problems thus raised to be intellectually formulated by the novelist. Indeed, it is quite possible—witness most English novels—to rest in a kind of comfortable empiricism, to concern oneself with particular, limited human and social situations, and to be entirely unaware that any larger problem exists. Alienation most often manifests itself as a diffused and undefined pressure to which the novelist responds obliquely. As one might expect, an important set of responses is religious in nature; yet these produce surprisingly few really great novels. There is a kind of neo-Platonic response in which objects are placed and given significance by being the symbolic manifestation of a transcendental reality. This, of course, is the descendant of the traditional Christian metaphysic; what is new is that the god is veiled and ambiguous; reality may be divine or diabolic. Of this kind of reaction Melville and Kafka are perhaps the major representatives. As against this, by believing that the divine is also totally immanent, one may simultaneously celebrate God and life in all its particularity; parts of Tolstoy's work are here the best example. Finally, one can accept the entire contingency of the phenomenal world as it is humanly experienced and leap, like Kierkegaard, across the void between the breakdown of reason and the acceptance of faith. I cannot recall any great novel which dramatizes this position; Dostoievsky comes closest, I suppose, but does not quite fit into this or into any other category. Roquentin makes part of the journey and comes to the edge of the void, to the absurd; but he can go no further since God is absent from his universe. Sartre, to be sure, subsequently makes the leap to a total faith. But this is irrelevant to his fiction; indeed, perhaps it killed him as a novelist.

The significant reaction, in fact, has not been so much religious as aesthetic. One thinks, for example, of characters like Mrs. Ramsay whose sensibility works on the raw data of her experience in a typically aesthetic way, composing relationships into harmony, translating her gastronomic triumph into a symbolic celebration of human love. One thinks of all those novelists—the Mrs. Ramsays of that craft— who have written novels exploring the preconditions necessary to the writing of a novel. One thinks of the rise of the *Bildungsroman*. Most significant of all, perhaps, one thinks of Roquentin's faint hope of escape from the world of nausea; he, too, however feebly, can rejoice, having to construct something on which to rejoice. Why can Roquentin hope that the writing of a novel will make some sense of his life? Because the work of art—viewed as a self-sufficient artefact—is a necessary and not a contingent thing. It is a thing wrenched from the chaotic flux of the experienced world; it has its own laws and its own firm structure of relationships; it can, like a system of geometry, be held to be absolutely true within its own conventionally established terms.

Many modern novelists have found consolation in this view which has consequently affected their creative practice. While few novels can be derived from it in any philosophically rigorous sense, it is clearly no accident that autonomy theories of art have concurrently become dominant. Connected with these theories there is another kind of aesthetic response to the fact of alienation which is important to the substance and the implied values of many modern novels. In an autonomy theory of art the cardinal sin is didacticism. By this I mean any attempt on the part of either writer or reader to *use* the work of art. On this theory the artefact both arouses and completes emotion; the aesthetic state is one of stasis. Kinetic responses—those which carry over from the artefact to life—are at best irrelevant and at worst vitiating since the work of art is a sufficient end in itself, containing its own values. In the post-Kantian, liberal ethic endorsed by most novelists, the human being has much the same status as that accorded the work of art by this type of aesthetic. Man is an end in himself; we must respond to him as an autonomous being; the cardinal sin is to use or to manipulate him, to reduce him to a mere thing. The fields of aesthetics and ethics have a common frontier; thus one may easily understand how many novelists will therefore dramatize the moral substance of their novels in aesthetic terms. Aesthetic value becomes a metaphor for moral value; if man, in his alienated state, is reduced to a thing, then the novelist responds by asserting that he is at any rate a very special *kind* of thing—a work of art. Ethical discrimination merges into aesthetic discrimination; good taste becomes nearly synonymous with good sense and right feeling.

Here again, Virginia Woolf is a relevant example, especially if one sees her as sharing an ethos derived from G. E. Moore:

> By far the most valuable things, which we know or can imagine, are certain states of consciousness, which may be roughly described as the pleasures of human intercourse, and the enjoyment of beautiful objects. No one, probably, who has asked himself the question, has ever doubted that personal affection and the appreciation of what is beautiful in Art or Nature, are good in themselves; nor, if we consider strictly what things are worth having *purely for their own sakes*, does it appear probable that any one will think that anything else has nearly so great a value as the things which are included under these two heads.[7]

But it is probably Henry James who has most consistently, richly and subtly exploited this interplay between aesthetics and ethics. Let us examine briefly, therefore, some aspects of *The Portrait of A Lady*.

V

In the education of Isabel Archer no lesson is more bitter or more important than this recognition of what Osmond and Madame Merle have done to her:

> She saw, in the crude light of that revelation which had already become a part of experience and to which the very frailty of the vessel in which it had been offered her only gave an intrinsic price, the dry staring fact that she had been an applied handled hung-up tool, as senseless and convenient as mere shaped wood and iron.

(Chapter 52)

This perfect example of the sin against human autonomy—of use and exploitation, of the person reduced to a thing—gains part of its force from a context of imagery which persistently renders human experience in aesthetic terms. This is particularly true when applied to Isabel herself; thus, early in the novel, her cousin Ralph thinks of her:

> "A character like that," he said to himself—"a real little passionate force to see at play is the finest thing in nature. It's finer than the finest work of art—than a Greek bas-relief than a great Titian, than a Gothic cathedral. It's very pleasant to be so well treated where one had least looked for it. I had never been more blue, more bored, than for a week before she came; I had never expected less that anything pleasant would happen. Suddenly I receive a Titian, by the post, to hang on my wall—a Greek bas-relief to stick over my chimney-piece. The key of a beautiful edifice is thrust into my hand, and I'm told to walk in and admire." (7)

As Isabel is seen in aesthetic terms, so she sees others; thus Lord Warburton is "a hero of romance" (7) and in Caspar Goodwood "she saw the different fitted parts of him as she had seen, in museums and portraits, the different fitted parts of armoured warriors—in plates of steel handsomely inlaid with gold" (13). So her moral life, too, is defined in these terms; of her relation with Madame Merle, "it was as if she had given to a comparative stranger the key to her cabinet of jewels. These spiritual gems were the only ones of any magnitude that Isabel possessed" (19). The notion of the key is, of course, recurrent and related to the persistent image of the house, both conveying the basic themes of independence, invasion and possession. Similarly when Ralph tells Isabel, "Don't question your conscience so much—it will get out of tune like a strummed piano" (21), his simile perhaps gains a resonance from the literal, emphasized fact of Madame Merle's skill at the piano; she *plays* on Isabel as well.

This brings us to Madame Merle and Osmond, and to one of the central problems confronting James in this novel. Madame Merle and Osmond must be made to *seem* fine and impressive, at least in Isabel's eyes; otherwise her sensibility will be coarsened and her value as moral agent diminished. If she is to be deceived then at least she must be taken in by a very good imitation of the real thing. But she *is* deceived; Madame Merle and Osmond must be seen by the reader only as *seeming* what Isabel actually takes them to be. James's major techniques for solving this problem are not relevant here, but clearly the problem *is* closely related to the view of human beings as aesthetic objects. Thus many critics have noticed the limiting qualification in James's description of Madame Merle: "Of painting she was devotedly fond, and made no more of brushing in a sketch than of pulling off her gloves" (19). Similarly, Osmond *appears* a fine aesthetic object:

> He suggested, fine coin as he was, no stamp nor emblem of the common mintage that provides for general circulation; he was the elegant complicated medal struck off for a special occasion. (22)

But the fine coin proves to have too great an admixture of base alloy; Osmond is like the precious coffee-cup flawed by a minute crack (49). The human failure is suggested in aesthetic terms; thus Madame Merle admits that "his painting's pretty bad" (19); thus Rosier (whose testimony we tend to trust since he sacrifices Art for Life by selling his bibelots) thinks that much of Osmond's taste is bad (37); Ralph, while allowing to Isabel that Osmond is "the incarnation of taste," comes as near as he can to savagery by telling her, "you were meant for something better than to keep guard over the sensibilities of a sterile dilettante" (34). Osmond himself reveals his human-aesthetic flaw. He dismisses Madame Merle thus; "Oh, the imagination of women! It's always vulgar, at bottom. You talk of revenge like a third-rate novelist" (49). Yet within a few pages he too becomes the third-rate novelist:

> Osmond turned slightly pale; he gave a cold smile.
> "That's why you must go then? Not to see your cousin, but to take a revenge on me."
> "I know nothing about revenge."
> "I do," said Osmond. "Don't give me an occasion." (51)

Naturally these two predators regard Isabel in similar terms:

> What could be a happier gift in a companion than a quick, fanciful mind which saved one repetitions and reflected one's thought on a polished, elegant surface? Osmond hated to see his thought reproduced literally—that made it look stale

and stupid; he preferred it to be freshened in the reproduction even as "words" by music. His egotism had never taken the crude form of desiring a dull wife; this lady's intelligence was to be a silver plate, not an earthen one—a plate that he might heap up with rich fruits, to which it would give a decorative value, so that talk might become for him a sort of served dessert. He found the silver quality in this perfection in Isabel; he could tap her imagination with his knuckle and make it ring. (35)

Even before this Isabel has conceived of herself in a like way:

> She only felt older—ever so much, and as if she were "worth more" for it, like some curious piece in an antiquary's collection. (32)

This, of course, is precisely what she is destined to become; part of the tragedy of her relationship with Osmond is in the metamorphosis from "silver plate" to "an applied handled hung-up tool, as senseless and convenient as mere shaped wood and iron."

The examples I have quoted in this brief analysis are not isolated; such imagery is dense in *The Portrait of A Lady*. It is a concern, moreover, which persists through much of James's work; one thinks of *The Princess Casamassima* and *The Tragic Muse*. From it James derives many of his most beautiful effects; I can think of few more lyrical passages in his work than his description of Strether's walk through the French countryside in the eleventh book of *The Ambassadors*. Yet in the margins of this translation of human experience into aesthetic terms there remains a faint question mark. How adequate, after all, to the complexity of life is this view of human relationships as a matter of connoisseurship? If Osmond regards Isabel as a work of art, so do Ralph and Lord Warburton; if Osmond regards his daughter thus, so does Rosier. But unlike them, Osmond has a base and improper aesthetic sense; unlike them, he wants to *use* the work of art. It is precisely in these terms that James achieves the desired moral discrimination and, in doing so, achieves also a masterpiece. Nevertheless, the question remains; the balance between aesthetic vehicle and moral tenor is a precarious one; the traffic between the two areas is often equivocal and ambiguous. This is the reason, surely, why the attitude of the Ververs to their captive Prince has caused so much critical debate.

For a symbol of this mingled strength and weakness, this combination on the reader's part of admiration and marginal doubt, we may turn to another novelist. Aschenbach in *Death in Venice* is truly representative of many writers whose dilemma and response I have tried to describe. His artistic life has been dedicated to the wrenching of a classic order out of the delirium and flux of life. Yet behind the order lies the dream of a Dionysiac revel; life reasserts itself, fascinating, corrupt, chaotic, a jungle. In face of this, "his art, his moral sense, what were they in the balance beside the boons that chaos might confer? . . . Knowledge is all-knowing, understanding, forgiving; it takes up no position, sets no store by form. It has compassion with the abyss—it *is* the abyss.

Yet before he plunges into the abyss of life, immersing himself for the last time in the destructive element, Aschenbach once more asserts his identity and dignity as an artist, "and fashioned his little essay after the model Tadzio's beauty set; that page and a half of choicest prose, so chaste, so lofty, so poignant with feeling, which would shortly be the wonder and admiration of the multitude."

It is a heroic stance, compelling respect and compassion. The artist for the last time tames the multitudinous seas, before breaking his magic staff and drowning into life. Yet even here we hear the whisper of our marginal doubt. Do we ever really believe in that page and a half of exquisite prose? Is the purity of the aesthetic response ever adequate to the challenge of a corrupt, contingent, chaotic world? Can a last-ditch defence ever become a proper base for further explanation?

NOTES

1. In the preface to *Roderick Hudson*.
2. "Charles Dickens" in *A New Spirit of the Age* (1844).
3. G. Steiner, *Tolstoy or Dostoevsky*, p. 50. London: Faber and Faber, 1960. The quotation from *Madame Bovary* is from the translation by Francis Steegmuller (New York, 1957).
4. V. Woolf, *To the Lighthouse*, Part I, Section 17.
5. J. P. Sartre, *Nausea* (*La Nausée*), pp. 174–5. London: Hamish Hamilton, 1962.
6. J. P. Sartre, *Nausea* (*La Nausée*), p. 169.
7. G. E. Moore, *Principia Ethica*, pp. 188–9. Cambridge University Press, 1959.

ALAN FRIEDMAN

The Stream of Conscience

Innocence in the novel is apt to be a slippery affair: let me quote from the most innocent fiction I know.

> A tall man of 29 rose from the sofa. He was rarther bent in the middle with very nice long legs fairish hair and blue eyes. Hullo Alf old boy he cried so you have got here all safe and no limbs broken.
> None thankyou Bernard replied Mr Salteena shaking hands and let me introduce Miss Monticue she is very pleased to come for this visit. Oh yes gasped Ethel blushing through her red ruge. Bernard looked at her keenly and turned a dark red.

The bashful specimen comes from *The Young Visiters,* misspelled and composed by Daisy Ashford at the age of nine.[1] Unquestionably, the book is some sort of masterpiece: it has a brilliantly managed, complex, and unified plot, a broad and sensitively rendered social milieu, a large number of astonishingly varied and vividly realized characters, a luxuriant surface of sensuous and material details integral to the psychological moment, technically admirable suspense and a firmly controlled point of view, incisive insight and deep irony, even a final fullness of meaning—all filtered through immature spelling and punctuation, and the immature, if not altogether innocent, mind of its author. Written at about the turn of the century and preserved in manuscript—penciled notebook—until it was published in 1919, it constitutes not only a precocious unconscious parody but also a very reasonable facsimile of the genus Novel for the first two centuries

From *The Turn of the Novel.* Copyright © 1966 by Alan Friedman. Reprinted by permission of Oxford University Press, Inc.

374

of its existence. Perhaps it deserves to be honored as the last traditional novel, the *reductio ad absurdum* which looks backward, as
Joyce's looks forward. Forward or backward, nowhere else can we
learn so easily what we want to know about the genre as a whole.
The Young Visiters reveals everything: it is utterly defenseless.

> Well said Mr Salteena lapping up his turtle soup you
> have a very sumpshous house Bernard.
> His friend gave a weary smile and swolowed a few drops
> of sherry wine. It is fairly decent he replied with a bashful
> glance at Ethel after our repast I will show you over the
> premisis.
> Many thanks said Mr Salteena getting rarther flustered with
> his forks.
> You ourght to give a ball remarked Ethel you have such
> large compartments.
> Yes there is room enough sighed Bernard we might try a
> few steps and meanwhile I might get to know a few peaple.
> So you might responded Ethel giving him a speaking look.

As the excerpts suggest, Daisy Ashford's novel, like all novels, is
about morals, manners, marriage, and money; it gives us all of this in
movement. And its movement begins in innocence.

> . . . she ran out of the room with a very superior run throw-
> ing out her legs behind and her arms swinging in rithum.
> Well said the owner of the house she has a most idiotick run.
>
> .   .   .
>
> Mr S. skipped upstairs to Rosalinds room. Good-bye Rosa-
> lind he said I shall be back soon and I hope I shall enjoy
> myself.
> I make no doubt of that sir said Rosalind with a blush as
> Mr Salteena silently put 2/6 on the dirty toilet cover.

Whose innocence? That of its tender author, age nine? Or of her
creature, Miss Ethel Monticue, age seventeen—"quite a young girl"
. . . "who did not really know at all how to go on at a visit," but seems
used to "staying" with apparently anyone, Mr. Salteena or Bernard.
When after barely thirty-six hours Mr. Salteena departs, leaving young
Ethel in Bernard's hands, our child author has him remark solicitously

I do hope Ethel will behave properly.
Oh yes I expect she will said Bernard with a sigh.

And the very next time we see Bernard and Ethel

I was thinking he said passionately what about going up to
London for a weeks Gaierty.
Who inquired Ethel in a low tone.

Clearly *both* heroine and author know what they are up to. And
when Bernard and Ethel engage adjoining rooms at London's Gaierty
Hotel, lingering doubt vanishes.

The best shall be yours then said Bernard bowing gallantly
and pointing to the biggest room.
Ethel blushed at his speaking look. I shall be quite lost in
that huge bed she added to hide her embarassment.
Yes I expect you will said Bernard.

If Ethel Monticue is "innocent," the concept allows for a bit of
sharp practice and may require some sharp definition.

To bring matters to a sharper, not to say glaring, focus, it may be
useful to consider one of the least innocent fictions and one of the
earliest English novels, John Cleland's classically dirty book, *Memoirs
of a Woman of Pleasure* (originally published in 1749, just nine years
after Richardson's first effort, *Pamela*). In the opening pages of her
memoirs, Fanny Hill writes that her "foundation in virtue was no other
than a total ignorance of vice, and the shy timidity general to our
sex." [2] And although on page 125 she writes that experience "soon
stripped me of all the remains of bashfulness and modesty," the intention of this sentence is clearly to remind us that even after one hundred
salacious pages she still possesses some remnant of those qualities; after
161 pages, she manages to accept "a proposal which my candor and
ingenuity [ingenuousness] gave me some repugnance to"; after 204
pages, she is still protesting, "I had not, however, so thoroughly re-
nounced all innate shame as not to suffer great confusion at the state
I saw myself in." And so on.

Now although Fanny Hill's protests, like the blushes of Ethel Monticue and the endless guarantees of Pamela ("don't be frightened—for

—I hope—I hope, I am honest!"—Letter XXV), are never entirely credible, all three girls somehow manage to convey *nevertheless* a most unreasonably strong sense of innocence—their pure confusion perhaps about the impure stuff of their experience. Each girl, after all, is never entirely prepared for the next page. Admittedly, Fanny's case is special. Every new scene in *The Memoirs* exposes Fanny to a new "experience." The muck thickens; and it becomes Cleland's problem as a good pornographer to keep before the reader some (slowly crumbling) impression of Fanny's inner purity for purposes of titillation. And yet if we choose our words with greater care, we can say much the same thing about *Pamela* and *The Young Visiters*. No muck, less titillation; but each girl, as her innocence crumbles, is forever innocent of what the next chapter holds in store, unready—not quite ready—to interpret it when she arrives, unsure—not quite sure—of how to respond when it happens. Her innocence, if we may call it that, is the frame of mind on which the skein of action is wound.

There are differences of course. Ethel Monticue's innocence, confidently assumed by her author, is gradually and conclusively eroded by her story. Pamela Andrews' innocence must be circumstantially protested and re-propped so that Squire B—can assault it over and over again. But in both cases, innocence is the perspective which provides the necessary tension against which the events of experience may move. And the operation of that fundamental dynamism remains unchanged and essential—if subtler in its range of effects—elsewhere in fiction. Can we say everywhere?

Every central character must, in a sense relative to his story, be *relatively* innocent at the beginning of his book: that is, he must be more innocent earlier in the story than he is later in the story. On this agreement heroes and heroines shake hands: Moll Flanders with Molly Bloom, Joseph Andrews with Joe Christmas, Uncle Toby with Hans Castorp, Becky Sharp with Jane Eyre, Pip with Nick Carroway, Natty Bumpo with Bernard Profitendieu, and, for that matter, Lady Chatterley with Alice in Wonderland. To crash the world of fiction successfully, even a murderer, pervert, con-man, or whore must agree to respect at least one convention, the convention of his own innocence— Raskolnikov, Humbert Humbert, Felix Krull, Fanny Hill. The relative innocence of central characters is a truism; what is perhaps only barely less obvious is that "innocence" is a function of the organization of events, and may therefore serve as a very useful source for a theory of the dynamism—the motivation—of narrative form. At the outset of the form, even the most sophisticated of central characters must be innocent of what is going to come at him. Innocence in fiction establishes the crucial inner perspective because it is a pressure (as it were "outward") to interpret freshly for the reader the outer, oncoming experience. The latter, outer experience, exerts a reciprocal pressure "inward" upon innocence (whether upon a great innocence or upon a presumed sophistication which proves inadequate, not quite adequate). The result, moment by moment from the character's point of view, is a continuous stream or series of responses—in perception, in action—which constitutes his gradual rendering of himself and his world. Now the intense energizing function of innocence in fiction helps to explain in part why so many great novels have had central characters of exceptionally great purity, simplicity, or harmlessness. But with an eye on structure, we can perhaps justifiably lay stress on any specific traits of character. We can more generally and more usefully define the central subjective energy of the novel as an inward pressure not merely to engage with experience, but to interpret experience by responding to it.

For response, whether out of simplicity or subtlety, whether in action or feeling, constitutes interpretation.

> Ethel blushed at his speaking look. I shall be quite lost in that huge bed she added to hide her embarrassment.

We can, after all, imagine other responses than Ethel's blush; and other responses—if we or the author should insist on imagining them—would create other events, other characters, other stories; in short, another interpretation of experience.

> I screamed out, and fainted away. . . .
> When I recovered my senses, I found myself undressed and a-bed, in the arms of the sweet unrelenting murderer of my virginity. . . .   (Fanny Hill)

> . . . I sighed and screamed, and fainted away. . . . I knew nothing more of the matter, one fit following another, till about three hours after, as it proved to be, I found myself in bed, and Mrs. Jervis sitting upon one side . . . and no master, for the wicked wretch was gone. But I was so over-joyed, that I hardly could believe myself. . . .   (Pamela)

It was only then that her still face showed the least emotion, a tear or two beginning to trickle down.

"What are you crying for?" he coldly asked.

"I was only thinking that I was born over there," murmured Tess.

Over the long course of a novel, the flux of such responses not only creates or defines character, as it obviously does, but does so through a process which we can isolate: with all the energy of their crumbling innocence, characters are obliged to interpret themselves as they interpret a changing experience.

That double interpretative process is the primary imaginative movement in the novel, a movement that is never merely cumulative, never piling experience on inexperience *merely* (as in some earlier narratives, Nashe's *The Unfortunate Traveller*, for example), but always moving from innocence to experience, from relative unreadiness to relative adequacy. The stream of responses, which is a stream of interpretation, is therefore a fundamental moral process in fiction.

Now it is precisely in the moment of not-quite-readiness ("I was only thinking that I was born over there") and under the threats and opportunities of experience, that responses are made, characters are created, interpretations are formed, and fictional events occur. In that incessantly recurring moment and in its necessary momentum toward sophistication may lie a clue to the relation between ethics and events in the novel. We may be able to trace a theory of single events which will allow us to see the full trajectory of such events in the fictional experience as both narrative structure and ethical form.

Let us consider for a moment the plight of those assaulted servant girls who hold open the doors through which English fiction enters so rudely—Defoe's Moll, Richardson's Pamela, Fielding's Fanny, and Cleland's Fanny. Four very different girls chased by four very different squires: a world of ropes, ponds, hedges, purses, employment agencies, mothers, captains, and justices of the peace. The pell-mell momentum of threat and opportunity, response and interpretation, grows increasingly tense. Squire A— tempts Moll with a silk purse and silken promises; Squire B— commands lackeys to spirit Pamela away and keep her in an isolated house; Squire C— has Fanny Goodwill bound on a horse and abducted as a "rebellious" wife; Squire D— has his procuress terrorize Fanny Hill with threats of debtors' prison before he generously pays her rent. Against such harsh and subtle assaults, what sort of chance does innocence stand?

In describing the existence of the novel as a genre, Mark Schorer has spoken of "the intersection of the stream of social history and the stream of soul. The intersection . . . provides the source of those generic tensions that make [the form] possible at all." [3] Can we go further and say that that same intersection provides the source of tension in each individual event by which any given novel achieves its existence? If we can, then we will at least be in a position to understand the remarkable resistance the soul puts up against social history, the sort of chance innocence does in fact stand against the harsh and subtle assaults of squires. But each individual squire immediately and loudly objects: by what authority, he demands, do we make a servant girl a soul and himself a fact of social history? Still, let us overrule him for a moment and side—tentatively—with the harassed girl. From her point of view, the encircling arms of the squire are embarrassingly twofold: the world of impersonal force (social, historical, physical, and natural) and the personal world of character. For squires, lackeys, and lovers, though "selves" like her own self, are from her point of view parts of her world, forces outside her soul with whom she must cope and to whom she must respond. (Our analysis is of course relative to an arbitrarily fixed center; and the moment the squire's protests become persuasive, we can—for his soul—simply reverse our procedure.)

Now in the moment of innocence, when the susceptible squire seizes her about the waist, each girl's responses may also be divided, conveniently, into a dilemma: how to feel about it and what to do about it. And both together inevitably constitute her "interpretation": perception and action. Moll Flanders is often content to count her blessings; Fanny Hill and Fanny Goodwill sometimes cry and kick against the aggressors; Pamela, "sadly vexed," usually contrives to let her affairs drift to the sexual brink. This running interpretation of the heroine's world— the current of small outcomes all along the way—generates its energy, it is true, through a limitlessly complex and dynamic interaction of self and world: the full inner and outer experience of fiction. But if we divide that experience—abstractly—into an onrushing double response of the self (insight and deeds) to the onrushing double trouble of the world (personal and impersonal), we have at least a coherent and consistent analysis that can account for any given event in terms of the tensions between individual innocence and the onslaught of history and society: blushes and wishes; captains and employment agencies. By including within the term "world" not only society and history but everything "not-self," we can even account for the circumstantial detail of events, the physical and natural texture: ropes, ponds, and hedges.

That double onrushing confrontation constitutes the full flux of experience in a novel. In turning now to the structure of events in fiction, I want to distinguish the formal development of experience from the development of what we commonly call plot. (The word *plot* is heavily and traditionally associated with "action"—we habitually distinguish plot from character as related but separable concepts. By now the association of plot with "what happens," and why it happens, is too strong to break.[4]) In what follows, I intend to place a more reasonable emphasis on the self in the experience we call the novel, and to restore focus on what in fact "happens" in fiction: interaction, rather than action.

If the fundamental unit of language is the word, and the fundamental unit of discursive prose is the assertion, it seems reasonable to suggest that the fundamental unit of fiction is the event. But what is a "single" event? We turn the page. The event isn't over: it may seem to be finished, but it has refused to sign a treaty over boundaries, refused to stay "single," even when the chapter closes on it. The event doesn't close: just as it has incorporated within itself smaller events, it contains within itself potentialities for further events which inexorably incorporate it, and it is alive only in the stream. By looking at events as an onrushing confrontation of tensions (between responses generated internally in character, externally in the world), we sacrifice something —the convenience of considering events as closed "units" in a separable "construction"—but we come closer to a dynamic and true sense of structure in the novel. For it is in some such way that we do read fiction: at some moments more aware of the force and flow of the stream; at other moments more aware of the single and particular event —we pause in acknowledgment, we know that it has occurred. If we can agree that the event is the fundamental unit of fiction, then we should agree to go further and say that the stream of events is the fundamental form of fiction.

The fundamental unit of fiction, "one" event, might perhaps at this point be formally defined as the dynamic confrontation of two pressures, self and world, which issues in any clear outcome—whether in perception or action or both, whether on the part of the self, the world, or both.[5] Several provisos and amplifications follow.

Of course the definition obliges us in the first place to choose arbitrarily, but not injudiciously, one character as the center or focus of any event and to regard that character as the continuous inward center for the duration of any sequence of events. If we regard as inward whatever parts of the narrative pertain to the character as a self—his perception, feeling, action, and so on—then *everything* else can be considered as outward, that is to say, as *that* character's world—including, most notably, other characters. The pressures exerted upon him by the world (in this relative analysis) can then include, for example, the pressures of other characters' perception, feelings, words, intentions, and actions; of social institutions and conventions; of physical and natural forces—soft chairs, open doors, bad weather, snapping twigs, falling rocks.

Now in the second place, it is in the nature of fiction as a stream or a process that any inner-and-outer happening which strikes us as an outcome will normally also be, with respect to the next event, an inception. That is, any new relation of the self to the world which we *call* an outcome either becomes *part* (if new stresses are introduced) or constitutes *all* of the two new pressures of self and world which produce the outcome of the next continuous event.

Third, thanks to a definition by now rapacious (inner *and* outer), all has become grist to our mill of events: everything from the discernible ripple of a single superficial incident to the strong but indistinguishable eddying of many incidents; even such stubbornly irreducible shoals and islands in fiction's flow as long landscapes or detailed interiors, summaries of the past or character analysis, expository meditation or the stream of consciousness; all of necessity become the background, the potential energy, inward or outward, for the succession of outcomes which establishes the stream.

Looked at in this way, therefore, an event is not only "what happens"—though, heaven knows, if we call it anything else, we are obligated to show what blessings will eventually flow from our sophistication. An event is a moment in the process which creates for us the inward self, a moment in the flux by which the self consciously copes with and interprets the world—other selves, social institutions, conventions, values, sometimes nature itself. But to say *that* is to say that the novel structures the specific and essentially moral process of which the human imagination is capable, structures it in the full substance of narrative.[6] By its obligatory attention to the perceiving self, the flux of experience in the novel is also obliged to create (even against the novelist's will) an ethical form in process. The stream of events may therefore (but not against our will) be studied as a process or flux of the conscience: we can grasp the perceiving self's attempts to grasp—to come to grips with, in perception and action—the assaults and offers of the surrounding world. Without changing the terms of our earlier definition of an event, but concentrating on the self's responses as developing and related interpretations, we can regard that peculiarly novelistic continuum, the inner-and-outer dialectics of the novel, event by event, under the aspect of an ethical form. We have already suggested that, with respect to structure, the fundamental form of fiction is the stream of events. With respect to meaning, it seems reasonable to suggest that the fundamental form of the novel is its stream of conscience.

That is what we read novels for: to share in creating the experience of one more world of selves, and one more, and one more. This may seem hardly a process of the conscience. But the novelist arranges in advance the rules of play (style and ethics; time and pace) and the reader, with all the energy of his imagination, plays the book as his experience. Instead of a "willing suspension of disbelief" before the unreality of the theater stage, the co-operative reader submits to (the novel produces) another kind of suspension, which we regularly call identification—a suspension of dissociation before the intrusion of personality. An "other" becomes our temporary self. More precisely, others become our temporary selves, one after another, and we experience the fiction not from orchestra or balcony but from some center of the novel's world, through the temporary peephole of character, moving from innocence to experience on the subjective wedge that opens the future of narrative motion.

In that way the stream of events in the novel, just as we have described it, becomes the experience of the reader: the self and world in the novel become our self and surrounding world, so that the experience of reading a novel comes closer than does that of any other form of literature to our personal experience in time. The fundamental form of fiction in-forms the reader's self, and as a result consistent patterns of moral and emotional response in the novels of an era can and do take on the impact and authority of mythic information.

NOTES

1. Daisy Ashford, *The Young Visiters* (London, 1919). The various passages given here are quoted from the first fifty pages of the London, 1960, edition.

2. John Cleland, *Memoirs of a Woman of Pleasure* (New York, 1963), p. 30. Subsequent page references are also to the 1963 edition.

3. Mark Schorer, "Foreword: Self and Society," *Society and Self in the Novel, English Institute Essays, 1955,* ed. Mark Schorer (New York, 1956), p. ix.

4. Nevertheless, with the analysis given here one should compare Ronald S. Crane's analysis of the "working or power" of the novel, in an essay which considerably extends the concept of plot by viewing it as a "dynamic whole which affects our emotions in a certain way through the functioning together of its elements in subordination to a determinate poetic form."—"The Concept of Plot and the Plot of *Tom Jones,*" in *Critics and Criticism,* ed. by Ronald S. Crane, abridged ed. (Chicago, 1957), p. 91.

5. Compare the following definitions: "The unit of fiction is the event. . . . We may define a fictional event as the representation in language of any psychic or psychological phenomenon which is observed as a process rather than as an entity"—Marvin Mudrick, "Character and Event in Fiction," *Yale Review,* L (Winter 1961), pp. 210 and 207. (The two passages have been excerpted in reversed order.) "The surface of a novel is made up of items concretely represented and temporally arranged (the temporal arrangement includes plot and other kinds of pattern), enabling us to perceive the immediately felt qualities of a human 'world,' experiences in the imagination, not through any one sense"—Joseph E. Baker, "Aesthetic Surface in the Novel," *The Trollopian,* II (September 1947), p. 98. "Most novels develop their meaning through a communication to the reader of the imagined adventures (psychological and physical, occasionally only one or the other of these two kinds) of imaginary characters"—David Daiches, "Problems for Modern Novelists," in *Accent Anthology* (New York), p. 549.

6. Compare Lionel Trilling's emphasis: "For our time the most effective agent of the moral imagination has been the novel of the last two hundred years. It was never, either aesthetically or morally, a perfect form and its faults and failures can be quickly enumerated. But its greatness and its practical usefulness lay in its unremitting work of involving the reader himself in the moral life, inviting him to put his own motives under examination, suggesting that reality is not as his conventional education has led him to see it. It taught us, as no other genre ever did, the extent of human variety and the value of this variety. It was the literary form to which the emotions of understanding and forgiveness were indigenous, as if by definition of the form itself."—"Manners, Morals, and the Novel," *The Liberal Imagination* (London, 1951), p. 222.

B